Black Atlas

Black Atlas

GEOGRAPHY AND FLOW IN

NINETEENTH-CENTURY

AFRICAN AMERICAN

LITERATURE

Judith Madera

DUKE UNIVERSITY PRESS

Durham and London 2015

Designed by Amy Ruth Buchanan
Typeset in Quadraat and Quadraat
Sans by Copperline.

....

Library of Congress Cataloging-in-Publication
Madera, Judith Irwin, 1977–
Black atlas : geography and flow in nineteenth-century
African American literature / Judith Irwin Madera.
pages cm
Includes bibliographical references and index.
ISBN 978-0-8223-5797-1 (hardcover : alk. paper)
ISBN 978-0-8223-5811-4 (pbk. : alk. paper)
1. American literature—African American authors—
History and criticism. 2. American literature—
19th century—History and criticism. I. Title.
PS153.N5M23 2015
810.9'89607309034—dc23
2014046636
ISBN 978-0-8223-7595-1 (e-book)

....

Cover art: Alison Saar, *Inheritance* (2003).
Wood, ceiling tin, and cotton. 72 x 29 x 29 in.
(182.9 x 73.7 x 73.7 cm). Copyright Alison Saar,
courtesy of L.A. Louver, Venice, CA.

CONTENTS

....

ACKNOWLEDGMENTS vii

INTRODUCTION On Meaningful Worlds 1

CHAPTER 1 National Geographic:
The Writings of William Wells Brown 24

CHAPTER 2 Indigenes of Territory:
Martin Delany and James Beckwourth 69

CHAPTER 3 This House of Gathering:
Axis Americanus 110

CHAPTER 4 Civic Geographies and
Intentional Communities 151

CHAPTER 5 Creole Heteroglossia:
Counter-Regionalism and the New Orleans Short
Fiction of Alice Dunbar-Nelson 190

EPILOGUE Post Scale: Place as Emergence 211

NOTES 219

BIBLIOGRAPHY 261

INDEX 285

ACKNOWLEDGMENTS

....

Black Atlas was conceived of in New York and came into form in the North Carolina Piedmont. Both places have taught me about the ways environments shape our stories, and for that I am grateful. At the Graduate Center of the City University of New York I was fortunate to work in a lively intellectual community made most vibrant by David S. Reynolds, Robert Reid-Pharr, and Jon-Christian Suggs. Thanks for having faith in this project in its earliest stages, and for galvanizing my ideas in ways too numerous to list here. Meena Alexander, David Harvey, and the late Neil Smith also changed the ways I wrote about space. They amplified the thought-ways I know to be community. It has been a privilege to learn from each of you. I must also express my gratitude for research support to the Institute for Research on the African Diaspora in the Americas and the Caribbean at the CUNY Graduate Center, the JFK Institute at the Freie University of Berlin, and the Office of the College of the Dean at Wake Forest University. I am grateful for the support I have received from the Melvin Dixon Prize Foundation and the Dunn and Riley Families Award for Scholarship and Faculty.

The Office of the College of the Dean at Wake Forest University has been particularly generous, aiding my research through the Archie, Dingledine, and Faculty Development Funds. Thanks especially to Rebecca Thomas for ongoing support and to my chairs in English, Claudia Kairoff, Scott Klein, and Dean Franco. Also thanks to the 16 beaver group in NYC, the Counter Cartography Collectives of the Research Triangle, and the Wake Forest Humanities Institute for inspiration.

Along the way, a number of people contributed to this book with their matchless intellectual generosity: Houston Baker, Sarah Banet-Weiser, Susan Gillman, Caroline Levander, Bob Levine, Chris Lukasic, Ana María

Manzanas Calvo, Ross Miller, Fred Moten, Michelle Stephens, and Priscilla Wald have made this book possible. A special thanks to Michelle Stephens, who encouraged me as a writer and illuminated my arguments with her extraordinary knowledge of Caribbean literature and art, and to Caroline Levander, who is such a thrilling thinker and presence. This book is much better because of her lucid critiques. Courtney Berger at Duke University Press believed in this project from the outset. She offered indispensable, clear-sighted advice and a nuanced eye for the craft of criticism. Courtney is a stellar editor and it has been an honor to work with her. Also, my appreciation to Willa Armstrong and Sara Leone at Duke University Press.

I am grateful to a number of colleagues at Wake Forest University. Gillian Overing was invaluable support as I wrote this book and remains my finest interlocutor on process and flow. Dean Franco is an esteemed friend, reader, and discussant. My sincere thanks to Dean for his good humor and for bringing some vitality to the commons when it was most welcomed. Mary DeShazer graciously read the full manuscript and provided much in the way of assurance. "What wisdom can you find that is greater than kindness?" My thanks to Mary Foskett, James Hans, Jefferson Holdridge, Herman Rapaport, Olga Valbuena, Ulrike Wiethaus, and Eric Wilson, all of whom have sharpened my ideas and contributed to this book in very different, catalytic ways. I am so grateful to Hope Cooke, Meredith Farmer, Omaar Hena, Melissa Jenkins, Daniel Mulcahy, Janet Neary, and Mark Rifkin for discussing the writing process with me. At Wake Forest the women in my Landscape and Humanities research group, Transnational Feminism and Diaspora faculty seminar, and American/Medieval seminar brightened my afternoons with their wit and warmth. Kind thanks are due to Connie Green and Peggy Barrett, the administrative coordinators in the English Department where I work. My research assistant Rochelle Davis has my continual appreciation, as do my hardworking, inquisitive students at Wake Forest University. And a particular debt of gratitude to the Winston-Salem Friends, who have lent some of their light along the way.

Above all, my family, my parents and siblings, Anita, David, and Charles —thank you. I am especially beholden to my extraordinary mother whose own Atlantic storylines motivated this work. If I had a second mother, it would be Mary Mulcahy, whose grace and compassion have sustained me and my family. There really is no way to return all the kindness you have shown. I think we can only give it to our children. And of course, the three graces. Siguen brillando: Nicola Madera, Bridget Day, and Lucia Inéz Mulcahy. Dònal, thank you for sharing this walk with me. Thank you for being there for me through it all. This is book is dedicated to you with love.

....

ON MEANINGFUL WORLDS

Black Atlas is about the ways literature reflects and composes place. I begin from the position that places are sites we imbue with meaning. They are constituted by our ways of knowing. Just as importantly, they are imprints of feelings and attachments. The pages that follow look at the ways places are generated through processes of participation. They take the view that places are about how we use them, how we share them. I further argue that place resists the closure of any singular mode of representation. Place is something semiotic (between concept and symbol) and something material with real conditions. It exceeds any private experience. In making these claims, it is necessary to foreground the stakes of my argument—what a reinvigorated understanding of place means for more specific communities in time. I am particularly interested in what place means for those whose histories have been vernacularized, or simply overwritten in the dominant records of a culture. *Black Atlas* is about these kinds of communities and about their stories.

This book takes up with African American literature from the volatile period between 1849 and 1900, an era of massive national expansion and hemispheric ambition. The period encompasses the radical abolitionist movement, the Civil War, Reconstruction, and Jim Crow. From an artistic perspective, it might be called "the rise of the black novel period," because the decade of the 1850s alone launched the first generation of black novelists, including William Wells Brown, Frank J. Webb, Harriet Wilson, and Martin Delany.[1] But to limit the story of black place aesthetics to this midcentury literary surge is to hem a complex record of print expression into a too-narrow scope of periodicity and genre. Late-century literature gains its projection in relation to earlier writing. And the range of midcentury textualities considered here actually comes into relief against later, post-Reconstruction fiction in a variety of ways that do not align with imposed historicizations.

Black Atlas thus begins with the supposition that place pushes against assimilable forms. Place unsettles sweeps of development-based histories. It also interrupts ideas of black history as a march of progress, or a story of protest within a national frame. Thus, to better attend to the complexities of literary place aesthetics, I extend this rise of the black novel, as I am calling it, to a longer view of literature. I start with the first novel to be published by an African American author, William Wells Brown's 1853 Clotel, and close with the end-of-century literature by authors like Pauline Hopkins and Alice Dunbar-Nelson. Theirs was the kind of fiction that tied the specters of the past to the flows of a new black cultural history, poised at an uncertain but impending modernity. Across this expanse, these pages consider the ways literature stages the processes of place as a discursive struggle.

I should state, too, that the readings that follow are not sequenced around a series of symbolic spaces. (Here I think of Melvin Dixon's Ride out the Wilderness: Geography and Identity in Afro-American Literature [1987], which reads modernist black narratives as quests for belonging in relation to the mythico-real spaces of wilderness, underground, and mountaintop.) Nor do I organize Black Atlas as a collection of topical sites in black history, which I then examine through the lens of literature. Instead, what I keep at the center of my discussion is how African American literature itself arranges geographic meaning. I go on to argue that discourses about place can effectively produce experiences of space, and that what African American literature does with a lucidity and richness is make place into a theatre of deliberation. Place in African American literature is a complex of meaning that cues different worlds of necessity and possibility.

This book brings into focus a group of authors, all from the critical half-century, beginning with William Wells Brown, Martin Delany, Frederick Douglass, James Beckwourth, and Frances E. W. Harper and extending to Pauline Hopkins and Alice Dunbar-Nelson, among others. It encompasses political editorials from black serials (the North Star, Anglo-African, and New Orleans Daily Creole), detailed travel writing and exploratory accounts, and midcentury national maps of hemisphere.

Yet the authors I look at here are unified less by the worlds they inhabited than by the worlds they invented. Most centrally, they are united by the prominence of geography—*geo* (world) and *graphia* (writing)—in their literature. Their writings, I argue, reflect not just the times, but the processes of place. That is, their work is about the complexities of place—and place has a valence outside of fiction. In terms of organization, I have tried to select texts that most clearly illustrate my claims about the relations of the literary to the geographic. However, my argument is less about patching together any synthetic canon than it is about the centrality of territorial relationships and geographic materiality to meaningful correlations between race politics and black literary aesthetics. I especially arrange the chapters to locate and historicize something that African American literature showcases in respect to other narrative traditions in the Americas: the highly interstitial scope of placement blacks worked through—both materially and perceptually—in the United States.

I further argue that although nineteenth-century African American authors did write about scenes and sites frequently inaccessible to white U.S. and British readers, they did more than present stories about how the other half lives, or make "peculiar" witness for popular print commodity. Instead, to gain representation in the symbolic structures of white territorialization, black authors had to write over white principles of containment. They had to dismantle dominant organizational codes of place. They did this by revealing the contingencies of dominant discourses and the different fabrications that took the form of geographic fact. They also got close to something I think of as parallel invention. As the following pages consider, nineteenth-century African American literature produces subject mappings. It creates worlds and effects sensibilities and relations to those worlds. So what I try to attend to are the ways literature stages place and simultaneously breaks with scales of geography that abrogate the local as a function of the national, or that collapse hemisphere into nationalist paradigms of influence. As I will describe shortly, literature confounds the logic of scale.

Finally, I suggest that what animates the literature I look at here is its engagement with deterritorialization. Deterritorialization, as a dislodging of geographic contexts and descriptors, takes different forms in each of the following chapters. It can be about presenting a world and presenting how to undo it. It can also be about posturing in one world and moving an agenda forward in another, or passing through the codes of a given space outside the modalities that systemize control. Regardless, it is a leading mode of representative practice in the literature I consider here. Deterritorialization partitions territory. It moves boundaries. And so it has the potential to be generative since, by realigning territories, it can alter the overall map. The approach to deterritorialization I pursue in *Black Atlas* connects to the ways literature configures black flow (the currencies that traverse space—be they speech acts or the movements of cultures and capital) in nearly all of these texts. It also connects to what I suggest is the creative potential of deterritorialization. This is an important consideration in the subsequent chapters. African American authors and intellectuals understood that it was only through decoding dominant registers of power that they could find openings for different forms of actualization. The authors I examine used their writing to interrupt racist ordering systems. They used it to make contours for spaces of dissension. That is, they used it to yield new forms.

Spaces of Dissension

The term "spaces of dissension" is influenced by Michel Foucault's early archaeological-styled work on discourse formation and the accidents or contradictions that keep a dominant discourse from ever being fully self-contained. These contradictions pose certain openings whereby new discourses can emerge.[2] As Foucault contends, spaces of dissension are always in subtle negotiation with the agendas of power. They belong to no specific domain, and they reconstitute in different places. In my treatments here, I read spaces of dissension and discursive deterritorialization as modes of a similar thing: I take them both to be interactive forms of a black aesthetic that is always in negotiation with other circulating discourses. But additionally, the body of literature I examine prompts a further recognition. African American literature shows that spaces of dissension are more than reactive, rhetorical gestures toward a real "out there." They are not just declamatory expressions against a backdrop of material history. Rather, they are fields of invention that mediate different worlds.[3] So instead of taking the production of such spaces to be inevitable cracks in the coherence of some pervasive ideology, or quasi-attached resistance acts that defy the sense of a system (as Foucault would suggest), I look at them as deliberate narrative strategies.

I say "narrative" because that is how they reach the modern reader—through the records of writing. But they could be constituted by any variety of practices: life practices, escape acts, performances. What African American literature shows is that spaces of dissension are produced on purpose, to effect new modes of figural representation: they are aesthetic figurations of a process. And this process is the business of feeling out the normative organizational codes that cohere in oppressive power systems, and then finding disruptions in, contradictions to, and corridors through these codes. This is what black flow is about. Its forms are virtually endless because it does as it makes.

Black Atlas traces a portion of this deterritorializing work geographically through nineteenth-century black literature since the literature itself is so invested in gauging and reformulating different exercises of power. It is literature that narrativizes different schemes of possibility for black positioning. For example, dispersed through the plotlines of Martin Delany's serially released novel Blake (1859–62) is an instructional counteratlas. In chapter after chapter, the author illustrates devices for black escape via land knowledge (moss growing on the north side of tree bark), river knowledge (crossing sites and the names of steamer captains), basic astronomy and navigational technology (lodestone and compass), and an array of performances in the gaps of white custom. All constitute the material of black passage out of slavery. All feed a black counter-discourse of place that takes shape against other cartographies.

Literature, I argue, serves as an important vehicle for those interested in understanding the operations of place as creative strategies for living. It gives purchase to places that fall outside of historiographical landscape accounts, spaces termed obsolescent, nonproductive, or generally removed from the scenes on which real modern action is believed to transpire. It also confers shape on spaces that go unrepresented in traditional cartography. Fiction poses questions about what is mappable and which sites cast shadows; it opens dwellings and it opens the spaces of memory. It writes not just known spaces or the negative aesthetics of dislocation. It makes a relationship between scenes of experience and worlds that can be imagined.

In writing this book, I have also had occasion to reflect on the ways space is about stories. Our stories are constantly augmented by the spaces we inhabit. The scales and vantages espoused in narratives are, in effect, maps of times embedded in space. Thadious Davis understands this when at the beginning of *Southscapes* she writes, "approaching space as a site of struggle over value and meaning necessarily involves engagement with the structures underpinning and driving narration itself."[4] Geographical knowledge is produced through narrative, and as this book illustrates, narratives negotiate geographies of power. Moreover, stories yield insight into the ways users design their environment—even as these environments seem to determine them. Stories, I claim, are archives of movement and spatial representation. They are a circulating commons. "Every story," Michel de Certeau writes, "is a travel story—a spatial practice."[5]

And insofar as the readings that follow connect stories to spatial practice, I think it is necessary to consider, at least briefly, what space means in relation to place, especially because space is so frequently equated with freedom and place with enclosure. I mean that for all the possibility space ostensibly hosts, we associate it with emptiness. Space suggests extension—without a set course.[6] Humanist geographers tend to interpret space as something abstracted from the particular.[7] It is a framework for configurations shaped by time and somehow subject to scientific law. Computer scientist Paul Dourish argues that despite major gaps of legibility, space has come to be seen "as a natural fact—a collection of properties that define the essential reality of settings of action."[8] Processes flow through space, but it evades our scope of causality and ideas about closure. Its range makes it largely unmeasurable.

By contrast, place has a rather different set of associations. Place is attached to our sense of values, *genius loci*, and our experiences of boundedness. In terms influenced by Martin Heidegger, place constitutes the boundaries through which presencing can begin. Without such boundaries for presencing, there can be no being, no identity or identification.[9] This distinguishes place from space's infinite extension: place is closer to us and closer to our connections. From Henri Lefebvre to Fredric Jameson, space represents surface and synchronicity, a kind of vertical history. Place, on the other hand, contains times as practices; it spans a horizontal axis of forward experience and backward recollection. Sociologist Anthony Giddens argues that places reveal time by tradition (a point we will return to in the later chapters dealing with region).[10] And Yi-Fu Tuan, whose work perhaps best defines the turn to humanistic geography beginning in the 1970s, emphasizes the ways individuals and people bond to settings, calling place "a center of felt value."[11] Though geographers on the whole recognize place to be one of the field's most contested concepts, certain understandings come together as convention. Political geographers Erica Carter, James Donald, and Judith Squires state this paraphrastically: "Place is space to which meaning has been ascribed."[12] We superimpose our frameworks for meaning on place, and space, ostensibly, lays its claims on us.

Yet the literary histories I will examine here turn on an understanding that rejects the dominant dualism of space and place—namely, the presupposition of an absolute space from which place can be particularized, and the primacy of space over place. As I argue, such divisions tend toward a succession of reductions. This is particularly the case when it comes to examining represented spaces (spaces in discourse, spaces in art) because, among other things, spaces become legible to us by the ways they orient the human subject. We can read spaces if they enable structures of meaning, or if they present a world of sensations. Thus, we know space like we know place: by the practices it "presences." But my main concern is more simply that the division proves misleading. It unnecessarily foreshortens our views into the ways actual life spaces work, how they are made and get into circulation. And it leads to the equation of place with representation, which is actually another kind of closure, much like making time the particularization of historical occurrence.[13]

This leads to the issue of periodicity, something I do not want to leave aside in this preliminary discussion about geographical approaches. One point I should make at the outset is that I take the foregrounding of place as process to be part of the generative, critical work I see that is bringing forward a newer set of benchmarks for the organization of African American literature. These benchmarks are more geographically inferential than they are sequential. For example, recent scholarship in black diaspora and hemispheric studies has gone quite a distance to expose the kinds of exceptionalisms inherent in the project of containing literary aesthetics and discourse circulations in national forms (Carr, Gruesser, Gruesz, Kazanjian, Levander, Levine, Nwankwo).[14] From another angle, works like Stephen Knadler's *Remapping Citizenship and Nation in African American Literature* and Ivy Wilson's *Specters of Democracy* trace within the aesthetics of citizenship a foundational reflexivity, a spatial indeterminacy that lies at the base of any projection of the national. Knadler, for example, looks at the border spaces between comparative cultures for alternative contexts to the meaning of democratic self-making. And

Wilson follows a pervasive shadow presence, an undercurrent that comes alive in the echoes and recesses of national form. For Robert S. Levine in *Dislocating Race and Nation*, an attention to the conspicuously fictive, provisional qualities of a national culture—what Levine aptly calls an "unknowingness" undergirding a culture's assemblages—is just as valuable an opening for the modern critic as the forms of consensus that inform any "rising national literature" paradigm.[15] And in the project of expanding an expressly African American frame of reference, Eric Gardner's *Unexpected Places* illustrates the breadth of frequently overlooked textualities from the black periodical press that can be recovered (just as Gardner himself archivally recovers) by extending our views of a literary landscape to a much broader range of print publication venues.

In contrast, a sequentially driven, horizontal analysis of cultural history is generally configured to obscure from view events and scenes that do not point toward a given conclusion. Indeed, such arrangements hold together long-standing chronologies of African American aesthetics—whether it means the culmination of black agitation after slavery into a proto–civil rights movement, or a staging of the Harlem Renaissance as the flowering of the Great Migration from the rural South. These older historiographies, which I see no need to single out here, are by no means poor conceptualizations. On the contrary, they offer organized and compelling frames for symbolizing African American national experience. And they remain valuable for their conductive role in bringing forward an African American literary tradition—which at the present time of writing, I suppose, we are no longer inclined to view as a somehow singular tradition.[16] But place-based histories frequently prove most interesting when they do not adhere to such chronographies—when they run aslant of temporal encapsulations. This is because geographical approaches can provide a wider aperture for inspecting counter-histories or counter-movements that do not directly lead to a given historical junction. Thick descriptions of place may be less valuable as an organizing motif for sequential-axis histories because of their inclusive nature. Yet the point remains that many paths in cultural expression do not work as designs leading to some determined end.

And so I begin from the claim that nineteenth-century African American literature is starkly geographic. The readings that follow intervene in major period debates about free soil, regionalist scales of production, Indian deterritorialization, internal diasporas, color line spatialities, pan-American expansionism, and hemispheric circuitry. They do so because the literature I examine did so first. I also argue that African American literature reconfigures geographic contexts by intensifying sites of identification and sites of defamiliarization. It manipulates the signification of different geographies in ways that make openings for black aesthetic emergences.

Having previously addressed periodicity, I should also make a claim for genre. Most basically, the generic category of novel in the black rise of the novel begs qualification. (This is discussed in detail in the first chapter of this book.) The nineteenth-century black novel did not exist in any bracketed specificity. There was not an integrated sense of readership for it. Nor was there a more unified or nationalized commercial market to tap, as was the case during the rise of the novel in eighteenth-century England. Nineteenth-century black authors targeted multiple publics. For instance, Brown's first edition of *Clotel* was directed to a white, primarily British, antislavery readership, while Delany's *Blake*, published just a few years later, was written for a literate, largely urban, black magazine subscription base. And in as much as it appealed to different constituencies, the black novel borrowed from many conventions. It was, in fact, something closely intertwined with parallel innovations in other narrative forms, including autobiography, serial fiction, natural history, and political theory. *Black Atlas* takes all these genres to be constitutive of nineteenth-century African American literature. But it keeps in focus the era's most incisive and developed writing about place, writing found in the radical genre-bending work of a number of the period's important authors.

Finally, I think it is important to describe how I mobilize the subject of geography in this book: I pursue a characterization of place as something both material and invented, which is actually indicative of geography's reach. That is, the literary analyses that follow do not have to subtend geography's disciplinary function in some way, since geography is a practice already attached to both writing and human apportioning of landscape. As geographic historians have argued, geography is a compound field of study. What separates geography from related domains like geology or topography is that geography is about places as interconnected, interactive phenomena. It poses questions about the nature of places and the ways they are organized, not as contiguous sites but as interwoven spatial forms. Geographer Michael Curry argues that the history of geography as a scientific discourse predates printed English, and that since its earliest traceable appearance, it was a compound branch of learning. Accordingly, geography from the time of Ptolemy (born approximately 100 CE) joined together topography (the writing about discrete places), chorography (the writing about region), and geography (the study of the earth as a whole).[17]

The point of this genealogy is not to identify the perhaps obvious scalar movement from *topos* to *choros* to *geos*, an arrangement from small to large. Nor is it that contemporary practices of geography have somehow swallowed other traditions of thinking about space (although that might be an interesting arena of philological debate). Rather, it is that geography shares in the articulation of spaces as multimodal. Geography is about places as limit situations and places as possibility. In addition, geography is at the intersection of both place and text: it describes worlds out of sites; its purview is interactive place. African American literature reflects this multiplicity of modes, and it does so in a way that is amplified by the strikingly interstitial relationship to places that African Americans in the United States historically experienced.

The Land Stakes

Throughout the first decade of the African American novel, the black population in the United States existed without political representation in a nation whose very federal structure appeared to be on the brink of dissolution. The vast western land accessions of the 1840s and the growing competition between federal and state claims for primacy created a broad-based uncertainty about the status of nation in the U.S. popular imagination. Slavery had already made the vast Nebraska Territory slave country. It was a decisive issue in carving out from the Mexican Cession of 1848 the slave territories of Utah and New Mexico. In 1853, the same year that the first African American novel—Brown's *Clotel*—was published, President Franklin Pierce authorized the Gadsden Purchase, buying from Mexico the southern corners of what are now New Mexico and Arizona to make a route for a transcontinental railroad across the South. It was territory that was conspicuously opened to slavery. Slavery was also deeply implicated in designs for the movement of capital, as thousands of miles of railroads and hemispheric steamboat routes reshaped national pathways. As figures like the black explorer, author, and journalist Martin Delany feared, slavery had the potential to shape the country's seemingly voracious future growth. In 1849 Delany wrote: "That the question of Free Soil is henceforth to become the great leading political topic of this country, is now admitted by all."[18] Little was more pressing than the subject of national geography for midcentury African Americans. Slavery made the lands stakes very high.

At the same time, the African American authors I examine saw beyond the spatial teleologies of Northern freedom and Southern bondage. From Brown and Delany to Harper, Hopkins, and Dunbar-Nelson, they wrote about the webs of wider hemispheric geographies and how they came together in known worlds. Even authors like Sutton Griggs, whose best-known novel *Imperium in Imperio* (1899) described an intranational black breakaway republic, secretly headquartered in Waco, Texas, were fascinated by the wider arc of black territorial imagination. He described the anticipation with which midcentury African Americans greeted news of black revolt in Cuba: "In proportion as the Cubans drew near to their freedom the fever of hope correspondingly rose in the veins of the Imperium."[19] Writing for the *North Star*, both Douglass and Delany scrutinized technologies of connection between nation and hemisphere. They closely followed the transit and communication spreads (submarine telegraphs, steamer hubs, and capital flows) linking proslavery U.S. nationals and Caribbean landholders. Such circuitry reflected what Delany called, "the Southern Confederacy of America."[20] This was a confederacy that did not simply concentrate itself along North-South or industry-agriculture polarizations. Viewed on a map, it was not the other half of the Missouri Compromise or the proslavery side of the Mason-Dixon Line. Finally, it was not the Southern landscape purveyed by some of the most proslavery of Democratic legislators, figures like South Carolina's John C. Calhoun, who in an 1850 Senate address depicted it as a grounded, agrarian space of quiet that maintained a national equilibrium.[21] Rather, it was an expansive vision of slavery's alliances as an "Axis Americanus," a capitalist network that swelled beyond national structures. Slavery's topographies were designs on land and water. They went over and under the 36°30' latitude lines thought to contain slavery. As David Kazanjian has observed, U.S. imperialism is itself a circuit that stages nationalist vistas: "The entrenchment of racial formations depends on the enhancement of U.S. imperialism."[22]

And as the following chapters describe, the story of black placelesness in national schemes of affiliation does not end with the abolition of slavery or postbellum reunification. The Civil War brought little in the way of resolution to black experiences of internment in white models of underdevelopment. By the second half of the nineteenth century, concerns about black figuration in national representation proliferated as some of the most written about and publicly debated issues in African American life. For blacks, it was about getting through jurisdictions, through the relation of law to land. And it was about survival when as late as 1896, John Marshall Harlan—the only dissenting Supreme Court justice in the *Plessy v. Ferguson* decision—conceded that what national law was now bestowing on African Americans, this "large class of our fellow citizens, our equals before the law," was "a brand of servitude and degradation."[23] Chapters 4 and 5 address the ways African American authors had to develop geographic literacies to move through coded restrictions after Reconstruction. Late-century authors like Charles Chesnutt and Alice Dunbar-Nelson described these adapted forms of movement in their literature. They both knew firsthand what it meant to be outsiders from American plenitude. They knew about social stratification and racial difference under the banner of a free nation, and their stories certainly reflect this.

Yet African American authors took seriously the idea that systems of meaning, just like the ordinances that determined their own national lives, were dynamic and fluid. They knew that power could be manipulated and subversively reappropriated in different contexts. Ways of knowing, their writings demonstrate, might be ways of reading material places in their configurations and their phrasings. Black geographical literature, I argue, is the textual reclaiming and reconstituting of actual places. In fact, although it has been little examined, geographical inquiry into the ways places were organized as overlapping sites of access and sites of surveillance reads as a persistent subtext in the African American novel. Writing about the United States as a fugitive in England, William Wells Brown addressed the spaces of the slaveholding household from Missouri to New Orleans, as well as the conflation of domestic production (slavery and industrialization alike) and planter politics in both the national capital and the capital of the Confederacy, Richmond, Virginia. Martin Delany extensively researched the presence of internal diasporas, situated within the spaces of some thirteen slave states and the Choctaw Indian Nation in Arkansas. His writings insist that the dimensions of black diaspora, from the Guinea Coast in West Africa to the Niger Valley and colonial Cuba, absolutely mattered for slaves on U.S. plantations. James Beckwourth's travel literature cartographically illuminates questions about frontier and Crow Indian border knowledges vis-à-vis statist territorializations in the lands of the North American West. Pauline Hopkins fashioned a black public sphere within the urban geography of Boston at the end of the nineteenth century in relation to interracial legacies from postcolonial Bermuda. And Alice Dunbar-Nelson looked to regional space to remap the locales of late-century New Orleans. She wrote a regionalism that was consciously creolized and transnational.

But even in outlining the sites that were meaningful (or most made to mean) in literature, another point of consideration looms large. Black geographic literature is more than representation and more than taking apart dominant spatial coding. It is literature that produces subject mappings. So whereas the texts I look at here do challenge normative representations of places, they are further suggestive for their engagement with something closer to nonrepresentational geographies. Nonrepresentational geographies are deliberations about the ways places get produced rather than the outcomes of that production. Put another way, they are about the relations that come together to make place. These might be thought of as scenes of flow or mediation, or the ways places can be constituted by interruption. More theoretically, they can be described in terms of deployment, as "processes of delegation or translation." Bruno Latour calls the processes of nonrepresentative theory "traceable associations."[24] For Latour, it is about flattening the social to get at its movements and interactions, to get at its makings. For black authors in the nineteenth century, it was also about unfolding space—to get across. To be clear, relating nonrepresentational theory to nineteenth-century textualities is not about dubbing some anachronous sensibility onto earlier constructions of space. It is more a way to think alongside projects that question the making and enforcement of dominant geographies. And it is no less a way to do justice to the multiple material and semiotic relations and experiential depth recorded in African American literature. For nineteenth-century African American authors, print representation was already the work of thinking around dominant geographies.

Process Geography

David Harvey has noted that the history of geography, at least from the eighteenth century onward, reads primarily as a tool of domination of the powerful over the weak. He writes, "retrospectively we see how geographical dynamics have proven central in the quest to dominate nature and other peoples, to build and perpetuate distinctive power structures (such as a capitalist class or imperialist systems) or social identities (such as the nation state)."[25] Harvey's thinking recalls the observation of cartographer and historian J. B. Harley that the social history of geographical information and maps exhibits "few genuinely popular, alternative, or subversive modes of expression" and rather reads more as "a language of power not of protest."[26] Indeed, like other discourses, geography is reproduced through narratives that give coherence to places by sequencing them according to scales of development and underdevelopment, inclusion and exclusion. Geographer Doreen Massey summarily observes that "not only under modernity was space conceived as divided into bounded places but that system of differentiation was also organized in a particular way. In brief, spatial difference was convened into temporal sequence. Different 'places' were interpreted as different stages in a single temporal development."[27] Massey's broader argument shows that one major outcome of this process is the reduction of space to a dimension that could display a particularization of time.[28] A second outcome is the diminishing of the flow that is space and time to something more like sliced historical occurrences. These could be popular periodicities or some version of what Susan Gillman critiques as "forced chronologies," the kinds of frameworks frequently pinned to national histories.[29] Forced chronologies take different shapes, and one could conceivably argue that all chronologies are, at best, approximations of some collective experience. But what I want to draw attention to is the ways such readings amplify time and conduct space through its chambers. They make place the realm of receivership for history's outworkings.

From another converging angle, colonial historian Walter Mignolo makes clear the presumptions underlying dominant geographic discourses. Writing from a perspective that tries to encompass the coloniality of modern history, dated loosely from the European Age of Discovery and the beginning of Indo-European contact in the Americas in the long sixteenth century, Mignolo claims that by linking geographical boundaries to temporal hierarchies, colonialism's outside—its "others"—could be exteriorized and denied a "co-evalness." He writes that "at the end of the nineteenth century, savages and cannibals in space were converted into primitives and exotic Orientals in time."[30] Mignolo's work is particularly suggestive when it comes to the residual *epistemes* of colonial encounters. He argues that subjective projections of time (as calendars, as histories) have consequences for space. For example, the colonialist Atlantic imaginary he constantly circles—so as to keep in sight—is described as a story about sequencing, about world history that began with Europe. Applied via different regimes of conquest, it made the Americas a place without a history before the present, before the colonial encounter. Such an imagination of space, for Mignolo, produced "the formation and transformation of the modern/colonial world system."[31]

What bringing together accounts by Harvey, Massey, and Mignolo focalizes for this discussion are the more starkly geographic dimensions—indeed, geographic consequences—of official histories. These histories generate normative temporalities, productions of time and space. They are produced and exercised by those in power. And they influence what gets told and how.[32] So one reason why dominant discourses play the role of antagonist (or, more accurately, secondary subject) in *Black Atlas* is because they are discourses that inter space into modes of temporality. As the work here dealing with cartography especially considers, such mobilizations were often invisible, even during U.S. slavery, and blended into matters of fact or presented as the terms of the debate. Yet I also want to argue that African American literature deploys its own vibrant counter-discourses, which reassemble these dominant discourses. It shows them to be fictions that can neither correspond to material space nor cohere as systems of order. If the written literatures, records of civilizations, political documents, and narratives of development in U.S. history are at the same time records of offsetting others into static chronologies of placement, then it is through an attention to heterogeneous counter-discourses that we can read beneath dominant institutionalized knowledges. African American literature is one site among others where the particularity of the local and, at the same time, its imbrications into wider patterns of geographical uneven development, can be narrativized and reimagined. It is literature that is preoccupied with generating what I describe as panic cartographies and side sites in contention with official discourses.

Thus, in framing this discussion about African American geographies, I have found it useful to draw on the work of geographers influenced by compositional, nonrepresentational approaches to space. Although such writing frequently treats debates related to market and labor dynamics, and is more likely to address the spatial structures of global finance rather than those of the novel, "process geography," as it can be called, helps open the terms of analysis for the study of place in literature. Such an approach might read place in terms of its connection to movement, to something geographers Mike Crang and Nigel Thrift call "*space as process* and in process."[33] Process geography looks at place as transient network systems. And it makes geography as much about the coproduction of meaning as it is about any topographical domain. Further, thinking of space as process is potentially significant for new critical studies in literature. A more concentrated focus on flow, migration, and the interlaced networks of relations that constitute location can offer valuable insight into the ways discourses lend shape to place.

Actually, one challenge that process geography poses for readers of literary texts is its insistence on understanding place as dialectical, not merely a backdrop on which historical causality can unfold toward a conclusion. In *Postmodern Geographies*, Edward W. Soja argues that in literary studies the tendency is that an "already-made geography sets the stage, while the willful making of history dictates the action and defines the story line."[34] This is a common figuration in both literary criticism and the literature classroom alike. For example, character dynamism takes shape against a static backdrop of representation; development is temporal action. Place is the background. If it does not support structures of character ambition or movement, it is an obstacle. But in its recognition that landscape is a composition of ideas and struggle for meaning, process geography might be modeled as a way of reading. In the same sense that we tend to think of setting in the novel as scripted place, it is the practice of cultural geography to examine the means (be they mechanisms or imaginaries) by which places come into being—essentially how spaces are scripted.

Terrain

The subsequent chapters are in keeping with the suggestion that place not be thought of as the closure of representation, but rather something closer to an actor itself. For this reason, they approach literary geographies in a number of different modes. Moreover, all of these modes are deliberately sewn through with openings for spaces of dissension. For every posited form, there is an attention to disruptive openings or sites for new emergence. So the first chapter looks at geographies of nation. It also probes the sorts of subnational ruptures that break through the frontpieces of national symbolism. The second is about intra-national territory and also the deterritorialization of landscape. The third chapter considers cartography and mapping as spatial syntaxes. It assesses hemispheric geographies as taking shape through the terms of the connection, and it reads black counter-maps designed to undo world metropole maps. The fourth chapter looks at civic geographies and the subsites of gendered organization via a late-century print public sphere. The final chapter considers the complexities of hemispheric regionalism under the surface of a national membrane. In my inquiries I am deliberate not to impose a geographical scaffold or some scalar hierarchy onto nineteenth-century literature. Rather, I try to delineate the forms that literature makes most suggestive.

To be more specific, chapter 1 considers the ways African American literature both posits and destabilizes foundational fictions of a national *geografía*, an account of national coming together. It looks at the performative qualities of national geographies through a historicized reading of Brown's body of literature, including his midcentury slave narratives, European travel narratives, American traveling catalogue, *Original Panoramic Views* (1850), and the four editions of *Clotel* published between 1853 and 1867.[35] The chapter further examines the ways Brown's literature both formally and thematically presents challenges to the validity of a national republic as exemplary landscape, something that can underwrite social contract and natural law. His panorama and blended fiction, I claim, can be read as counters to the influential Jeffersonian-influenced vision of land usage and territoriality, a model of agrarianism that claimed the natural landscape as a corollary of Enlightenment fulfillment. I also illustrate the ways that *Clotel* knits disparate landscapes together into a larger, knottier amalgam, to give new literary form to a crisis-prone nation. Brown's literary topographies are particularly interesting, too, because they are arranged as sites of intensity and convergences of crisis. They are textual outworkings of a rhizomatic geography from beneath the expanse of national landscape. And they play out against geometries of order like the public squares and street plans of Washington, D.C. that Jefferson had overseen as president in 1801. Chapter 1 thus describes the ways the black novel form facilitated something that exceeded earlier forays into the popular, but more narrowly framed, first-person slave autobiographies. The novel gave authors like Brown a way to approach a deeply disjunctive, antebellum national space as a malleable field of knowledge. This was a major development for black literature.

The second chapter moves from tracing the geographies of nation to an examination of one of the most debated concerns in nineteenth-century African American print records: issues of territory. Two mid-century authors are particularly suggestive for their investigations of territory: One is Delany, whose writings constitute the most in-depth study of black diaspora by any nineteenth-century intellectual. (The chapter looks at a number of Delany's major texts published between 1851 and 1862, his most pivotal years as writer.) The other figure remains relatively unknown in a climate of postnationalist American studies. But James Beckwourth's *The Life and Adventures of James P. Beckwourth: Mountaineer, Scout and Pioneer, and Chief of the Crow Nation of Indians* (1856) reveals a geography of tensions embedded in frontier quests. An early nineteenth-century black explorer in the Rocky Mountains and the Sierra Nevada ranges, Beckwourth's expeditions opened the North American West to the mappings of famed national figures like "the Pathfinder," John Charles Frémont. Beckwourth's extended ruminations of a life on the make are particularly compelling for the ways they frame concerns about intranational Indian territory during a period of rapid U.S. expansionism as issues of deterritorialization.

The chapter explores how blacks politicized the idea of territory as a way to get out from behind white ownership—from being the object of property. It further reveals different dimensions of deterritorialization, including the ways territory can be unmoored from its significations, and the ways print discourses can functionally strip meanings from a particular landscape and rearrange spaces of identification. Drawing upon the writings of Gilles Deleuze and Félix Guattari, I argue that Delany's literature enacts a kind of positive deterritorialization; it multiplies forms for black spatial production (travel technologies, flightlines, and star atlases). It also advocates for new spaces of recognition in the folds of dominant cultures. Beckwourth's life and travels, though, lead to negative deterritorializations. At the end of his tales, he is left with legalistic invocations to land claims, but without the flows of emigrants or capital he envisioned. In his *Adventures* he even offers his knowledge of Indian lands to the War Department for contract work, and for first rights to discovery. Negative deterritorialization is revealed to be a vicious circle of captures and closures.

Perhaps most suggestively, the chapter's comparative approach brings into relief questions about territory, not just as a theatre of contest, but as a scope for affiliation. I move from the argument that literature itself produces territorial identification to an assertion that a major, but underexamined, interest of both authors is the intersection of black and American Indian *epistemes* in Indian lands, for example, the ways stories themselves produce land affects frequently in contention with land-to-law jurisdictions. For example, under midcentury federal policy, African Americans were denied ownership of their labor and the land they worked, while Indians were offered incorporation through land cession, incorporation by ceasing their labors. I argue that both Beckwourth and Delany knew that the very exclusionary constructions of citizenship made available to Indians were made with wider goals of geographic dispossession, and that their texts pose questions about the layered, ancestral geographies subject to erasure in the march of progress.

Whereas chapter 2 is framed by a processual account of territory (territory as process), the chapter that follows is an elaboration on how process geographies can function as spatial grammars, or structured language relations. Chapter 3, "This House of Gathering," makes process geography a critical methodology and puts it to the task of reading spatial representations. This chapter examines the cartographic qualities of mid-nineteenth-century African American literature alongside the textualities of leading period maps. It is concerned with the ways African American authors interpreted and rewrote hemispheric cartographies during the precipitous 1850s, during a period of heightened U.S. ambitions for an American archipelago, or what I call an Axis Americanus, in the Caribbean. To illustrate the spatial qualities of this axis, I look at the ways premier midcentury U.S. mapmakers/atlas affiliates

(J. H. Colton, D. G. Johnson, and A. J. Johnson, and others) print-produced hemispheric space as national space across a number of separate national maps during the 1849–59 decade. Through a number of cartographic devices (transport trails, transposed imagery, perceptual groupings), their maps gave form to contemporary U.S. expansionist drives into the Caribbean—radiating from the scripted spaces of a U.S. nation. At the same time, these leading maps presented a picture of a magnetically holistic nation, gathering in its hemispheric neighbor, especially what was the then the richest colony in the world, Cuba. I further assert that that U.S. possession claims were naturalized into expansionist rhetoric after President James Polk (1845–49) revitalized the Monroe Doctrine to sponsor U.S. acquisitions in the Caribbean and Gulf of Mexico.

Yet, black journalistic discourse tells a parallel story about black hemisphere, and it presents important counter-mappings. The chapter assesses the ways authors such as Douglass and Delany engaged directly with visual representations of the Caribbean in order to challenge the gridded logic of national form. For Delany, Cuba was a plane of projection for African American initiative. For Douglass, it was a site of human traffic and the ambit of empire. Both used their writing to deterritorialize space, to unmask the terms of its making. Delany specifically deployed the languages of mapping to pull apart imperialist codes and to show "white gaps" or contours for black passage. In an era when international propaganda campaigns and violent filibusterism received near-constant coverage in such African American papers as the North Star, Anglo-African, and New Orleans Daily Creole, black discourses about the Caribbean were starkly geographic, and conversant with leading cartographies. This chapter on the whole is an attempt to broaden our understanding of cartographic literacies and to locate textual records of black geography in nineteenth-century literature.

If chapter 3 is about the intersection of cartography and discourse, chapter 4 is about geographic genres in literature. The fourth chapter identifies three waves of literary place aesthetics in the black nineteenth-century novel: 1850s-era fugitive spatialities, color line geographies, and turn-of-the-century black public sphere. This is a critical genealogy to traverse because it informs the book's wider shift from the macro theatre of hemispheric cartographies to what I call practice geographies. Practice geographies, I contend, are those that privilege sites of interaction and the forms that participation takes. They operate in terms of context.

The chapter works out from a broadly New Historicist premise (that texts respond to the conditions of their production, and that literature is itself embedded in culture) to examine Hopkins's literature alongside the geographies it records. It focuses on *Contending Forces*, Hopkins's most enduring effort to vivify the dynamics of black civic space. I claim that this text adjudicates two expressly masculinist, black civic platforms (those I attach to her contemporary rivals, Booker T. Washington and Massachusetts's own W. E. B. Du Bois) and that Hopkins ultimately argues for a protofeminist black women's deliberative arena. In this context, the work of feminist geographers and public-sphere debates by Seyla Benhabib and Judith Butler are important for their explicit challenges to normative publics in the work of civic self-fashioning.

Additionally, a major focus within chapter 4 is the position of the black church (as a structure and network) in the formation of literary civic geographies. I argue that although *The Souls of Black Folk* (1903) has been credited as the first Afro-anthropological examination of the black church, Hopkins—three years earlier and in careful detail—portrayed the church's geographic specificity as a kind of civic circuitry in the pages of *Contending Forces*. I further claim that Hopkins inverts state into church to make an embodied black counter-public in a way that parallels Puritan lease-taking on the spaces of a new nation. I thus compare Hopkins's black civic hagiography, a kind of apostolic procession of black church leaders, to Cotton Mather's corporatization (body making) of an emblematic Puritan citizenry. What these ecclesiastic, geographic processes localize (both embody and make proximate) is the work of fiction: Print produces spaces of identification. It produces a rhetorical New England. And readers of Hopkins's turn-of-the-century fiction encounter more than ethnic spaces, unified by common race experiences or a common inherited ethnicity. They encounter intentional communities that share the same aims as the novel: the joint work of demographic self-fashioning and protofeminist civic organization. Using devices associated with regionalist expression, Hopkins portrayed black Boston as a counter-public, a setting within a setting that could be transformed into a route for black participation.

The final chapter extends the treatment of literature geographically, to the idea of region as matrix, and generically, to the short story. It considers the work of black regionalist authors within the genre of late-century regionalist writing, and it accords particular attention to the

New Orleans–based author Alice Dunbar-Nelson and the two fiction collections she published in her lifetime, *Violets and Other Tales* (1895) and *The Goodness of St. Rocque* (1899). Dunbar-Nelson's writing has received less critical attention than that of other regionalists. But her work is particularly interesting because it presents a counter-tradition within a tradition. As a recognized regionalist author, she took some of the most identifying traits attributed to regionalism and subverted them.

In her fiction, the use of dialect, local character names, customs, and geographical settings like Mandeville, the Bayou Teche, or New Orleans's Third District all complicate the presentation of region. And while nineteenth-century regionalist discourse is associated with both spatial and temporal landscape preservation after the Civil War, Dunbar-Nelson wrote about landscapes and communities constantly in states of revision. In her writing, place is always connected to conflict and movement. Place is constituted by flow. Moreover, whereas regionalist literature has been commonly characterized as popular writing for the cultural tourist—depictions of national difference without being "immigrant," portraits of provincialism directed toward an elite readership base—Dunbar-Nelson's black regionalism does something different. It explicitly rejects the plantation idiom of the post-Reconstruction rural South. Instead, following the elusive metaphor of race as signifier, I look at how her fiction occasions the broader themes of creolization and place as exchange. Dunbar-Nelson's fiction shows how local scales transpose wider, transnational movements. This includes the turn-of-the-century fruit trade with Central America, which, in turn, polarized African American and Irish labor within the New Orleans shipping industry. And it further encompasses the ways southern Louisiana Creole culture elided boundaries of ethnicity and racial specificity. Local space and local circuitry, I suggest, warrant further consideration precisely because they do not fold back neatly into the discursive and social parameters of nation. Drawing upon the first half-century of African American literature, from Brown to Dunbar-Nelson, I seek to situate local arenas of activities that can actually destabilize and subvert more official national histories and borders.

The different chapters of *Black Atlas* arrange geography and cartography in the context of African American literary aesthetics. They indicate major figural modes for a postnational black geography. At the same time, they show the ways African American literature performs the work of refiguration. That is, it unfolds actual spaces. In his recent book, *Geography and the Production of Space in Nineteenth-Century American Literature*, Hsuan Hsu makes a related argument, not only about what geographic methodologies bring to the study of literature, but also about how literature, in effect, translates and transforms geographic imaginaries. Examining literature's connection to thinking space, Hsu argues that "literary settings produce real spaces by instilling and manipulating readers' geographical identifications. Literary settings distribute *privilege* itself by containing and facilitating hierarchized dynamics of production, reproduction, labor, migration, and commodity circulation."[36] Such suggestions about sites of privilege and geographic identification have a particular valence for literary scholars because, among other things, they connect the act of making to the act of writing. Literature does not only describe the world in the manner of postmimetic practice or symbolic synthesis. It makes the real.

Philosopher Ian James makes a parallel point worth drawing attention to here. Describing Jean-Luc Nancy's own layered account of space, he infers: "Prior to any traditional distinction between mind and body, ideality and materiality, and prior to cognition per se, there is the passage of sense as a bodily event, as an opening up of meaningful spaces and a meaningful world."[37] As I have argued throughout *Black Atlas*, it is precisely through its potential for narrativizing the sites of belonging, and its transformational capacity to enrich and reconfigure nearly any discourse, that literature opens vital geographies. African American literature is about that opening up of meaningful spaces. It is about the search for meaningful worlds. And black geography is about possibility. Katherine McKittrick reaches a similar position in "Stay Human," the concluding chapter of her landmark study of black women's cartographies of struggle. She writes: "The geographic meaning of racialized human geography is not so much rooted in a paradoxical description as it is a projection of life, livability, and possibility."[38] These inscriptions of possibility draw this introduction to a close. Black geographies configure multiple maps. They are stories that are like paths. They are shaped by pursuits of connection. Stories open place.

....

CHAPTER 1

NATIONAL GEOGRAPHIC

The Writings of William Wells Brown

Just as none of us is outside or beyond geography, none of us is completely free from the struggle over geography. The struggle is complex and interesting because it is not only about soldiers and cannons but also about ideas, forms, about images and imaginings.—EDWARD SAID, *Culture and Interpretation*

William Wells Brown's *Clotel or the President's Daughter: A Narrative of Slave Life in the United States* (1853) has the distinction of being the first novel published by an African American. Yet during the bulk of its one-hundred-fifty-year literary existence, it has received little more than passing attention. Remarking on what at that time accounted for over a century's worth of criticism, J. Noel Heermance concluded in 1969 that *Clotel* was "not a work of sculpted unity resting on American soil," but rather "a nineteenth century 'deus ex machina' mobile, propitiously hanging from the sky."[1] In the 1970s during the social ferment of Black Power, *Clotel* proved to be a problematic foundational piece for race scholars assembling an African American literary tradition. The novel's frequent characterization as a forerunner text for what would come to be known as the tragic mulatta trope was the source of repeated criticism.[2] Even when *Clotel* was, in effect, recovered at the end of the 1980s in critical race studies by Bernard Bell and Blyden Jackson, it was still difficult to place. It was slotted as a sort of bridge venture between slave narrative forms and the presumably more complex and race-conscious kinds of black literature that emerged at the end of the nineteenth century. To complicate matters, Brown retooled and republished the novel three additional times in the decade after 1853, changing the title and plot details as he went.[3] As John Ernest archly observes, "critics have been so frustrated by the presence of so many sources and plots in one text that they have trouble seeing the one in the many—a unified artistic achievement greater than the sum of its parts."[4]

Recently though, Brown's writings have gained footing as major works of nineteenth-century literature. They have been historicized by scholars such as John Ernest, Ezra Greenspan, Robert Levine, Christopher Mulvey, and Hollis Robbins precisely for their literary appropriations and for the ways Brown renegotiated the difficult terrain of nineteenth-century race culture.[5] What is most striking to contemporary readers of *Clotel* (or later editions like *Clotelle* or *Miralda*) is the sheer thickness of subject materials.[6] In *Clotel* alone Brown combined firsthand knowledge of black slave life and regional slaveholder practice with Victorian melodrama, the nineteenth-century historical romance, frontier humor, and religious oratory—all to expose the institution of U.S. slavery across the widest spectrum of national life. Yet within this breadth of textualities, a major component of Brown's representative practice still entreats further consideration. By taking the unwieldy archive of antislavery writings that transect *Clotel* as a starting point, this reading seeks to examine this novel—so long criticized on the basis of its structure—directly through its discourses on a national geography. Brown's geography is both referential and discursive. That is, the novel brings together stories and sketches in the outlines of referential, material space. Aesthetic representation frequently turns on some kind of spatial referencing (for example, a setting, core, backdrop). This is not necessarily new. But in the rich archives of nineteenth-century black print culture, inclusive of editorials, graphic broadsides, dictated narratives, serial fiction, and the bounded book, what gives Brown's literature its specificity is the ways it reveals how nation is materialized: through performances and travels.

Nation is a discursive struggle that is actualized into nonfictional boundaries. More than just an imagined frame for belonging, it imposes meaning on movements and segments the body's access to space and resources. At the same time, what the novel form facilitated was a way to approach the formative geographies of the United States as something more than a record of physical sites. As a genre, the novel was a malleable structure for organizing stories of human projection in the world with scales of knowing and belonging. It could gather different stories to effect new relations to place. This was a major development within early African American literature.

Second, but just as important, Brown's 1850s-era collective writings, including his multiform travel narratives, challenged the validity of a national republic as a kind of exemplary place, a manifest landscape underwriting claims about democracy, expansion, and the free exercise of republican virtue. Like his contemporary Martin Delany, he unseated notions of national territory as cohesive or of a piece. In the following pages I approach *Clotel* as a kind of textual outcrop from beneath the expanse of a U.S. national landscape. The novel tells a story about physical, indexable, North American spaces that do not feed back into any self-evident, iconic national form. This context then reveals a sequence of subnational sites, arranged to expose the inherent geographical tensions between the United States as a centralizing unit and the shapes of life that overlapped in regional culture. I term such sites "panic cartographies." Panic cartographies are spaces of dissimilitude, straining against their containing form; they are alternately sites of eruption and sites of quietude. But in their form they house the potential to undo not only what is close or proximate, but the broader collective.

Finally, *Clotel* is about the ways places were made. I argue that Brown first had to leave the United States before he could see the outlines of a form he subsequently mobilized in his fiction. The outline was nothing less than nation. Nation in *Clotel* is presented as a kind of political fiction, but it is a fiction with real-life consequences for national inhabitants. For example, *Clotel* is a layered deracination of Jeffersonian agrarianism in its strained mid-nineteenth-century forms and ongoing plantation practice. It was Jefferson who wrote in an 1801 letter to James Monroe that "it is impossible not to look forward to distant times, when our rapid multiplication will cover the whole northern, if not the southern continent, with a people speaking the same language, governed in similar forms, and by similar laws."[7] These topographies of sameness could not, in Jefferson's words, "contemplate with satisfaction either blot or mixture on that surface."[8] Jefferson was of special consequence for Brown. Among other things, he saw the former president as a leading contributor to a particular kind of nationalist landscape mythos, one supported by ideals of a national husbandman, land cultivation, and race-science. But *Clotel* goes further than this. Through its tangential plotlines, it appraises models of industrialism associated with the growing northeastern middle classes, which sustained dominant spatial practices. It also examines the kinds of slave-powered land and labor systems that had grown up in places like Missouri, where Brown himself came of age; such spaces were linked through water traffic to the slave markets of the Deep South. Brown's novel is thus a trove of archives, fusing narratives of national race culture together with voices, idioms, and variants of domesticity that showcased profoundly unstable national locales.

Transatlantic Correspondence: Narrative of William Wells Brown and The American Fugitive in Europe

In 1852 William Wells Brown, a fugitive St. Louis slave lecturing throughout Britain, delivered a speech titled "An Appeal to the People of Great Britain and the World." In it he condemned the U.S. federal government's sanction of slavery in both the Southern and Western states. He claimed: "Although the holding of slaves is confined to fifteen of the thirty-one States, yet we hold that the non-slave holding States are equally guilty with the slave-holding."[9] One year later he reiterated this statement in *Clotel's* concluding polemical chapter: "The free states are equally bound with the slave states to suppress any insurrectionary movement that may take place among slaves. The Northern freemen are bound by their constitutional obligations to aid the slaveholder in keeping his slaves in their chains."[10] Brown's insistence on national complicity in maintaining the institution of slavery, a foundational premise of the 1853 version of *Clotel*, could be traced to at least two formative developments. They were interlinked: his travels throughout Europe in the early 1850s and the passage of the Fugitive Slave Act as part of the Compromise of 1850.

In 1849 Brown began what would be a five-year tour as an antislavery lecturer in Britain and France. His travel journals from this time reflect a growing interest in narrating cultural interactions (often the gaps between expectations and encounters) and the ways a given landscape might enlarge or restrict one's sense of self. For Brown, the experience of a new place could unfold practices and ways of knowing advantageous to black self-fashioning. The opportunity of traveling "to other climes" to "look upon the representatives of other nations" also invigorated his writing insofar as he came to experience the ways tourism engendered new forms of subjectivity.[11] Traveling helped him reframe what the concept of nation could mean, and how epistemes of enclosure operated. In 1849 Brown served as a delegate to the World Peace Conference in Paris, and by 1852 he could list such luminaries as Victor Hugo, Alexis de Tocqueville, Alfred Tennyson, and Charles Dickens among his European friends and contacts. These encounters were detailed in what is considered to be one of the first travel narratives published by an African American, Brown's *Three Years in Europe* (1852). Most importantly, Brown's European travel offered a new window into licensed mobility without being subject to arrest or forced fugitive transfer.[12] Announcing his arrival in Liverpool to William Lloyd Garrison in the pages of the antislavery *Liberator* in 1849, this escaped Missouri slave and national noncitizen concluded: "In the so-called Free States I had been treated as one born to occupy an inferior position; in steamers, compelled to take my fare on the deck, in hotels, to take my meals in the kitchen; in coaches, to ride on the outside; in railways, to ride in the 'Negro car;' and in churches, to sit in the 'Negro pew.' But no sooner was I on British soil than I was recognized as a man and an equal."[13] Frederick Douglass made a similar pronouncement following his visit to Eaton Hall, "one of the most splendid buildings in England." Contrasting his ready access with a long list of banned sites of entry in the United States, he wrote: "As I walked through the building, the statuary did not fall down, the pictures did not leap from their places, the doors did not refuse to open, and the servants did not say, '*We don't allow niggers in here!*'"[14]

Brown's first European narrative also shared something in common with his 1847 *Narrative of William W. Brown, A Fugitive Slave*, and the prefatory "Sketch of the Author's Life" in the 1853 edition of *Clotel*. In each text of personal enterprise, what is instrumental to the author's narration of life movements away from slavery is an understanding that place is constituted by performance and expectations.[15] In his second European travel narrative, *The American Fugitive in Europe*, Brown recalled in close detail an incident he experienced at the World Peace Conference in Paris. The incident was significant because it demonstrated the ways users' expectations made place within spaces. It was an encounter with a slaveholder from the United States: "Just as I was leaving Victor Hugo . . . I observed near me a gentleman with his hat in hand, whom I recognized as one of the passengers who had crossed the Atlantic with me in *The Canada*, and who appeared to be the most horrified at having a negro for a fellow-passenger. This gentleman, as I left M. Hugo, stepped up to me and said, 'How do you do, Mr. Brown? . . . O, don't you know me? I was a fellow-passenger with you from America; I wish you would give me an introduction to Victor Hugo and Mr. Cobden.'"[16]

The incident was further remarkable for Brown because it signaled how a change of physical locale might desituate behaviors. Slave subjectivity, the travel narrative illustrated, was prescriptive; it moved with its contexts. By disembedding the actors in this uncomfortable configuration (a lawfully enslaved African American and a "proslavery gentleman") from their physical domains, place performances became very different. Wrote Brown: "The man who would not have been seen walking with me in the streets of New York, and who would not have shaken hands with me with a pair of tongs while on the passage from the United States, could come with hat in hand in Paris, and say, 'I was your fellow-passenger.'"[17]

Like Frederick Douglass, who posted transatlantic correspondences to Boston from England and Northern Ireland in the mid-1840s, Brown realigned his own positionality in the United States as a result of his travels.[18] Travel prompted further questions about cultural conditioning, about something Mark Simpson more widely terms the "politics of mobility," or "the compensatory processes that produce different forms of movement, and that invest these forms with social value, cultural purchase, and discriminatory power."[19] Brown's travels produced the formative impressions of place he developed throughout *Clotel* and conveyed through anecdotes of Virginia slave escape in *My Southern Home* (1880). European travel gave the author a sense of common ground on which he would be taken as a man—a curiosity in many cases. But he was certainly no slave in Europe. At the same time, travel—and not excluding forced transit—in the United States gave Brown his subject material. His extended contacts with slaves on U.S. waterways—first as an enslaved market assistant and riverboat steward, heading South; and later as a fugitive steamboat operator, transporting slaves to freedom on the major ports of Lake Erie, including Sandusky, Detroit, and Cleveland—were the sources for many of *Clotel*'s patchwork anecdotes. Literature bridged place to performance. It could concentrate sites, infrastructures, and the very flows he facilitated on the Underground Railroad between 1834 and 1843. It was also a way to work out different frames of geographic attribution, like those that made landings of a coastline or districts of some homesteads. Literature gave expressive output to exploration. But it did not itself engender material access. In fact, for all his florid descriptions of England's literary heritage sites, Brown still exhorted other would-be fugitives not to come to England. His letter to *Frederick Douglass' Paper* makes clear, "there are numbers here, who have set themselves up as lecturers, and who are in fact little less than beggars."[20]

Actually, filtering through Brown's oftentimes tedious compendiums of European museum visits, famous residences, and hotel stays is the insight that on both sides of the Atlantic, whether it be the United States, Canada West, Jamaica (with its postemancipation indentured labor schemes), or England, was the understanding that even the most kindred of places were shaped through conflict. Place was thus about its negotiation of that conflict. The work of inscribing a U.S. territorial imaginary, one that illustrated the ways nation at once absorbed annexation, militarization, and federalist collusions with a "sectional" slavery into its domestic union, was a project of moving parts. What *Clotel* does is map these parts, not into some neatly synthesized, conceptual economy but rather into something that best befit Brown's own mode of storytelling: Nation reads as a kind of sensational, affective cartography. Like other slave autobiographers, Brown exposed the U.S. nation's domiciles and shrouded locales. But the novel form takes this exposure further and aggregates these sites as constitutive pieces of nation.

The travel narrative Brown produced in England a few years prior to publishing *Clotel* demonstrates this very transitivity of local knowledge, the ways places could be made exportable through artifacts, or implements of technology. In *The American Fugitive in Europe* he wrote about the incredulous looks he received from British customs officials in 1849, when his luggage was ransacked by custom handlers during general port arrival inspections. In his trunk inspectors uncovered an iron collar worn by a female slave on the banks of the Mississippi. As he told it, the object stopped further search.[21] To his viewing audience, the collar was an uncomfortable piece of freight. It signified a relationship to place and experience that could not easily be categorized in a customs log.

The reaction caused by the iron collar—for its very dissimilitude— would come to indicate the subsequent shape of Brown's literary production. Following the abolition of the international slave trade in 1807, British public attention was increasingly directed away from transcontinental narratives of the Middle Passage. These were the writings of eighteenth-century authors now associated with black Atlantic literature: Quobna Ottobah Cugoano, Olaudah Equiano, James Albert Ukasaw Gronniosaw, and Venture Smith, among others. Compared to their restless oceanic struggles and port narratives, the nineteenth-century Southern plantation seemed stable. It was dreadful in its own way, no doubt. But it was sectional. It was this veneer of stability that Brown's entire literary corpus aimed to disrupt.

In fact, for an antebellum American abolitionist sent abroad to seek support in Britain, there was a real urgency in locating a more vitally interactive voice of witness. Slavery was more than some localized residualism. Since torture tools like the iron collar could be attributed by a British public to a presumably extinguished and illegal slave trade, Brown was faced with the task of bracing his claims with connections to existing, current space.

What still needed to be said was that these implements of slavery were more than traces of some now-resolved, reducible past. Slavery was an open circuit in the western hemisphere. It was not closed, nor could it be represented in a way that suggested closure. For instance, though Equiano described an iron muzzle on a female cook on a Virginia planter's estate in The Interesting Narrative (1789), even more gruesome uses for irons could be found in British colonial holdings such as Montserrat and St. Kitts.[22] Equiano bears convincing witness to this: "It was very common in several of the islands, particularly in St. Kitt's, for the slaves to be branded with the initial letters of their master's name; and a load of heavy iron hooks hung about their necks." He wrote, "Indeed on the most trifling occasions they were loaded with chains; and often instruments of torture were added. The iron muzzle, thumb-screws, &c. are so well known, as not to need a description, and were sometimes applied for the slightest faults."[23] The iron collar could have been a British relic. But for Brown, colonial complicity was less the point than was a living, fleshed-out struggle.

And so it was from within the contemporary institutionalization of domestic U.S. slavery that Brown located his material. Print was the mechanism, and the novel the genre for reproducing and interpellating the particular landscapes and artifacts of a place as charged—and making them disruptive. As the iron collar exemplified, indexes of place could be dislodged from their cultural context to effect new reactions to local custom. Local custom was itself a site of cross-hatched meaning.

To use a phrase from phenomenologist Edward Casey, the antebellum locale was the kind of "grasping together" of arrangements that yielded meaning.[24] Indeed, it was through this very kind of pieced-together work that the earliest black novel depicts nation—as a place made strange.

The Fugitive Slave Law: Intra-National Material

No greater proof existed for Brown that there was a national complicity in maintaining chattel slavery as prevailing land-cultivation practice than Congress's passage of the Fugitive Slave Act as part of the Compromise of 1850. In a speech to the National Free Soil Convention at Pittsburgh, Frederick Douglass called it "a law fit only to trampled under foot," and he suited the action to the word. He threatened that "the only way to make the Fugitive Slave Law a dead letter is to make half a dozen or more dead kidnappers."[25] In *Three Years in Europe* Brown shared this sentiment. He also politicized the injunction, concluding that "the Fugitive Slave Law has converted the entire country, North and South, into one vast hunting-ground," later portraying tracts of Mississippi in *Clotel* as just that: human hunting grounds.[26] He concluded that the Fugitive Slave Act "could never have been enacted without the votes of a portion of the representatives from the free States."[27] Promoted in Congress as a measure to preserve an already embattled Union, the Fugitive Slave Act gave slaveholders the power to retrieve escaped slaves from free states and provided for the deployment of federal agents to aid slaveholders in their claims to human property. It also threatened severe fines or imprisonment for any person found to be aiding a runaway. Blacks living in the northern states had considerable cause for alarm. Any African American suspected of being property could be claimed by a slaveowner or an owner's "agent" who furnished proof of purchase. Furthermore, blacks in the geographically demarcated free states were denied trial by jury and had the burden of documentation as free men or free women. Consequently, black suspects would also have to pay any legal costs incurred in the ordeal—provided they could even prove they were free.

The Fugitive Slave Act extended the territorial reach of slavery and readjusted the political geography of free and slave states. In addition, it made slavery transportable into both free territories and free states because it enforced the legality of human chattel, not only north of 36°30' latitude, the line established as the border of free territory in the Missouri Compromise of 1820, but even in places such as New York and Massachusetts.[28] The act was a matter of serious concern for Brown, a famed runaway slave who had lived publicly in Massachusetts since the success of his first, immensely popular *Narrative of William W. Brown* (1847). While he initially arranged to spend a year on the antislavery lecture circuit, touring continental Europe and Great Britain in 1849, he extended his visit after receiving news from abolitionist friends about the law's passage. (It helped that he was enjoying himself in Europe, and that he had marital problems at home.) He would ultimately spend five years in Europe and publish *Clotel* from England.

But the Fugitive Slave Act also gave nineteenth-century African American authors something to work with. In important ways, it brought abolitionist sentiment together with free states' defiance of what was widely perceived to be a Southern concessionist law. And it gave authors like Brown impetus to produce a new form of literature about African American slavery, one that might both nationalize the contemporary landscape of slavery and decenter the dominant logic of nation—a logic that *Clotel* suggests took its shape through claims to a manifest natural landscape. However, while the plot in *Clotel* unfolds primarily across various Southern slave states, Brown leveraged his critique in such a way that he did not atomize the South as the seedbed of the slavery institution. To do so would have enforced a belief, possessing more currency in the United States than in Britain, that slavery was a regionally specific concern and not reflective of the nation as a whole. Instead, *Clotel* references the national text of slavery, ultimately showing it to be spatialized in the architectural layout of Washington, D.C., and most prominently in the human geography of the capital of the Confederacy, Richmond, Virginia.

Brown's first major move in making *Clotel* a national story was to put nation "material" into the struggle of the titular namesake, Clotel, and make her the object of national practice. The story's central premise is that the national Enlightenment icon and author of the Declaration of Independence, Thomas Jefferson, fathered two daughters with his former housekeeper and slave, Currer.[29] The union's progeny are Clotel and her younger sister, Althessa. Although in the early nineteenth century it was widely rumored in numerous black communities, starting in the state of Virginia, that Thomas Jefferson had sired slave children with a slave mistress, Brown was the first black author to take this sort of creative license with details not yet deliberated as public memory. It was a freedom of characterization that he no doubt felt freer to pursue in Britain, where he first published the novel in 1853, than in the United States.[30]

In fact, the first edition, published by the London house of Partridge and Oakey (by far the most readily available version of the novel today), is notably the only edition to incorporate Thomas Jefferson into the fiction in any substantive way. It is also the only edition to sustain its detailed critique of nation—as distinguished from region—as a central premise of the work. The first U.S. edition of the novel, revised and retitled as *Miralda; or the Beautiful Quadroon*, would not appear until some eight years later in serialized form in the New York–based black journal, the *Anglo-African* (the same journal that published Delany's *Blake*). For the installment edition, Brown renamed almost all of the novel's characters and extracted "the President's Daughter" nominative from the title, making vague the Jefferson relation. Only upon the heroine's death does Brown write: "Thus died Isabella, *a descendant* of Thomas Jefferson, the immortal author of the Declaration on Independence" (emphasis added).

The movement away from nation toward region is even more pronounced in the third edition of the novel, this time retitled as *Clotelle: A Tale of the Southern States* (1864) and published during the Civil War with only fairly minor revisions from the *Miralda* text. It was released as part of James Redpath's Books for the Campfires series, marketed to Union soldiers. In the third edition, Clotel's mother becomes Agnes, a woman who boasts that she is the daughter of an American senator, while her two daughters are said to be fathered only by "a young slaveholder." Because of the edition's intended readership, complaints against the federal government are generally ameliorated. Lastly, the fourth and final edition of the novel (substantially revised despite the similar title to its precursor), emerged some three years later as *Clotelle, Or the Colored Heroine: A Tale of the Southern States* (1867). It marked a different moment in Brown's articulation of geography and power in areas of the deep South. In this version Brown reversed the trajectory of the first novel from slavery in the United States to the realization of freedom for the slave in France. Instead, Clotelle (who was Clotel's daughter in the first novel) and her husband, Jerome, remarkably travel from France to the Civil War battlegrounds in Louisiana, where they join the Native Guards during Union occupation of Louisiana and Mississippi. At the end of the novel, Clotelle goes on to found a Freedmen's school on the site of a former Mississippi plantation, an endeavor that would prove popular in later Reconstruction-era African American fiction like Frances Harper's *Iola Leroy* (1892). Across the progressive revisions, a pattern emerges: As Brown adjusted the novel to different cultural and political eruptions, he also recast its units of geographic attribution (transatlantic, national, regional).

The blend of scales responds to the shifting political orders that produce space. In fact, a careful consideration of nineteenth-century African American publication histories illustrates the ways genre takes its meaning through double milieus: the geographies that enable community, but no less so, the circulation of that community through communication, such as print dissemination. This point is key since it signals the ways places in literature are at once discursive, social, and material sites. So more than plot just being a kind of map that drives emplacement, and genre being both the categorical output and the spatial form recognized by readerly convention, revisioning gives new temporalities to spatial configurations.[31]

Hence in an overview of these texts, Brown's antebellum *Clotel* proves rather unusual because it is a critique of the federal government and its commercial and political investment in chattel slavery, not a critique of sectional politics like the subsequent editions. In the first edition, Brown's insistence on the figure of Jefferson functions largely as a matter of representative politics in a contest for national space in the years leading up to the Civil War. Jefferson, who could claim he heralded in the new national century as U.S. president (1801–9), was a leading print authority in establishing claims about race, land usage, and territoriality in broader national culture. These claims were ostensibly issued to reach a domestic support base. But Jefferson also targeted international opinion, especially after the widespread broadside distribution of his drafted Declaration of Independence in 1776, which captured critical attention in Britain, France, and other European colonial powers. Less known is that even his most nativist-appearing late work, *Notes on the State of Virginia*, was composed in response to a series of eco-geographical queries from the secretary of the French legation at Philadelphia, the Marquis de Barbé-Marbois, and published in London in 1787—presumably following intelligence of an unauthorized (illegal) French publication.

Brown's purpose in *Clotel* was, of course, very different from Jefferson's in crafting a natural history. But it was yoked to a similar range of concerns. Already sharing a print language with his British readers, Brown also opened a landscape to give tangible form to his claims about slavery abroad, a landscape containing histories and narratives not exported across the Atlantic in official histories and dispatches. Brown did not reiterate earlier challenges to the racial philosophy Jefferson advanced in *Notes*, something already invoked by earlier writers like Benjamin Banneker in direct correspondence with Jefferson in 1791 and the abolitionist David Walker, whose widely circulated pamphlet, *David Walker's Appeal* (1829), was a more militant excoriation of Jefferson's ethnographic allegations. Instead, Brown took a different angle.[32] His redress of antebellum race culture began on the very ground from which Jefferson in 1787 had inscribed the natural landscape as a corollary of Enlightenment fulfillment, on the soil of Virginia. Brown wrote about the city that Jefferson was to successfully name as the state capital when he became governor of Virginia in 1779: Richmond.[33] The *Clotel* character plot actually has its beginning, middle, and conclusion in the politicized geography of Richmond, Virginia's state capital and, by the decade's end, the capital of the Confederacy.

Geographers Gearóid Ó Tuathail and John Agnew have argued that setting, geopolitically conceived, is never merely a backdrop but more resembles an actor in scripted social scenarios. They write: "To designate a place is not simply to define a location or setting. It is to open up a field of possible taxonomies and trigger a series of narratives, subjects and appropriate foreign policy responses."[34] In terms of *Clotel*, a closer examination of Richmond's domestic spaces reveals a set of local subjects not monumentalized in the city's legacy of first families and national heroes, but no less determinant of the successes of its domestic economy. This is the first family of Brown's novel, the family of the title's namesake, Clotel. Brown's Virginia geography thus begins in the gendered Victorian space of the home. It was a space frequently designated in nineteenth-century popular market literature as an apolitical women's realm. But it is most cohesively a place that Brown exposed to be deeply contiguous with both an industrial and an agrarian social economy, the old standbys of a statist institutionalism that constituted the market forces of slavery.

Confederacy Capital(s) and Domestic Production

As nineteenth-century authors such as Lydia Maria Child, Harriet Jacobs, Harriet Wilson, and Frank J. Webb demonstrated in their literary treatments, the domestic was among the most vital of sites in the antebellum United States for reproducing slaveholding structures and extending slaveholder claims to property. Webb's *The Garies and Their Friends* (1857) and Wilson's *Our Nig* (1859) illustrate the ways the mixed-race domestic household in free states incubated inevitable rupture; in their tellings, the domestic shell of normativity could not withstand the pressures of a national race culture. The same can be said for *Clotel*, except that this story is set in the slave state of Virginia.[35] In fact, early in *Clotel*, the domestic plotlines open when the reader is introduced to a young Virginian aristocrat of inherited wealth, a midcentury Thomas Jefferson avatar named Horatio Green, who represents the future of planter politics in the late antebellum period. Horatio purchases the sixteen-year-old Clotel from a Richmond slave market, where she is auctioned alongside her mother and sister. Horatio and Clotel move to a secluded cottage, where Clotel resides as his common-law wife.[36] She falls in love with him. Her acquiescence to the cottage arrangement, and her willingness to be unseen, hidden from sight in a cottage covered by elaborate foliage, is what ultimately fixes her place in Richmond's domestic economy.

It is worth mentioning that Clotel's plight and Horatio's strategies for keeping her in it bear a resounding similarity to the experiences of Harriet Jacobs, later recorded in *Incidents in the Life of a Slave Girl* (1861). As a young teenager, Jacobs was terrorized by James Norcom, an Edenton, North Carolina, slaveowner. Norcom sought to isolate his young slave by building a concubine cottage for her, four miles outside of Edenton Center. Jacobs, who altogether refused to enter the residence, later wrote: "Hitherto, I had escaped my dreaded fate, by being in the midst of people."[37] Brown borrowed both the story of the man's purchase of a slave girl and the secret cottage residence directly from Lydia Maria Child's short story, "The Quadroons." But whereas Child's story was set in Georgia (without a Thomas Jefferson in the mixture), Brown places "the quadroon's home" just three miles outside of Richmond City, a somewhat unusual choice for a secluded cabin on a pleasant plain, if only for the fact that Richmond was the developed state capital. The location is further suggestive of the kinds of relations existing between capitalism and slavery, a principal thread woven through the fabric of nation that Brown picks apart in *Clotel*. [38]

During the period when he was preparing his novel, 1850–53, Richmond was one of the South's leading cities in the production of tobacco, processing of flour, and ironworks. It was also home to one of the nation's largest populations of African American skilled industrial workers, who were, in turn, largely responsible for maintaining the city's industrial infrastructure. According to Midori Takagi, a historian of Virginia, at the onset of the Civil War half of Richmond's male workforce was drawn from the local slave population. [39] *Clotel's* cottage is an architectural metonym of the wider city. It is described as "a perfect model of rural beauty," "surrounded by piazzas"—by which Brown in a nineteenth-century context likely meant verandas—and its "gateway rose in a gothic arch, with graceful tracery in iron work, summated by a cross." [40] Architecture mediates landscapes, and as William Gleason points out, "in the nineteenth century most American commentators understood built forms to have explicitly racial origins and connotations." [41] In this case, the iron railings signify the conflation of a particular mixture of industry, domesticity, and slavery in Richmond's economy.

Charles Dickens, who visited Richmond in March of 1842 as part of his American tour and recorded his observations of the city a year later, in *American Notes*, was particularly struck by the city's thoroughgoing reliance on a black workforce. After a visit to a tobacco manufactory, "where all the workers are slaves," he commented on the ways black workers were regulated by apparatuses of industry like clocks, meal bells, and even schedules, according to which they were permitted to sing while working. [42] Dickens's observations effectively underscore a feature distinguishing Richmond slavery and certain evolutions of urban slavery from other plantation-based, agriculturally driven forms of the institution. The problem can most clearly be isolated by briefly considering the labor politics undergirding Richmond's most important industry.

A leading reason why Richmond was chosen as the capital of the Confederacy was that it was home to the South's largest and most important foundry, Tredegar Iron Works, on the James River. Tredegar was the South's greatest producer of heavy munitions like cannons and artillery, as well as iron siding for the famous ironclad naval gunboats, the South's best technological innovation for countering the North's virtually intact prewar U.S. Navy. Tredegar was also a site of contention because it relied heavily on slave labor, both hiring slaves and purchasing them outright. When the Civil War began in 1861, half of Tredegar's nine hundred employees were slaves. This arrangement lead to massive strikes from white workers, who feared dispensability and a downgraded employee status—as well as their subsequent expulsion from the company in favor of less expensive slaves.[43] Consequently, Richmond came to be associated with the kinds of sectional crises that threatened to divide Southern cities: labor tensions centered not on the popular polarization of agriculture and industry, but rather between a slave-based industrial society and a unionized wage-labor economy.

This problem was perpetuated by the fact that in Richmond, a city that clearly exploited the cheap hire of its growing urban and enslaved populace, capitalist production ventures did not make slavery obsolete; rather, they generated new markets. In considering American slave production in the context of the broader African slave trade, Michael Hardt and Antonio Negri assert that "slavery and servitude can be perfectly compatible with capitalist production, as mechanisms that limit the mobility of the labor force and block its movements."[44] Indeed, places are about how they are practiced. The case of Richmond exemplifies such a mode of territoriality as an organizational system of captures. As Brown's fiction depicts it, the aristocratic Horatio Green, who apparently does not work, exemplifies how the slave system was fitted to local social structures that facilitated the planter class's territorial interests—as overlapping members of Virginia's powerful governing class—and protected the elite, at least in the short term, from the sorts of labor tensions that rocked urban life.

In Brown's political topography, Richmond is an early example of collusion between heavy machine industry, associated with the free labor North, and the pastoral ideal of the planter class. Richmond's centrality to the novel's plot underscores a broader point rehearsed across the author's collected writings: capital connects the North and South. It sutures the distance between the capital of the Confederacy and the production and trade-driven cities of the Northeast. Richmond also stands in socially for what I have suggested is a dominant theme in this version of *Clotel*—a broad and national complicity in maintaining the landscapes of slavery. The city's developed industrial infrastructure, facilitated by its black factory workers, suggests a greater similarity between generically conceived Northern industrial models and Southern modes of labor than was commonly indicated in antislavery writing.

In *Clotel* the domestic ultimately proves coterminous with Richmond's multi-tiered slave-industrial nexus. Clotel's union with Horatio as a kind of "marriage of understandings" precludes, by its nature, extensions into the world beyond the wooded cabin. After giving birth to a daughter, Mary, Clotel finds herself only further implicated in reproducing the terms of her social oppression. As slave authors themselves frequently pointed out, antebellum slaveholders' policy, codified in binding legal codes in the Southern states and the Western slaveholding territories, was that the line of descent followed what was commonly referred to as "the condition of the mother." (This policy made the United States the obvious exception to historian Seymour Drescher's observation: that ending the slave trade to a given slave society in the long run resulted in the abolition of slavery itself.[45])

What a geographical reading of Brown's Richmond illuminates is that place, in its specificity, is constituted not only by its modes of production, but also by the ways it produces race. Racial production reaches across scales (local, national, and transnational) insofar as the concept of race, particularly in the nineteenth century, was constructed around environmental debates about habitation and the suitability of areas for white settlement (especially in respect to colonial prospects for resource development and labor extraction). Writing about how empire haunts both the intimate and public landscapes of U.S. history, Ann Laura Stoler cites what she calls "domains of the intimate" as key spaces for the exercise of state power through "local knowledge and close encounters."[46] Such processes, in turn, shape entitlements. According to Stoler, domains of the intimate "are strategic for exploring two related but often discretely understood sources of colonial control: one that works through the requisition of *bodies*—those of both colonials and colonized—and a second that molds new 'structures of feeling'—new habits of heart and mind that enable those categories of difference and subject formation."[47] The point here is that race is imbricated in blended scales of belonging. And certainly structures of feeling extend to the sorts of sexual relations, child-rearing practices, and forms of racial admixture that underwrite categories of colonial classification.[48]

In fact, feminist geographers have long seen the privatized space of the home as a pervasive space through which ideas of authority and access are produced. A wide range of work on gender and body space illustrates the ways domestic sites and households shape networks of affective belonging, even as gender remains such a heterogeneous category of analysis. As Robert Reid-Pharr points out, a central feature in the antebellum "process of domesticity" was to fashion a distinctively raced subject, a subject who would later emerge as the black national citizen.[49] In Brown's Clotel, as in Jacobs's Incidents in the Life of a Slave Girl and Child's "The Quadroons," the same sorts of racialized social dynamics that shape domesticity also script contemporary U.S. slaves' movement. Having removed Clotel not only from the complex of African American life in the city, but civil society altogether, Horatio secretly courts the daughter of a wealthy benefactor, identified only as Gertrude. The two marry, his previous bonds with Clotel retaining no legal status. In terms of plot, Brown's novel generally arcs toward greatest disclosure and (significantly for this study), new geographies. Soon after Horatio's second marriage, the indomitable Gertrude learns about Clotel and the child through a channel of local gossip, which so happens to be confirmed by her new husband's nighttime murmurs. She orders Mary, a child of ten, into her home to be a special object of revenge. Gertrude also sees to it that Clotel is sold down South to a new owner in Vicksburg, Mississippi. However, Clotel's new home, conveniently a major port city, brings about unexpected opportunities for both black self-invention and new ventures into mid-nineteenth-century forms of mobility. Another node is thus presented in Brown's cluster of subnational spaces.

Bulwark and Conduit

"Vicksburg," Confederate President Jefferson Davis famously declared in 1862, "is the nail head that the holds the South's two heads together."[50] Certainly at the time Brown was writing his novel, near King's College on the Strand in London, Vicksburg was perceived as no less than a leading fortress city for the American South. Built on what were believed to be unscalable steep-faced bluffs, it connected the eastern and western sections of the Confederacy and controlled the middle reaches of the Mississippi River. Yet it is precisely from Vicksburg and its fortified port that Brown imagined a performance that could successfully launch slaves on a water route to freedom.

A reading of Vicksburg that emphasizes the relationship between regional geographical arrangements and scales of civil authority is suggestive insofar as it can direct attention to the discontinuities between what is topographically physical (cliffs and river inlets) and what gets made into a "fact" of place design (harbors and outposts). Brown's story shows that what made Vicksburg hold the Confederacy together—its holds or, to use the terminology of Bruno Latour, "stabilizing mechanisms"—were its concentrated slave markets.[51] Whereas Richmond in this novel functions as its own microdrama about a nation enduring a crisis of self-definition at the federal level, Vicksburg has a different purpose. It is portrayed as a place that is at once zoned, classed, and racialized—a spatial bulwark for proslavery economies and a major commercial port for trading, auctioning, and commissioning slaves. Vicksburg was, in fact, a leading steamboat city for cotton, supplying factories in the Northeast and Europe. Furthermore, its physical geography supported its primary economic geography. Brown writes: "The town of Vicksburgh [sic] stands on the left bank of the Mississippi, and is noted for the severity with which slaves are treated."[52] But at the same time, it also proves to be a route out of slavery for Clotel. As I will suggest, even the most strategic strongholds of slavery, places like Vicksburg, were not finite arrangements of place determinants, but rather points of variability with knots and openings.[53] Once again, getting through was a matter of place coding.

Despite Vicksburg's fortifications, it was vulnerable and as much constituted by its potential undoing as it was by its claims to Confederacy dominance. As a port city, it presented physical gaps in security for maintaining propertied persons. Like Natchez, it had more opportunities for black anonymity and information exchange, factors that slaveholders understood as ever-persistent threats to their human property. As Douglass commented in his 1845 Narrative, "a city slave is almost a freeman, compared with a slave on the plantation. He is much better fed and clothed, and enjoys privileges altogether unknown to the slave on the plantation."[54] For city slaves, the presence of free blacks, along with increased opportunities for employment beyond the immediate oversight of a master, created better possibilities for networking outside the confines of monitored slave relations. Christopher Waldrep, for instance, writes that for slaves residing in antebellum Vicksburg, permission passes might be used to effect escape: "Some—perhaps most—knew where to go for a forged pass: a white man named Red Jack."[55]

Brown, who first "hired" his labor as a slave in St. Louis, was no stranger to falsified slave passes and would have understood the value of a city's more extensive flows of and access to transportation. In fact, a limited number of Vicksburg city slaves were even known to operate their own businesses. Although the better part of any profits from such ventures usually ended up in the hands of slaveholders, a slave "hiring" his or her own time came into contact with a wider range of people and generally maintained some measure of control over labor conditions, experiences notably different from those of blacks in the cotton fields, which dominated the greater expanse of Mississippi's landscape. Additionally, an urban slave had far improved chances for escape than the same slave would have living on a plantation. Being close to a harbor helped.

Port cities were vitalized by the flow of black seamen who worked in waterfront industry and commercial shipping. Abolitionists like the clothier David Walker knew this and made sailors conduits of abolitionist discourse. Walker's known tactic was to disseminate his antislavery tracts from his home shop in Boston by sewing them into the linings of sailors' coats so that they would reach major port cities in the South, including Richmond, Savannah, Wilmington, and New Orleans.[56] As Douglass described it, his access to the Baltimore shipyards and weekly wages as a "hired out" slave facilitated his own 1838 flight to freedom. For Brown, as I discuss below, access to steamboat technology and a familiarity with river port culture were the final factors that put him in proximity to freedom.

So in terms of a politics of location, slaveholders' control over the middle Mississippi and Vicksburg's strategic clutch hold of the wide Yazoo Delta did represent the appropriation of something fluid in an effort to solidify control. A long tradition of thinkers on power and spatial practice from Antonio Gramsci to Michel Foucault, Edward Said, Henri Lefebvre, David Harvey, and Doreen Massey have since shown how power is territorialized. Power is embedded in spatial orderings and development. The spatialization of power in any given topography is produced by the flows of capital and people that pass through its physical structures. But what is important to black performance vis-à-vis Brown's fiction is that the characters populating the plotlines (modeled on real-life slaves Brown encountered during his midcentury travels) are made to recognize that successful escape required personal adaptability. Escape required fluidity, an ability to imagine oneself as performance in the exchange systems that comprised the social. It required an ability to make with the surrounds.

Clotel's very passage through the "fortress city" of Vicksburg is achieved through reversing the marks that assign her to a specific race, class, gender, and even general able-bodied status. She manages to execute an escape from Vicksburg by impersonating a sickly, aristocratic, Italian man in green glasses. Also included in the performance is a darker-skinned fellow slave from Clotel's new home, not incidentally named William, who poses as her servile manservant. Brown modeled the Clotel and William escape plot on that of the fugitive slave couple Ellen and William Craft, who fled Georgia for Boston in 1848.[57] (Brown, who was instrumental in both the London publication and promotion on the British abolitionist lecturing circuit of the Crafts's narrative, *Running a Thousand Miles for Freedom*, in effect took authorial compensation for his efforts. He grafted the Crafts' story into his narrative as he would with the stories of others, appropriating it for his composite design.)

Thus, although Clotel's transformation into an Italian passenger traveling through Mississippi seems like an odd and not altogether inconspicuous choice, when considered in light of antebellum Vicksburg's ethnically diverse population, the posture reveals that the presence of more ethnicities in a given space generates more code to mobilize and more figurations for character performance. Brown's adaptation of the Crafts's story and his choice of Vicksburg discursively restage what was widely depicted in midcentury antislavery literature as a static, closed, and nativist deep South. But it was not only that: Vicksburg from the 1830s to the time of the Civil War was home to a sizable contingent of Irish Democrats as well as smaller populations of Italians, the latter entering the United States through the port of New Orleans and settling in river cities, including Natchez. It was also home to Jewish groups from Alsace-Lorraine and Bavaria, whose members found employment as merchants and peddlers in the antebellum city.[58] The presence of such groups created a markedly more cosmopolitan space in which a broader range of communities could take root than in neighboring farmlands.

None of this is to suggest that Vicksburg was not a deeply racist, authoritarian place—even in a midcentury U.S. context. Not surprisingly, the city exercised deep restrictions on the movements of its black population as well as a wary regard for those comprising its social fringe.

In significant ways it represented a closed vision of society, where social order was maintained from the inside out. Citizens' vigilantism (as opposed to Northeastern reform societies) was the preferred social safeguard for keeping the Vicksburg "lower orders" and riverboat influx subordinate to older established families. Violence and racial division were never far from the city's social surface. However, there were still cultural openings to be exploited. As Christopher Morris, a historian of Mississippi, argues, women, immigrants, slaves, and landless populations "were all freer in Vicksburg than in the surrounding countryside."[59] More generally, Claudia Goldin and Richard Wade argue that slaves in urban areas like Richmond or Vicksburg had a greater exposure to ideas about freedom than those living on plantations or in agricultural communities.[60] In any case, Brown's novel suggests composite forms within Confederacy capitals, and the plural as a kind of vitality that enabled the politics of mobility.

Brown's character William exploits one social opening: he plays with the coding that links race and caste in antebellum Vicksburg. ("Slaveholders have the privilege of taking their slaves to any part of the country they think proper," William Craft reminded his readers.[61]) It is as a slave that Brown's William travels up the Mississippi River, connecting to the Ohio River with a stop in Louisville, Kentucky. (The journey Brown describes can be followed on a map of primary U.S. waterways.) Inside the boat, Clotel isolates herself at every opportunity in her cabin quarters due to her said malaise, and William plays the part in the servant's quarters, bragging loudly about his supposed master's wealth: "Nothing appeared as good on the boat as in his master's fine mansion."[62] After a required transfer on land and a stay at the exclusive Gough's Hotel in Louisville, where the radical slaveholding politician John C. Calhoun is also said to be a guest, the two fugitives board a second steamboat for Pittsburgh, where they reach freedom.[63] In Brown's novel, it is ultimately one variant of his heroine's cosmopolitan imagination (presumably her sense of affective internationalism and innate ability to think outside the parentheses of domestic race culture) that translates into movement and change on the ground. At the same time, cosmopolitan designs divorced from local knowledges bear out in this novel to be mere variants of fantasy, an amnesia of place.[64] All told, it is only through Clotel's performative risk and a renegotiation of her immediate space as a Vicksburg domestic that she can move across the gridlines of domestic race culture—not by hitching her dreams of future freedom to the vague transatlantic promises of a profligate young slave keeper.

Forks of the Road

In Brown's authorial trajectory of development, the experiences of travel and story gathering grew from the root of requisite labor. Like another of his contemporaries, the fugitive author Henry Bibb, of Shelby County, Kentucky (near Louisville), Brown spent his Missouri adolescence in service to various submasters, who worked him under the lash. Such experiences gave him an early exposure to the circulation of blood capital in the United States frame. But like Douglass of Baltimore, Brown's early experiences as a city slave, sent around St. Louis to earn maximum profits for his master, brought him knowledge about the kinds of labor that permitted the widest berth for unmonitored movement. Indeed, it was Brown's rather unusual behind-the-scenes labor experiences in slavery that gave him working knowledges of slave market traffic patterns and spaces in the antebellum United States.

As a teenager, he was forced to work as an assistant for a St. Louis slave trader, James Walker, a man he accompanied on three trips up and down the Mississippi River by steamboat from St. Louis to New Orleans during 1832.[65] Brown described his time with Walker as a period of great personal difficulty—"the longest year I ever lived"—and he never forgot what he saw or the stories he took from fellow steamboat passengers.[66] Preparing Missouri River Valley slaves for market, Brown became familiar with a number of infamous professional slave trader depots.[67] In his body of writing, these sites stand in a kind of counter to his transatlantic destinations in France and England. But to the contemporary reader, they reveal far richer stories of what Brown called slavery's "lower countries."[68]

Such place accounts reach the twenty-first-century reader of *Clotel* as site histories of slavery's buried thoroughfares. Many of the places Brown details were river settlements that lost their angle on modernity with the development of railroads in the latter part of the nineteenth century. One major slave market was Rodney, Mississippi. Once among the busiest river ports between New Orleans and St. Louis, it is now an abandoned town, administered by a hunting community in Jefferson

County, Mississippi. Brown described it in his *Narrative* as the St. Louis slave coffle's first major stopping point on the steamboat voyage toward the Gulf of Mexico.

Another site Brown wrote about was particularly notorious. Often considered the grim terminus of a slave's transit South, it was one of the leading antebellum slave trading cities: Natchez, Mississippi. In 1833 Brown learned that his beloved sister, also a slave, had been transported here. Natchez was a place whose practices and people affected him personally. Indeed, it was a city so permeated with slavery that its slave markets, by all accounts, did not run on auction models. Instead, the city was more like an open slave mall. During the high tide of steamboat transport, slaves were traded on the shop-lined waterfront at Under-the-Hill, Natchez. Martin Delany wrote that "it is customary among the slaves when any of their number are sold, to say that they are gone 'under the hill,'" so notorious was Natchez.[69] Slaves were also traded in city shops, at the Natchez courthouse, and in greatest numbers at a market Brown knew well: Forks of the Road Market, one of the South's busiest slave-trading venues and just a short distance east of Natchez. Here slaves silently, joylessly cavorted for display. In an irony that was probably not lost on Brown, the market was located at a famous Y intersection, where Liberty Road and Washington Road met.[70] Indeed, Brown looked critically at such entitlements of nationalism, even renaming the slave transport steamer that Walker used to transport slaves to market in his novel "The Patriot."

Like other hubs of slave traffic, Natchez's Forks of the Road Market would be removed starkly from its midcentury chain of meaning during the Civil War. The same market was made into a refugee camp for liberated slaves by the Union Army in 1863. By 1864 its buildings that housed various traders who came to town to move their human cargo were demolished. Such spaces, nonetheless, were recorded in Brown's memoirs, speeches, and plotlines as traces of a process. They crystallized the deep-reaching destructiveness of slavery. They were spaces that importantly were not dead ends. Rather, they were formative assemblages that gave meaning to nineteenth-century nation.

Yet St. Louis served as a kind of origin for the various sites and subsites in *Clotel*. It was Brown's first and primary site for extracting slavery's shared stories. Though born in Kentucky, St. Louis was the space of his early attachments, where he came to understand how slavery interfused with domestic intimacy, home life, and employment. St. Louis's streets and waterways colored his spatial imaginary. Returning to St. Louis from New Orleans, he reversed the trajectory of slavery that other, less-fortunate slaves could not. His perspective on his departure city, a city that opened into such traffic, must have shifted as well. St. Louis became a place for restocking human cargo. It became a port of entry into a landscape of slave trading, characterized by will-breaking and familial destruction. It became what Eric Gardner aptly calls "a 'gateway' to the heart of slavery, 'a representation designed to challenge the depictions of St. Louis as the gateway to the West (and thus to America's future) that dominated white texts from guidebooks and city directories to early St. Louis newspapers.'"[71] This point is particularly suggestive, too, because Brown staged St. Louis as a geographic gateway to nation as early as in his 1849 *Narrative* and as late as in his 1880 *My Southern Home*. The notion of place as gateway further connects to an important fact about African American literature in the nineteenth century: place mapping is a major component of both black autobiography and the early black novel. Just as geographies are simultaneously sites of performance and witness, they are also networked spaces, hosting flows and circuitry that literature can make deeply suggestive. For these reasons, it is a valuable next step to consider the ways Brown gave form to black mobility.

Ohio River Stories: Scenes of Counter-Transit

In the writings of nineteenth-century African American authors whose careers spanned both the antebellum and postbellum periods—authors such as Douglass, Brown, Delany, and Harper—it is easy to identify an ongoing preoccupation with the profusion of forms (legal, commercial, spatial, and so forth) generated by slavery. The literature documents slavery's spheres of influence and its reach across Reconstruction and Jim Crow. It also investigates new paradigms for the postslavery black subject in search of defining stories, new definitions. For Brown, black self-positioning was closely tied to geographies of experience. In *Clotel* he detailed the geographies of slavery's seams, its slippages and passes where a slave could make free. Delany, whose writings I will consider in the next chapter, did a similar thing. He worked out of an even wider range of Atlantic space to effect black counter-mappings. Such counter-maps not only protested the boundaries of white stratification, but also subversively realigned the militarized sites of surveillance in the United States and Cuba. Yet what links writings by a Douglass or a Harper (whose work I will look at in chapter 4) to someone like Delany has to do with the ways they envisioned black mobility as an evolving relation, not just to history, or to what Kenneth Warren more subtly describes as a "politico-historical relation," to Jim Crow.[72] They envisioned black self-projection as tightly linked to place and to the geographies they summoned in their literature.

Certainly most of Brown's contemporaries did not possess his archival imagination. His writing remains notable insofar as it describes with particularity and extension the means slaveholders used to exert geographical control over landscape. He collected slavery's treatises and witness statements alike. He documented slavery's reward and punishment systems, its scope of influence on legislation and trade. He also had firsthand experience of slavery's black codes and spatial privations. But like the black novelists who would follow him, he showed place as multidirectional and formative. If it was in place that the human subject could be racialized or made the object of property, taking place apart and looking at how it came together gave purchase to new possibilities. This is central to what I take to be the more radical aspects of black textuality. Brown, for instance, was fascinated by the varieties of black enterprise that found coverage gaps. He used *Clotel* to brandish a number of real-life examples of the ways slaves played to the situatedness of slavery. This was the very situatedness that for many U.S. slaves was a condition of how they came to understand their places in the world.

Thus, one approach to destabilizing routine geographies and infusing place with new forms of movement (in practice and in writing alike) is through something that might be thought of as counter-transit. Perceived through the lens of nineteenth-century African American literature, counter-transit reads as a kind of modal motion. It is something enacted on different registers: necessity, improvisation, choice, or chance. But counter-transit is also, in an underlying sense, what nineteenth-century black geography was all about. It was a way of tracing place as fugitive possibility, as the terrain of misrecognition. It was both travel across physical space and travel as subject transition. The idea of counter-transit is connected implicitly with both representational and nonrepresentational claims about space. In Brown's antebellum novel, it reads as a kind of bodily travel into possible worlds. One could gesture to his transatlantic correspondences that described the realizations and reorientations produced through travel. But counter-transit exceeds Brown; it inspired his authorial practice.

Numerous nineteenth-century fugitive narratives are animated by counter-transit. One example is Elisha Valentine's 1838 escape from North Carolina slavery on open roads. He began by deploying implements of slavery and an identity attached to slavery, "first securing a bridle from the stable, as a ready proof that he was hunting a horse, and as a quiet answer to impertinent inquirers."[73] Fugitive David Johnson played on variations of presumed black domesticity. He arranged for a "well-known laundress" to smuggle his wife, a domestic, in reasonable comfort in a large, well-padded laundry basket on an express wagon boarding an Ohio River ferry.[74] And Andrew Jackson of Kentucky detailed his own bold escape efforts, built right on top of the inequities embedded in modern travel, where servants were frequently compelled to follow coaches, often haphazardly, in the thrall of their masters. Jackson actually took to waiting at carriage passes on the open road: "Whenever I met any one I would appear to be all anxiety and inquire 'how far ahead master's carriage was.' This plan worked admirably, and I was enabled to travel more than half a day with one assumed 'master'—always managing to be absent when he stopped, and not far behind him when he traveled. . . . I thus went on changing, until I reached the Ohio river, at a place called Barker's old Ferry, where I crossed into Illinois, in the county of Gallatin, and began to feel secure."[75] What these accounts all illustrate are the ways fugitives used slave epistemologies (what slaves knew and how they knew) to find routes beneath slaveholder expectations.

Counter-transit represented a way out of slavery, a variety of escape. As a kind of code switching across both the physical spaces and the organizational claims of slavery, counter-transit plays out most clearly in several of Brown's intertextual anecdotes of slave escapes. The Ohio River sketches, as they can be called, are short accounts of what Brown insisted were verifiable escapes. Packed into the late middle chapters of *Clotel*, they are compiled alongside the winding plot of Brown's heroine. The interstitial stories emphasize ingenuity and risk.

In one instance, Brown related the story of a slave spotted one day on a high road of a border town in the interior of Virginia, heading toward the Ohio River. The man had neither coat nor hat and appeared to be a local farm laborer, driving a pig. To everyone who inquired, the slave claimed he lived "jist up de road," and that the pig was a favorite of "marser's."[76] In this manner, the man traveled some fifty miles through slave territory without a written travel pass, something required for all slaves conducting business outside their immediate neighborhood. After crossing the Ohio River, the man sold the pig, and in nine day's time reached freedom in Canada. Unlike Clotel, the slave played the local, not the stranger. His mode of operation was familiarity; and most important, he was convincing in his performance. A second anecdote included in the novel takes place just a few weeks later on the same high road. In this case two slaves were traveling together: "One was on horseback, the other was walking before him with arms tightly bound, and a long rope leading from the man on foot to the one on horseback." On the road, they attract more attention than ordinarily desirable for two fugitives. But they have planned for it: "'Oh, ho, that's a runaway rascal, I suppose,' said a farmer who met them on the road. 'Yes, sir, he bin runaway, and I got him fast. Marser will tan his jacket for him nicely when he get him.' . . . And the slaves traveled on. When the one on foot was fatigued they would change positions, the other being tied and driven on foot."[77]

In Brown's story of the tie-and-ride troupe, the Ohio River is where the two men turn the horse loose and set out for Canada. Steamboat crossing sites along the Ohio River read as spaces on the edge of two different spatial regimes, separating Ohio and Pennsylvania, free states, from the slave states of Kentucky and Virginia.[78] The river was a moving stage. It was a physical barrier, a symbolic space of crossing, and finally something fluid. Breaking the fictional frame, Brown buoyantly interjected into his plotline the assurance that at least one of the travelers reached his destination because "the writer of this gave him a passage across Lake Erie and saw him safe" to Canada.[79] Clotel highlights a sense of adventure, the wildness of escape, and the possibility for blacks to unsettle registers of power embedded in the pathways of nation.

Counter-transit, Brown demonstrated, took on some of its most creative permutations in free states. In yet another scene packed into Clotel, a young slave—George, the future husband of Clotel's daughter, Mary—escaped his slave home in Richmond also destined for Canada. But no sooner had he crossed the Ohio River into the free state of Ohio than he finds two slaveholders on horseback in pursuit, mistaking him for one of their own escaped slaves. This rather serpentine plotline goes on to involve a white Quaker farmer, who also orchestrates a slave escape through his own performance—a kind of pantomime of slaveholder frontier conventions. Here the farmer's plan begins when he directs George in through the front door of his barn and closes the door behind him. Brown wrote:

> The Friend, for the farmer proved to be a member of the Society of Friends, told the slave-owners that if they wished to search his barn, they must first get an officer and a search warrant. While the parties were disputing the farmer began nailing up the front door, and the hired man served the back door the same way. . . . After an absence of nearly two hours, the slave-owner returned with an officer and found the Friend still driving large nails into the door. In a triumphant tone and with a corresponding gesture, he handed the search-warrant to the Friend . . . "Lend me your hammer that I may get the door open," said the slaveholder. "Let me see the warrant again." And after reading it over once more, he said, "I see nothing in this paper which says I must supply thee with tools to open my door; if thou wishest to go in, thou must get a hammer elsewhere."[80]

In Brown's telling, the tools must be procured elsewhere, off the printed page, and more time elapses. Yet once the barn door is finally battered and the hay inside thoroughly ransacked, the barn is revealed to be empty. The Quaker, who has clearly bested the indignant slaveholders, mildly intones: "Can't I do what I please with my own barn door? Now I will tell thee; thou need trouble thyself no more, for the person thou art after entered the front door and went out at the back door, and is a long way from here by this time." He also invites them to stay for dinner, keeping them off the road.[81] In this ornate display of counter-transit, the local functions as an intensity of place knowledges, both legalistic and topographic (based on terrains and transit duration). Much could be said about the manipulation of law in *Clotel*, since it is a power that is circulated and used by blacks, too, to confound their status as property. But by keeping the focus on geography, Brown's writing, like that of other fugitive authors, demonstrates how such place knowledges could amount to codings, or the kinds of explanations and interpretations that can be manipulated and made aggregate.

Lastly, the Quaker sketch demonstrates Brown's experimental method of frame-making in the novel. The episode makes a frame of reference by clustering scenes of slave life and travels in the skidmarks of fugitive presence. It renders place as real, traceable national landscape, and it makes the national both a transitive and ultimately interpretive space. Scenes of pursuit across the Ohio River and into free territory illustrate place as performance, composed by multiple actors who can facilitate black flow and make interference, sometimes at the same time and in the same site. This suggests again the radical potential of the earliest African American novel. *Clotel* casts places as sites for subnational user design, and it makes the bedrock of jurisdiction—the relation of law to land—the irony precisely because private property is the irony. Property is not so much a closure as it is something porous. The Quaker's inclusion (with representative Quaker diction and mannerisms) opens landscape to slave passage via allied players. The plotline plays on the theme of doors (gateways and concealment) and white challenges to slaveholder's writ—in this case, a freely issued warrant for search and seizure on behalf of slaveholders. Notably, it is issued at the time and expense of nonslaveholders.

Brown may have picked up this particular anecdote in Ohio in the early 1830s from the Quaker benefactors who aided him following his Cincinnati escape, and who inspired the surname he bore the rest of his life in tribute.[82] It might also have come to him during his years as a steamboat operator during the 1840s, time spent in transit between Canada and Buffalo, New York. In any case, he contributed significantly to the print circulation of Quaker stories, even devoting the thirteenth chapter of *My Southern Home* to tales of Quaker pluck and humor. What the Quaker episode gave *Clotel* aesthetically and politically was a further elaboration of the novel's panic cartographies. Scenes of slave travels in free states, specifically in Ohio, were occasions for the author to demonstrate the toll that maintaining the institution exacted on broader national economic life. Such incidents signaled how slavery's congressional supporters were able to elicit compliance and expenditure in sustaining the institution—from the very citizens of states where the practice was illegal.

To be sure, foundational claims to a logical national fabric were deployed by Republican unionists and Democrats alike in their respective geographical claims. On the side of proslavery Democrats, the late writings of South Carolina senator John C. Calhoun provide one illustration. In a speech to the Senate in 1850, Calhoun argued that "the equilibrium between the two sections in the government as it stood when the Constitution was ratified and the government put in action has been destroyed. At that time there was nearly a perfect equilibrium between the two, which afforded ample means to each to protect itself against the aggression of the other; but, as it now stands, one section has the exclusive power of controlling the government, which leaves the other without any adequate means of protecting itself against its encroachment and oppression."[83] The more overt claims to national cohesion were, of course, made by Republican unionists. Brown had carefully studied the writings and arguments espoused by the forerunners of proslavery economics, chief among these Calhoun (the firebrand slaveholding politician whom Clotel and her accomplice William are said to assiduously avoid in Louisville in the manner of the Crafts). Calhoun's arguments shared central assumptions with the kinds of anti-free market rhetoric that dominated proslavery discourse in the 1850s, the decade during which Clotel was published.[84] His most famous speeches drew on classical texts such as Aristotle's *Nichomachean Ethics* to argue that slavery was "a positive good," one that was, in fact, protected by the Constitution. In his famous 1837 Senate speech, Calhoun argued: "There is and always has been in an advanced state of wealth and civilization, a conflict between labor and capital. The condition of society in the South exempts us from the disorders and dangers resulting from this conflict; and which explains why it is that the political condition of the slaveholding states has been so much more stable and quiet than that of the North."[85] As Brown's construction of Southern regional geographies demonstrated, the conflict for which Calhoun claimed Southern exemption was nowhere more apparent than in the South's "quiet" places. The experience of national travel connected to the ways spaces unfolded in the human experience, and Brown would use travel as a vehicle for revealing these places.

Panoramic Dissimilitude

It is not difficult to trace a legacy of black Atlantic expression, beginning with Briton Hammon's 1760 account of slavery, spanning ports in Boston, Florida, and Jamaica as well as London; and Venture Smith's 1798 recordings of Atlantic sea travails between Africa, the Barbados, and the coastal farmlands along the Long Island Sound, where he labored to manumit his entire family. The legacy extends through the nineteenth-century spiritual biographies of black itinerant ministers like Zilpha Elaw, Jarena Lee, Sojourner Truth, James W. C. Pennington, and Julia Foote, and it goes much further. But from its putative beginnings, black literature maps the cognitive landscapes of homelessness. It presents contemporary readers with a history of spaces of exclusion, stories from the fringes. It also navigates different sites of quietude or seeming invisibility that would not have otherwise gained representation, and it holds these to the light. Black narrativity shows different modes of subject making in the interplay of established orders. Like much of what we characterize as American literature, it is a literature of witness. But more definitively, it bears witness to the contradictions in classifications of caste and economics. It attends to the flows the black subject must devise to traverse different reductions of order.

Counter-transit as trope leads to another question, too: What kinds of geographical knowledges are revealed through print inscriptions of travel in the early African American novel? Brown used travel to open circuits of geographical knowledge closed to the literate bourgeois readership he addressed in his literature. That is, he understood the value of his literature as a variant of North American travel writing with a particular attention to life in the slave states as part of a larger whole. It bespoke of a peculiar regionalism and detailed illicit relations and unimaginable witness—all subsumed under the system of slavery. In a chapter called "A Ride in a Stage-Coach," the peculiarities of national identity take center stage as Brown places Clotel, still in disguise, in a stagecoach as one of eight winter travelers on departure from Wheeling, Virginia (later West Virginia) in the direction of Richmond. This is quite an extraordinary reversal, since it sets the stage for the plot's final geographical exposition: Clotel goes back into slave territory in the hope of finding her daughter.

Wheeling, on the banks of the Ohio River that Brown had traveled by steamboat, was the terminus of the federally financed Cumberland Road, a project approved by Congress in 1806 that would ultimately stretch to Illinois. The Cumberland Road became landmark infrastructure for Western expansionism and development in the nineteenth century and was debated hotly in the Senate and House in the 1850s, particularly for its imbrication in the balance of power between free and slave states—as well as its role in extending slavery into areas where federal and commercial infrastructure existed to potentially support it.

Travel out of Wheeling is represented as nothing less than a political act, and the "genuine Americans" Brown puts in the stagecoach display their local solidarities on the eve of the presidential election of 1840, when—according to Brown—"every man is thought to be a politician."[86] The novel stages a revealing debate between two of the author's sojourners. One is described as pale, with spectacles and a white neckerchief. He is a "teetotaling" Connecticut preacher. The other is a Tennessee-born, New Orleans–based "white hat man," a Southern gentleman lacking a formal education but whose speech reveals him to be a highly capable raconteur. Both are devices for shaping poles of a kind of gothic Americana; each is fascinated with the lurid and subversive details of vernacular life—in regions other than those of claimed affiliation.

From the outset, these regional representatives reveal incongruent national values. Yankee morality is portrayed by its Southern detractor as an extension of fanatical capitalism: "You talk of your 'holy religion'; but your robes' righteousness are woven at Lowell and Manchester; your paradise is high per centum on factory stocks."[87] Southern decorum is a thin veneer for cruel sports and abuse of resources. In response to the Southerner's soliloquy, the New England preacher turns the urbane antebellum New Orleans into a space warranting savage indictment. He recounts verbatim a New Orleans newspaper account of a Sunday cage fightbetween a fierce grizzly bear and a bull with horns filed to sharp points, a spectacle purportedly attended by thousands. Gory public spectacles of bullbaiting, bearbaiting, and blind bear whippings, taking place on Sundays in arenas built for the purpose, were known to be popular British pastimes that came under repeated attack by Puritans. They were banned by Act of Parliament in 1835, but would likely have been known public spectacles to British readers. Brown attached these characterizations to American place practices. Like the iron collar he brought through British customs in 1849, the newspaper accounts of American blood sport are charged place modalities. At the conclusion of the verbal parrying between the stagecoach passengers in *Clotel*, though, there is no resolute balance of opposites as "The Clay Compromise Measures" suggested could be achieved. Rather, the whole stagecoach debate directs readers' attention to another fight that crossed the Mason-Dixon Line multiple times over. It was one from which neither the North nor South was exempt, and it was represented by the bear and the bull whose blood covered the arena floor in New Orleans. It was the market expectations between the bear and the bull that serviced the slavery industry through facilitating coastal trade in slaves from Baltimore and the wider Atlantic, played speculator to profitable returns from slave labor, and overall represented the antebellum fight for manufacture markets. It is notable, too, that even as Brown criticized social habits in the slaveholding South through his staging of various disruptive geographies, Massachusetts's commercial merchants and industrialist classes did not escape the censure they did in Douglass's antebellum writing. They are part of the same panorama.

Before publishing Clotel, Brown had experimented with the stories of slavery as a display of American anti-enchantment. In 1850 he completed A Description of William Wells Brown's Original Panoramic Views, a traveling catalogue of twenty-four personally commissioned illustrations, accompanied by Brown's written anecdotes and explanations. Each presented variations on the theme of slave life in the United States. Included in this collection was an auction scene sketch for what would three years later evolve into the story of Clotel's sister, Althessa, and her daughters. Another was a drawing Brown commissioned from George Cruikshank of a woman jumping from one ice floe to the next, desperately trying to cross the Ohio River in the dead of winter with a child in her arms. (This illustration would later become famous as "Eliza's Escape" in Harriet Beecher Stowe's Uncle Tom's Cabin, and is still commemorated as cover art in modern editions.) William Farrison, Brown's biographer, suggests that the panorama project was consciously influenced by the European vogue of exploration narratives and photography. Farrison mentions that Brown carried out the project in the summer of 1850 after seeing the London exhibition of the India Route Panorama, which attracted large crowds during a slow summer lecture season.[88]

However, Brown claimed his panorama was a project of recontextualizing geography, explaining in his display guide that that he was motivated by his visit to "an exhibition of a panorama of the River Mississippi" in the summer of 1847. While this was several years prior to his London exhibit visit, he nonetheless attributed the genesis of his panorama to the Mississippi River display, several years prior to his visit to the London exhibit: "I was somewhat amazed at the very mild manner in which the 'Peculiar Institution' of the Southern States was there represented, and it occurred to me that a painting, with as fair a representation of American Slavery as could be given upon canvas, would do much to disseminate truth upon this subject."[89] The work of panorama is significant because it illustrates counter-convergences of slave space, comprised through word and image. Panorama is the arrangement. Its anatomical logic is associative and inferential. In the same way Brown's *Narrative* made St. Louis into slavery's matrix through descriptions of slave geographies and transit, the panorama was itself a matrix of form, not just between image and language, but signaling the relationship between literacy and territory. The panorama enabled more points of view to be taken into the image. It stressed the connections that constituted a site.

Brown's massive rolling images no longer exist. They have been either lost or destroyed. They were inexpensively produced, and it is somewhat unlikely they would have survived a cargo transfer across the Atlantic. Yet the still-extant panoramic catalogue gives real indications of the author's intermedial method. "View First," for instance, describes a Virginia tobacco field with a slave dealer on horseback. It represents slavery in its "mildest form," as a system of handed-down instructions. But it also clearly indicates the ways slavery distances labor from meaningful personal investment. By the time Brown got to "View Eight," distance takes on another meaning. This view highlights the New Orleans Calaboose, where slaves were whipped on "order." It is a service site, which allowed the messy and often sadistic work of slavery to be yet again distanced from the slaveholder; it could be outsourced. The work of panorama though shows that slavery's violence could not simply be distanced from the geographical record.

Brown's deployment of the antebellum panorama extends to his novel treatments and presentation of territory. His chief textual device might even be called panoramic dissimilitude, a technique that combines both recognition as defamiliarization and vision as estrangement. Indeed, panoramic dissimilitude may be an apt metaphor for Brown's entire project in *Clotel*. It geographically cues a relationship between the kinds of narratives that draw together worlds ("a more perfect Union" or "one Nation") and landscapes that configure black constraints. By examining *Clotel*'s range of cultural expression through the textualities and practices of geography, readers encountered a narrative world that supported Brown's political vision of nation as a composite of discord. It was an expanse of space suggested by Douglass in "What to the Slave Is the Fourth of July?" (1852), which described a disparity embodied in landscape from New York to Virginia and the Pacific Northwest: "digging gold in California, capturing the whale in the Pacific, feeding sheep and cattle on the hillside, living, moving, acting, thinking, planning."[90] Such anachronistic spaces of citizenship were further enlisted by James McCune Smith, who in 1856 recomposed a scope of geopolitical space from Louisiana to California and Texas to Kansas, where the question was not the freedom of persons but "the freedom of [white] opinion": "The quarrel is between the friends of slavery about the degrees of slavery, not between slavery as such, and freedom as such."[91] As each of these authors certainly recognized, slavery constellated national geography into vernacular affiliations. It made a vocational warp in the agrarian order of things, and at the same time, it blighted the interlocking parts of national public memory. In fact, responding to *Clotel*'s problematic reception as a work of "unified" literature, John Ernest argues that the text should be taken as "an entrance into a world in which the work's apparent lack of unity and overabundance of materials are entirely appropriate."[92] In *Liberation Historiography*, he extends this point, observing that for Brown, "literary genres were less conventions to be followed or even reshaped than they were codes of cultural authority and modes of performance."[93]

Profiles of the Proscribed: Frontier Burlesques

Brown himself turned to frontier humor as a generic convention for transforming the unwritten and presumably quiet spaces of slaveholding into sites that subtracted from the tenability of an agrarian republic. Using subversively comical figures like the "squatty" and wide itinerant New York state preacher, the Reverend Hontz Snyder, a man with "the half-Yankee, half-German peculiarities of the people of the Mohawk Valley," he relayed stories about lonely travels in the rural South.[94] In a chapter called "The Poor Whites, South," Brown presents Snyder regaling an uncontemplative Natchez plantation overseer with tales of travels on his swayback horse across the Sand Hill district of Mississippi (some thirty miles from Natchez). Snyder claims that his arrival at what is supposedly "the best house" in that locality, actually a low log hut, generates a great deal of excitement on the part of the woman of the house, her nine children, and the few farm animals sharing space under the same roof: "'Clar out the pigs and ducks, and sweep up the floor,' she cries, 'This is a preacher.'"[95] Brown also packs in a story about a pious old woman whose husband and three sons are said to be sad characters with degenerate habits. An errant son's takedown by a rattlesnake in the cornfield inspires a prayer for more snakes and more bites.[96] Another anecdote is about a Sand Hill district funeral procession led by a plain horse cart pulling a coffin and a small crowd of "very shabbily dressed" attendants. This leads into a grotesque eulogy for the deceased, referred to as "this lump of mortality . . . a worthless, drunken, good for nothing vagabond."[97] The accounts are rife with stock elements of nineteenth-century frontier humor, with nearly every feature attributed to the genre: encounters with wild animals, analogies from outdoor life, and a pre-ponderance of burlesque sermons.[98]

But the point of region's comic portraiture was that it could be folded into a didactic sweep of commentary, intended to demonstrate the class-based injustices spawned not this time by slave-based industrial-ism, but by planter agrarianism. Brown's depiction of life in rural Missis-sippi is a further elaboration of panic cartographies, highlighting what in his fiction proves to be a fundamental disconnect, again between classes of whites in the South. It is through the mouthpiece of the quasi-anthropological Snyder that the rural poor of Sand Hill are painted as American primordials. They are in national space, but they are in their own world of time. Snyder insists that "the state makes no provision for educating the poor; they are unable to do it themselves, and they grow up in a state of ignorance and degradation. The men hunt and the women have to go into the fields and labor."[99] He compares their lives to those of the comparatively less impoverished, once again in Connecti-cut: "In Connecticut, there is only one out of every five hundred above twenty-one years that can neither read nor write. Here there is one out of every eight that can neither read nor write. There is not a single newspa-per taken in five of the counties in this state."[100] Slavery, Snyder claims, not only abridges the rights of the individual but "reflects discredit on industry" and "forbids the general culture of the understanding."[101] The critical deduction from the Snyder scenes is that slavery is the cause of white wretchedness in the South: "You see, no white man is respect-able in these slave states who works for a living. No community can be prosperous, where honest labor is not honored." Such claims echo those made by Brown in A Description of William Wells Brown's Original Panoramic Views.

The embedded Sand Hill episodes certainly point up extremes of regional landscapes of poverty through humor and exaggeration. But in their fictional context they are positioned less as efforts to separate the North from the South than as ways to highlight a split between the planter classes and poor rural whites. Snyder, readers learn, shares his stories in moments of repose in "a beautiful valley," nine miles outside of wealthy Natchez, on Poplar Farm. The sprawling plantation is owned by John Peck, a character who—as Brown repeatedly reminds the reader—is "a native of the state of Connecticut."[102] In spite of its prosperity and propriety, Connecticut continually resurfaces in Brown's fiction and nonfiction alike for its embedded racism. In his postbellum military history, *The Negro in the American Rebellion: His Heroism and Fidelity*, Brown wrote, "And yet Connecticut, with her proscription of the negro, and receiving their aid in fighting her battles, retains her negro 'black laws' upon her statute book by a vote of more than six thousand."[103] Again, the political quietude covering injustice stitches together these spaces: Mississippi and Connecticut. *Clotel* stresses nation and national geographies. The novel critiques the viability of a national republic that includes slavery by bringing nominally free spaces together with slave spaces to show parallel features of a contaminated union.

Subnational Geographic: The Declaration of Independence and Recouping Lincoln

Through an identification of such geographical themes as regional culture, racially based spatial encoding, uneven development, and the power geometries of planned space (the latter discussed at the end of this chapter), the picture of national fissure developed across *Clotel*'s expansive chapters comes into sharper view. Such geographically influenced writing (and reading) practices have been identified by Martin Brückner and Hsuan Hsu as ways of effecting a more heterogeneous place studies through literature. In *American Literary Geographies*, they write: "By historicizing American literature through the everyday practice of geography—its literary protocols and textualities—we discover how the fictional worlds created by early writers transform the literary stage from the homogeneous space of an expansive democratic empire to a multitude of qualitatively different spaces that varied significantly from prominent discourses on the history of human consciousness and emotions."[104] In *Clotel* this sense of national fracture is at once a result of Brown's panoramic dissimilitude and his thematic portrayal of internal life in slave states, particularly Mississippi and Virginia, and, as the novel's final chapters demonstrate, the landscape of Washington, D.C.

Thus, while Brown criticized the nation for slavery and racism in violation of its founding aims, even calling for mass boycott of the United States in *Clotel's* closing polemical chapter, his novel on the whole undermines the possibility that such a universal democracy could even be achieved as a national value. In fact, on Brown's original title page, he transcribed the opening sentence of the Declaration of Independence. But asserting mass equality and freedom as a unified value across, in Brown's words, "every foot of soil over which the Stars and Stripes wave," was ironic.[105] Brown had little experience on which he could base the prospect of real democratic access for blacks in the United States. In fact, following Abraham Lincoln's inauguration in 1861, Brown's skepticism that a war against disunion would realistically ameliorate the condition of blacks in the United States was made apparent through his continued support of black emigration to the Caribbean. In April 1861 he embarked on a tour of New York and Canada to promote an emigration plan to Haiti. Though he did reverse his position on emigration the following year by 1862, the geographic themes in his 1853 *Clotel* are nonetheless directed to the project of unsettling discourses of a universal-nationalist *res publica* and any accommodating discussions of territorial unity that might support such ideals.

Brown's 1853 *Clotel* heralds a moment of relations in antebellum agitation marked by profound pessimism and the sense of a nation that had clearly defaulted on the interests of blacks in the United States. But it nonetheless reflects a belief in the power of voices and ideas to proffer change and to announce the possibility of alternate identities—alternate constructions of place. Following the novel's publication, the work of union was soon being reclaimed in antislavery Republican perorations such as the most popularly circulated speeches of Abraham Lincoln. Among these were his "House Divided" speech at Springfield, Illinois, on June 16, 1858 ("A house divided against itself cannot stand. . . . It will become all one thing or all the other") and the "Address in Independence Hall in Philadelphia, Pennsylvania" (February, 22 1861), in which Lincoln inquired, "what great principle or idea it was that kept this Confederacy so long together. It was not the mere matter of the separation of the

Colonies from the motherland; but that sentiment in the Declaration of Independence which gave liberty, not alone to the people of this country, but, I hope, to the world, for all future time."[106] Additionally, Lincoln's first inaugural address, delivered in Washington on 4 March 1861, presented his most developed rumination on the inviolate perpetuity of Union, a self-referencing construction and "legal contemplation" that had found its apogee in the Declaration of Independence.[107]

Yet in the presentation of landscape as local systems without any solid borders separating the political from the literary (or the acquired from the invented), readers are directed toward a different kind of end than one that would culminate in union. It is important to clarify that at the time Brown was writing *Clotel*, he was not historically in conversation with a fictional Lincoln. Rather, he was reading Lincoln's own political references. Contrary to Lincoln, who cited the Declaration of Independence as the cornerstone of his entire political philosophy ("I have never had a feeling politically that did not spring from the sentiments embodied in the Declaration of Independence"), Brown was deeply ambivalent about the Declaration's leading author for his failure to live up to the democratic ideals he espoused.[108] Though Brown would come to champion Lincoln in later years, the Declaration's republican promise presupposed an expansive civil spatiality, a far-reaching equality that African American intellectuals could not help but view with guarded skepticism. It was, somewhat paradoxically, a skepticism that matched that of Jefferson.[109]

Is Jefferson's *Notes on the State of Virginia*, a text weighing heavily on *Clotel*, a retreat from the very anti-imperialist historical narrative Jefferson himself championed in the Declaration of Independence? The lifeline Brown grants to the president's progeny, Clotel, seems to suggest that it is. Jefferson's imperial grievances, enumerated in the Declaration, beckon him toward a strong advocacy of governmental transparency, and an acceptance of intra-national difference, the "naturalization of foreigners," their rights to own land, the free exercise of trial by jury, and the rights of representation. And yet the very relationship between word and world encountered in Jefferson's Virginia and in the national Capitol is staged in *Clotel* to undermine these very propositions. Peter Onuf presents one response to the question above. While conceding that the Declaration's narrative "made emancipation and colonization morally imperative," Onuf suggests that *Notes* was reconditioned with a nativist homogenizing vision, characterized by "the geopolitican's 'realistic' assessment of pervasive security threats to the American republic and the natural philosopher's scientific observations about 'fixed' racial differences that were grounded in nature—and beyond the kind of redemption in history that the American Declaration promised to oppressed peoples everywhere."[110] With a focus directed toward the makings of an early national geography, Martin Brückner complements this interpretation through his assessment that "the implied map of Virginia, though invisible throughout *Notes* as such," had the effect of laying "the groundwork for depicting Virginia as a homogeneous culture working the land collectively."[111] As *Clotel* shows, it was not just for blacks to contest the ideological instability of this foundational fallacy. That task could be taken on by any of the self-determining prototypes suggested in the novel, like the highly educated female anticolonialist Christian, Georgiana, or the freethinker she converts to antislavery, or any of those readers he petitioned outright in the preface and conclusion of the novel. These were Brown's proxies for influence, people who could assert sympathy and the primacy of black life experience over national polity.

Writing in England in 1852 and 1853 during a period of heightened American transformation through the growth of urbanization and the rise of factory towns all along the Eastern Seaboard, which further displaced artisanal and homestead production, Brown presented an assembly of overlapping landscapes as literary stages. In the fiction, these scenes related to divisions in the shifting market economy are repeatedly shown to be marked by a divisiveness connected to practices of slavery. The Northeast was only one such site for deterritorialization and cultural uprooting. Contrary to certain period overviews, American Southern planters did not convalesce in a preindustrial phase of antidevelopment. Rather, technological advancements in agricultural processing led to massive increases in productivity for propertied landholders and also signaled what opponents of slavery recognized as the threat of a broader cultivation of export markets, securing the perpetuation of the slave labor system. Brown wrote into a context where the vast western land annexations and territorial accessions of the 1840s, which brought in land from southern Texas to what is now Washington State (and with it, a fight for representation as free or slave states in both Houses), gave viability to slavery's geographic extensions.[112]

Ultimately, Brown's concerns about slavery's territorial reach and staying power pointed back to Thomas Jefferson, who proposed that slavery be excluded from Western lands after 1800, yet extolled an economic system that, if not altogether predicated on slavery, continued to depend on it for its greatest margin of profit. It is difficult to gauge from Brown's writings whether in the years leading up to the Civil War he was realistically concerned about a kind of agrarian-driven backlash against the implementation of Jeffersonian pastoralism, a romantic landscape ideal that by midcentury was already proving unfeasible—even among the planter class. Nonetheless, the sustaining ideological power of Jefferson's symbolic America not surprisingly continued to trouble the former slave throughout his European travels during the 1850s.

In fact, Brown's imaginative portrayal of life in rural Mississippi obversely parallels Jefferson's own concerns about slavery in Virginia, expressed in Query XVIII ("Manners"), in which Jefferson implied that slavery reaped a core divisiveness within white communities, "alienating" a master class from a "direct, unmediated relation to the land."[113] Jefferson claimed at the outset of his public life that America's great hope of redemption lay in the sustaining values of the national husbandman. He envisioned an agrarian republic in which slavery would gradually be phased out, colonization would ameliorate the race problem, and the nation would prosper as a commonwealth of small farmers. As he penned in his 1784 publication of *Notes on the State of Virginia*, the most popular eighteenth-century natural history and a key document in his bid for establishing claim to an American national identity: "Those who labor in the earth are the chosen of God. . . . Corruption of morals in the mass of cultivators is a phenomenon of which no age nor nation has furnished an example. . . . For the general operations of manufacture, let our workshops remain in Europe. It is better to carry provisions and materials to work-men there, than bring them to the provisions and materials, and with them their manners and principles."[114]

Yet Jefferson also recognized the space between ideals and national practice. As president in 1800, he revised his stance on American manufacture, coming to see it as a necessary measure for national growth and national independence of Europe. There was also perhaps a certain unavoidability, touted in reciprocal ideologies of frontier-driven manifest destiny, in the growth of manufacture in a country possessing a virtually unmatched wealth of forest, mineral, and agricultural resources. Leo Marx's well-known study of nineteenth-century America's cultural mediation between technology and pastoral ideals of landscape credits Jefferson with authoring the first fully articulated pastoral ideal of America. Yet it also presents a notable disclaimer. Marx reminds readers that in "detached moods, [Jefferson] recognized the restless striving of his countrymen, their get-ahead, get-rich, rise-in-the-world ambitions. Whatever it was they wanted, or, rather, that they *thought* they wanted, it was not the domestic peace and joy of the self-sufficient farm."[115] The point (for Marx, at least) is that the middle landscape was the pastoral ideal. It was iconic, but profoundly influential: "[Jefferson] kept it in view as a kind of model, a guide to long-range policies as indispensable to intelligent political thought or action as the recognition of present necessities."[116] *Clotel* brings to antebellum deliberations about slavery a double critique of what Brown shows to be a foundational legacy. First, the legacy was reflected in a version of national sustainability reliant on the very thing that defrauded the honest labor of Jefferson's salt of the earth: slavery. Second, Jefferson's legacy haunts Brown's novel, both as an emblematic father of the United States republic and as a lawmaker whose stake in partisan politics finally trumps the interests of Virginia's secret families—including his own. Clotel runs up against this legacy when her mobility is literally arrested en route to finding her daughter in Richmond, and she is jailed in an infamous Washington, D.C. slave pen, midway between the Capitol and the president's house. This striking geometry emphasizes spatially what Brown viewed as federal concessions to slavery's capital in the representative landscape of the national capital.[117]

Brown's novel personifies the ways power geometries are experienced from the perspective of a nineteenth-century, enslaved African American woman. Through the lens of Clotel, the author reveals that geographies of national scale work out to be systematized closures. Michel Foucault has argued in *Power/Knowledge* that space is something arranged according to histories of power, "from the great strategies of geo-politics to the little tactics of the habitat."[118] From his own genealogical reference points in the nineteenth century, Brown staged slavery's spaces as registers of circulating power, radiating from Washington, D.C., and connecting back, finally, to the city slave yard between the Capitol and the President's House. Accordingly, the architecture of *Clotel* moves from Horatio's hidden homestead in Richmond to the public squares and street plans whose development Jefferson had overseen as president in 1801.[119] The triangulation between the emancipatory symbols of a democratic nation and the Washington slave pen, described by Edward Abdy—a tourist who visited the city in 1833–34—as "a wretched hovel, right against the Capitol, from which it is distant about a half a mile, with no house intervening," is telling of the power wielded by slaveholders over the organization of national space.[120] More precipitously, it was telling of the human lives in the balance. The fact that slave trafficking remained legal in the District of Columbia until 1862, despite Congress's power to expunge it from the national capital, further evidenced the very forms of national complicity in the slavery institution that Brown highlighted across various environments throughout the novel.

For Clotel, imprisoned and awaiting to be shipped farther South, a return to slavery is not an option. She decides to make a final attempt at escape, bolting past her captors. But she is trapped on a high suspension bridge over the Potomac River, with Washington slave catchers on one side and three Virginian onlookers ready to aid in her capture on the other side. (Once again in this novel, Virginia has the curious distinction of being the cradle of democracy and the seat of slaveholders' government.) In sight of the Capitol, Clotel throws her body into the river, an at once heroic and suicidal gesture by which she demonstrates her final defiance of the grave that is slavery. Clotel is a casualty of the national legacy of first families and the American subaltern, landing herself at place zero. On the bridge, facing democratic promise in the shape of the Capitol and surrounded by topographies of oppression, she has little choice but to jump. Her life and death are a final testimony to what Brown's novel casts as a fundamental misalignment in the political geography of the nation-state: the overwriting of the black race in a deliberate landscape of monuments and prisons, and a nation divided by its own legal system. Yet Clotel's death does not mark the defeat of dissent, but rather a legacy of freedom that Brown somewhat attenuates into three final chapters in the story of Clotel's daughter, Mary, who he reminds the reader is Thomas Jefferson's granddaughter. (Mary's was a story Brown had previously told in Three Years in Europe.) But its inclusion in Clotel and Mary's eventual freedom, only obtained outside the U.S. national circuit in France, brings the capacious novel to its somewhat unbelievable, but nonetheless happy, ending.[121]

Writing as he did from Britain in the wake of the renewed Fugitive

Slave Act of 1850, Brown was acutely concerned that Congress had shifted what he argued was a profoundly moral issue for redress into a territorial and economic practice, a fact of process protected and regulated by federal laws. To a significant extent, he used *Clotel* to stir the waters of the current debate about slavery and national boundaries. In doing so, he made the African American novel into a form that grappled with the very premises of contemporary black life under law in a climate marked by slavery's territorial spread westward. A key issue *Clotel* polarizes is the enduring conflict within national space between the designs of federal government and state economies. This would, of course, prove to be one of the most significant sources of congressional tension in early U.S. history, and later, an issue that would transform into a principal cause of the Civil War.[122]

Ultimately Brown placed the case of the "peculiar institution" on a national register by taking it out of the domiciles of Virginia and the slave pens of the District of Columbia, where it was tucked away behind official dispatches of place, and insisting on its inclusion alongside the repository of legal documents, maps, and infrastructure registered in official histories. In addition, through the figure of Thomas Jefferson he emphasized the ways slavery nullified social contract and "natural law," purportedly the foundational premises of the U.S. national landscape. In these respects, *Clotel* can be read as Brown's midcentury inflection on the discursive complex that constituted U.S. national life. In such a complex as this, spatial thinking had the potential to reveal structural conflicts under the surfaces of encoded space.

....

CHAPTER 2

INDIGENES OF TERRITORY

Martin Delany and James Beckwourth

Among the leading issues circulated in mid-nineteenth-century African American print records were those connected to constructions of territory. The concept of territory was an expansive one, entering into nearly all domains of life. On one level, it made place a thing that could be possessed: it was a way to code place as operational or owned. On another, territory put a political frame on prospects of settlement. To hold territory required a writ or some record of recognition. And this was problematic because a black subject's attachment to a site of belonging was likely nonlegalistic and would not be honored as proper domain. Why territory was debated so extensively in black literature and letters of the 1850s reflects what was at stake for African Americans: For those long sequestered in place as the materialization of property, its achievement stood for an altered relation to land. Territory harkened to something outside the story lines of slavery.

The idea of territory as common land ownership for a collective or a people was central to discourses on African American emigration at midcentury. A successive series of legislative acts gave a real urgency to the whole prospect. Among these were the Fugitive Slave Act as part of the Compromise of 1850, which put the force of the federal government behind slave catchers operating above the 36°30' latitude lines of non-slavery and, more controversially, in free states. This was followed by the 1854 passage of the Kansas-Nebraska Act, which repealed the geographic limits of slavery set by the Missouri Compromise of 1820–21. In

1857 the Supreme Court ruled in *Dred Scott v. Sandford* that Congress could not prohibit slavery in federal territories. These major land-configuring rulings produced a climate of fear among African Americans. For many, they blighted hopes of future holdings. They prompted some several thousand U.S. blacks to migrate to Canada. This, in turn, resulted in intensive black print discussions about territory as something exceeding the national form. The goal of extranational territorial gains thus became a prominent feature of a new black geographic discourse.

Henry Bibb—leader of U.S. fugitive slaves, author, and editor of *Voice of the Fugitive*—announced land development projects in Ontario. Mary Ann Shadd—who published *Notes on Canada West* and the *Provincial Freeman*, the abolitionist newspaper she co-founded with Samuel Ringgold Ward—portrayed Canada West as the grounds for developing church life and civil society. So, too, did Martin Delany (1812–85). As contributing editor to the *Provincial Freemen* in 1858, Delany advocated large-scale Canadian land procurement—even as he solicited support for the Niger Valley Exploring Party, formed with the aim of obtaining African Americans land settlement contracts in West Africa. Black abolitionists James Holly and William Wells Brown (the latter returning to the United States from England) lectured on the possibilities for Haitian emigration, trying to subscribe potential émigrés during recruitment tours.[1] Though many free African Americans remained particularly cautious about white instrumentalism in advocacy of black colonization, territory was nonetheless enlisted as a kind of buffer from slavery's statist arm. It was more satisfying and, perhaps, seemed safer to envision territory an international outpost or elsewhere rather than a space that shared slavery's national infrastructure.

In literary and fictional texts about black self-making, territory occupied an important place. It was something caught up in entrenched orders and already embattled gains. Not surprisingly, it was the frequent subject of black editorials and transcribed speeches.[2] The theme surpassed any particular antebellum genre of writing. It was deliberated in midcentury slave narratives such as Josiah Henson's *Truth Stranger than Fiction* (1858), in which Henson described it as the necessary sequential achievement after ownership of labor.[3] Black experiences of territorial disenfranchisement were also at the heart of James Monroe Whitfield's *America and Other Poems* (1853). They were thematized in Harriet Wilson's blended novel of domestic Northern slavery, *Our Nig* (1859), and Frank

Webb's Philadelphia-based *The Garies and Their Friends* (1857). In both these novels, neither free state settlement nor property in place safeguarded against white territorialization. Indeed, issues of territory as a form for access or restriction posed few clear resolutions.

Two African American authors in the 1850s emerge as particularly important for the ways their major texts composed place as territory. These men were Martin Delany, author of *Blake: or, the Huts of America* (1859–62), and James Beckwourth, author of *The Life and Adventures of James P. Beckwourth* (1856). Though both approached territory as a site of contestation, beyond the category of nation and the transactions of the national, their texts are quite different. Delany's is a two-part novel about the American South and Cuba, published serially by the *Anglo-African*.[4] Beckwourth's extended ruminations on his life and perilous journeys through the North American West were dictated as "unembellished truth" to an amanuensis, Thomas D. Bonner, whose influence will be discussed shortly. Actually, bringing these works together for their preoccupations with territory presupposes that different generic conventions can be meaningfully read as parallel forms. Insofar as both texts focalize the concept of territory, and both territory and identity can be taken as expressions of belonging, a lateral reading is useful. It gives range and color to the projections of possession. The novel and the memoir of course call into view different schemes of subjectivity. They speak to different audience expectations and permit different modes of expression—even when the fiction is most canny of life and the autobiography is something untrue. Nonetheless, the subject position both of these authors claim, not necessarily for themselves but for heroic enterprise, frames the picture of territory extended in each story.

As the following pages consider, territory works on at least two levels in both texts, prompting an approach to it as something doubly made, or doubly making. First, territory is denotative. It indexes physical lands, identifiable material spaces in the formative Americas. Certainly it is relevant that Beckwourth and Delany applied their time and resources to acquiring land as territory. Beckwourth, the cofounder of Pueblo, Colorado, claimed first rights of discovery to what he believed would be a major wagon pass in the Sierra Nevada Mountains, the Beckwourth Pass. A speculator and land guide, he used his memoirs to vet his knowledge of Western Indian habitats for midcentury War Department and Internal Affairs work. He also touted his hospitality as a hotelier and land guide in the Sierra Valley community known today as Beckwourth, California. Delany, too, was an avid seeker of territory. In 1851 he claimed to have received news that he was duly elected "mayor of Greytown [Nicaragua], Civil governor of the Mosquito reservation, and commander in chief of the military forces of the province."[5] He never visited the place. But by the end of the decade he managed to obtain a treaty to settle unoccupied Egba tribal lands in what is now southwestern Nigeria. This treaty was later nullified by the Abeokuta Alake, or king. Delany moved on, seeking work with the South Carolina Freedmen's Bureau. To whatever degree a life's territorializing efforts can be offset from authorial forays into the subject is, of course, difficult to ascertain. Territory, as I will argue, is itself a relation. But as figures who actively pursued lands beyond U.S. dominion for political and financial "development," both Beckwourth's and Delany's major texts flex the concept of territory to account for everything from a rational form for the exercise of self-interest (Beckwourth) to a specific, occlusive good for the realization of a common people (Delany).

Second, both texts are less about the embodied realities of living inside someone else's conscription of territory as they are about the constitutive features of territory, and how territory—very much like empire—gets made through narrative projections onto physical space. (It is also not incidental that these projections are usually those of actors only temporarily connected to the spaces over which they assert claims.) So even if literary representation gets us only so far in recognizing the real flows of contact and the hard-edged outcomes of black expansionist plans, narrativity is still important because it structures both colonial discourses, anticolonial rhetoric, and whatever vantages one assumes in order to gain some hold on geographic perspective. And while it is useful to bear in mind Gayatri Spivak's criticism of Gilles Deleuze (or Michel Foucault, for that matter) for positing aggregate nomadic systems as though they could somehow exempt themselves from reenacting Eurocentric colonial discourses, there is still something that makes the spatial imaginaries of Deleuze and Félix Guattari heuristically interesting when attending to the ways territory gains meaning in African American literature.[6] It is perhaps fair to qualify that Deleuze and Guattari have far more to say about deterritorialization, or the undoing of territorial codes, than they do about physical territory or specificities of place-making. They offer very few developed or site-specific examples—whether these be of territory as an explicitly nationalist formation or of territory as a geopolitical theatre of empire. But across their writings, their (provocative) claims about territory have a particular resonance because they shape it as something determined—made corporal, put into the actual—by capital. At the same time, they insist on its discursiveness.[7]

So unlike numerous scholars who pit a transnational kind of diasporic consciousness against a presupposed center (whether this center be an imperial power, authoritative historiography, or some immobile setting), I do not want to conceive of territory as a settled state of affairs or a bounded culture that deterritorialization then undoes. Rather, I think that what African American narratives show us, quite explicitly, is that territory is unstable by its very constitution.[8] Territory is embodied. Identities are bound up in known spaces of belonging that overlap with sites of uncertainty. At the same time, territory is polymorphous; it is idiosyncratic and contingent. Spaces can change us, and they can change our intentions. As the literature I will look at here illustrates, territory is situated within complex tensions of empire, between construals of possession and fulfillment, and in unstable histories of financial gains and losses in lands little known. Beckwourth, for example, did not concern himself with questions of nineteenth-century African American overseas expansion or even with the black fugitive colonies established in Veracruz or Córdoba, Mexico, because he was so occupied with inserting himself into colonialist trade schemes in Native Territory near Santa Fe, New Mexico, or in gaining military advantage among the said-Upper Californians, geographically distanced from Mexico's seat of taxation and political power. Delany, too, wrote about cells of black, grassroots resistance in the U.S. South, fortified in resistance to distinctive regimes of national slavery. Yet he also envisioned these smaller groups ceding their powers wholesale to some abstracted, transatlantic black governance coalition that could not realistically represent their concerns.

The reason I draw attention to these characterizations of imperial venture is that I think they yield a more dynamic, nuanced lens for understanding territory in the ways it is shaped, especially through its representative practices. Representative practices could be maps or national literatures. But the key point the literature illustrates is this: Because territory is composed of multiple, unstable signifieds, it is entangled in its subjective undoing. This undoing can be foregrounded and, as Deleuze and Guattari make clear, must be brought into play as a starting supposition for any meaningful conjectures about the forms territorialization takes. They write: "Civilized modern societies are defined by processes of decoding and deterritorialization. *But what they deterritorialize with one hand, they reterritorialize with the other.*"[9] The undoing, I argue, is the threat attached to the opportunity.

For these reasons, a processual view of territory lends a fitting scheme for revisiting the nineteenth-century literary output of Delany and Beckwourth, both of whom extended a view of territory as mutually constituted by land, labor, and capital—and conversely made unstable through these same things. Through geographic discourse, Delany drew attention to white territorial practices precisely so that he might decode and reconstruct spaces for black passage. In a less sure-footed way, his writing grappled with Native American conceptions of space, which in no small way complicated his own expansionist agenda in the Americas. But on the whole, his work ultimately wrestles with issues of occupancy for blacks within competing frameworks of nation. Beckwourth, in contrast, literally deterritorialized Indian space, depicting himself as a primal map maker and white-affiliated conduit to Indian pathways. His narrative expounds an iconic map of Anglo expansionism in the Western Territories and suppresses already-networked Indian space to effect this image. This reading attends to the fallout: what he lays claim to through his allegiances but cannot account for through his long narrative of experience. And as this reading will try to show, when places are defined by their unmasking and the terms of their unmaking, they start to look more like characters. They are more like clusters of involvements and identities made through relations. This, in turn, confounds a view of landscape as a subject's background.

....

Perhaps no other individual represents both the aspirations and difficulties of a nascent, nineteenth-century black transnational movement quite as much as Martin Delany. In his lifetime he was known for his various vocations and accomplishments. He was an author, journalist, African explorer, doctor, inventor, politician, and ethnographer. Delany's most prolific period as an author was between 1852 and 1862, in the ferment of U.S. abolitionism. During these ten years he authored his first book, *The Condition, Elevation, Emigration and Destiny of the Colored People of the United States* (1852), the treatise that established him as a leading nineteenth-century black intellectual in advocacy selective emigration. He also delivered his long keynote address on reterritorializing the Americas, "Political Destiny of the Colored Race on the American Continent," which was later reissued by the U.S. House of Representatives in 1862. By the end of the 1850s, Delany had founded the Niger Valley Exploring Party with the aim of encouraging black emigration to West Africa. Though this venture was quickly dismantled by excess debt, he managed to publish the *Official Report of the Niger Valley Exploring Party* in 1861, today recognized as the first African American ethnographic study. Concurrent with this, Delany worked through the installment novel form, publishing his epic romance *Blake* in the New York-based *Anglo-African Magazine*.[10]

Blake was the serial compilation of a decade of intellectual investment and political work in the service of African American enfranchisement. It was dedicated to a black readership and took up the issue of a hemispheric black diaspora, concentrated in the U.S. South and Cuba, a rangy theme Delany editorialized about in the *North Star* as early as 1847. The text marked a critical shift in Delany's apprehension of place from the earlier *Condition* and "Political Destiny." To an even greater degree than any of his previous writings, *Blake* attached questions about territory to deterritorialization, to the creative destruction of white materialist space-as-production. The novel romanticized the scope for transnational antislavery resistance, with blacks from the United States, the Guinea Coast, and Cuba brought into alliance. At the same time, many of *Blake's* most interesting reflections on territory emerge from the ways the novel gives form to spatial strategies for a fugitive insurgency in U.S. national space. *Blake*, I will show, is an excursion through subspaces within the United States, which the author, in turn, mined for their deterritorializing potential.

Toward very different ends, James Beckwourth was also involved (both in life and print) in the reorganization of national geographies. Beckwourth's recitation to T. D. Bonner, published as *The Life and Adventures of James P. Beckwourth: Mountaineer, Scout and Pioneer, and Chief of the Crow Nation of Indians* (1856), is not a novel, but nor is it quite nonfiction. It is an extensive record of a life, built through heroic self-embellishment and novelistic detail. Though it claims to be an "unvarnished statement" of Beckwourth's exploits as an Indian chief, hunter, and mountain guide in the Rocky Mountain hunting lodges and Sierra Nevada mining camps, early historians of the American West have mostly been skeptical about its facticity (and to a certain extent, Bonner's role in the making of all these claims). Western historians Hiram Chittenden, Francis Parkman, and J. Frank Dobie have each pointed out Beckwourth's penchant for self-glorification over fact.[11]

But rather than try to peel away degrees of reliable detail from exaggerative winnings or write off Beckwourth's text as a distortion of fact, it makes sense to approach *The Life and Adventures* for what it offers to modern readers. It is a rich cultural document of oftentimes convincing, firsthand stories about travels through the North American West. It also is about intimate encounters with the little-documented Crow Indians. Beckwourth claimed he was elevated to Chief (or least a war chief) of the Crow. Although this has been the subject of some debate, it is less contested that he was the Indian trader most intimately acquainted with the Crow and their lands, a vast expanse straddling what is now Montana and Wyoming.[12]

Absent from Beckwourth's conscriptions of contested Western space is the very thing Delany viewed as most significant in the shaping of national territory: slavery. This would, of course, be a stark omission from an African American author. But it is one that has wider implications for what Beckwourth's extended self-story reveals about efforts to exact U.S. geographical space for profit. Reading *The Life and Adventures* alongside *Blake* brings the theme of achievable space into relief, since for both Beckwourth and Delany territory was about physical possession of land. It was also about a subject's position in relation to an object of quest.

Delany's Forms: Contestation on the Inside

Delany's print work reveals his ongoing preoccupation with the competing claims of democracy and empire in late antebellum United States, a subject that has also sustained him as a figure of interest across different climates of twentieth- and twenty-first-century scholarship.[13] Though more currently featured as a leading voice in the contemporary critical frame of the Black Atlantic (Eric Sundquist, Paul Gilroy) and in growing work on black hemispheric studies (Robert Levine, Ifeoma Nwankwo, Jeffory Clymer, Andy Doolen, and Jake Mattox),[14] the recent emphasis on postnational venture has somewhat obscured the ways a figure like Delany extensively adjudicated the territories of national form.[15] Delany never fully abandoned his efforts to work within the United States to promote greater civic and political parity for African Americans. His focus on the United States as a physical site for staging black resistance is apparent in Blake, especially in part I of the novel—which will be my focus in this chapter. Simply considered, the United States was the country Delany knew best and wrote about the most. From federal Emancipation in 1863 until 1877, when President Rutherford Hayes authorized the end of federal Reconstruction, Delany worked solely in the United States. He supported the Union cause during the Civil War as an army recruiter in Connecticut, and was also the first commissioned black major in the U.S. Army. After the war he accepted a federal Reconstruction commission for the Freedmen's Bureau in South Carolina.

None of this detracts from Delany's diasporan constructions of racial identification, views that were important in shaping his ideas about territorialization. The following chapter ("This House of Gathering") focuses on the author's hemispheric geographic identification. But the point here is that Delany also matched the idea of nation to a subject's territory; nation was a requisite form for black enfranchisement. He also made nation an exportable entity that a group could pack up and take somewhere. Nation could be reconstituted in space.

Another innovative feature of Blake is its use of physical geography to represent radical African American deterritorialization from the inside. Writing as an American subaltern, a son of a slave, denied a lawful education in Virginia and in Massachusetts, Delany made textual deterritorialization not only the project of resituating the United States in relation to the wider Americas (during an era of volatile U.S. filibusterism in Central America). He also directed it to the work of contestation within the national form.[16] This territory "within" is the converse of dominant slaveholder spatialization. In Blake the trope of mapping is dually a means for inscribing place and a means for effecting representation. The novel enlists the vocabulary of cartography, spatial ordering, and geographic navigation to focus attention on inroads for viable black enterprise. But, as I argue in the following pages, Delany's methods are aligned with his eponymous hero's usages, specifically Blake's modes of navigation. These modes include the compilation of travel technologies; the black survey for the collection of local, place-based knowledge; and the star atlas as key visual axis. All come together in the service of route making, which, in turn, means the decoding of white slaveholder practice in search for what Delany called, "white gaps."

2.1. John C. Lewis, *Lewis' Free Soil, Slavery, and Territorial Map of the United States.*
New York, 1848. Map reproduced courtesy of the Norman B. Leventhal Map Center
at the Boston Public Library.

One way to open a discussion about Delany's counter-mapping strategies in *Blake*, especially the cartographic themes and forms in the first
part of the novel, is by referencing a map the author knew well: *Lewis' Free
Soil, Slavery, and Territorial Map of the United States* (1848; figure 2.1). Under
Delany's *North Star* co-editorship with Frederick Douglass, he com-
mended abolitionist John Lewis's map at least twice, once in 1848 and in
1849. The map is described by the editors as something that "presents
at a glance the aggressive and greedy character of the slave power so that
he who runs may read."[17] Such a description could have been angled to
the fugitive sense of place that both Douglass and Delany drew upon in
their writings. More likely, it referred to the map's instantly accessible
visual presentation. Though it featured dense columns of text (harangu-
ing slaveholders as weak, self-serving, less-educated), it offered a simple

visual scheme that illustrated the representative claims of slaveholding within a national landscape. It was a map deeply critical of national landscape apportionment.

Thematically, the Lewis Map illustrated slavery as a kind of menace. Slavery was an inky grey spread. It moved up from the bottom of the contiguous states, threatening to subsume the sunnier, yellow-colored prospects of free states, and the light blue futurity of the new territories. In fact, when the *North Star* in 1849 republished notice of the map, it excerpted complaints from the *Newbern N.C. Republican* newspaper, which blasted the "foul spirit of abolitionism" that had bled into journalism. The southern paper lamented that "the slaveholding States are shaded so dark with India Ink that it is difficult to read the names of some of the places." For the *North Star* editors, these were the very qualities that gave this map its edge. They called it a "new mode of impressing the northern mind with the importance of this subject."[18]

Like Delany, Lewis cast slavery as a contest for political occupation of real, material spaces. Both pictorially and rhetorically, his map illustrated the ways slavery eroded the material of nation: "*The slaveholders say they have an equal right to the Territories with the Free Interest; if that is admitted does it follow that a joint owner in a land has a moral right to introduce a nuisance on one half that lot, and thereby destroy the value of the other half? . . . Look at the vast and unreasonable representation already in Congress, founded on almost uninhabited country, and what the Slave Power calls cattle. That is, one slaveholder, owning one hundred negroes, has the power of Sixty freemen in the Free states. This is a sad commentary on equal rights.*"[19]

In *Blake* Delany took the opaque ink spread that mapmakers like Lewis used to represent national slavery, and turned it into a black menace on the institution itself. Delany had long visualized African American interpositions into white nationalist mappings, describing the work of the 1854 Convention of Colored Men in Cleveland as disruptive of proslavery geographical plans. It was, he wrote, as "though our great gun was leveled, and the first shell thrown at the American continent, driving a slaveholding faction into despair, a political confusion from which they have been utterly unable to extract themselves."[20] By the end of the 1850s, he was working through the long novel form as a way to imaginatively conjure a black counter-state. The creative potential of these deterritorializing goals is realized in *Blake*.

Reterritorialization

Delany's leading character is an aggregate of places important to the author in his vision for African American nationhood and enfranchisement. First, Blake embodies in his person the networks of slavery. But importantly, these features of slavery are retooled into the grounds of self-actualization: Blake is a multilingual, free-born Cuban hero of pure African descent who actually has very little in common with most midcentury U.S. plantation blacks. His insertion into plantation life is astoundingly voluntary. He has lived both as one of the enfranchised and as a slave, and thus knows the institution from the inside and the outside. His perspective is that of the Atlantic, and what he brings to the story line is a kind of middle knowledge between freedom's access and slavery's forms.[21] Blake cannot be fully realized as either a character or a principle of action until he engages the problems of territory. He needs to emerge from white reterritorialization and ruin the border integrity of various slave states by acts of crossing. A freeman in the clothes of a slave, he is essentially programmed to do just this.

The concern with achieving black parity through territory had occupied Delany throughout the 1850s, both before and after *Blake* reached print. In *The Condition* he wrote: "A freeman in a political sense, is a citizen of unrestricted rights in the state, being eligible to the highest position known to their civil code."[22] Later in the same text, he claimed that a freeman required "unrestricted soil; free to act and untrammeled to move."[23] Throughout the decade he alternated between different emigration sites in the Caribbean, South America, and Africa. But he was very consistent in his printed work about the need to achieve physical territory. He repeatedly argued that it was the essential first requirement for enfranchisement.

In "Political Destiny," Delany quoted British Prime Minister George Hamilton-Gordon's House of Lords speech in support of Britain's entry into the Crimean War on the side of the Ottoman Empire in 1854: "One thing alone is certain, that the only way to obtain a sure and honorable peace, is to *acquire a position* which may *command* it; and to gain such a position *every nerve and sinew of the empire should be strained*."[24] Delany called this "the essential basis of self protection."[25] In "Political Aspect of the Colored People of the United States" (1855), a proposal presented by Delany in support of black emigration, he stated: "The only successful remedy for the evils we endure, is to place ourselves in the position of potency, independently of our oppressors. All intelligent political economists and historians know this, our oppressors know this."[26] A lecture in the second half of Blake (staged by Blake) summons these points for Delany's novel project, insisting that the first principle upon which "all great nationalities" must depend is "territorial domain."[27] It was a point Delany made again after he returned from Lagos in 1861, when he argued that "the selection and security of a location" was the most important step in building a political economy.[28] Read against the backdrop of Delany's territorial declarations, Blake's ideal, but as of yet unrealized, citizenry positions to achieve territory. If, as Delany insisted, territory was the goal, deterritorialization was the means.

Blake alters space as he moves through it. His vehicular composition as a character of continuous action suits a project of deterritorialization, where deterritorialization reads as dissolution of imperial white cultural space at the "joints and sinews of empire."[29] Such an effort works on the level of depicted space. It presents a world and presents how to undo it. Deleuze and Guattari have looked at the fiction of Franz Kafka for what they claim is its immediate intervention in politics and deterritorialization of the world. They argue that literature has the potential not simply to comment on the political, with the political remaining external to its form, but instead be that very realm for adjudication. They claim that a minor literature can enact the political in its form. Such literature generates a world and stages desire. More specifically, it stages desire's outworkings and the structures of power through which it swims. And then literature shapes these into new understandings.[30] Blake, too, showcases these claims. The novel is about bodily movement through space—across rivers, forests, farms, and oceans, guided by maps of capital, human knowledge, land knowledge, and the zodiac. And it is about something radical and minoritarian that is shaped into an epic about undoing human bondage. Blake is Delany's most grandiose literary endeavor. Its aim is to identify and then destroy the enabling institutions for the pre-war organization of U.S. space through black initiative, and in doing so, "fatally" disrupt the circulation of capital and the networks of slavery.

A figure consistently associated with action metaphors and transportation technology, Blake first moves against the proslavery mappings imposed on the U.S. nation's imagined surface—this would be the space depicted by mapmaker John Lewis in 1848 as determined by slaveholding extension. Blake's earliest appearance in the text signals a spatial reversal of slaveholder trajectories. He enters the novel at sunrise, returning to Colonel Frank's plantation from a distant errand aboard the steamer, Sultana, puffing up the Mississippi River. As a generation of former slave authors attested in print, especially from the early 1840s to the 1860s, the most dreaded punishment for the slave who had little else to lose was to be sold south of Virginia to a slave-consuming state. The very threat of enduring the most difficult forms of hard labor on large rice, sugar, and cotton farms along the Mississippi Delta prompted slaves to risk all and run North. Instead, Blake literally comes up from the lower South on the same Mississippi River slaves were sent down, not resembling an article of chattel at all, but rather returning as a thoroughbred horse handler, sent to oversee some operational details on Baton Rouge's racetrack syndicate. Other spatial interruptions of slave territory are lined up and executed systematically. Blake's first series of actions are thus reconstitutions of the black subject in space; his movement and agency are the extensions of a counter-geography.

A self-appointed leader, Blake sets out to study the spaces inhabited by his would-be electorate—and the impress of human activity within those landscapes. Traveling undetected, under cover of night, he (somehow) arranges meetings as he passes through Mississippi, Louisiana, Texas, Arkansas (including the Chickasaw and Choctaw Indian Nation), Georgia, North and South Carolina, Virginia, the District of Columbia, West Virginia, Tennessee, and Kentucky, all played out in the space of ten chapters. As a global hero forged from many spaces and time zones, Blake moves rapidly through the United States. He sacrifices depth only for breadth and speed. Because he holds "but one seclusion on each plantation," his progress "was consequently very rapid, in whatever direction he went."[31] As Delany shows it, Blake exists in a sort of alternate temporality, at once a fugitive and a tourist, passing through hundreds of landscapes and sewing these places together into his sweeping vision of united action.[32] Blake is the black menace embodied, the counter-black in the black spaces of Lewis's map.

The relative enfranchisement Delany accorded his exemplary Blake in the spaces of the Southern U.S. slave states, where the details of his illegal abduction mean far less to white landholders than his status as a fugitive black man, is suggestive of something further. Blake is, of course, an exceptional human being. But he is also a sentinel for another kind of potentiality, which the novel depicts as generally untapped by enslaved African Americans. It was something that could be accessed not only by enfranchised transnationals like Blake, but by enslaved, deterritorialized populations such as the blacks of the antebellum South. This undervalued resource was the power to mobilize local knowledges within national space. Local knowledges could be routes, timetables, or specificities of place. This was the material that did not show up in mappings with agglomerative shows of possession. But it was the work of deterritorialization from the interior.

Delany's fiction—as separate from his period political treatises, which turned to emigration forecasts—postulated that African American progress out from "the slave huts of America" required a special kind of geographical syncretism. It was not a principle of doubleness, fabricated from a primal African memory or a pan-African linguistic community. (These were lineages Delany had previously explored in the early 1830s, when he founded the Theban Society during a phase of high vogue Egyptology.) Rather, it was a syncretism born directly from African Americans' at once specific and liminal (that is, in but not of) relations to place.

In the first part of *Blake*, Delany works out the idea that blacks could most effectively challenge the assumptions and implements of bondage through an enhanced understanding of place. Rather than making slave spaces static, Delany characterizes them according to their openings, their potential flow, which Blake then excites. Blake's subnational geographies are formed in process by connecting elements of local knowledge, taken from a slave's daily life, to a greater understanding of modern mechanized transit. The goal is to form an embodied network, a revolutionary underground.

In the first part of the novel Blake travels widely by drawing on his familiarity with modern transportation and navigation technology—especially the American steamboat, which by midcentury had transformed the Delaware, Hudson, Mississippi, Potomac and their tributaries into principal transportation routes and zones for commercial enterprise. But no less valuable to him are local *epistemes*, ways of knowing a local space. A compiler of erudition, Blake is able to relay all the names of masters of steamers on the Upper Mississippi. This specific network knowledge comprises the black survey. Blake's river crossings are listed in summary fashion. He approaches the Red River "after crossing a number of streams, as the Yazoo, Ouchita, and such."[33] Later, seeking passage across a tributary of the Red River, he casually mentions "Captains Thogmorton, Price, Swan" to demonstrate that he is a tried traveler and permitted free passage, even within slave states.[34]

For instance, in his early travels away from Colonel Frank's Natchez plantation, Blake keeps a careful record of plantations he passes so that "when accosted by a white, as an overseer or patrol, he invariably pretended to belong to a back estate, in search of his master's race horse."[35] Encountering slaves, he makes pointed inquiries to assess the value of their labor specializations and field-based understandings. Together such information is the basis for a collective counterintelligence. Attendant to the fact that most slaves could not read, and hence were highly dependent on oral modes of communication, the literate (and also literary) Blake places a high premium on word-of-mouth transfer. He spreads news of his organized slave revolution through direct spoken communication. Once again, the work of black mapping is connected to its efficacy and immediacy. Blake's goals (just like Delany's) are always arch, always about connectivity. He collects geographical information to undermine the organizing principles of national space. But what is interesting, too, is that Delany seems to suggest here that if slaves looked modally into the rehearsed, colonized routes of movement, they would find paths leading out. They would find lines of flight. It was a matter of subverting the stabilizing codes, the expectations of usage.

In *A Thousand Plateaus*, Deleuze and Guattari describe "lines of flight" as passages toward "virtual," nonorganized, nonhierarchical space.[36] They are motions that partition strata, or the dominant manifest networks of modern societies. Strata represent forms, like spheres of influence, for the rationalizing abstract machine. In their theorization of it, the abstract machine covers multiple operations. It striates space and makes the grid, the inside and outside of the majoritarian norm. It also determines forms of subjectivity, the constitution of bodies, and the domain of proper enunciation (fitting expression). It claims normativity by announcing and replicating what is correct signification, or entrusted organization. To be noncompliant is to be "deviant," or substandard, or simply "just a tramp."[37] But Delany and Beckwourth would both show the peregrinations of the seeming tramp as far from unsystematic. Such designs have their own logic and can be pieced together into systems that can be invisible to dominant cultures.

Second, Delany's novel shows that local knowledge is not only small. Here it is worthwhile to deliberately reject Deleuze and Guattari's suggestion in "What is a Minor Literature?" that local knowledge exists in "a narrow space."[38] Rather, by taking the view of the local as a unit of the subject's extension into place intensity—be it affective place, physical place, or political place—the notion of the local as a narrow projection proves to be rather inadequate. Local knowledge can exist in wide spaces as tools of usage or reproducible epistemes. It can also be cast, as it is in Blake, as a way to contract a national expanse by framing it against wider mappings. Actually, one of the most remarkable features of Blake's part I is the ways local scriptings push out beyond "nested hierarchies of scale," to use a critique by geographer Nigel Thrift, where the global subsumes the national, and the national subsumes the regional, and so forth.[39] The local is not about affirming bounded space, but more an assertion of the self's differentiation. It is like what Edward Soja describes as a "rippling outward" from self to setting.[40] And for Delany, the impact of local knowing exceeded white enclosures. Beyond the purview of slaveholders' claims, Delany imaginatively drew up a firmament. Beyond slavery's confines were the stars, illuminated in the pages of Blake.[41]

Delany's novelistic dramatization of celestial navigation was part of his broader drive for scientific discovery. It was something that the Blake character is shown as bringing to blacks, and something Delany considered a black-positive science with Egyptian roots.[42] In Blake, stars make the shape of a flight atlas in spaces of confinement. Blake instructs Mississippi slaves on how to escape North to Canada using diagrams of the North Star and pointer stars in the handle of the Big Dipper. With its numerical pointers, degrees, lines, and dotted lines, Blake's star map is an embedded pedagogy, transcribed into the pages of the Anglo-African Magazine. (It actually reads as a raw transcription from Delany's astronomy studies in 1859, when he published two articles in the Anglo-African Magazine: "The Attraction of Planets" and "Comets.")[43]

Blake relays that during the night the Big Dipper continues to change its position in relation to the earth. He connects the study to a pedagogy of cardinal directions for slaves: "When your face is to the north, your back is to the south; your right hand to the east, and your left to the west."[44] In tandem with Blake's didactic display of celestial orientation, Delany modeled a pedagogy for a fictional audience he depicted as simple plantation blacks. One quality of meaningful geographic knowledge, the text suggests, is its immediate applicability. Land knowledge is thus made the material of counter-maps.[45] On terra firma and as a print record in the black newspaper, all this gets presented as a navigational tool. In the novel, celestial movement is modeled into the shape of transitive local knowledge. It is applicable in near spaces and across spaces unknown.

A key part of the counter-cartography tendered in Blake is the flight line, the route out—or to use the terms of the North Star, what it is that "he who runs can read."[46] Blake is on hand for this, too, teaching his listeners how to use land signs as a guide: "Feel, in the dark, around the trunks of bodies of trees, especially oaks, and whenever you feel moss on the bark, that side on which the moss grows is always to the north."[47] Having equipped his understudies with proximate land-first knowledge, he apprises them of an inexpensive, yet invaluable technological tool. He explains what a compass is and how it works: "The hand or finger is a piece of metal called 'loadstone' or 'magnet,' and termed the needle of the compass; and this end with the little cross on it, always points in one direction, and that is to the north."[48] Technology is thus made ancillary to tactile, geographic knowledges. It is not a competing system, but a means of facilitating and enhancing exploration. The compass presentation is also important for this reason: Measurement, Blake shows, need not only be a unit of masters' time, a territorialized, striated, episteme of the machine.[49] Rather, technology can be allied with a vocabulary of flow, bringing features of mechanization, modernization, and navigation through the doors of usage and into the knowledge systems of those he instructs.

Finally, Blake presses on the message Delany developed many times over in his literature: The prime mover in the organization of national space was capital. To oil the wheels of movement and white cooperation, Blake insists that whatever else they do, plantation blacks must acquire capital.[50] Capital could invert the subject-object relations between master and slave by making territory objectifiable for a free subject. Capital is the passport across a topography of systems, through the name-generating features of maps. In the second part of *Blake*, Delany suggests that capital is what made Atlantic trade maps in the first place; it flows below and above the flags of different ships. (The novel shows how refitted Baltimore clippers, operating as transatlantic slavers, protected themselves from British West Indian cruisers by hoisting different sailing flags after leaving harbor.[51]) The examples are summoned to make the point that deterritorialization and reterritorialization exceed national processes. Delany's message in part 1 of the novel is that capital will get an enslaved and subaltern people across physical expanses of space. The ability to accumulate capital, he argues, will break the social system of master-slave relations and pave the way to higher social positions for blacks. Even before leaving Natchez with two thousand dollars around his waist, Blake reminds local slaves that successful escape plans require capital: "Keep this studiously in mind and impress it as an important part of the scheme of organization, that they must have money, if they want to get free. Money will obtain them everything necessary by which to obtain their liberty. The money is within all of their reach if they only knew it was right to take it."[52] On a Texas cotton plantation, he repeats this theme, claiming, "money is your passport through that White Gap to freedom. . . . Money will carry you through the White mountains and across the White river to liberty."[53]

Blake's revolutionary purpose in the first part of the novel is ultimately that of super agent. He brings together seemingly disconnected species of knowing and combines them into himself, the representative whole of black liberation. But poised for a revolutionary, black filibuster strike into Cuba in the second part of the novel, all this amassed local knowledge gets left behind. It is as if it never happened. How the massive reconnaissance might be processed into the counter-regime is never addressed. The novel steers off course into another, albeit parallel, struggle (discussed in chapter 3 of this book). Nonetheless, reading Blake's underexamined national peregrinations through a perspective influenced by geographic process directs attention to the novel's site mappings, its partitions of nationalist territory. It foregrounds the relational qualities of territory and the material pivots of flow. It also represents the work of black deterritorialization as something that moves boundaries. Moving boundaries is generative, or at least has the potential to be generative, since by realigning territories it can alter the overall map.

Authenticity in an Errant Land

Delany opened with the counter-map, which effectively primed geographies of the southern United States to get beneath white territorializations and undo them. For James Beckwourth, his story was also one of tensions embodied in territorialization: these were the more conventional contests between savagery and civilization, but also something connected to the heroic subject's correlation with nature. Beckwourth made claims for an authentic relationship with the real that lay beneath the mapped forms he helped make. In a climate of postnationalist American studies, Beckwourth has received considerably less critical attention than Delany.[54] Less has been said about Beckwourth's position as a prospector and land guide of the North American West. Nonetheless, his stories of pursuit reveal the ways landscape is discursively made into territory, and the ways territory is shaped through what I will describe as nonexclusive self-positioning.

Beckwourth's life story is told as a voyage out into unsettled trapping lodges in the Rocky Mountains and Sierra Nevada mining camps. His was "a career of wild adventure and thrilling romance . . . dearly purchased."[55] He freely admits to wanting wealth, glory, Indian wives of convenience. But the nature of his quest is open-ended, and attainments only satisfy him briefly. In painting a life's movement from the Crow lands of Montana and Wyoming to the Cheyenne networks of New Mexico, his story takes the form of careening extensions into lands beyond the measured tract. What underwrites all this is cast as a primal relation to land. Describing the stories told by "scores of emigrants" en route to California, those who stopped at his late-in-life Sierra "hermitage" in Beckwourth Valley, Beckwourth assumed the wizened position: "When I recurred to my own adventures, I would smile at the comparison of their sufferings with what myself and other men of the mountains had really endured in former times."[56]

Though Beckwourth's narrative charts movement beyond the ragged edges of what nineteenth-century readers knew to be civilization, it undermines indigenous possession and cedes to dominant territorial codes of representation. That is, *The Life and Adventures* depicts a manifest landscape for a nationalized subject. This is different from Delany's achievement in his novel. *Blake* advocated minoritarian political movement (the black survey, the slave's counter-map) even as it envisioned these as a vitality that needed to be turned into directed action from the outside. This was something that the confederate form that is *Blake* is continually tapped to provide. In *The Life and Adventures* the frontier is importantly not a trial space for character development, or some crucial zone for the human will and spirit, as it appeared in James Fenimore Cooper's contemporary *The Pathfinder* (1840) or *The Deerslayer* (1841), or in Sarah Royce's epic restaging of the California gold rush in *A Frontier Lady*, written years later in the 1880s. For Beckwourth, it is more a space of free play, where self-interest can be attached to whatever form best serves it. By the final chapters of his narrative, it is clear that what Beckwourth proffers—even off the grid of settlement—is the closure of property. Within Beckwourth's tale of pursuit, landscape is channeled into territory, and territory is an exploitable form to accommodate self-interest.

Beckwourth's relationship to territory was conditioned by the kinds of releases he pursued away from settled life; it was conditioned by the ways he tried to decode space (land guide, scout, surveyor, trapper) and the sort of familiarity he claimed to find especially in the Rocky Mountains of the 1830s. In considering the relationships between deterritorialization and what the narrative presents as landscapes of venture, the notion from *Anti-Oedipus*—that territory is produced by capitalist drive, the great "social axiomatic" that rides over other assemblages, among them tribal affiliations—is interestingly enough borne out in narrative form.[57] Indeed, it is capital, or pelf, that is Beckwourth's avowed driver, and it is ultimately capital that he understands to be opening a new, white West.[58] Taking the quest for profit, not only as his life aim, but as his view of what makes white territory into territory in the first place, Beckwourth positioned himself as an adventurer on the endless make. In his story of struggle, he is "the hardy mariner, whose compass guides him through all parts of the pathless ocean."[59] But for Beckwourth, the seas he explored were the lands he prowled as an early American mountaineer.

One of the first issues that needs to be considered in any reading of *The Life and Adventures* is the text's status as dictated narrative. This matter is particularly important here since it figures prominently in the forms of deterritorialization evoked in the story lines. *The Life and Adventures* is a romance about traversing cultures that in itself is a collaborative formation, a compound of voices. Beckwourth's autobiography was transcribed by Thomas D. Bonner, a self-described "wanderer" and itinerant justice of the peace in the midcentury gold mining camps that sprung up in California at the end of the 1840s.[60] Bonner was a colorful figure and no stranger to bold, literary endeavor. Before the gold rush, he published *The Temperance Harp: A Collection of Songs* in 1842. For two years he also ran an investigative weekly temperance paper, *Cataract*, from Massachusetts. He went so far as to moonlight as a temperance detective to come away with salacious stories about alcohol.[61] He may have been a first-hand participant in any number of these "investigations."

Hardly a quiet background figure, Bonner was a tradesman of letters, a medium in his own right. His voice cannot really be taken as subordinate to Beckwourth's. On the contrary, Bonner's involvement as amanuensis was constitutive. Describing the role of the amanuensis in the first century of African American autobiography, William Andrews has noted the difficulty of "distilling an authorial essence from the clouded stream of edited and dictated Afro-American autobiographies."[62] Andrews goes on to suggest that such autobiographical form might be treated more like a "complex of linguistic acts on a discursive field" than as historically referential, or even as a particular captioning of self in history.[63] Thus, rather than seeking a representational product, authenticated by presence, taking both voices to be part of a discursive complex presents readers with the most interpretive options intertextually. Indeed, questions of attribution, inclusion, and braided voices can all be productive in pursuing a comparative literary analysis of territorialization as something both discursive and physical. In another sense, formal questions related to the telling or withholding of an amanuensis actually resonate with the themes of placelessness and uncertain possession that repeatedly present themselves in any critical approach to Beckwourth's long narrative.

Though Bonner claimed in his preface that the thirty-seven chapters of biography were "taken down literally as it was from day to day related," and that his role in formation was simply "to put . . . upon paper" what "fell from his [Beckwourth's] lips," this is clearly misleading.[64] For one thing, it diminishes Bonner's own role in shaping a story framed to print conventions already in place. In conveying Beckwourth's Rocky Mountain life among the Crow Indians, Bonner appears to have angled the text to the frontier adventure reader or, in any case, the reader with an appetite for ongoing horse raids and picaresque episodes of narrow capture and escape in the golden West.[65] Blake Allmendinger has inferred that the majority of Beckwourth's contemporary readers would have been familiar with the ken of white trappers and frontiersmen, "both real and fictitious (such as Daniel Boone, Davy Crockett, and Natty Bumppo), in the mid-nineteenth century."[66] A newspaper founder and venturer on many fronts, Bonner probably hoped to strike market success with the Beckwourth contract. He very likely did target the sort of audience that Allmendinger suggests. Beckwourth also dreamed of "renown" and even solicited Bonner's participation in the project after learning that he had been a newspaperman before coming West.[67] On the whole, the forceful collaboration was favorably reviewed in *Harper's New Monthly Magazine*, as "at last something really genuine about the privations of the mountaineer; something to be relied upon relating the inner life of the savage; the vail [sic] has been lifted, and although somewhat rudely done, the scene is before us in its deformity and beauty."[68] If the product was "rudely done," as the review suggests, this was not a bad thing. It was as much a reflection of the transparency and authenticity of Beckwourth's account as it was credit to Bonner's packaging.

As literature of vernacular (Western) expression, framed by certain generic conventions, Beckwourth's tale thus reads as a kind of double-voiced projection into the topographies of the North American West. It elaborates alcohol's destructive (literally deterritorializing) influence on the Cheyenne of New Mexico and shares an appeal to sensation and the panoplies of human folly that were hallmarks of Bonner's earlier 1840s-era temperance verse.[69] (These themes gradually converge as illustrative modes for the kinds of drama that could be elaborated in the more prolix adventure memoir.) Though *The Life and Adventures* passes itself off as "free indirect discourse"—something that Henry Louis Gates in *The Signifying Monkey* identifies as a defining component of the black, speakerly text—it is mediated by a white voice. In respect to Bonner, the voice was not peripheral at all, but generative of form and meaning. It was certainly complicit in masking Beckwourth as a white man, an avowed "American citizen, friend of my race."[70] Beckwourth's is the voice of a racial insider in an errant—but, importantly, "native"—land. He is someone claiming to have "saved more life and property for the white man than a whole regiment of United States regulars could have done in the same time."[71] As the narrative shows, questions of territory and resource expropriation are addressed in relation to a white subjectivity.

Roots

The child of a slave mother and white overseer father, Beckworth's race identity was something both he and Bonner buried under a long story of wilderness peregrinations in the Rocky Mountains and the Sierras of California. Early on in the narrative, Beckwourth presents his father as setting out with his family and "twenty-two negroes" for the frontier of Missouri. The number of slaves may have been exaggerated, like many other details (scores of warriors defeated, scalps taken, and so forth).[72] But by enumerating his fellow sojourners as just that, numbers, Beckwourth distances them in favor of expressing his own father's wealth and nonblackness. In Blake the track lines for motion are black, "pure black." For Beckwourth, the first journey out is the white campaign westward. His slave mother, whom he likely never knew, is written out of his story completely. In stark comparison to Delany, who boasted of royal African lineage on both sides, Beckwourth masks his genealogy. He quickly moves past his murky family life in St. Louis, in favor of compiling anecdotes of his many Crow Indian wives and detailing the adversarial relationship between whites and Indians, a dividing line he depicts himself as traversing repeatedly.

While Delany worked among the black populations of Pittsburgh and Canada West, placing African American political enfranchisement at the center of all his undertakings, Beckwourth ultimately found only disappointment in returning to town life, especially in St. Louis. Coming back for a visit after fourteen years away, he learned of the deaths of his father and the scattering of others fondly remembered. Enemies proliferated; they approached him on the streets and circled him in saloons. As a known black man, his freedom of movement could not have been the same as it would have been in the Rocky Mountain region, where he could independently contract himself to fur companies, set up his own exchanges, and act as a land guide. The momentous return to civilization, as his visit is initially cast, turns into a way to deflect all future connections from place-based African American communities in St. Louis.

Against normative, settled life (also a restricted life for a manumitted man of color, though he does not say this), his "Indian home" becomes the "vivid coloring in relief."[73] His inevitable return to the Crow confirms that he is truly "a wanderer upon the earth." In the West, his fields of flight are far more expansive than what is portrayed as the material of town life: constrained connectivity.

Just as Delany made the black international fugitive the bearer of incipient land knowledge, Beckwourth cast himself as an American fringe. He is the unregenerate "tramp," the man unmoored. But even though he formed no absolutist citizenship, he could still legitimize his takings in the service of nation.[74] For Beckwourth, the midcentury mountaineers were the ultimate agents of American land making. Mountaineers, the topography-referencing name for the early non-Indian fur trappers, scouts, and route makers in the Rocky Mountains, produced a knowledge beyond the printed map. More pointedly, their work made the map: They made wilderness into territory. Early in his narrative he relays his (volatile) time spent during the summer of 1824 as part of General William H. Ashley's overland expedition along the Colorado River northward as the labor of territorialization. His group made the tracks for civilization. In twilight mode, Beckwourth claimed: "The forts that now afford protection to the traveler were built by ourselves at constant peril of our own lives . . . no roads before us but trails temporarily made."[75]

In fact, as Beckwourth told it, he was chief among discoverers and hunters. A bodily tactical sense guided him in incorporating Indian trails (their values neutralized by Beckwourth) into designs for company movement. He followed land features like forks in the river beds, and divided prairies in search of streams where wild geese and teal ducks were abundant. He detailed the canyons and the deep river passes through mountains as places to track the movement of the North American buffalo. Beckwourth's biographer Elinor Wilson notes that the physical pathmaking work by figures such as Beckwourth made it possible for the more frequently cited mapmakers of the West to lay claim to discovery: "The mountaineers were becoming the geographers on whom the future Corps of Topographic Engineers would rely for guidance. They were the pathfinders without whom the Pathfinder, John Charles Frémont, might never have attained his sobriquet. Still later, the United States Army would rely on these mountain men as guides and interpreters, and even as commanders in the seemingly endless Indian wars."[76] Beckwourth may have been a fringe, but he provided the actual groundwork for government contractors who, in turn, produced officialized knowledges, official maps.

Beckwourth constructed a mountaineer's life as a service life. It was like a soldier's life. Many are the tales of bloody loss, scalpings, and maimings. And through it all, he insisted that his efforts aggrandized the state. He was the roguish nondissident for midcentury U.S. Indian policy in Western territories. A mountaineer's acquisition of "Indian habits" was an advertisable, in fact, hirable, quality for white reterritorialization of the West.[77] He boasted: "I know that with five hundred men of my selection I could exterminate any Indian tribe in North America in a very few months. But so long as our government continues to enlist the offscouring of European cities into our army, and intrusts [sic] the command to inexperienced officers fresh from West Point, just so long will they afford food for the Indians in and about the Rocky Mountains."[78] As Beckwourth told it, his knowledge would make the difference. But his experiences outside of white civilization did little to change the lines of contestation between savagery and civilization. These were his guidelines, and they remained in place. He did not challenge dominant territorial ideology, even though the basis for his judgments was later shown to be subverted by the very life experiences he shared with Indians during his time among the Crow.

Internal Diasporas

Beckwourth accurately described the territory claimed by the Crow as larger than the state of Illinois: "Portions of it form the choicest land in the world, capable of producing anything that will grow in the Western and Middle States."[79] Yet in expanding the known map, he also laid bare his interests in deterritorializing Indian lands—in splitting place from indigenous practice. What might be characterized in any number of American romantic texts of the period as vital environment encounters, openings into what nature could provide the spirit, Beckwourth made into advertisements for capital development. In Crow lands he enumerated the crystal streams of clear water that "would afford power for any amount of machinery."[80] He also told of a blazing mountain in the darkness of night, describing how he surrounded it with a group of warriors. He first thought it to be alight with enemy fires. His real discovery,

2.2. Crow Indian chiefs captured at Custer battlefield, Montana, 7 November, and imprisoned at Fort Snelling, Minnesota, 15 November 1887. Photographer unknown. War Department. (1789–09/18/1947), ca. 1881–ca. 1885.

though, was that this majestic spectacle was a mountain of coal on fire: "I immediately drew off my forces, as I was fearful of an explosion."[81] This realization is briskly marshaled into an exposition on the potential for anthracite coal mining. Claimed Beckwourth: "No part of the United States contains richer deposits of anthracite coal than the territory I am speaking of, and my conviction is thus founded."[82] In this sweep, the narrative makes territory by translating Crow environment for industrial usage. Beckwourth was also clear that his primary interest in the Crow was profiting from them through their access to hunting territory. Such an association he viewed as beneficial to the Crow, whom he could influence against excessive, loss-incurring tribal wars—for the sake of plying the fur trade. More directly, it was beneficial for him and for his employers at the American Fur Company, whose trade he expanded.[83]

It is here where Martin Delany's operative contrasts are most apparent. Delany clearly romanticized Indian knowledge. He imagined relatively unlikely alliances between Indians and blacks in a way Beckwourth

2.3. James Beckwourth, early American trapper and fur trader of the West. Photographer unknown. Daguerreotype, 1860. The Smithsonian Institution, Washington, D.C. Scanned from Geoffrey C. Ward, *The West: An Illustrated History*.

did not. That is, he envisioned blacks and Indians coming together, albeit in mostly unspecified ways, as a force that could resist dominant white nationalism and upend the spread of U.S. slavery.[84] Indians represented landholders under radical encroachment, a dispossession that presaged annihilation. They were without legal claims to land. African Americans were without claims to their own labor. Both were deterritorialized. Both lived in internal diaspora within state structures. In Delany's framing of worlds, both existed as nations within nations. He described this recognition in *The Condition* as "a people who although forming a part and parcel of the population yet were from force of circumstances, known by the peculiar position they occupied, forming in fact, by the deprivation of political equality with others, no part, and if any, but a restricted part of the body politic."[85] This was the condition U.S. blacks shared with Indians.

Throughout *The Condition* he treated diaspora in quite a different sense than it has frequently been deployed in black Atlantic theory today. For example, Paul Gilroy, in his influential contention that "national units are not the most appropriate basis for studying this history for the African diaspora's consciousness of itself has been defined in and against constricting national boundaries," frames diasporas as overwriting the national.[86] They are depicted as overreaching nation via different tropes of attachment and translation. But for Delany, diaspora signified not only physical removal from a putative homeland, but internal divisions that broke apart processes of self-determination and forms of territorial sovereignty among specific groups within existing national structures. By 1852 Delany concluded that diasporic subjection was something deeply complicit with the structures of the nation-state, "especially," he argued, "among those nations laying the greatest claim to civilization and enlightenment."[87] His thinking in this respect is most resonant with that of more recent subaltern scholars like R. Radhakrishnan, who write about the ways national identities are constructed from the outside and diasporan cultures are interwoven with national space.[88]

Blake in the Indian Nation

In a nineteenth-century context, there is no starker case for the comparative existence of nation within nation than that of Native American communities. One of the most illuminating spaces Delany's Blake enters on his counter-state reconnaissance mission is what he calls "the United Nation of Chickasaw and Choctaw Indians," near Fort Towson in Arkansas, a bracketed nation within a political state.[89] The Indian Nation's geography was significant for a number of reasons. Fort Towson, since its 1824 establishment as a U.S. Army outpost, had been a symbolic frontier line settlement. It was built with the aim of policing the border between the United States and Mexico (of which Texas was then a part). In depicting the Indian Nation, Delany suggestively packed into his novel a space of subaltern potential inside dominant national orders. The Indian Nation stands in as an American subspace between two sides of international territorial conflict.

As Choctaw scholars beginning with Grant Foreman have discussed, Fort Towson was also intended as an intra-Indian buffer between the Comanche, Kiowa, and Pawnee of the West and the "Civilized Tribes" (the Cherokee, Chickasaw, Choctaw, Creek, and Seminole), following their

Jacksonian-era expulsion.[90] Shortly after the U.S. war with Mexico, which vastly enlarged United States territorial possession, the "frontier fort" was turned over to the Choctaw, who made it their tribal capital. The Chickasaw were made to settle there as well.[91] Fort Towson was, then, a nation within a nation on two levels. It was a place of refugees from two nations in crisis, brought together under the statist arm of another nation. In fact, when Delany visited the Chickasaw in 1839, most of them would have been temporarily encamped near Choctaw settlements, as a district tribe with a chief reporting to the Choctaws.[92] Although the Indian Nation was a temporary compound formation between distinct tribes of North American Indians who entered into treaty in 1854, Delany's novel depicts it as a singular space of holism amenable to Blake's revolutionary revisionism. It is made into a ready unit of Blake's diasporic reunification scheme.

Pure in his purpose, Blake targets it with the specific goal of forging alliances between blacks and Native Americans. However, one major problem looms over this otherwise commodious occasion: the Indian Nation is also a slaveholding nation. While Blake maintains he cannot be reconciled with such principles, the narrative that ensues largely mitigates Native slaveholding, even to the extent of offering up a rationalization for it. Chief Culver, whom Blake regards as a wise man, proffers that it is simply better to be enslaved by Indians, explaining "the difference between a white man and Indian holding slaves. Indian work side by side with black man, eat with him, drink with him, rest with him and both lay down in shade together; white man won't even let you talk! In our Nation Indian and black all marry together."[93] In "The African Diaspora in Indian Country," Tiya Miles and Sharon Holland caution against such romantic constructions of past alliances between Indian communities and African Americans. They write: "Black expressions of alliance with Indians often sideline the parallel history of adversarial relations between African Americans and Native Americans, in which Southern Indians owned black[s] as slaves and black buffalo soldiers served in the U.S. military as a unit charged with crushing Native resistance movements and enforcing Native detention on reservations."[94] Though Miles and Holland direct their focus toward black sojourns into Indian territory after the end of Reconstruction in 1877, what they caution against is already apparent in Delany's pre-war expectations about diasporic affiliation.

Indeed, what is particularly important to note is that this issue of Indian slaveholding is not resolved in Blake and is, in fact, ultimately transferred into a much broader rationalization, motioning toward the central tenets of Delany's midcentury pan-racial thinking. This was something he called original priority. Most synoptically, he describes it like this in Blake: "The western world had been originally peopled and possessed by Indians—a colored race—and a part of the continent in Central America by a pure black race. This . . . gave them an indisputable right with every admixture of blood, to an equal, if not superior, claim to an inheritance of the Western Hemisphere."[95] Original priority is thus a readily packaged rationale, not for African American emigration per se, but for a more directive black territorialization in spaces that could leverage an advantage. The Chief Culver character applies the concept: "The squaws of the great men among the Indians in Florida," he claimed, "were black women, and the squaws of the black men were Indian women. You see the vine that winds around and holds us together. Don't cut it, but let it grow till . . . it git so stout and strong, with very many little branches attached, that you can't separate them."[96] In effect, Delany's argument for original priority translates directly into blacks' prerogative to preside among (and also over) indigenous cultures within the Americas and later, Africa, based on the understanding that they were all colored. What Delany fictionalized in Blake was already anticipated by The Condition, chapter 21, "Central and South America and the West Indies," and chapter 24, "A Glance at Ourselves."

The mode of all this should also not be overlooked: It is through the female replication of bodies that the rhizomatic vine of the land can be established. Some fifty years later, the author and journalist Pauline Hopkins, who studied Delany's work as political literature, investigated the problematics of this position in the serial Winona (1902). She treated it as the failed hope of counter-colonizing along black and Indian lines. But for Delany, black and Indian intermarriage was less about genealogical rewiring as it was suggestive as a model for cooperative alliances. Writing during a period where Indians were widely offered incorporation into the affective nation through land cession and where African Americans were not, he envisioned intermarriage as a means of enhancing political positioning.[97] He depicted black fugitive excursions into Indian landscapes as openings for a border knowledge, not a knowledge that issued from any local context, but a story of encounters as resources.[98] It would take the work of Pauline Hopkins to expose the more fundamental ineffectiveness of Delany's interbreeding suggestions, both because it did little to reclaim some primal territory and because it did nothing for women seeking greater gender parity.

Against Alliances

By contrast, Beckwourth (and Bonner) placed territorial sovereignty on a single, closing line that played to a contest between savagery and civilization. Indigenous scholars such as Taiaiake Alfred have criticized the ways the concept of sovereignty has been framed as "exclusionary" and "rooted in an adversarial and coercive Western notion of power."[99] Vine Deloria Jr., for instance, has argued that sovereignty's "statist" genealogies "originated as a means of locating the seat of political power in European nations."[100] As *The Life and Adventures* spins out Beckwourth's wild adventures, it keeps pace with a staunch polemic. Civilization conquered disorder; it conquered what was not in place: nonindustry, nonagriculture—meaningless pursuits. Beckwourth's text offers a mid-nineteenth-century rationalization of this logic from the perspective of ineluctable reterritorialization: "But it is impossible to confine an Indian to a steady pursuit—not even fighting; after a while he will even tire of that. It is impossible to control his wayward impulses; application to profitable industry is foreign to his nature."[101]

The text presents Indian pathways through landscapes of the West as analogues of rootlessness nonhistory. As Beckwourth tells it, the Indian "is a vagrant, and he must wander; he has no engendered habits of thrift or productiveness to give him a constant aim or concentration of purpose."[102] This fits War Department policy, which Beckwourth explicitly appealed to at the end of his narrative.[103] According to Indian Commissioner William Medill's "Annual Report on Indian Affairs" in November 1848, "apathy, barbarism and heathenism must give way to energy, civilization, and Christianity; and so the Indian of this continent has been displaced by the European; but this has been attended by much less of oppression and injustice than has generally been represented and believed. . . . Where in the contest of civilization with barbarism, since the commencement with time, has it been less the case than with us."[104]

Repeatedly, narratives of capitalist land development are accorded the backstory of a viable, sequential history, which Indian place histories are not. Indians are denied the locations of possession. Maureen Konkle writes that the work of U.S. liberal imperialist narratives "wasn't just a product of blind racial prejudice or ethnocentric cultural misunderstanding; it stripped away history, geography, political life, and traditions from indigenous people to produce an abstraction that demonstrated that they didn't and couldn't own land and form legitimate governments."[105] On one level, *The Life and Adventures* plays into this reasoning. Territorial treaties made with Indians and annuities paid to them are deemed "worse than fruitless." Treaties were only for those "caught at a disadvantage, and reduced to enter into a compact." But once the "controlling power is withdrawn . . . they can repeat their depredations with apparent impunity, no moral obligation would restrain them."[106] At the same time, despite echoing dominant nationalist phrasings, Beckwourth extolled these very qualities of "savagism" as just the kinds of opportune traits that served him best on the frontiers of the North American West. Beckwourth is slippery on alliances anyway. Though he funnels Indian difference into white hierarchies of power-as-possession, he also frames a diversity of Indian life, Indian languages, punishment modes, and communication strategies. It is a deep playing ground, and Beckwourth is Bonner's ultimate inside man. But for all of Beckwourth's winnings, the loss of utility value for Indians starts to add up.

Deleuze and Guattari characterize deterritorialization, which they affirm is always "inseparable from correlative reterritorialization," as assuming both negative and positive forms.[107] Negative deterritorialization is when a broken down assemblage reforms or is reconstituted (reterritorialized) in such a way that it impedes further lines of flight. It becomes a "conjugation" in a system of capture.[108] Its expressive autonomy is lessened. A positive deterritorialization, by contrast, opens into productive connections that flow from a reserve of freedom. A positive deterritorialization increases freedom and increases connections. A negative deterritorialization though results in further blockages, more boundaries imposed, and usually a carry-over from previous regimes. Beckwourth plays into the latter.

In Cheyenne country in New Mexico, Beckwourth implicated himself most distortedly as an agent of "civilized" reterritorialization, opening a trade of fur for alcohol. For sixty gallons of whisky mixture, he alleges, he took from the Indians more than 1,100 robes of buffalo and eighteen horses. This was an extraordinary yield, even for a vaunting trader as himself. In scenes such as these, the obvious tensions between profiting from Indian "generosity" and advocating Indian destruction becomes most apparent. It is here too that what William Andrews has termed "the division of literary labor" shows itself most starkly: the "fire water" merchant Beckwourth and temperance-driven Bonner apparently part attributive company.[109] In the Cheyenne country passages, the tone shifts toward clear opprobrium: "The trading whisky for Indian property," the narrative reads, "is one of the most infernal practices ever entered into by man. Let the reader sit down and figure up the profits on a forty-gallon cask of alcohol, and he will be thunderstruck, or rather whisky struck."[110] Bonner describes Beckwourth's deeds as vitiating community and family life and wasting the labor of Indian women, who "toil for many long weeks to dress these . . . robes. The white trader gets them all for worse than nothing, for the poor Indian mother hides herself and her children in the forests until the effect of the poison passes away from husbands, fathers, brothers." The buffalo, too, the narrator points out, "are becoming gradually exterminated, being killed with so little remorse that their very hides, among the Indians themselves, are known by the appellation of a pint of whisky." That an agent of the trade such as Beckwourth would hail his efforts in this way is unlikely, especially since the effects of this all are not simply written off as externalities or the cost of doing business.[111]

Out of Space: The Surrounds

Indeed, though the narrative passes quickly through various sites of Northwestern landscape, often giving only a glimpse of the trading forts Beckwourth established and lived among, these sites do collect over the course of some five hundred pages. It is impossible not to consider the ways Beckwourth as trader and Beckwourth as prospector changed the shape of the lands he left behind. The reader recalls the kinds of compound alliances he forced in order to edge profits, for instance, with the Black Foot and among the Grovan tribes. Beckwourth appeared to understand that his successes were not without attendant losses, traces of defeat left somewhere.

And for the Crow, theirs is the impasse of the surround. They are cast as the deterritorialized element, just like the buffalo. "Doubtless," Beckwourth asserted, "much of the land which [the buffalo] now roam over will be under the white man's cultivation, which will extend inland from both oceans. Where then shall the Indian betake himself? There shall be no more Mississippis to drive him beyond. Unquestionably he will be taken in a surround, as he now surrounds the buffalo; and as he can not assimilate with civilization, the Red Man's doom is apparent."[112] Apart from sparse tobacco, they do not raise crops. As the narrative tells it, all they have is the buffalo and the rituals of the hunt.

The text's invocation of inevitable destruction for the Indian in the anticipated sweep of white civilization is ultimately less prescient than procedural. It reproduces a frame of reference and policy that Beckwourth had to have known from his own participation in the Seminole Wars in 1837 as a civilian employee of the army and, more notoriously, as the leading land guide to the Third Regiment of the Colorado Volunteer Cavalry in 1864.[113] In actions he would later purportedly regret, Beckwourth guided Colorado militiamen under John Chivington to the Cheyenne and Arapaho village at Sand Creek in southeastern Colorado Territory for the brutal mutilation of approximately a hundred Indians, about two-thirds of whom were women and children.[114] Beckwourth was also among the first to advocate in print the extermination of the buffalo through poison and planted, land "pitt falls."[115] He cast his work as supportive of "the expanding development of civilization."[116] But in his narrative, civilization takes the form of a dragline through the morass of other life outcroppings. As a free agent, he claimed he could offer "some counsel" to the War Department on the "most certain method of quelling their Indian troubles."[117]

What preserves this text from the flats of imperialist chronotype with the well-hewn storylines of civilization versus savagism is something two-fold. It can be found in the details of Crow expression and ritual from inside the camps. Beckwourth describes medicine lodge practices, marriage arrangements, elderly Indian lifestyles, and ceremonies involving animals. Though he is quick to weary of any one place, the narrative lingers on the surface of Indian territory. In oftentimes remarkably generous detail, he gives accounts of interactions and dealings among the Crow that do not synthesize well into any concept of savagery. Secondly, the narrative impels itself into stories of mountain adventures and territorial wars, where gains are lost and losses are regained to such an extent that any shape of territory gets attenuated; it appears as a profoundly unstable, displacing entity. It is no more choate than the contour trails

2.4. Pierre-Jean de Smet, *Map of the Upper Great Plains and Rocky Mountains Region. Respectfully submitted to Col. D. D. Mitchell by P. J. de Smet.* 1851. Mansfield Library Map Collection, the University of Montana. The Crow Territory is northeast of Utah, in the center of the map. De Smet's map used boundary lines to mark tribal lands from Missouri to the Columbia River.

of quest. Because territory is so fraught, the narrative's phrasings on civilization-as-progress appear particularly hollow, especially when attached to an exposition that undoes them from the inside.

Life among the Indians is dramatized as a continuum along the lines of increasingly immersive excursions into lands unknown. And land knowledge repeatedly recedes into Indian knowledge, which represents a deeper relation to a land consciousness. In Beckwourth's text, this consciousness reads like something structuralist geographers identify as "locale." This is simply the shape of space, and the kinds of institutions (formal, but especially informal) that make a place what it is.[118] The *Life and Adventures* relays Indian knowledge as subverting white normative territorialization. Indians answer to neither white entitlements nor white restrictions. They cannot be brought into white land epistemes. He states: "The Crows, as a nation, had never credited any of the representations of the great wealth, and power, and numbers of their white brethren." They are motivated by a pride in their own territorial governance: "They have always refused to send a deputation to Washington, although repeatedly invited."[119]

The Crow are attached to a land, Beckwourth suggests, but not a specific dwelling. Their "locality," as he configures it, is actually a relation. It is not fixed by spatial coordinates, but by modes of knowing. Indians can "make" with the land as they encounter it on the run. They know the mountains and gorges better. And where there are plains, they outstrip an army's coverage of distance. He writes, "To attempt to chastise Indians with United States troops is simply ridiculous; the expense of such campaigns is only surpassed by their inefficiency." His reasoning is this: "The Indians live on horseback, and they can steal and drive off the government horses faster than it can bring them together."[120] The locale of the Crow is also the space they cover. It is the space they use, and it runs counter to War Department creeds of land as waste until white (or, presumably, black) labor is applied.

In spite of a narrative that unveils Indian land dependency to the projected white reader as an exploitable vulnerability ("if the government is determined to make war upon the Western tribes, let it be done intelligently") Indian technologies are not easily interred into white land knowledge.[121] If the metric is maximizing a resource's yield, and not simply maximum profit extraction, the Indians are far more efficient. They take for necessary, projected use. Western Indians (the Crow, Blackfoot, Sioux), he claims, travel better. Accordingly, Crow Indians, "have no stationary villages, they can travel faster, even with the encumbrance of their lodges, women, and children, subsisting themselves on buffalo slain on the way, than any force, however richly appointed, the country could send against them."[122] They can move dry goods more expediently. He describes himself as "greatly edified" by the Crow's way of bringing freight across the Missouri River. By using ballasted "hide tubs" and by running puckering strings through buffalo robes until they "assumed a globulated form," they make ready transport lines. These can then be used to convey guns and dry goods across the river "in a very short time."[123] In terms of communication, they work with the elements made ready to them. They telegraph by fires at night and by smoke in the daytime, and use mirrors to communicate. Beckwourth discloses that their communication exceeds the speed of any "officer" intelligence in the Rockies.[124]

The narrative makes explicit that even though Indians can be killed, they cannot be decoded. They do not share the prospectors' land-to-language registers, the very notions that hold together the "white man's" concept of territory. Western Indians align themselves differently to place, and their language shows this. He states, "I would here remark that the name 'Crow' is not the correct appellation of the tribe. They have never yet acknowledged the name, and never call themselves Crows. The name was conferred upon them many years ago by the interpreters . . . The name which they acknowledge themselves by, and they recognize no other, is in their language Ap-sah-ro-kee, which signifies the Sparrow-hawk people."[125] To get into their land knowledge would be like getting into their language. At best, it is an estimation. What is more, the gap between Anglo and Indian signification systems is mirrored in the wider project of *The Life and Adventures*. Beckwourth's narrative is largely diegetic. The teller advances the text, not the characters. Character opinions are not weighed, at least not enough for them to have any real motivations unless the narrator wants to abdicate responsibility for an undesirable outcome. But it also seems that for someone like Beckwourth, whose literary market identity was forged on his experiences as a Crow chief with transient Crow marriages and specialized land knowledges, the Indians he depicts really cannot be told. That is, they cannot be told as characters in the kind of history he advances. They do not match the plot's presumptions of progress.

Indian knowledges and polities have, of course, long been suppressed from view in settler land claims since they did little to advance notions of white territorial advantage. Remarking on "signaling systems" employed in the Americas by Roger Williams some two centuries before Beckwourth's dictated narrative, Matt Cohen makes an important point about white refraction of Indian linguistics. He writes: "When settlement texts are read with an eye to [the] serious competition European communications networks faced from indigenous ones, confident narratives of conquest and settlement begin to show anxieties—anxieties that would spawn a long history of worrying about how American Indians represent themselves."[126] But there is another point to consider, too: Indigenous communities might also have thought about geography differently insofar as they took it to be the sum of connections to history. Put another way, Indian place/space condenses chronology into geography. Vine Deloria Jr. suggests as much when he claims that in Indian oral traditions "every location . . . has a multitude of stories that recount the migrations, revelations, and particularly historical incident[s] that cumulatively produced the tribe in its current condition."[127] The idea here is that place is a storehouse of spirits. It retains histories as composites, as layers of experience that reach us in the form of stories.

So even as Beckwourth featured his personal accomplishments and extraordinary battle mettle, which elevated him to a war chief of the Crow, he cannot but wonder at the unthinkability of the Crow's land communalism. He marvels at their willingness to proffer goods, guns, horses, clothing, traps, and praise. He also tells of how one brave offered him animal skins after a day he trapped no animals: "'Take them,' said he, 'you are my friend: your traps have been unlucky to-day.'"[128] What would be taken as private property for the white man is for the Indian "the gift of the Great Spirit," to be shared among them as an inheritance.[129] This is how they view the buffalo. They, too, are a gift to them as they live out the relationality of space. In contrast, U.S. territorialization, at least as it is constructed by Beckwourth, is legalistic. It represents a closure of the common. It appropriates resources for consumption and promotes such processes as viable infrastructure. Development is thus equated with a privatized sectioning, or a marking of land for developmental purposes.

The Life and Adventures concludes with Beckwourth's discovery of the Beckwourth Pass, a northwestern California land route through the Sierras. This is pitched as his would-be crowning accomplishment after a kind of raw life in process, a closing chapter. But Beckwourth's failure to gain recognition for his discovery, or useful mountain traffic due to rumors of alkaline waters and plants poisonous to cattle, disrupts everything. He ends up a "capture" in the very cycles of reterritorialization he enforced as a free agent. The opening of the Isthmian Railroad in 1855 further stems flow through his pass. In the final passages of the narrative it is all glum reminder of the fraughtness of human proprietorship of place. Beckwourth is an explorer forever consigned to be outside the land he claims.

Beckwourth's freewheeling life on the make, his epic extension of self against the mapped grid, gets reduced by legalistic itemization. He airs questions about tolls. He discusses his rights to discovery, and his work to obtain a "subscription list setting forth the merits of the project."[130] He documents witnesses: "I imparted my views to three of my companions in whose judgment I placed the most confidence. They thought highly of the discovery."[131] Obviously the narrator does, too. But it proves a poor investment: "Sixteen hundred dollars I expended upon the road is forever gone, but those who derive advantage from this outlay and loss of time devote no thought to the discoverer."[132] Beckwourth's last lament is that he cannot "roll a mountain into the pass and shut it up."[133] The Beckwourth Pass is a final, fitting land analogue for the logic of territorialization. Insofar as he reterritorialized Indian lands, he cannot escape the induction of deterritorialization.

....

For texts that share similar major devices (episodic narratives without character development, fringe explorers who come home to find themselves by traversing different worlds) and similar concerns (land reconnaissance, organizing for wars, and North American Indian life), Beckwourth and Delany's literature move the concept of territory in very different directions. Delany's is a novel about intra-national territorialization and African American resistance through programmed cells of revolt. Beckwourth details the reaches of a dominant nationalizing form on an already-peopled, already-nationalized continental land mass. Delany's use of geographic discourses opens up questions of bearing and emplacement. Blake reads as a counter-discourse to slaveholder spatializations. Its hero is a mobile model of resistance large enough to fill the hemispheric spaces of antislavery activism with his presence.[134]

Beckwourth, too, soliloquized self-enterprise. He viewed himself as an endless wayfarer, claiming what he could in the way of individual property. But his guiding interest in landscape was steered by a quest for personal wealth. Even at the end of his life, he sought out War Department contracts that could provide him money at the expense of basic Indian survival. He did not hide these motives, but showed them as the operative forms of American citizenry.[135] "Experience," he claimed, "has revealed to me that civilized man can accustom himself to any mode of life when pelf is the governing principle—that power which dominates through all the ramifications of social life, and gives expression of the universal instinct of self-interest."[136] Territory was the output of the "natural" man, or at least the man acting naturally; and it was the commodity at the end of action.

Axiomatically, Delany did not differ, though he consistently wrote about black meritocratic ownership of land, ownership by the skilled, "the intelligent"—even if this ownership could be of already-occupied lands throughout Central and South America and Western Africa. Nonetheless, he envisioned a general welcoming of African American counsel and leadership for the aim of black reterritorialization, specifically cued to challenge midcentury U.S. imperialist venture. His own commitments reflected his view of place as an ongoing social contest toward the closure of consensus. At the same time, actual decision-making across his various writings is consistently directed outward, past any locus of embodiment toward a signifier of embodiment (Blake), and toward international coalitions of hemispheric counter-elites. These are, in turn, made corporate, made into a body, in the ideal of an organized, diasporic, black emancipation circuit. Indeed, the ways that territory is navigated in both texts point to its composition as a kind of double bind. It was an essential and material form for black self-positioning. But its forms were realized through extension, through a kind of nineteenth-century variation of what sociologists like Anthony Giddens describe as distanciation, or the elasticity of place integration, beyond claims based on presence.[137]

As this reading shows, territory for midcentury African Americans was something physical, something at the juncture of power/knowledge systems, and something textual. Textually, it reads as a frame of reference for attainment and a frame for sequencing action. Both Beckwourth and Delany continually—diachronically—foregrounded place as part of a territorial struggle. Delany found the expressive potential of territory in acts of deterritorialization: fugitive movement is pivotal in the mounting, serial form of Blake. The entire book turns on it. For Beckwourth, first rights to discovery and profiting through the territorialization of Indian lands were his ongoing quests. This is what The Adventures is about. It is not about the relation of law to land (jurisdiction). It is about the relation of land to territory. Beckwourth gets close to his prevailing idea of territory, but the most he seems to have at the end of his life are stories of the pursuit. Delany, too, never achieved his dreams of African American empire in Africa. His last joint stock company for a Liberian emigration mission fell to bankruptcy. Nonetheless, for both authors, territory appears to be as much about an enclosure of the imagination as a space of projection. Both imagined that the possession of territory meant the opening of a meaningful world. As their works illustrate, environment matters differently to different people.[138] Bringing the story lines together only highlights how these differences might look.

....

CHAPTER 3

THIS HOUSE OF GATHERING

Axis Americanus

A confluence of texts from the early 1990s, each putting forward a view of America beyond the bounded United States form, signaled what was to become known as the postnational turn in American literary studies. Among these were Gustavo Pérez Firmat's critical anthology, *Do the Americas Have a Common Literature?* (1990); Amy Kaplan and Donald Pease's frequently cited *Cultures of United States Imperialism* (1993); and possibly the most debate-defining essay of the "turn," Carolyn Porter's 1994 "What We Know That We Don't Know," in which Porter envisioned an American literary studies "reconstellated by a historicized politics of location."[1] Though written toward different field and disciplinary formations, all contributed courseways for the expansion of a turn-of-the century hemispheric American studies. Indeed, some twenty years after Pérez Firmat outlined methodologies for tracing literary continuities across comparative topographies, the fast-growing body of hemispheric literary criticism is still about the terms of its locations. It is about terraining textualities and making contingent places marked by colonial difference.[2]

Though postnational U.S. literary studies on the whole tends to eschew the formative vocabularies of postcolonial criticism (deployments of rootlessness, liminal subjectivities, or general polyvalency) in favor of more materially referential, historicist spatializations, it has generated its own common signifiers as well. One of the most prominent tropes to emerge has been mapping.[3] This is quite fitting. As a heuristic device, cartography speaks to issues of design; it is a form for tracing cultural production and its dissemination into spaces beyond the conscripted nation. Literary cartographies can also designate a subject's standpoint or bodily space. They can reference political arrangements and cognitive models. Actually, the preponderance of the map trope speaks to a richness of possibilities in hemispheric scholarship.

But perhaps due to the transitive qualities of mapping (in relation to communities of meaning) or its semiological flexibility (between sign and representation), the term has been used more to describe forms of critical repositioning than the denotative, material objects that are maps. This results in real omissions. As land-print technologies, maps are themselves texts to be read; they reveal stories of territorialization. Maps proliferate traceable code. They scale material places into systems of organization. Itala Vivan describes the modern map as a "prospect," calling it, "a representation of spatiality and at the same time temporality."[4] In one of the most sustained accounts to date of media history through maps, Martin Brückner's *Geographic Revolution in Early America* emphasizes the ways the intersection of literacy practices and print geography produced nation in British America.[5] Brückner positions geography as "a material form and stylistic device of literary production (to write)."[6] Kirsten Gruesz and Ileana Rodríguez also demonstrate they ways geographies are languages that produce frames of hemispheric belonging; they produce perceptual encounters.[7]

The following pages are influenced by such approaches to mapping, those attendant to its functions as a kind of literacy. I also look to insights from late critical cartography that explore maps as propositions about the world, as premises for self-positioning.[8] In other words, this chapter considers the implications of what it means to look at place as a composition, and it traces cartographic claims through narrative. The speculative reading developed here examines geographic representational modes for the ways they convey political scopes of attachment. I further suggest that geographies are produced through stories, and that discourses give shape to place. Like other forms of cultural production, maps and literature articulate space as limit situations and as frames for possibility. They are multi-modal.

Specifically, I will examine U.S. maps of a nationalized hemisphere from the middle of the nineteenth century. These 1850s-era maps were broadcasts of Pan-American space during one of the most volatile periods of United States national formation. Nonetheless, they presented readers with pictures of a kind of magnetically holistic nation. They placed the United States at the center of an American archipelago. It was a nation that could gather in its hemispheric "neighbors." As I will further suggest, in the very ways maps coded space, they coordinated political frames for inclusions and exclusions. National maps reflected professed federal and sectionalist interests in bringing the Caribbean into a zone of influence. In the maps included here, the United States of the 1850s is cast as a hemispheric control axis. Such geographical positioning was actually something naturalized into expansionist rhetoric after James Polk revitalized the 1823 Monroe Doctrine during his presidency. (Polk was himself elected in 1845 under the slogan "54'40 or Fight," the coordinates of U.S. land claims in western Canada up to Alaska's southern border.) By 1848 he claimed success for stretching the Monroe Doctrine to new geographic lengths to support acquisitions in the Yucatan and the Gulf of Mexico.[9] In tandem with this renewed federal interest in hemispheric protectionism, period maps presented the United States as the hub of the Gulf of Mexico and featured the Caribbean as adjunctive U.S. space.

But African American period literature tells another—albeit intertwined—story. It polarizes mapping's discontinuities. It shows that what maps presented as openings for national expansion were also lines of entrenchment for North American slaves. Put another way, though maps exhibited expansive national orbits, they also closed horizons. Maps gave form to an expanded print-land base for hemispheric, North American chattel slavery. They rendered a political vision that Cuba would be a future state for Southern interests. Certainly the organization of Caribbean space in antebellum cartographies would have appeared far from slavery-neutral for free blacks even remotely attentive to the network spreads of slavery in the Americas. It was all very immediate for Martin Delany, the nineteenth-century African American author most opposed to pro-slavery incursions into Caribbean spaces. As Delany's midcentury literature reveals, national slavery's future, its sustainability, depended on attaching its practices to spaces where profit could be extracted.[10]

Blake's transformative geographies have already been explored by scholars such as Bruce Harvey, who examines the text's embodied transit networks as extensions of black agency, and Robert Carr, who interestingly suggests that Blake might be read as a blueprint for a formative black nation state, which could undermine Southern big cotton and place Africa at the center of a new commercial trade empire.[11] But a cultural-materialist assessment of contemporary cartographies draws attention to the terms of Delany's cartographic imagination. Bringing Delany's editorial writings, speeches, and serial fiction together with key cartographies of the period shows the ways black antebellum literature was very much about redistricting. It was about the creative potential of deterritorialization—ways to undo or make insolvent, to peel away practice from place, to destabilize domains of imperialist development.[12] And it could also cogently foreground different kinds of connections. Additionally, a comparative approach underscores Delany's own argument: that the slavery institution's material extension was dependent on representative claims to such potential places. Leading maps displayed such claims, pictorializing a hemisphere that was malleable to a U.S.-controlled slavery in America's "sugar tropics."

As I will try to show, an intermedial reading of literature and maps inflects both on questions of race as situated subjecthood and on race as absence. These are absences reproduced in nineteenth-century American maps. Geographer Timothy Oakes asserts the value of such a comparative approach, arguing that fiction can work as a kind of "template" for representing a "terrain of modernity" in its paradoxes and contradictions. He writes, "the open-ended and complex quality of literary representation allows the crisis-prone interactions between space, human agency, and abstract historical processes to come sharply into focus in a way social science is often unable to match."[13] Bruno Latour makes a similar point in relation to literature's capacity to configure "actants" as agents, morphing figures against landscapes. Describing why sociological theory might do well to borrow from narrative theory, he outlines what he calls a "freedom of movement" via literature. Claims Latour, "the diversity of the worlds of fiction invented on paper allows enquirers to gain as much pliability and range as those they have to study in the real world."[14] In a related way, Delany's writing tenders a kind of national landscape storyboard. His serial fiction shows hemispheric arrangements and attaches a sequencing to them. This sort of sequencing works less as a traditional literary plot with rising action, crisis, denouement. Rather, it is Delany's way of sequencing time to accommodate what he envisions as hemispheric black revolutionary action.

On Literature and Cartographic Claims

Delany's literature is starkly geographic because it is driven by its focus on the logics of national territorial expansion. It also takes as its subject matter the network power/knowledges (as discourses and injunctions) used in the organization of slave space. Second, Delany's 1850s-era writing plays on similar tropes to maps. By tropes here, I mean figurative turns deployed to make representative experience, devices that configure. Reading Delany's epic serial novel *Blake* alongside period maps draws real attention to the terms of a midcentury debate about a U.S. takeover of Cuba. Indeed, a comparative approach shows that the devices for cohesion in cartographic representation work out to be more like narratives—held together by forms of fabrication. Thus, no less integral to my focus here are the ways literature and cartographic media are expressive forms.

In part II of *Blake*, Delany drew attention to Cuba as a space that polarized the scales of colonial possession. Its island form made it vulnerable. It was a nearby object of U.S. expansionist interests and a wealthy Spanish slave colony among British-claimed islands. By building on themes and devices associated with cartographic representation, Delany staged a hemispheric geography for African American horizons via Cuba. Horizon here refers to the background against which character and ambition are actualized. But it is also a way to understand the routes that are out there and that can be picked up for imagining other storylines. It is like a suggested futurity. In *Blake*, Cuba functions as a house of gathering for African, American, and European trade circuitry. It is Delany's horizon for the revolutionary subject. That is, Cuba comprised black political communities Delany believed could be organized to upend Cuban slavery and Southern ambitions in the Caribbean.

Delany previously argued in *North Star* editorials such as "Annexation of Cuba" (1849) that Cuba was pivotal to the commercial and geographic "binds" of hemispheric slavery. He viewed Cuba as a revelatory space for the course of an agglomerative United States imperialism in the Americas, calling it "the great key-of-entry to the United States from the East" and "the great western slave mart of the world."[15] This was a view that circulated in other abolitionist papers. In an article simply titled "Cuba" (1847), William Lloyd Garrison's antislavery *Liberator* reported: "England sees that if America be permitted to get a foothold in the West Indian

Archipelago, she will never rest till she has possession of the whole. America sees that if England obtain possession of the key of the Gulf of Mexico, it may be used in her hands to unlock her own house of bondage."[16] Since slavery's position within a still-forming United States was already so divisive, and the international slave trade had supposedly closed, many North Americans tended to view slavery as a national, or peculiarly regional, problem.

However, abolitionists such as Delany (and Garrison, for that matter) countered such a narrow view. In fact, Blake spatializes Cuba from the joint perspective of a networked, Atlantic proslavery cabal (a statist outside) and from the perspective of a black Cuban inside. The following pages take seriously Delany's convictions about U.S. proslavery expansionism, revisiting Blake in relation to a number of cartographic modes for representing empire. These include arrangements within control ambits, the collapsing or attenuating of distance, and the transposition of labeled places onto other places. The reason for emphasizing this comparative approach is that such cartographic conventions constitute the very terms of the debate that Delany announced for a black counter-insurgency. In Blake, Delany drew on contemporary journalistic captions of place used to validate U.S. territorial interests in claiming the island. Among these claims were—to quote from an article in the New York Sun—Cuba's proximity to current U.S. holdings ("almost within cannon shot and sight of the United States"); territorial aggrandizement ("the possession of Cuba will complete our chain of territory"); and certainly not least, strategic use ("Its vicinity to the Gulf of Mexico gives it a commanding position in relation to the rich commerce of this country which seeks an outlet through the Mississippi and the Gulf").[17] Blake makes these issues (transit, territory, and geopolitical strategy) the business of black-directed abolition. Cartographic claims to space thus become the features of a counter-geography, a story of place written over for black enterprise.

Throughout the 1850s Delany argued that Cuba was black-occupied space and its investments and wealth could be taken by black force. He wrote, "three-fifths of the whole population of Cuba being colored people, who cannot and will not much longer endure the burden and the yoke. They only want intelligent leaders of their own color, and they are ready at any moment to charge to the conflict—to liberty or death."[18] As might be expected, the horizon of black action comes to the island from the United States under the wingspan of Blake, who represents Delany's "intelligent leadership" principle. Blake is the corporealization of hemispheric action in his very person: a United States-dwelling, "pure black"[19] Cuban of royal African extraction. He is the possibility of black America, written as a model of authority and organization on the landscape of Cuba. Cuba has made the earliest version of Carolus Henrico Blacus, Blake's Latinized, but not quite Spanish cognomen. But Blake also makes Cuba. In part II of the novel, he returns to take charge of an anticipated Africana overcoming, announcing: "I am the lost boy of Cuba."[20] He is the fruition of Delany's Cuba interests from The Condition, Elevation, Emigration and Destiny of the Colored People of the United States. "On this island," Blake declares, "we are the many and the oppressors few."[21] This is a foundational claim for a black Cuba.

Collective Representation: Reproducing Land in Print

While it is one thing to claim Blake is an inversion of imperial-styled United States cartographies, it is another thing to look at how an imperialist U.S. map functioned and, more specifically, the print devices through which midcentury maps presented archipelagic space. For this reason, I have selected a cluster of authoritative, 1850s-era maps of the United States (highly detailed, up-to-date, informative maps from leading mapmaker/atlas affiliates) for the ways they give form to midcentury geopolitical arrangements. Geopolitics is a conceptually wide, mostly twentieth-century term—predicated on both geography and politics. But as Gearóid Ó Tuathail in Critical Geopolitics reminds us, "some codifications trace it back to antiquity and Aristotle, while others locate its origins in the late nineteenth century."[22] This is all to say that it is relevant to U.S. abolitionist frameworks. In combining the term with a view of geography as discursive power/knowledge, a view of textuality influenced by Jacques Derrida and Rodolphe Gasché, Ó Tuathail advocates for what he calls a "hyphenated" geopolitics.[23] This is an understanding of geopolitics that "does not mark a fixed presence but an unstable and indeterminate problematic."[24] It approaches critical geopolitics not as a general theory or logocentric infrastructure, but rather an assertion of the textuality of geography.[25] This kind of approach is particularly useful here. First, it applies to the territorialization strategies within the slavery-driven economies of the Americas. And second, it foregrounds the discursive practices that dominate social realities.

What the leading national maps of the mid-nineteenth century concertedly show is an arrangement of space that places Cuba as the U.S. nation's island. The maps corroborate imperialist claims—or, at any rate, stage such claims. They apply the same kinds of scalar organization and mobility that Delany's fiction first addresses and then tries to reverse. In *Blake* Delany took apart the frame for a Southern cosmopolitan politics of representation, where U.S. accession interests could be naturalized into a sense of geographical affinity through maps and rhetoric. In fact, the geographical nexus between Cuba and the United States is at the center of *Blake*'s most developed and complete serial run in the *Weekly Anglo-African* (1861–62).[26] But in a print climate galvanized by the U.S. Civil War, it is a charged network of black revolt and the schema for organizational efforts between antislavery blacks—not just proslavery capitalists and Creoles.

In a late antebellum era of general border uncertainty and rapid territorial expansion by accession and annexation, maps were vital in generating pictures of national form; basically, they showed national publics what nation looked like. Abolitionist maps such as John Lewis's *Lewis' Free Soil, Slavery, and Territorial Map of the United States* of 1848 (figure 2.1), praised in the *North Star* under Delany's co-editorship with Frederick Douglass at least twice (once in 1848 and in 1849)[27]; the later G. W. Elliott's 1856 *Map of the United States, Showing by Colors the Area of Freedom and Slavery*; and William Reynolds's 1856 *Political Map of the United States* (figure 3.1) all depicted a nation divided by slave interests.[28] Other maps of the period simply inferred the kind of union only made achievable by North and South concessions on slaveholding. Such maps will be the focus here because they tell a different story about homeland. They make it a cogent form against a backdrop of continental drift. Nation's own cohesiveness is underscored by its configuration within a western hemisphere.

Thus, a consideration of authoritative contemporary maps from some of the most important midcentury U.S. mapmaking firms—maps Delany would have encountered while writing *Blake*—prove quite revealing for the ways they present homeland. The maps show the modes through which cartographic representation came to naturalize the land of Cuba as United States domain. Maps made union something larger than the contiguous states.

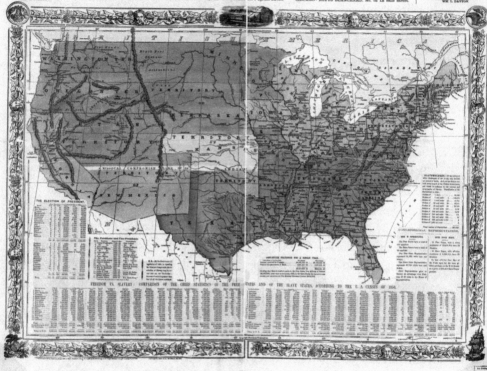

3.1. William C. Reynolds, *Reynolds's Political Map of the United States*. New York: Wm. C. Reynolds and J. C. Jones, 1856.

At this juncture, it is perhaps necessary to qualify that my aim is to look at the ways maps, seemingly descriptive, verifiable surfaces, enact imperialist pictures of space. I am not undertaking an analysis of map-maker backgrounds or biographies. The latter has been a line of inquiry in mapmaking archival histories. It can certainly be of value in assessing atlas target audiences and printing commissions. (It is not irrelevant, for instance, that collectors speculate that D. Griffing Johnson, the leading New York City map engraver and designer, probably came from a Southern family and died in a Civil War battle near Richmond in 1862. His sense of regional affiliation likely impacted the expressive content of his U.S. maps.)[29] But rather than attributing political designs to principal engravers or press owners, I am concerned here with the modes deployed through maps to make representative spaces—for the purposes of comparative literary study.

There are, of course, different field constraints between cartography and the novel that should be (briefly) enumerated. Delany's fiction filled pages of newsprint with burgeoning story lines of Blake's exploits. What are boundaries of time, expanses of space to a hero such as Blake? They are set pieces that collapse under his performance. Thematic nineteenth-century mapmakers, on the other hand, worked with more fixed arrangements. Map layout, even in the earlier part of the century when land knowledge and measurement were far less extensive, was a project of accommodating detailed site data, or what mapmakers today call map elements. Relatedly, in the maps considered here, matters of design tend to reflect matters of division. They are ways to parse an abundance of information.[30] Delany's fiction, by contrast, speaks to questions of inclusion, questions about why spaces are called into national mappings, and what spaces are hidden from representation. Blake examines the logics of expansion shared by proslavery U.S. nationals, as well as network knowledges such operators deployed to achieve their goals of space and capital. Maps more directly showed an outcome, a produced space, whereas political hemispheric literature such as Delany's showed processes or machinations of spatial production.

Yet in both Delany's geographic novel and in midcentury U.S. maps, decisions about form and organization, what thematic cartographers call a map's "intellectual scheme," were about two focal things: the apportioning of space and the projecting onto/inscribing of space to give prominence to possession. Even though maps were constrained by scalar forms like land masses, cartographers did have expressive devices at their disposal in projects of composition. In fact, in the antebellum United States theirs was a craft situation driven by opportunities for new inclusion, as well as opportunities for problem-solving and collaborative venture.

Map Firms and Affiliations

In terms of cartographic output, a public interest in up-to-date maps with current land and water routes created a situation where graphic work such as engravers' plates needed to be rapidly modified. This interest was compounded by heavy landscape territorialization and border adjustments throughout the 1850s. With an explosion in westward American pursuits for gold and opportunity, reliable information on land routes, and especially information about railroads from the Missouri River to the Pacific Ocean, was generally wanting. In the cartography industry, access to census information and geographical statistics, as well as news about rapid railroad development, had to be readily translatable into print.[31] The most profitable mapmakers worked together to pool resources. One of the most important midcentury mapmakers, Joseph Hutchins Colton, founder of the premier New York City–based firm of J. H. Colton, was not an engraver at all, but rather a copyright consolidator. Among the elite map firms considered here, the Colton imprint is particularly prominent across the decade of the 1850s. The firm purchased copyrights to maps, and shaped itself into a variety of useful partnerships with such mapmakers and atlas affiliates as D. Griffing Johnson and Alvin Jewett Johnson (respectively publishing as J. H. Colton, D. G. Johnson, and A. J. Johnson).[32] Thus, it is important to bear in mind the compound nature of period maps, made by contract engraver's art, statisticians' geographical data, and copyright consolidation.[33] Mid-nineteenth-century maps need to be approached as collectively produced forms. They were not forms of fact, but rather cultural compilations. They brought together information and illustration to shape print modes of territory.

Official U.S. maps, "entered according to act of Congress," as their mastheads frequently proclaimed, constituted a discourse of space that a text like *Blake* was premised on challenging. That challenge was made more difficult because mass-produced maps were popularly regarded as factual material and overall land guides. They were presented to readers as self-evident, reliable sign systems. Yet, maps openly indicate that the United States could gain space through language acts of designation. Maps reflect imperialist interpretation, a type of episteme that Delany warned in 1852 gave power to authoritarian structures in all areas of life by making slavery supporters and enablers "both translators and com-

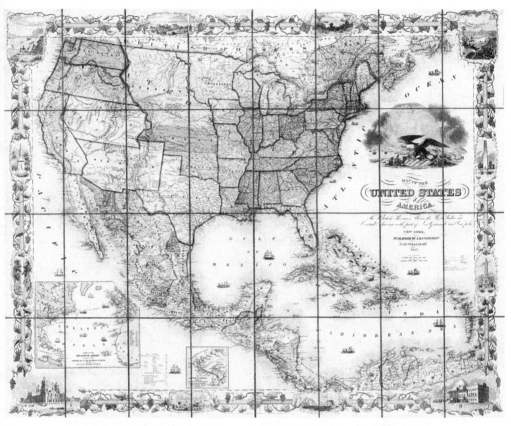

3.2. B. W. Thayer and Joseph H. Colton, *Colton's Map of the United States of America, the British Provinces, Mexico, the West Indies and Central America.* New York: Thayer and Colton, 1859. Image courtesy Barry Lawrence Ruderman Antique Maps/RareMaps.com.

mentators," just as he claimed transpired within religious interpretation during slavery.[34] To be at once a translator and commentator is to hold the terms of the debate. It is to lay claim to a frame and designate its signification. Maps show traces of such processes. They present an outer-lining of how power/knowledge can look when it gets mobilized into law (congressional authorization of an official map), and into print circulation. They fixate claims that directly reference territory. Indeed, one of the most striking features about several of the midcentury maps produced by leading mapmakers such as Colton and affiliates is the apparent disjunction between map titles and viewing surfaces. Here the terms of the debate lie in the play of elision.

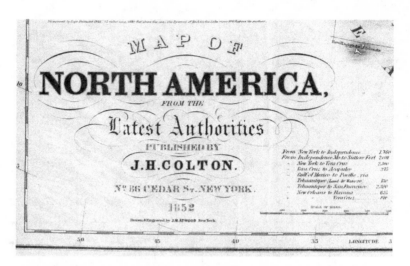

3.3. Detail of the Colton imprint from *Map of North America from the Latest Authorities,* 1852. Image courtesy David Rumsey Historical Map Collection, www.davidrumsey.com.

The Politics of the Frame

As leading maps illustrate, titling is as much connected to geographical organization as it is to textual fabrication. In the 1859 map by B. Thayer and Colton, for instance, the title appears to be *Colton's Map of the United States of America* (figure 3.3). It is only on closer examination that spindly, cursive letters indicate: *The British Provinces, With the West Indies and Central America with Part of New Granada and Venezuela.*[35] Quiet subheadings, which cast very big spaces like the detailed entirety of Mexico as ancillary, are actually most conspicuous in Johnson and Johnson's 1857 map (figure 3.4). The map reads: *A New Map of the Union/Islands & Countries.* Only minutely lettered vertical script, functionally hidden in a portion of decorative flourish, infers the relation between the Union and the Caribbean: *with the Adjacent* (figure 3.5). With similar devices, the *Republics of North America* map of 1859 (figure 3.6) also buries the connective phrase visually. Each map smoothly makes the geographical implications of language acts appear transparent, or coordinated to something real. Hiding a prepositional phrase on the viewing plane creates a notable effect. In this instance, it clearly alters a map's meaning since the title appears to suggest a union that includes islands and countries. Hence, beyond showing a clear bias toward expansive views of nation and national im-

3.4. Alvin J. Johnson and D. Griffing Johnson, *A New Map of the Union, with the Adjacent Islands & Countries, from Authentic Sources.* New York: D. Griffing and Alvin J. Johnson, 1857. Image courtesy David Rumsey Map Collection, www.davidrumsey.com.

portance, maps such as those by Colton and the two Johnsons present a way to read nation.[36] They make naming into a principle of overwriting space, and they channel landscape into language.

Though not a device typically studied by cartographers, maps pictorialize nationhood through something that might be called cartographic transposition, the overlaying of scenes or frames into an otherwise occupied representational plane. One example of transposition would be the prominent use of vignettes in these maps. Nineteenth-century vignettes were landscape scenes usually blended (unbordered) into the viewing surface. Vignettes were the sorts of enhancements a skilled engraver like

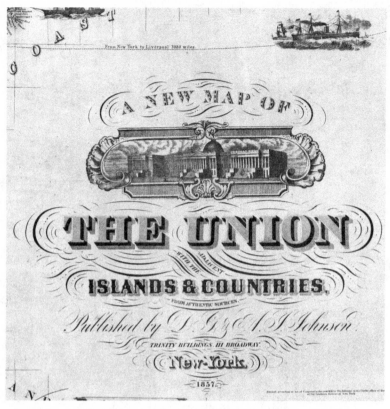

3.5. Detail from Alvin J. Johnson and D. Griffing Johnson, *A New Map of the Union*. Image courtesy David Rumsey Map Collection, www.davidrumsey.com.

D. G. Johnson used with mastery, and his placement of them in his 1857 *Union* map is particularly striking. This map displays an original engraving of a California gold mill, Sutter's Sawmill, which Johnson composed on site when gold was discovered in 1848. Beneath this vignette is an elaborately bordered, sharply detailed illustration of a gold rocker. The topical value of these pictures is rather obvious in an epoch of California gold quests. Nonetheless, these etchings from the West Coast are printed into waters of the eastern Caribbean, due east of the Leeward Islands, near Antigua and Guadeloupe. Extracting terms from Jean Baudrillard's work on American signage, the transposed vignettes appear as an extension of national portraiture, brought "in" or "upon."[37] The same could be said for the 1859 Colton map's transposition of a massive eagle mounted on an American flag and anchor, against what looks like a rolling-hilled

Caribbean harbor (likely Havana) with ships of commerce. This scene is placed directly in the Atlantic Ocean; the waters in the vignette blend into the middle Atlantic. Map readers are thus presented with projections of Western symbols of territorialization in spaces where no Union existed, and where no claimed territory rested either. The vignettes read as symbolic, national overdraftings of oceanic spaces beneath.

Beyond simply offering an expansive view of nation, midcentury maps were picture-language reproductions used to solidify hierarchical arrangements of meaning. But such processes were not necessarily framed as points of view. On the contrary, in the maps discussed here, the leading kind of cartographic deployment for working archipelagic space into a picture of national holism could simply be considered organizational. Organizational aesthetics could account for a map's visual focus, how its content was shaped, and how its relations to an outside were mediated—much as form did in the midcentury serial novel. So on one level, drawing the archipelagic spaces of the Caribbean into domestic purview is merely a matter of achieving organizational balance. For example, in Colton's 1859 map, the surface balance is tilted toward maximum inclusion of the Caribbean islands. In that map and the two maps presented here by D. G. Johnson and A. J. Johnson, the Gulf of Mexico is the optical center; map elements are visually arranged around the Gulf.[38]

Yet, as the maps show, organization itself tells a story about the reaches of place-claims. Colton's map frames the sheet's lower quadrant in such a way that it makes the Gulf of Mexico and connecting sea into a kind of lagoon, closed by an L frame. Both the Gulf and the Caribbean appear as an apparently closed space—with the United States as axis. The whole mass is punctuated by an elegantly vine-encased vignette of the National Capitol in Washington, squarely covering Venezuela. In effect, the borders foreground oceanic space by bringing it into bay. The borders make a "within," which includes the Caribbean islands. And "within" this all, the biggest island of Cuba sits tight along Florida's strait. It appears as an island off the U.S. mainland. It is proximately and symbolically placed into a frame of national destiny.

Referring to oceanic spatializing strategies within late capitalism, Carole Boyce Davies and Monica Jardine make a point clearly germane to Cuba's geographic position under nineteenth-century colonialism. They write: "The issue of geography and empire can be best preliminarily understood as a series of remapping exercises in which various land spaces are acquired and located within an orbit of control. In this context, the opposition between land space and ocean space becomes negligible."[39] Overwhelmingly, islands of the Caribbean have played host to territorial formations that take their coherence in terms modeled by colonial power. For instance, the nautical space between Spanish-speaking Puerto Rico and French-speaking Guadeloupe, though actually quite small, is scaled as a distance through languages, product imports, and relations to a perceived outside. A Caribbean "within" is still partitioned space, a zone of oceanic distance from seats of colonial power.[40] Maps enforce such conceptualizations. They reproduce colonial territory through print description; they rearticulate zones of influence. Distance is revealed as an attenuation of "center."

In respect to the Caribbean, this process geographically enacts what Walter Mignolo describes as "colonial difference." Colonial difference encompasses not only "the space where coloniality of power is enacted," but "the space where the restitution of subaltern knowledge is taking place."[41] It is thus an internalization of distance vis-à-vis potential hemispheric neighbors. It is also an interior phenomenon, not just the work of an outside imposed on an inside. Instead, colonial difference is reproduced in the knowledge systems of the post colony. Anthony Bogues infers that what is missing from stories of colonial modernity are less questions of its historical "underside," but rather questions about "how the stubborn legacies of colonial modernity operate," and what the consequences of these legacies are for populations in the Caribbean.[42] Michelle Stephens cites Jamaican poet Louis Simpson's description of colonial mentality as characterizing modes of knowing produced by spatial distancing: "Among legacies of a colonial culture is the habit of thinking of creative sources as somehow remote from itself."[43] Delany depicts it as a kind of emaciated agency: The Cuban slaves, he writes, "were ripe for a general rising . . . but God only knew where they would find a leader."[44] Such foreshortened prospects, of course, clear a very wide swath for Blake, a hero bigger than Cuba. But they also reveal traces of process. Agency gaps, like spans of affiliation, reflect place investments and how distances are manufactured. They show how distances are manufactured and how cartographic organization—what is brought into a purview or sectioned into a national frame—produces affective spans of affiliation.

In Blake, colonial difference as colonial legacy most starkly manifests in the presentation of Haiti. In the novel's overarching project of an orchestrated black revolt with multiple Africans, North Americas, and Caribbean enlisted in the struggle—but held in abeyance by Blake even through the novel's conclusion—Haiti is left out of the picture. Delany has surprisingly little to claim for Haiti's geographic location, or for its black independence. At one of his hero's many, elaborate meetings in Cuba, an antislavery patron, Madame Montego, is apprised that black Cuba will receive little help in its struggle from an independent Haiti or her "sister islands" in the British colonies. The reason for this, she is told, is that "they are a constituent part of the body politic, and subject alike of the British government and laws which forbid any interference in foreign affairs by any of her Majesty's subjects."[45] Such declarations are clearly problematic for Delany's wider project in *Blake*. They undermine the very premises for the plot, and they undermine the novel's ostensible political collateral: that a black coalitional nexus bleeding out from the barracoons of western Africa to the mouth of the Gulf of Mexico is in motion and will dramatically change the course of hemispheric slavery. The novel's qualifying claims about (post)colonial dependencies more quietly move the scope of black-directed action to something further in the future. What might be a plot-based occasion to address, for instance, the ways colonial partitions overpower either intra-island proximities or racial affinities, is left outside the scope of *Blake*'s part II.

This parallels something that happens in the movement from the first part of *Blake* to the second. The reader is still left to imagine why it is that much of the novel's research into United States slave life on different plantations in some thirteen slave states is suddenly abandoned when Blake gets to Cuba, or why the accumulated knowledges Blake has spent much of his time gathering are just as suddenly devalued as slave practices. Haiti's material disconnect reads in a similar fashion: It separates a key space of contestation from the very network the plot tries to energize. Certainly, as the first black, independent nation in the Western hemisphere *and* a nation established through the modern world's most successful slave revolt, Haiti has precedence in this expansive struggle. But in *Blake* it does not. It is only mentioned in passing: "Hayti is a noble self-emancipated nation, but not able to aid us, excepting to give such of us shelter," Blake allows.[46] Yet, the text begs the questions: Why is Haiti in its postrevolutionary moment made into a closure? Are there not resources for the fight? Is it that Haiti's global recognition as a black republic does not stem the flows of Atlantic slavery that are the subject of *Blake*?

Frederick Douglass's late writing leads us to one response. In the last print edition of *The Life and Times* (1892), his final autobiography, Douglass ruminated on the disappointments of public life as former U.S. minister to the Republic of Haiti. He bitterly remarked on the "clamor for a white minister" among Haitians, despite their postcolonial independence from slavery and the general optimism in the neo-state.[47] His comments are revealing about the sites of citizenship and which might take precedence—black diasporan identification with abolitionist struggle or national inclusion. In his view, prior to U.S. abolition, the threats of U.S. slave market extensions were simply too great to justify circum-Atlantic connections. He wrote:

> I am charged with sympathy for Haïti. I am not ashamed of that charge; but no man can say with truth that my sympathy with Haïti stood between me and any honorable duty that I owed to the United States or to any citizen of the United States. The attempt has been made to prove me indifferent to the acquisition of a naval station in Haïti, and unable to grasp the importance to American commerce and to American influence of such a station in the Caribbean Sea. The fact is, that when some of these writers were in their petticoats, I had comprehended the value of such an acquisition, both in respect to American commerce and to American influence. The policy of obtaining such a station is not new. . . . I said then that it was a shame to American statesmanship that, while almost every other great nation in the world had secured a foothold and had power in the Caribbean Sea, where it could anchor in its own bays and moor in its own harbors, we, who stood at the very gate of that sea, had there no anchoring ground anywhere. I was for the acquisition of Samana, and of Santo Domingo herself, if she wished to come to us.[48]

Douglass's avowal of national expansionism and support for the development of a U.S. ambit of power in the Caribbean were certainly the obverse of Delany's aims in *Blake*. Throughout his adult life, Delany advocated African American expansion through colonial settlement and western African resettlement, but never U.S. expansionism. (Though he explored the Cavally River in Nigeria with Alexander Crummell to look at settlement lands, he staunchly rejected the already-settled Liberia.) Yet, Douglass understood that U.S. extension into the Gulf of Mexico and the Caribbean was practically inevitable. He had good reason to view this as the general course of "development." Doctrine and process came together in late-century pan-Americanism and Big Sister policies aimed at Latin American markets. During the decade of the 1890s, acquisition talks were already directed at the projected canal in Panama, lands in Samoa, and the islands of Hawaii. And still, U.S. interests in an Antillean Haiti prefigured these developments by nearly a century. There were clues, so to speak.

For instance, in the so-called Toussaint Clause of 1799, the United States authorized trade with the revolutionary black Caribbean state in a gesture of recognition—recognition for profit. Such recognition signaled tacit support for a nearby (potential U.S. slave contact zone) government born of violent slave revolt. In fact, trade relations with Haiti's anticolonial government were initially supported, not only by political orchestrators like John Adams, Alexander Hamilton, and Thomas Jefferson (who used the conflict for the gain that was the Louisiana Purchase), but by protrade Southern republicans as well.[49] Taking a cue from David Scott's postcolonial history, *Conscripts of Modernity*, Michael Drexler synthesizes a key insight about the turn-of-the-century stakes of U.S. recognition of Haiti: "If trade relationships with insurgent Saint-Domingue furthered national sovereignty by winning points against imperial antagonists, it was possible to overcome racism temporarily to further these goals."[50] Geopolitically speaking, race prejudice could have been a factor in shortening the arm of hemispheric commerce. But it was not. Prejudice only hurt the potential for black-directed action, or the sorts of race leadership positions that most attracted a Delany or Douglass. In earlier texts charting African American emigration in the Americas (*The Condition* and "Political Destiny"), Haiti was a space Delany left outside his purview. *Blake* even suggests that Haiti could do little for the millions of enslaved black Americans. By contrast, the United States had a far greater stake in Cuba, especially in its acquisition. For these reasons then Cuba emerges as the grounds of contest in the fiction.

Cuba as Parallel Space

So while Delany's novel obscures genealogies of black representative struggle, making Haiti into a kind of closure, Cuba evolves as a space of openings. It is a space of undercurrents, established through layers of time. In effect, the counter-connecting to Cuba represents a certain aesthetic achievement of the novel. What Delany manages to do in *Blake* is decode formations of distance by making time a more fluid thing. He poses alternate frames for bringing together spaces manufactured as distant in axes of colonized time. This is one central feature of the literary counter-map: the remaking of a place's time. For example, *Blake* takes its meaning against an expansive geography *not* limned into nation-based timelines, where white stories of development, white benchmarks of progress and overcoming, constitute a historical setting. Rather, the novel describes National Fete days, Creole revolutionary activity, palace galas, and parades honoring the Infanta Sovereign of Spain that color in the vexed spaces of midcentury Cuba in tones not easily absorbed into United States aesthetic categories of *common grounds*. The pageantry and festivals depicted in *Blake*, alternately celebrated and subverted by island blacks, reference histories that are not the commemorative property of the United States.

Delany dramatizes the reframing of Cuba across two party scenes, staged on the same night in Havana: one is at the Palace of the Queen's Nativity, presided over by the white creole countess, Lady Alcora; the second is a grand celebration at the estate of Madame Cordora, "a wealthy widow mulatress."[51] During the first party, the countess relays a dream "of being in the interior of Africa surrounded entirely by Negroes, under the rule of a Negro prince, beset by the ambassadors of every enlightened nation, who brought him many presents of great value, whilst the envoy of Her Catholic Majesty sat quietly at the foot of the African Prince's throne."[52] It is a dream that profoundly disturbs the royal imaginary since, among other things, it relocates the ill-defined interior of Africa as the center of a transatlantic empire. No longer is Africa envisioned from its slave-trading shores and coastal barracoons, but rather from its largely untapped interior. No less so, this mythic interior supplants both a Castilian Spain and the colonial sugar capital of Havana as a subterranean site of circulation. But this all is interpreted differently by party guests. Some suggest the royal dream means a fresh cargo of blacks will be arriving from Africa, "very likely among will be some Negro prince, catering to your orders." Others view it as a presentiment of general insurrection, realigning the power grid of Cuba.

The second view is ultimately more prescient, especially when cast in light of the fact that a number of key domestics have secreted to another party, where they take on counter-identities as part of a revolutionary army. Most noticeably missing is the countess's favorite, Gofer Gondolier, known for his skill on the Spanish guitar and African banjo, "especially the latter instrument, in which he had few, if any equals."[53] In the context of his absence, Gofer's missing music is no longer a domesticated version of exotic song, but an invocation of a chorus elsewhere— at the very Cordora party, where an antislavery orchestra sits upon a stage and a new pan-Africanism is announced. This new regime, readers are told, borrows from "no denomination, creed, nor church: no existing organization, secret, secular, nor religious; but originated by ourselves, adopted to our own condition, circumstances, and wants."[54] Again, the common ground is taken out from beneath black life in the United States and the future figurations of black global action. Delany envisioned new histories being made in a new compass of power, and Africa was central to all this—albeit not very well specified by the author. Instead, what the novel's final chapters generate are nomenclatures for future embodiment. Toward the end of the novel, Blake, in a somewhat offhanded manner, is notified by his cousin: "And now let me inform you, that we have had our gatherings, held our councils, formed our legions, chosen our leaders, and made Henry Blake General-in-Chief of the army of emancipation of the oppressed men and women of Cuba!"[55] What follows is a laundry list of a new group of counter-elites, mostly previously unintroduced, under whose leadership the forms of black diaspora presented by Delany between the United States, the Caribbean, and Africa will be bound together:

> The provisional organization consisted of Placido, Director of Civil Government; Minister of State, Camina; Minster of Justice, Carolus Blacus; Minister of Foreign Affairs, Catina, Postmaster General, Antonio Blacus; Minister of War and Navy, Montego. The Army regulations were: Henry Blake, Commander in Chief of the Army of Emancipation; Juan Montego, General of First Division; Pedro Castina, General of Second Division; Ferdinand Recaud, General Third Division; Stephen Rivera,

General of Fourth Division; Gofer Gondolier, Quartermaster General. Thus organized, the oppressed became a dangerous element in the political ingredients of Cuba.[56]

So what does black initiative *between* nations mean for the central genus of Delany's Atlantic imaginary, Cuba? Maybe the most obvious thing is that Cuban genealogies connect to different schemas of experience. Cuba is presented as a parallel space. But it is a space of difference, too. Susan Gillman invokes a suggestive range of historiographic possibility for the continuum and circuit that is parallel space in "The Epistemology of Slave Conspiracy." Rejecting what she terms "Comparative History," with its models of nationally centered activity and "forced chronological frameworks," she suggests that a more synchronically interactive history can be found in the spaces between nations.[57] Eric Sundquist also makes a significant point in relation to Delany's use of historical compression in depicting the comparative spaces of Cuba and the Southern United States. He argues that the author's "telescoping" of 1840s-era Cuban political events and 1850s-era United States legislation such as the Compromise of 1850 and the Dred Scott decision of 1857 into the novel's shorter frame of time highlights the Atlantic dimensions of slavery. The outcome is "a fictive world in which Cuban and American slavery are yoked together into historical simultaneity. *Blake* is neatly divided into two parts, but the temporal movement is not forward, toward the moment before the Civil War, when the novel was published, but back and forth."[58] As Sundquist points out, Delany's nonlinear novel time brings attention to the ways U.S. expansionism and Cuban revolution were interlinked.[59] That is, it draws attention to spatialities, to proximate, dynamic landscapes. It makes the U.S. South and Cuba shadow sites, parallel spaces of a master-slave republic. In a novel with little that can be claimed as formal device, such alignment is noteworthy.

By contrast, even decorative and ornamental features of a Colton 1850s-era U.S. map intern time in pictures of national space. Rococo-styled map borders, actually a specialty of high-end firms like Colton's, which exported maps to Europe, were far from being stately garnish. The border decorations tell a story about national landscape portraiture. Studded by national monuments and scenes of national/natural extension from the Willamette Falls of Oregon to Mount Holyoke, Massachusetts, map borders caption a story about a people's progress into nature. They enclose a story of abundance, of land as plenitude. At variance with such depictions, Delany staged movements that countered the striated space of slaveholder republics. American subalterns such as black slaves, North American Indians, Africana renegades in the Dred Swamps, and blacks in lines of flight to Canada populate the text. They diffuse any clear chronologies of unified, fulfillment-driven migration.

For instance, it only takes Blake twelve very short paragraphs of action in the novel's 34th chapter to leave Canada West, sail past Albany on the Hudson River, and find himself at the corner of Broadway and Franklin Street in lower Manhattan. His sharp eye just happens to observe the festivities of an elegant, well-dressed party of women and naval officers whom he *overhears* matching Broadway's metropolitan pleasures to Havana's: in "Cuba, where in a few days they would be, recreation and pleasure were quite equal to that of New York."[60] Anticipation mounts in Blake's heart, while his body is seemingly everywhere all at once. Delany's character embodies black flow, taking on many forms to manage his interests. He is a counter-state unto himself.

But even more archly, the novel's plot can reach no conclusion in the spatialities of nation. Rather, it signals the scope of the conflict, and the clandestine connections between the United States, Cuba, and Western Africa. This will be discussed further in the final section of this essay. But what all these movements that constitute *Blake* lead to is a literary counter-mapping of expansionist U.S. maps. The counter-map suggests proslavery momentum in claiming Cuba to be a dangerous and very costly misadventure. So whereas in the major period maps, transit trails were the realm of signs for staging possession (as Anglo-American landscape tableaux) and directed movement as national destiny, *Blake*'s crosshatched story effectively reveals wider New World contexts for framing black experience.

In fact, to rewrite the map, *Blake* must do something else, too. It must challenge divisions that adhere within Cuba. Cuba's midcentury racial cartography is initially presented as divided and divisive: "The four great divisions of society were white, black, free and slave. . . . The free and slaves among the blacks did not associate, nor the high and low among the free of the same race. And there was among them even another general division—black and colored—which met with little favor from the intelligent."[61] The author claimed it was the project of the intelligentsia (Blake's group) to suture these forces and make a

3.6. D. Griffing Johnson, *Johnson's New Illustrated & Embellished County Map of the Republics of North America with the Adjacent Islands & Countries, Compiled Drawn & Engraved from U. States Land & Coast Surveys, British Admiralty & other Reliable Sources.* Designed by Alvin J. Johnson, engraved by D. Griffing Johnson, J. H. Goldthwait, W. S. Barnard, Wm. Wright, G. Rae Smith, F. H. King, James Duthie, and J. L. White. New York: D. Griffing and Alvin J. Johnson, 1859. Image courtesy David Rumsey Map Collection, www.davidrumsey.com.

"policy for their remedy," Yet what the novel actually shows is something different. It shows that the Spanish state concentrates its own problems by making a unified, revolutionary, black island interior—remarkably supported by Creoles—through its enactment of Negro Laws.[62] (Such laws were real. They were formed to curtail the freedoms of potentially dangerous colored populations in close proximity to slaves, and bring all under white submission. Negro Laws gained publicity after the colonial authority's handling of an alleged slave revolt in 1844, known as *Conspiración de La Escalera*, or Ladder Conspiracy.[63]) But in *Blake* the laws prove revolutionary in another way. They galvanize two populations: black and white. Blacks outnumber whites, and the laws close black ranks: "Succeeding this despair there was a reaction. A new vigor seemed ever to actuate, and a new impulse given to these faithful men and women determined to be free."[64] What this leveling of all nonwhites produces in Delany's fiction is a unified struggle, a mass of antislavery among the island's people of color.

From this juncture, the parallelism becomes most clear. Unlike the tri-tier race systems in many other Caribbean and Latin American countries (Venezuela, Colombia, and Brazil), Cuba's 1850s-era race system was much closer to that of the United States. Aline Helg writes, "Cuba had a two-tier racial system close to, but not identical to, that of the United States, and it helped Afro-Cubans mobilize on a scale unrivaled in other regions of Latin America. Conversely their mobilization prompted white-elite repression unmatched in other Latin American societies and in many ways parallel to the repression in Anglo-America."[65] The intrinsically volatile entities of black struggle and capital become the material of cohesion in Blake's binding together of antislavery cells. As I will discuss in the final sections of this chapter, parallel features of Cuban and U.S. slavery were evoked by Delany to make an affective topography, a black counter-map.

Accession

At the center of *Blake*'s plot is the leading concern that animated both period maps and Delany's Cuba writings ("Political Destiny" and *North Star* editorials). It was the reinvigorated contest for Cuba that officially emerged in political discourse in 1848 when President James Polk offered over one hundred million dollars to Spain to take full ownership of the lucrative sugar-producing island. Spain, for its part, refused flatly to sell its "Antilles Flower." Cuba was by that time the richest colony in the world, its economy fueled by African slave labor, sugar production, and several hundred million dollars of Spanish investment. With continued pressure from proslavery politicians, the United States throughout the 1850s became involved in a variety of both official and highly unofficial ventures in aims of acquiring Cuba. Highlighting the unofficial was a set of filibuster expeditions launched by Narcíso Lopez, the Venezuelan-born Spaniard whose chief economic and military support base came from United States proslavery advocates. Beginning in 1849, he embarked on a series of raids in the attempt to conquer Cuba for the preservation of slavery. His American army of paid soldiers from Kentucky and Louisiana was defeated by the Spanish army. A second takeover attempt in 1850 was also repelled by the Spanish. On his final attempt with a militia of some 435 United States men (only five of whom were purportedly Cuban), Lopez was caught and executed by firing squad. In New Orleans, Lopez's associates went on to form the Order of the Lone Star, which ultimately had some fifty chapters throughout eight Southern states and an estimated membership of 15,000-to-20,000. Their aim was to develop a plan to capture Cuba for the preservation and extension of slavery. Spain, however, discovered the conspiracy in 1852 and again thwarted this Southern proslavery takeover.[66]

In light of such activity, the United States's interest in officially annexing Cuba was by the middle of the century a matter of public record. In his 1852 inaugural address President Franklin Pierce announced his interest in purchasing Cuba, stating that he would "not be controlled by any timid forebodings of evil from expansion."[67] Maps such as Wellington Williams's 1851 *A New Map of the United States upon which Are Delineated the Vast Works of International Communication, Routes across the Continent, &c. showing Canada and the Island of Cuba* (figure 3.7) read like a cartographic blueprint for the political expansionism iterated by Pierce. Williams's map was notably pitched to tourists. Unlike the other New York–based cartographers previously mentioned, he worked from Philadelphia, and primarily produced affordable travel guides (issued each year after 1851), which included folding maps. "Every attention will be paid to keeping the work up to a standard of usefulness," the prefacing pages of his 1851 *Traveler's and Tourist's Guide through the United States of America* stated.[68] His lithographic map was a glued fold-out in the backboard of the travel

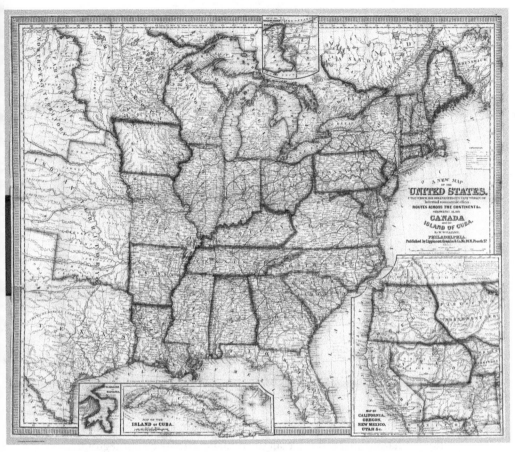

3.7. Wellington Williams, *A New Map of the United States upon which Are Delineated the Vast Works of International Communication, Routes across the Continent, &c. showing Canada and the Island of Cuba.* Philadelphia: Lippincott and Grambo, 1851. Image courtesy David Rumsey Map Collection, www.davidrumsey.com.

book, a book advertising that it detailed current steamboat, stagecoach, and canal routes, and "the Principal Places of Fashionable and Healthful Resort."[69]

Yet, perhaps to a greater degree than any of the Colton firm maps, the Williams map captions Cuba into United States belonging in a way that would have been useful for commercial traffic or harbor reconnaissance. A diptych-styled depiction of Cuba, placed on the U.S. map, gives it a two-window prominence (figure 3.8). One side of the inset, titled "City and Harbor of Havana," even features squares for houses and set-

3.8. Detail from Wellington Williams, *A New Map of the United States*. Image courtesy David Rumsey Map Collection, www.davidrumsey.com.

tlements along the harbor. Noteworthy, too, is how Williams makes figural the harbor space: It is a contained shape with its own foreground. The land is background. In an epoch of rampant filibusterism, Cuba is made into a site of landing, an island with an opening. The second inset shows the entire expanse of the island. By way of a comparison, Florida, entered into proslavery statehood in 1845, is not even depicted in its entirety. It is missing its peninsula tip. But Cuba is hyperimposed directly onto the map in a gesture of interest. It looks as though Cuba were an accession, or something marked for accession. It is not a territory of the United States, not yet. But it appears fitted to a rhetorical position argued in the 1854 Ostend Report, drawn up in Belgium by proslavery American ministers to Spain, England, and France. The report declared that the United States should annex Cuba to preserve slavery and that "Cuba belongs naturally to that great family of states of which the Union is the Providential Nursery."[70]

Cuba, embroiled in conflict between Creole landholders and a Spanish colonial government, and attacked the same year of publication (1851) at Bahia Honda by Narcíso Lopez's annexation army, was indeed a site of colonial contestation. But as Matthew Pratt Guterl details, it was just as much a scene of ambition for U.S. infrastructural export: "The railroad cars, sugar, boilers, and locomotives brought to modernize Cuban sugar production came from American companies."[71] These were strategies of midcentury New World imperialism. U.S. colonization could not be achieved by army occupation alone, but rather through the more supple and far-reaching arms of commerce. Delany knew this. It was the field of capitalist connections that he had to undermine, that he had to project as risk. The logic was: The greater the expanse of claim, the more opportunities for deterritorialization—ways to undo or make insolvent, to peel away practice from place, to destabilize domains of imperialist "development."[72] So the question then follows: How does literature mobilize the revolutionary subject in relation to possible domains of deterritorialization?

Maps present the scope of territory but tell only part of the story. Just as John Lewis's map (figure 2.1) in the North Star shaded in the slave states as a national space of peril, an inky, spreading threat to union, Blake's second half paints Cuba as the space of impending black revolution. It is a dangerous place for a white slaveholder: "A sleeping death or waking sleep, a living death or tormented life is that of the Cuban and American slaveholder. For them there is no safety."[73] Noting Cuba's proximity to a free black Haiti and a known-violent, black, British-emancipated Jamaica, Ifeoma Nwankwo rightly observes that Delany "could just as easily have set the second half of the novel in Brazil during that period, or in any part of the Americas before emancipation. That novel, however, would certainly not have had the same potential to inspire fear as this one because of the emphasis in contemporary discourse on Cuba in particular."[74] Indeed, though Blake's travels are said to have taken him to the far South Atlantic and to coastal Brazil, it was white fear of regional volatility that gave charge to Delany's selection of Cuba as the appointed site of black revolution. Delany colored the future of Cuba black. As he wrote in Blake, "the blacks have everything to hope for and nothing to fear, since let what may take place their redemption from bondage is inevitable."[75] Blake's armies move through it all.

Along with his information gathering from U.S. periodicals and African American newspaper accounts, Delany relied on some sorts of illustrative maps to depict the sites and cities of Cuba in his fiction—their relative proximity to the United States, and the division of colonial townships. *Blake* readily references geographies where slaveholders made their villas, and where Blake's organization gleans its counterintelligence. In fact, so quickly embedded in Cuba is Blake, apparently, that after only a short stay on the island, he can confidently assert that there is a "complete" and "systematic" organization of slaves across Havana, Matanzas, Principe, Trinidad, St. Jago de Cuba, and Fernandina.[76] To be sure, Delany did not have to look any further than U.S. maps from the 1850s to extract this information. Cuba's locality (its street-level action, its buildings) was claimed cartographically, as maps such as Wellington Williams's (figure 3.7) demonstrated.

Yet, far from blazoning nation as the achievement of the frame (what cartographers monumentalized on top of wider spaces with U.S. symbols: the Washington Monument, the U.S. Capitol, the eagle, the California gold rocker), Delany made it alive with conflict. It was a space of terror, close to both national and private holdings. In effect, the geographic arrangements underlying *Blake*'s sprawling part II transform proximity between the United States Gulf South and the hotbed of Creole discord and filibusterism that was Cuba into a threat against white sovereignty—if that white sovereignty entailed slaveholding. The rationale for Cuban annexation on the basis of proximity is thus fictionalized into the very thing that made Cuba most unsettling to U.S. citizenry: black insurrection.

Cuba was at the front of Delany's journalistic mind as he was writing the second section of his novel, even as he began considering African emigration toward the end of the 1850s.[77] Although questions of Cuban accession commonly appeared as U.S. news items in both Northern and Southern newspapers and editorials throughout the 1850s, black newspapers gave particularized coverage to the prospects of incipient black revolt on the island, especially following the Ladder Conspiracy discussed above. In 1848 the *North Star* reprinted a news item from the *New York Evangelist* that claimed: "Large number of slaves, trained to war, and massacre in Africa, are ready to enlist in any scheme of plunder and bloodshed, however small may be the prospect of securing their freedom. They only need competent leaders to excite their passions and direct their movements. Such leaders are found among the free negroes."[78] *Frederick Douglass' Paper* published William Watkins's transcription of Thomas Benton's remarks in Congress that the "emancipation of Cuba would, it seems, furnish a scene of dire contemplation to the United States, or which is about the same thing, the Southern portion of the Union."[79] And in 1856 the *Anti-Slavery Bugle* reprinted from the *National Era* an article by George Weston that highlighted the threat of Africanization as determining geographic priority: "If we can rely on Gen. Jackson as military authority, the 'naval strategic key' of the Florida Pass is not Havana, but the Dry Tortugas. It is not because the Moro castle threatens our shipping, but because the possible Africanization of Cuba threatens the plantations of Georgia and Florida and *ascendency in the Gulf of Mexico*."[80] In the same way that Spain supposedly promoted an image of Cuban conflagration to discourage U.S.-sponsored filibusterism or annexation attempts, black journalists such as Delany developed this picture in his serial literature for similar purposes, not the least of which was dramatic effect.[81] Annexation could mean new and dangerous problems. Fire was contagious.

Yet, though having worked as a journalist in two countries (in the United States since his 1834 launch of the Pittsburgh *Mystery*, and as a contributing editor to the *Provincial Freemen* after relocating to Canada West in 1856), Delany accorded very little attention to the roles of language communities in making national configurations. This may have been a purposeful omission on his part: Language differences posed obvious problems in situating African American leadership in Cuba or, for that matter, any of the other Central and South American sites of interest he suggested in *The Condition*. In fact, *Blake* tells a story about meaningful networks of activity that claim little for the reaches of print circulation within black communities. So-called "morning journals" like *El Diario*, circulating on the streets of Havana, produce "absurdities," which confuse eager populations about the real dynamics of slave struggle.[82] The author's fairly ambivalent textualization of print communities can, of course, be considered from the perspective that what he was interested in was a physical call to arms, not a print/protest-based revolt. He imagined a Haitian-styled black-led revolution, which would establish a new Toussaint L'Ouverture or Jean-Jacques Dessalines as black national champions and international figures.[83] It should not be overlooked that the radical story lines posed in *Blake* had to do with mobilizing the actual physical subject, and not only circulating print (or even capital) without the body.

Transit and Tracking

Like *Blake*, Delany's major nonfiction (*The Condition*, "Political Destiny," and *Official Report of the Niger Valley Exploring Party*) addresses the ways mobility could be modeled to reinforce presence, to make a mark or give code to a place. What his fiction does more constructively than his nonfiction is draw out the connections that shape place. Period maps also inferred a connection between the United States and the Caribbean based on functional transit. In the 1857 *New Map of the Union* (figure 3.4), such lines of transportation are made elemental to an organization of American space. The Johnson *Republics* map of 1859 (figure 3.6) goes even further, using tracking lines for oceanic travel routes to impart directional force to the Gulf of Mexico space. Marked transit lines through Texas, Mexico, and Cuba appear like radial spokes, tracking out from a centrum. The lines direct the viewer's attention to the Mississippi Delta in Louisiana, which looks like a hemispheric axis. They enhance the ocular pull of the United States Visually, the River Delta is the center of a half wheel. As both maps show, representations of travel are conductive.

In *Blake* characters are cast as embodiments of transit.[84] Their broader identities and occupations are formed by the spaces they travel and the traffic they impose upon others. These lines of transit could produce multiple outcomes. Blake's wife Maggie, an unremarkable, underdeveloped character like almost every other in the fiction with the exception of Blake, moves from capture to capture before release. Helen-like, she prompts the general insurrection after she is unwillingly sold by Blake's Mississippi owner to a Captain Garcia of Havana. (Here she loses her memory and hair color until Blake's immanent arrival.) Perhaps needless to say, such a profit-depleting reversal of slave traffic would have been unlikely—albeit no less improbable than the fugitive hero's extraordinary maneuverings in the slave states. Still, the abduction and sale of Maggie do underscore that what happened in Cuba mattered to blacks in the United States. It was as personal as the breaking up of black families with bills of sale.

Representing territorialization and populating the traffic schemes binding Cuba and the U.S. South are some of Blake's most formidable opponents: U.S. nationals who function as individual representatives of the wider international crisis he illustrates. One such character is a Northern legislator named Judge Ballard, a proprietor of a large Cuban estate, staffed by Afro-Cuban slaves. In following his commitment to whatever general government structure will facilitate unrestricted free trade and offshore investment options, he supports the proslavery antebellum position in respect to one of the most debated international affair items of the 1850s: the projected United States takeover of Cuba. Ballard airs the very position Delany in late 1840s North Star essays like "Annexation of Cuba" and "Redemption of Cuba" identified as the most serious threat to abolition—proslavery expansionism: "Cuba must cease to be a Spanish colony, and become American territory. These mongrel Creoles are incapable of self-government, and should be compelled to submit to the United States."[85]

Blake, by contrast, reverses trajectories. His movements are calibrated to disrupt imperial gnoseological axes, those with connections to the New World Atlantic slave trade. As African American papers reported it, Atlantic transportation and transit lines were not to be taken as subject-neutral formations (faster technologies, the general course of development) for blacks in the pre–Civil War United States. They were potential networks for slaveholding solidarity and hemispheric expansionism. Certainly the abolition of slavery the freeborn Delany fought so hard to achieve appeared at its most hopeless, its most unlikely, when transnational parties in shipping and tobacco were investing in its continuity, and when development of the resource that was slave labor was supported by domestic/oceanic transport lines.[86]

Transit encompassed networks of slave space in a climate where connectivity had real growth consequences. As the December 1856 New Orleans Daily Creole reported: "It is said that parties have been for some time in correspondence with the Cuban and Spanish authorities for the privilege of laying a telegraph line between Cuba and the United States."[87] Technologies of connection, like the lines of oceanic travel in Blake's part II, signify the transnational alliance's manifest stake in expanding the institution. Blake takes a journalistic tone when the third-person narrator reports: "It is confidently believed upon good authority that the American steamers plying between Havana and New Orleans, as a profitable part of their enterprise, are actively engaged in the slave trade between the two places."[88] On the whole, the novel gives fictional projection to an argument Delany previously made in the North Star: That Cuba was "the great channel through which slaves are imported annually into the United States."[89] The novel's Atlantic expanse, reflected in the full title—*Blake; or, the Huts of America: A Tale of the Mississippi Valley, the South-ern United States, and Cuba*—signals the scope of hemispheric slavery be-tween the United States, the Caribbean, and a slave-producing West Af-rica. But it also more intimately reflects the scope of what Delany called "the Southern Confederacy of America."[90] Conceived of geographically, the Southern Confederacy was not simply one half of the Missouri Com-promise, or the slave side of the Mason-Dixon line. It was not the ob-verse of Northern legislation and Northern cartographies. Rather, it was an alliance between proslavery U.S. nationals and Cuban landholders, which Delany claimed in *Blake* already comprised Havana, New Orleans, Charleston, and Richmond.[91] As he depicted it in his Cuba writings, this Confederacy was both a unit of more widely conceived Southern space and something that worked its way into and beyond national structures. Its geography was generative. The alliance's chief aim was capital, and capital produced its own forms.

Particularly with California poised to join the Union as a free state, the Confederacy looked to expand its sectional leverage with new land-holdings, potentially in the Caribbean and Central America. An 1849 edi-torial in the *American Literary Magazine* reported: "The temptations offered by Cuba are such, that the slavery interest will undoubtedly greet the new movement with great delight."[92] In "Confederate Cuba," Caroline Levander crystallizes the dynamics of struggle Delany tried to shape into his literature: "Approaching the U.S. South not from the usual van-tage point of its relation with the increasingly abolitionist states to its North but from the vantage point of its dependence on the slaveholding regions to its South reveals the Confederacy's location within and de-pendency on a hemispheric framework—a framework that elucidates the complex interdependencies between slaveholding Spanish Ameri-can nations such as Cuba and the United States."[93] The wider suggestion about remobilizing critical frames to desituate entrenched spheres of influence is particularly useful in assessing Delany's own interests in site mappings. Delany propped his fiction on spaces he viewed as most piv-otal to the contemporary crisis that was hemispheric slavery.[94]

Delany valued cartography and studied Caribbean maps at least as early as 1854, when he delivered his address to the National Emigration Convention of Colored Men in Cleveland. In it he unveiled a classification system for the colonial and political divisions of the Caribbean islands: French, Danish, Swedish, Dutch, Venezuelan Spanish, British, and then the Haitian and "adjunct islands," as he put it. So detailed was he that he included a description of the aggregate area in square miles "of smaller Islands, belonging to the Little Antilles, the area and population of which are not known, many of them being unpopulated."[95] But more than simply being illustrative of colonial incursions, the purposes of his colonialist compendium were broadly educational.

In nearly all of his major 1850s-era publications, he copied and published actual longitudinal coordinates of exploratory sites within Africa to ascertain their suitability for emigration (Condition; Official Report; Blake).[96] He used the languages of mapping (coastline measurements and lines of latitude) to describe places as schemed settlements (of his own making), assessing the potential of topographical features like plateaus, table lands, and stone formations (Official Report).[97] Cartography, he further valued, as a political science. In the detailed "Appendix" to The Condition he developed a plan for dispatching an exploratory party of knowledge extractors, in search of a settlement location for African Americans beyond the territorial claims of the United States. The Board of Commissioners, as he titled them, were land surveyors. "Their business shall be, to make a topographical, geographical, geological, and botanical examination, into such part or parts as they may select, with all other useful information that may be obtained; to be recorded in a journal kept for that purpose."[98]

Finally, although the author compiled map information and land guides to present cartography as political knowledge about how places were organized, the novel's most conclusive gestures piece the hero's missions to a wider architecture of Atlantic venture capital. Blake depicts the Atlantic as a crowded convergence of signs and identities that inflect on land-based territorialization. The novelistic counter-map presented in Blake is actually a cogent rewiring of the American axis established in dominant maps. It is a picture of deterritorialization. As Ronald Bogue observes, "all deterritorialization proceeds via a process of becoming-other, a passage between entities or categories that sets them in meta-morphic disequilibrium."[99] *Blake*'s part II shows that the act of transposing (passing against) oceanic slave networks is an act of enterprise that enlarges the gaps and makes new forms for black potentiality. Subverting white geographic usage is the first step. *Blake*'s counter-transit, its tracking devices, come into view most clearly through a number of such key reversals. First, in a trip aimed at both research and revolution, Blake travels the infamous Middle Passage in reverse, from Matanzas in Cuba to the Guinea Coast, and then back again, as shipmaster of a Spanish slaver. He claims his plan is to incite sea mutiny and commandeer an armed vessel for the purpose of making a strike on Cuba.

In the Atlantic scenes of transit, Blake is stationed in the forecastle, perfecting his plot under the open sky while the African slaves in the hold are defined in terms of their suffering and dispensability. This separation of Blake and the bulk of slave bodies populating the ship is significant at the formal level of the text, too, so that Delany's depiction of the Middle Passage is foregrounded, and so the terrors and ritualized violence of the hold might at least momentarily loom as large as a hero who can literally cut through cartographic space right to the hub of the transatlantic slave trade. But it is also within this profound decentering at the heart of the Middle Passage that Blake most signally becomes his purpose. Looking at the base map of his revolutionary plan from above, he is presented as the novel's black axis, a thoroughly modernized force of reterritorialization, able to knit together disparate representatives of diasporan life in a unifying struggle.

If the pure black, Caribbean-born, American-dwelling Blake is the axis, then it makes sense that most effective conduits for Blake's plan of resistance are the multinationals aboard the slaver. Such figures bridge together in their own persons the geopolitical gyres Delany viewed as most pivotal for black revolution. One is a Sudanese woman, identified as Abyssa, whose background Delany reveals at length. A Muslim by birth, she converted to Christianity after moving into the Eba country, where she established herself as successful dry goods merchant. Sold to Dahomi after a raid by the Ibadans, and then again sold into Caribbean slavery, she is a representative identity of the trade's interior in the Republic of Benin, one of the principal sites supplying slaves to America and Europe. She also happens to speak "good English."[100] Her strength is rooted in her versatility and adaptability to potential markets where

Delany himself envisioned African American leadership. (Among these were the Egba lands in Abeokuta of what is now Nigeria, where in 1859 Delany obtained a treaty for the right to African American settlement. The treaty was revoked in 1861 by the Egba king.) A second natural leader Blake selects on the *Vulture* is Mendi, a "native chief," who can command the other slaves, and in Delany's terms, "could meet with many of his race whose language he understood, and was thereby better suited to them than many others among them."[101] Like Abyssa, his status as a transnational makes him versatile, and not conscriptable into any narrow nationalism or a predetermined sense of racial heritage. Back in Cuba too, Blake has already secured the interests of a choice black family who represents the African Caribbean nexus, born of the Atlantic slave trade, but shaped into creolized positivity. By their African name they are Oba; in Cuba they are called Grande. He writes, "The family of a superior order proved to be native African, having learned English on the coast, French Creole at New Orleans, and Spanish at Cuba."[102] The history of this family reflects a functional transnationalism that Blake identifies as useful for future development in his insurgency scheme. In their own diasporic history, each of these figures represent disparate participants in the black Atlantic struggle, and all will be "powerful" accessions to his forces in Cuba.[103]

Such a black counter-filibuster regroupment late in the story line appears designed to fill the potential political unit Delany envisioned in Cuba with different players from the eastern hemisphere. For instance, whereas Narcíso Lopez originated his plan and army in Louisiana, Blake strikes back from the Guinea Coast of Africa. Delany himself sailed this coastline in 1859, traveling between Grand Cape Mount in Liberia to Lagos, with high hopes for new traffic from Niger Valley's interior: commercial cotton.[104] He must have thought about the way the East Atlantic deterritorialized Africans from articles of trade to pieces of a commercial capital.[105]

Cartographically, all this rising plot action might look like the overlay of Africa into the same Gulf spaces corralled into national holdings by maps and rhetoric during the Polk and Pierce administrations. The *Blake* narrative vividly describes a panoply of revolutionary bodies, converging on Cuba, and primed for violent takeover. But nearing Cuba, a second layer of reversals comes into view. The novel's purported sea mutiny is literally called off by the stoic Blake, and supplanted with a more nuanced reclamation of speculative value. As it transpires, the value of this apparently abandoned rebellion is actualized upon landing in the Bay of Mantazas in Cuba. Secret agents on land "affecting concern for the interests of the traders" circulate fake press postscripts detailing their mutiny at sea.[106] Posing as slave speculators, the agents manage to reduce the price offerings of the "restless spirits among the captives" to minimum price.[107] They are subsequently purchased by Blake's agents, as the hero turns his attention back to building his forces in Cuba. Again, oceanic commerce networks are foregrounded by Delany for their capacity to make land transactions insolvent; they unbind land categories. They are distributional forces of territorialization and its flows, and a whole different set of dashed transit signifiers on the midcentury Pan-American map.

Blake's resolution (if the novel can be said to have one) lies in its deterritorialization, its taking apart not only the claims but the contexts of imperialist maps. So what the novel illustrates is not just a critique of dominant white cartographies, but rather a resituating of the terms of the debate, an unfixing of context. This gives Delany's presentation a certain complexity—its engagement with mappings as forms of expression, as subjective frames. Conceived of internationally, one of the most significant spaces Delany wished to see reconfigured through black agency was not a territory as much as a network. It was the wide commercial culture of the Atlantic. To the author, the Middle Passage was not a dead zone, an international stigma of an earlier triangular trade between Europe, Africa, and the Americas. Nor did he view it as a kind of psychic space, an unresolved wound in black consciousness. Rather, it was a wild and live circuit, symbolizing an international underground. It was the space of transnational exchange, where human lives lay piled in the balance.[108]

To a greater extent than his contemporary abolitionist authors Frederick Douglass and William Wells Brown, Delany viewed slavery as compatible with the demands of industrial capitalism. In fact, he was acutely concerned about the dangers the growth of free trade posed for the exportable and outsourceable labor unit that was the chattel slave, particularly in areas tapped for "development." High-speed technology such as nineteenth-century railways, steam engines, refitted merchant fleets, and telegraph systems between Havana and New Orleans, were thus chief concerns, specifically because they translated into more facile trade and an easier transfer of capital into expanding transnational markets.

Yet, Delany believed that there were significant code gaps or lapses within what appeared to be the monolith of entrenched international profit cartels.[109] These were spaces for black deterritorialization, spaces through which powerful social and economic structures could be seriously disrupted.[110] The challenge, sewn into Blake, was for blacks to exploit and ultimately reclaim these openings as operative spaces for action. Such spaces were uncharted by maps but known to blacks. (In western Africa's coastal waters, Blake claims to have had "full command, as no white men manage vessels in the African waters, that being entirely given up to the blacks."[111]) Throughout both parts of Blake, Delany implored his black readership to learn about these gaps. Blake's middle knowledge stands as valuable navigational intelligence of slavery's North and South Atlantic passages and slave routes.

Atlantic transit in period maps may have been depicted as a kind of national unfurling, an arranged movement around a hub. But Blake's counter-cartography shows it as contours into spaces that were not so easily conscripted into national pictures. Instead, it is a space for counter-coordinating American development. The limited accountability of any one nation operating in nationalized space made the Atlantic into a place where sanctions of international law and geographical coordination were relatively porous.[112] The Atlantic was a space between national legitimations, where excrescences of human greed could operate with few tactical restraints. But Delany saw potential; he saw something that Paul Gilroy a century and a half later would call "the liquidity of a culture," and how it could be explored in the spaces between nations, in the ambits of an axis Americanus (Interview, Transition).[113]

Ultimately, for Delany what was at stake in Blake (and The Condition and "Political Destiny") was the future of black communities. Throughout his antebellum writings, he envisioned African Americans as having the potential to be something more than passive subjects of industrialization and burgeoning, trade-driven hemispheric capitalism. It was through his geographical revisioning that he most radically explored this potential. Maps gave view to terrains of emplacement. They also showed routes for navigation. A comparative reading of Blake demonstrates that maps posed the very structures of presence Delany had to first address, and then reshape in his fiction. To get at black embodiment, Delany had to get at geography, at the spaces underlying black corporeality and flux. To get out from being determined in someone else's history, Delany wrote over places for black enterprise. While interpretive practices in literature frequently separate thematic concerns from formal arrangements, maps more overtly show that form is thematic and that form is itself politically charged. In a similar way, *Blake* and its cartographies illustrate the intermedial ways places are transformed through print.

....

CHAPTER 4

CIVIC GEOGRAPHIES AND
INTENTIONAL COMMUNITIES

On the surface there appears little to link Martin Delany to the post-Reconstruction African American novelist and journalist Pauline Hopkins. Their best-known works were produced nearly half a century apart. While both lived through the Civil War, Reconstruction, and Jim Crow, they belonged to different generations of African American experience. Hopkins was born in 1859, the same year Delany's serial novel *Blake* first appeared in the New York-based *Anglo African*. Delany was the son of a slave, escaping the institution himself only because his mother was a freedwoman. He grew up in stark poverty and the first eleven years of his life were spent without the benefit of a legal education in the slave state of Virginia. Hopkins was born in Portland, Maine, and moved with her family to Boston in early childhood. There she enjoyed a firmly middle-class existence. She was educated in Boston's integrated city school system and called Boston her home until her death in 1930.[1] Today her house at 53 Clifton Street, North Cambridge, is a city landmark. Delany, by contrast, was less affiliated with any single place. In his lifetime, he traveled restlessly and settled sporadically in various communities in Canada and the United States. Much of his late work was devoted to soliciting finances for African American settlement projects in areas of western Africa.

Despite such differences, Delany's antebellum literature signaled many of the same concerns that occupied Pauline Hopkins throughout her professional life. As novelists and career journalists, both used their writing to reorganize the situations that determined the lives of contemporary black Americans. They pulled apart the environs of black experience for material. Yet while Delany's writing during his most prolific 1850s period is characterized by its broad scope and hemispheric concourses, Hopkins's most important contributions to African American print looked to turn-of-the-century spheres of community action to produce frames for local knowing.

Among other things, the movement from Delany to Hopkins signals a movement from territorial geographies to relational, practice-based geographies. By practice-based geographies, I simply mean geographies about the ways spaces are enacted. They can be about any number of arrangements since they ally place to its interpretations and encompass myriad ways of knowing. But to try to get beneath what it is that gives practice geographies their specificity, it makes sense to think of them as arenas of interaction. They are mediated by their participants, and they privilege interactive spaces of communication. The kinds of practice geographies I will consider in this chapter are interpersonal and shaped by the forms that participation takes in everyday life. Tracing such geographies in the literature of late-nineteenth-century African Americans, readers encounter spaces unified by a common race identity and drawn together by a range of inherited experiences. But there is another layer, too. Hopkins, in particular, wrote about consensual communities, communities of intention, organized around the goals of black enfranchisement and the development of a women's public sphere.[2] The following pages examine the ways Hopkins inscribed civic geographies. More widely, I look at her writing to discuss the forms of local citizenship that produced place at the end of the nineteenth century.

I begin from the premise that Hopkins's novels are all driven by their settings. From *Contending Forces: A Romance Illustrative of Negro Life North and South* (1900), her first and most widely read novel, to the subsequent magazine fiction—*Hagar's Daughter: A Story of Southern Caste Prejudice* (1901–2); *Winona: A Tale of Negro Life in the South and Southwest* (1902); and *Of One Blood; or, the Hidden Self* (1902–3)—the author brings into play a panoply of settings that condition black characters' movements and memories. These are places such as Canada West, a Civil War Kansas, Kentucky, South Carolina, and even a mythico-archeological Ethiopia in *Of One Blood*. However, one novel develops a literary place aesthetics in a more complex and detailed way than other texts. Its plot and configuration take depth from their depiction of the same community that Hopkins envisioned as her readership. This was *Contending Forces*, the only novel she published in book form.[3] The community she reconstructed in her writing was Boston's South End, a neighborhood made from layers of buildings and waves of migration. It was also Hopkins's own base of operations during her most prolific years as a writer. Beginning in the 1880s, it housed the largest population of the city's middle-class blacks. Its inhabitants are presented as players in a new black demos in turn-of-the-century New England.

This chapter first places Hopkins's work historiographically within the rise of the black novel, something useful for locating her in competing practices of the late-nineteenth-century literary marketplace and also for following the shifts from midcentury to late-century black literary place aesthetics. It then examines Hopkins's demographic modeling of black Boston as subject-fashioning civic work, made choate through devices associated with regionalist expression. I argue that what undergirds regional representation in the novel are different organizational sites for voluntary citizenship. In the case of Boston, black intentional communities link first to a fairly complex ecclesiological history. Drawing on post-Habermasian public sphere theory and Sacvan Bercovitch's contentions about the print-driven work of federal hagiographies (or the "figuration" of Massachusetts's Puritan church histories), I examine the ways Hopkins's novel casts the black church as both a structure and network. The aesthetic treatments of a Boston-based civics radiate from different modalities of belonging associated with church life.

But if the streets, homes, churches, and folklife make a community core, they are also seedbeds for a number of contested metanarratives presented in the text, each claiming "direction" for black civic organization at the end of the nineteenth century. This tension is something I frame as a kind of demographic contest between Pauline Hopkins's representative women's civic society (Hopkins was herself an active participant and chronicler of black women's club life) and plans espoused by her better-known, contemporary "race men": the post-Reconstruction rivals W. E. B. Du Bois and Booker T. Washington. Drawing on feminist geographical approaches, I show how *Contending Forces* accords civic centrality to households directed by women and to women's community spaces. It draws civic space around a female character never allowed to participate in meaningful community life. (Her name is Sappho.)

The last part of this chapter more directly examines Hopkins's framing of a diverse black public sphere within the topos of local life. Hopkins, I claim, constructed civil society as already a counter-public, already the world of a differentiated group. Black Boston is a setting in a setting, steered by gendered, urban spatialities. But the point of her discursive geographies is not simply to show blacks as seeking normative representative status in the already-made frame of some white political space. Rather, she circulates contending models for a black, deliberative political forum, settling finally on the system that she identifies as a progressive women's sphere.

Three Waves

In keeping with the larger framework for this book, I should note here that Hopkins's presentation of setting represents a marked departure from first-generation 1850s-era novels by authors like William Wells Brown, Martin Delany, Frank Webb, or Harriet Wilson, where the ongoing maintenance of a color line runs through plot designs and form. The color line establishes the overall spatialization of character movement. It runs deep, too. It determines the alignments for black private life as they are depicted in both free and slave states.[4] From a variety of angles, what a geographic reading of the midcentury novel most seems to expose is an arrangement of places organized simultaneously into sites of control and sites of subordination. The concept of race works as a principal signifier for maintaining the black and white divide—and the novel's organization. These early novels do present openings for black emergence. Extraordinary protagonists—race heroes— can and do push through structural blockages. But the color line is dominant, and it is rarely, if ever, escapable.

Nonetheless, it is not particularly surprising that Hopkins's work would depart from such midcentury race treatments. After all, she wrote into a different situation. Major social and political shifts (emancipation, Reconstruction, and migration) had changed the landscapes of African American experience. Such changes could certainly occasion a thematic shift from fugitive geographies to stories of U.S. settlement. Writing, of course, reflects the times. In fact, it could be convincingly argued that *Contending Forces* was clearly influenced by the geographies of what I am calling the second wave of the African American novel, beginning loosely after Brown's fourth version of *Clotel* (1867) and Frances Ellen Watkins Harper's *Minnie's Sacrifice* (1867). A wider pattern coheres in these second-wave texts: They are stories of travel between a kind of generic Northeast and the postwar, Reconstructionist South. This is a circuit scholars have already recognized in African American slave narratives. In *From Behind the Veil*, Robert Stepto identifies a narrative trajectory of black American life, not hedged by a specific time frame. It is a pattern of movement between the constrained and enslaved "symbolic South" and a relatively free "symbolic North." Stepto calls the journey to the symbolic North an "ascent" from the space of the symbolic South, which he identifies as a place that maximizes oppression. Nonetheless, this same South is also a place where the most elemental and enduring personal, familial, and communal bonds are established. The comparable freedoms associated with the symbolic North are more individualized and frequently come with the added cost of geographical and psychological isolation from the communities of the symbolic South. Ascent and journey as themes are thus linked to estrangement. As Houston Baker describes it, the "daughter's departure" and optimistic journey North are leading tropes in Afro-American women's poetics. But what the journey reveals is the hegemony of white patriarchic forms. These forms are implicit sites of violence, and for the daughter they undermine the world that has thus far sustained them.[5]

But Hopkins's use of such dominant second-wave geographic tropes as journeying and departure is geographically distinctive. *Contending Forces* tells a story of indexable, materialist place not present in the stories of escape and value-shaping peregrinations from the South that appeared in James Howard's *Bond and Free* (1886) or in Frances Harper's *Sowing and Reaping* (1876–77), *Trial and Triumph* (1889), and *Iola Leroy, or Shadows Uplifted* (1892).[6] Indeed, for an author such as Harper, the South emblematizes familial bonds. It houses the creative spaces of black folk culture. Northern figures travel South to find their roots and grow into them. Yet, for someone like Hopkins, this is all reversed. The North literally bestows black connectivity. Read heuristically, what *Contending Forces* does within the black rise of the novel is install and give civic purpose to the very expressive forms of women's arts and culture that are simultaneously threatened by dominant orders in the North. Further, the novel makes an auxiliary dominant order out of something different: Popular black concessionism platforms, something Hopkins specifically attributes to the parochial Southern insistencies of a Booker T. Washington, are the anticivics of Hopkins's participatory black demos. I will discuss this in further detail in the section, "Politics of Place."

At the outset, though, I establish this genealogy to suggest that Hopkins's writing and journalism might be seen as geographic inversions, or a directional revisioning of the spaces of African American literature. To be sure, Hopkins was clearly influenced by the forms used by African American authors who came before her. Mutual readers of both Harper and Hopkins, for instance, can trace Harper's influence on the younger Hopkins. Hopkins gave print tribute to Harper in her "Literary Workers" installment in the *Famous Women of the Negro Race*, a collective biography written for the *Colored American Magazine* (1901–2). In fact, *Contending Forces* adapted many thematic and formal devices from books like *Iola Leroy*, published only a few years earlier—everything from dual romance lines to an evil "uncle" who consigns the light-skinned black heroine to a sexualized slavery from which she must escape.[7] Like Harper (in *Minnie's Sacrifice* and *Iola Leroy*), Hopkins suggested separate sphere models for post-Reconstruction uplift. One sphere was allocated for the development of black cottage industries and vocational work, especially for Southern freedpersons; and another for a relatively fluid race-leader class, skilled in debate and council-based community organization. These race leaders are always connected to the Northeast by birth or dwelling. The North is associated with a civic collective. It is a center for race thinking. Yet civic action itself remains the property of the individual.

However, distinctive from her literary forebears, Hopkins by 1900 had arrived at a fairly proprietary story of place. That is, she used the fictional form of *Contending Forces* to make a play for the cultural stewardship of black bourgeois North America from the hosting city of Boston. Setting her story in 1896, she pronounced Boston to be a locus for what she called "the great plan of life as practiced in an intelligent liberty-loving community . . . in the free air of New England's freest city."[8] To this end, she transformed the city into a critical setting for an experiment in black living. *Contending Forces* is a community novel about black life and black memory, told from the inside. The novel is almost exclusively devoted to black life in its various permutations and interconnections, much in the way an earlier novel like *The Garies and Their Friends* was devoted to pre-Emancipation, black Philadelphia. But in Hopkins's text there is a greater attention to embodied, practiced modes of space within open-system communities. The local's specificity comes through in its pool of historical imprints and the currents of interactions that can bring these imprints into modern action.

What Hopkins gives weight to, then, is more than a people's length of history or ancestral traces. For instance, *Of One Blood* and *Winona* invoke the ancientness of histories interlinking people of color in Ethiopia and in Erie County, near Buffalo, New York (on Seneca lands), as something that constitutes spiritual place claims. But these kinds of inheritances do not have a tacit durability. They are in there among competing claims, including incorporation into new models of development. *Contending Forces* is especially notable for the ways it focuses on local geographies of transformation, or the collection of transformations exercised in a place. In a way, Hopkins's model for a black civic geography comes down to stories of subject-making encounters and the use of place resources.

Further, unlike the tragic race heroes in contemporary fiction by the better-known Charles Chesnutt, Hopkins's characters produce space through affirmations of black identity and an affirmation of gender as expressive modes of becoming. They are not just produced by a space and shown as passing through its codes. For instance, readers of the later Chesnutt's *House Behind the Cedars* (1900) encounter characters whose movements are lived through an angle of life first learned in Patesville (the thinly disguised Fayetteville, North Carolina). Patesville's streets and its organization of space contain tradition, and they contain resentments. They shape lives. Describing the worldview of Rena Walden, a woman suddenly poised to pass into white society, Chesnutt wrote: "Patesville life was not far enough removed to have lost its distinctness of outline."[9] In Chesnutt's subsequent *The Marrow of Tradition* (1901) or Paul Dunbar's *The Sport of the Gods* (1902), white territorialization makes the space for black mobilization—how far a protagonist gets until running up against the fences of white constraint. In such early twentieth-century fiction, which I tend to think of as early black realism, representations of place retain frameworks for black social regulations. Places do not typically liberate.[10] This may well be because spaces embody the contradictions and ambivalences of those experiencing them, those narrating them. Unlike the other authors this book has treated in depth, Hopkins did not know the South. Instead, her main concerns in *Contending Forces* related to how blacks structured the geographies she could herself envision and make alive. Attached to this was her interest in the ways (both potentially and actually) African Americans might exercise ownership over their inhabited spaces, a theme that extends into her later serial fiction.[11] As this chapter will display, one of Hopkins's most developed achievements within *Contending Forces* is the means by which she shaped black Boston's diverse neighborhood into a coherent, self-managed public sphere and geographic space.

South End Geographies

It initially appears somewhat paradoxical to approach *Contending Forces* as a text about regional spatialities insofar as the novel is itself a story about city life. Especially in the years leading up to 1900, Hopkins's choice of setting would hardly qualify as vernacular or somehow underserved in print circulation. On the contrary, Boston enjoyed a superlative place in the nineteenth-century literary imagination. From a publishing perspective, it launched into mainstream American print culture such authors as Harriet Beecher Stowe, Henry Wadsworth Longfellow, James Russell Lowell, Oliver Wendell Holmes, John Greenleaf Whittier, Julia Ward Howe, Edward Everett Hale, and dozens of others. The Ohio-born William Dean Howells, who settled in Boston and became editor of its premier literary journal, the *Atlantic Monthly*, described in 1871 the "literary situation" he encountered. The city had the greatest concentration of literary celebrities and academics in the United States. In "Literary Boston as I Knew It" he added that "Boston stood for the whole Massachusetts group, and Massachusetts, in the literary impulse meant New England."[12]

Boston's geography was also well recorded as a representative cultural landscape for modern life mappings. American authors from Nathaniel Hawthorne to the leading nineteenth-century fireside poets (Whittier, Longfellow, and Lowell) effectively reproduced the city's landmarks and architecture as affective spaces of belonging. Howells detailed such places as the Old Colonial House, the State House, Boston Common, Beacon Street with the Hancock House, Commonwealth Avenue, and other streets of the Back Bay in his catalogue of Boston impressions. In dominant literary discourse this was the civic material that veritably inspired the flowering of an American literary aesthetics.[13] Yet alongside its well-memorialized landmarks existed another Boston of specific interest to Hopkins. As a working journalist deftly conversant with contemporary nineteenth-century literary culture, Hopkins understood that an important side of the city had been overlooked in local print lime-light. It was largely absent in Boston's representations in literature and mostly unrepresented in the volumes of literature produced in the city itself. This was black Boston.

The spaces Hopkins detailed in her novel were the very neighbor-hoods and buildings used by the largely unwritten life of the city's black community. These included the older neighborhoods in the West End, an area now known as the North Slope of Beacon Hill, and the emerging black working-class communities moving into what became identified as Boston's South End—at the terminus of the area's railway lines. Her depiction of local life did not begin in the "old city" though, but rather in the South End, a neighborhood that at the time she was writing *Contending Forces* was undergoing a major demographic transition. The South End was built up from a tidal marsh in the middle of the nineteenth century for the purpose of retaining an upper-middle-class residential tax base inside city zoning limits. The current residents of this neigh-borhood of interest to Hopkins certainly did not belong to this intended tax base. Even those in the "most respectable part of the South End," Hopkins wrote, lived "with a heavy mortgage."[14] In fact, beginning in the early 1850s much of the upper and middle classes began exiting Boston for the suburbs, a move that followed an influx of new immigrants into the city, many from famine-stricken Ireland. By 1896 the South End had become home to the city's largest black population, following the exo-dus of the intended community for nearby Back Bay and Roxbury around 1880.[15] The African Americans whose lives Hopkins charted in her novel represent a second wave of South End residents.

The South End is both a captioned space and a conduit. First, it is a microcosm of the local black community at the center of Hopkins's fic-tion. At its heart is the Smith family's impeccable, but steeply mortgaged, boardinghouse at No. 500 D Street. The boardinghouse is an important site in *Contending Forces* because it centers the local black community. It is run by the Smith family, consisting of a widowed mother, Ma Smith, and her two young adult children, Dora and Will. All lodging house tenants and all the patrons are black. The neighbors, described as living in rows of neat bow-front houses near expansive avenues and residential parks, are also all black. They constitute the black middle class.

At the same time, the Smith family boardinghouse is a halfway structure for a wider pattern of migration: It channels the movement of post-Reconstruction blacks at the end of the nineteenth century from the South to the major cities in the North and Midwest. In Hopkins's contemporary Boston, many of these newer implants came to the city from Tidewater towns, along the east of Virginia and the Carolinas, or from farms in the upper South.[16] Many were connected by a close degree to slavery, and many were former slaves. According to Elizabeth Hafkin Pleck, in *Black Migration and Poverty: Boston 1865–1900*, by 1900 the population of migrant Southerners represented 53 percent of Boston's black population.[17] The boardinghouse is thus significant for the ways it compiles different waves of migration. It assembles arrivants into a model of civic society with modes of work sharing as a dominant threadline. So unlike the New York City boardinghouse situated at the center of Dunbar's *Sport of the Gods*, which conducts the Great Migration immigrants from the post-Plantation South to ruin, Hopkins makes the setting affirmative—affirmative of self-directed action.[18] Smith's tenants are viable figures in a black economy, even though they must "work at the scantiest remuneration."[19] But despite the constrained labor choices available to them, they define themselves as professionals; they define themselves in terms of their occupations. Much like Du Bois's early twentieth-century journalistic writings, Hopkins's novel belies a taxonomic interest in patterns of employment held by city blacks.[20] Both authors show that labor situates subjects and gives view to the realm of situations traversed in any story line.

As Hopkins displayed in her novel, access to the resources of white Boston was offset by employment limitations. Many employers would not hire nonwhites, and African Americans were discriminated against openly in terms of employment. Wrote Hopkins: "a man, though a skilled mechanic, has the door of the shop closed in is face here among the descendants of the liberty-loving Puritans."[21] In another instance, a black character in the novel comments, "you give us a bootblack stand in the corner of the State House, and think we are placated."[22] Du Bois, who authored a series of five articles for the *New York Times* "The Black North: A Social Study," wrote that only 62 percent of Boston's blacks found "gainful occupations, a smaller proportion than in other cities" (a comparison to Philadelphia and New York).[23] This statistic at once points up the economic hardships and lack of employment opportunities available to late-century blacks in Boston. Yet it is also interesting that in *The*

American Negro, Du Bois attributed blacks' low level of employment to "a larger number of children in school and a larger number of mothers and daughters making and keeping homes."[24] His reasoning reflected two features of late nineteenth-century black life that figure dominantly into Hopkins's novel. The first was an emphasis on public education as a gateway to future successes; the second was a pattern of women's home ownership, and the cottage industries borne of this development. By 1900 women headed more than half of Boston's lodging and boarding-houses, the greatest concentration of which could be found in the city's South End.[25] All this comes together in the undertakings and ambitions of the Smith household. Labor and education become pillar issues in Hopkins's proposed civic sphere model.

Indeed, throughout the early chapters of the novel, Hopkins moves through a range of observations about Boston's economic landscape as a way to frame space, to craft black Boston into a novelistic setting. Her attention to setting, to the labors that make worlds, is part of the novel's structure. The fiction builds slowly through episodic elaboration, as characters emerge from within the vista of local life. Spatial meaning, Hopkins suggests, is generated through participation. And places also make stories. "Space," Michel de Certeau wrote, "is practiced place," and the work of literature is to "carry out a labor that constantly transforms place into stories."[26] In *Contending Forces*, the presentation of a Boston boardinghouse is also a site story, intertwining fictional plot with represented space.

The House and Incorporation

Finally, to speak of a public sphere as something that can be explored or, for that matter, negotiated through literature begs at least a brief glance at the normative public sphere described by Jürgen Habermas. In brief, Habermas influentially designated the bourgeois public sphere as a site in modern societies distinct from the state and the official economy; it was a site for the circulation of discourses about common affairs, enacted through the medium of language.[27] Of course, a variety of correctives to (and reservations about) the ideal public sphere, including Habermas's own, have emerged in the two decades following *The Structural Transformation of the Public Sphere*. Most central to the reading here are those accounting for the exclusion of workers' experiences in the public sphere and the inclusion of home workers and part-time workers, notably the very groups excluded in Du Bois's period demographies.[28] Additionally, the work of the Black Public Sphere Collective has been signal in articulating the exclusionary arrangements of dominant national spaces and the ways political discourse constitutes such spaces. Thadious Davis and Houston Baker, for example, exactingly look at constructions of black civic geographies as interactive sites of contestation and as sites of ongoing struggle.[29]

This all bears on ways to read Hopkins's nineteenth-century mobilization of a black public sphere, since Contending Forces presents place as a kind of intra-discursive enactment. First, the novel stages representational spaces where different trial civics can come together. Included among such spaces are the boardinghouse, which hosts discussions and musical evenings, and the black church, discussed below. Both places are platforms for a debate-centered public sphere. But I would argue, too, that Contending Forces aggregates and then reworks the components from another literary model of black public sphere, one presented earlier in Harper's multifaceted novel of black recognition, Iola Leroy.

Hopkins includes in Contending Forces key elements of civic design from Harper and readjusts them for a different geography. For example, nation in Iola Leroy is constructed in two discursive arenas. The first is based in black folk culture and built by rural, Southern blacks who have passed through the crucible of slavery. They participate in a national consciousness through civic exercises like legal marriage, property management, cottage industries, and, in general, the activities of everyday life that call upon former slaves to exercise their quasi-legal identities. They also provide the folk discourse of nation in their prayer services and rituals. The second arena for national participation is depicted through the activities of the black bourgeois, those with formal (and mostly Northern) educations and inclined toward professional achievement. This group enacts citizenship through participation in structured debate and national conventions. They are responsible for narrating the renewed nation. They restructure the terms of official political discourses and rhetoric as they go on to establish educational facilities. Harper's vision of reconstructive nationalism brings together these two clearly stratified groups, forging them together into a sort of vertical community through common commitments to family, education, and public service—all grounded in a common black religious mission. Nation is built on recognizing political commitments, which in *Iola Leroy* include women's rights, service to the poor and those injured in war, and promoting self-help through church building and mutual-aid societies. Readers of *Contending Forces* will recognize the irrepressible postplantation wits at work, the emphasis on legal marriage for freed peoples, the cottage industries, the transcribed speeches on uplift, and multiple school-founding plotlines in the novel.

The main difference is that Hopkins blends the separate spheres together to effect a less class-centered black demos. As she observes in *Contending Forces*, "among the white Americans who perform domestic or personal service, how rare it is to meet the brilliant genius of a Frederick Douglass; but with this people it is a common occurrence."[30] And later describing a Boston race symposium about black Southern disenfranchisement and federal complacency, she writes: "They came from towns remote, from the farm, from domestic service in the homes of wealth and from among the lowly ones who earn a scanty living with scrubbing-brush and pail. Doctor, lawyer, politician, mechanic—every class sent its representatives."[31] Debate is not the property of the educated classes alone, nor are the conditions for viable civic organization.

Far from exhibiting the spatial/organizational forms of a nineteenth-century European bourgeois public, late-century, black civic geographies are intertwined with "private life" through the communal home. That is, the major players in Boston's black public sphere all share a residence. So instantly, a fundamental distinction between public and private that Habermas insisted upon does not adhere in Hopkins's black Boston. This is the "strict separation of the public from the private realm in such a way that the public sphere, made up of private people gathered together as a public and articulating the needs of society with the state, was itself considered part of the private realm."[32] In Boston and other eastern seaboard cities like New York and Philadelphia, workers in the late nineteenth century oftentimes lived together. The public to private spatial politics is different, the class-based diversity is greater, and workers' experiences are included. There is more vertical depth. In effect, the house itself draws together the different spheres of Harper's civic architecture and aligns them into a floor plan of civic organization, all under one roof.

First, stationed in the basement of the house are the colorful and seamlessly integrated cottage-industry components of black civic life.

Throughout the entire text, they constitute a vibrant undercurrent that stitches together characters and storylines. From the basement, they give the house its sense of foundation and its roots. They are Mrs. Ophelia Davis and Mrs. Sarah Ann White, long-standing friends from Louisiana who together journeyed North after the Civil War.[33] They establish a laundry business out of the Smith boardinghouse, and the business flourishes: "They became the style; and no young bride on the Back Bay felt that she was complete unless 'The First-class New Orleans Laundry' placed the finishing polish on the dainty lingerie of her wedding finery."[34] Davis and White also represent the creative-labor component of local experience, similar to what Houston Baker referred to as "women's expressive production" (inclusive of "handicraft, blues, culinary originality, quilting, expertise, dynamic conjuring, brilliant oratory, superior storytelling, and belles letters").[35] These are the same sustaining arts that Hopkins returns to later in the novel, as she elaborates the potential of a coalitional civic society through the women's sewing circle.[36]

Not all experiences are amenable to Hopkins's deliberative public, even if they do represent black bourgeois achievement. For instance, the house also attracts black professionals of the immigrant generation like John Langley, the jilted fiancé of Dora Smith. Langley enters the fiction as an amoral lawyer. An orphaned youth from North Carolina seeking his fortune in the North, he is described derisively by Hopkins as "a descendant of slaves and Southern 'crackers,'" something she claims is "a bad-mixture."[37] Unlike the laundry owners, Langley represents a model of success that is mercenary and does not promote black community. In his offices in the business district of the city, he prefers not to hire blacks but rather employs a white stenographer and a white office boy. He participates in the culture-forming aspects of the house. He is always there at "musical evenings or reception nights," instituted by the Smiths.[38] But what he achieves through his positioning in the house he undoes in his position outside it. That is, his villainy on one level of the romance's surface is produced by his unwillingness on another level to help other African Americans through labor.

In this schema of local cross-development, Mrs. Smith is consistently placed in the parlor. She is the receiving element from a family installed in Boston since the federal period. Yet, as the novel details, their roots are in creolized race genealogies produced by colonialism, migration, and the Atlantic slave trade. Their first Boston ancestor, readers learn, was Jesse Montfort, the Bermuda-born son of a wealthy white plantation owner and his Creole wife, whose own race is left ambiguous. In the opening pages of the novel, the Montforts are reported to have voyaged to North Carolina to outrun emancipation in the British colonies, supposedly entertaining the idea of a more eventual manumission in the Southern slave states. Hopkins suspends these connections between the present-day house dwellers and the Montfort clan until the end of the novel. However, what the Smiths share with the postbellum migrants can be traced to this Jesse Montfort: It is a symbolic heritage of connecting through relocation, the search for future promise in a place, and the drive toward building intentional communities in what Hopkins shows to be the outlines of historical space. These fortify the civic geography of *Contending Forces* as something more than just postslavery life.[39] Effectively, Hopkins places Will Smith at the highest point of the house of incorporation: "Will declared himself in favor of an attic chamber."[40] Will represents the would-be "head" of a deliberative public in Hopkins's civic geography. He represents the potential of a black bourgeois leadership, which brings international horizons (shaped in Boston and Heidelberg) to local life.[41]

The house mediates wider national citizenship on one level, and on another, it is itself a node of civic life. It encases a multiplicity of histories by the ways it frames, and outwardly gathers different stories. What is interesting, too, at least formally, is that by the time Hopkins gets to developing a kind of intra-textual, oratorical model of public sphere, which she does in the debate chapters in the middle of the novel, readers have already encountered a fleshed-out embodiment of a prospective community: The Smith boardinghouse is that already present culture-forming public sphere. Any discursive public-sphere models presented in the debate chapters must at least account for this community. It is a notable orchestration, which prefigures other civics to be unpacked in the narrative.

Defamiliarizing Landscape: Street Magic

Having established the centrality of the boardinghouse to Boston's black migrant populations, Hopkins uses the arrival of Sappho Clark in the South End to quite suddenly accelerate the plot—and flex the expressions of a local place aesthetics. Sappho is an audience for the civic unfolding of black Boston. As a character, she functions as a kind of regionalist device. She is the cosmopolitan stranger, a narrative figure brought in from the outside, usually representative of modernity. Like the stranger in regionalism, her known ties to some other main vein are obscured to foreground the new, vital world into which she is placed. What readers do gather up front is that Sappho is a glamorous but bereft New Orleans Creole woman. She is described as mixed-race, fair, and a stenographer by trade, newly arrived in Boston in 1896. Yet, as a stranger, she can absorb scenes of the local, and she can acquaint herself with local permuations. In the narrative, she works out to be a conduit of everyday life since her own unveiling comes through her immersion in the novel's locale of action.

It is also through Sappho that Hopkins makes Boston a site for defamiliarization. As a lens through which Hopkins can show the distinctiveness of black Boston, Sappho makes strange the setting. Throughout much of *Contending Forces*, the third-person narrator doubles as a tour guide, a *periegetes* (from the Greek for "guide"), connecting people to place. "Piloted by Dora," Hopkins writes, "Sappho became well acquainted with ancient landmarks of peculiar interest to the colored people."[42] Depicting local life through the eyes of this new character, she invites the reader on a virtual insider's tour off the well-inscribed, beaten path into what she calls Boston's "Negro Quarter." Here she points to landmarks like the Underground Railroad station that was the Lewis and Harriet Hayden house and relays stories about an older generation of black citizens, settled in their tiny Beacon Hill homes.[43] These are caulked, cracked, and tightly quartered wooden homes, and they are structures literally poised to be destroyed and overbuilt.[44] But their presence in the fiction signals both a collective and contingent sense of landscape.

Hopkins was attracted by fiction's capacity to capture and preserve places as they appeared in time. As she stated in the preface of *Contending Forces*, "fiction is of great value to any people as a preserver of manners and customs—religious, political and social. It is a record of growth and development from generation to generation."[45] Yet, in depicting the local, she was not interested in treating it as a time loop, a space of slower momentum or a tucked-away spatialization. Rather, *Contending Forces* is continuously attentive to movement. It records tides of migration, forms of community revision, and the lives of blacks caught up in a living history.

In a way that is similar to Alice Dunbar-Nelson's detours into Creole homes and "old world" shops in her New Orleans–based short fiction, Hopkins brings readers into the texture of black Beacon Hill. But this is not a case of regionalism as realism. Magic is interwoven into the tapestry of the city. It is an ungovernable mode of knowing that kinetically gets into the fabric of a place and its citizens. It is part of a place's distinctiveness, its particular mixture. And it permeates the lives of oldest residents most thickly.

Seen through the jumble of black back streets on the north slope of Beacon Hill and black churches and clubs in the West End, the novel illustrates the ways longtime residents such as the aged Dr. Abraham Peters constantly reinvent themselves vis-à-vis magic. Like the Uncle Julius character in Chesnutt's Conjure Woman stories, Peters represents black folk life with its seeming eccentricities that are actually deterritorializing sorts of know-how. Peters is a former slave who operates at the edge of different systems, living on the make. He is also a West Ender of many trades who has learned how to capitalize on the superstitions of both blacks and whites. He claims that when he was a slave, he was known as possessing an "evil eye." However, after moving North and becoming involved with the Christian Scientists, the New England–based faith-healing movement headquartered in Boston, he became "jestified an' concentrated so that I got the blessin'." Through changing location, he thus rechannels his magic. His is a topos of flow—not of removals, but of reinvention. Thus, he finds a way to profit from his discovered gift of the healing touch and, "knowing something of medicine and nursing the sick, had advertised himself as a magnetic physician."[46] As a survivor of different regimes, Peters symbolizes place as accretion and place as merger. He fuses his two great interests, scientific research and Christianity, into his current affiliations. He is a janitor at the Tremont Temple Baptist Church in the West End and a healing artist, who also keeps a small bootblack stand around the corner from the church. This is his second office.

Another character residing on the hill makes new territories for the imagination by revealing obscured connections within the everyday through the economies of magic. She is the mysterious, turbaned Madam Frances, a professional fortuneteller who is said to unveil real-life destinies in her hired-out ten-foot wooden building. Magic is her site story, and its schematic possibilities are found in the often-hidden, postslavery circuitry of black Boston. (This is something that Hopkins later illustrates to be bound up in the syncretic, open nature of black churches.) A window into her home, past her parlor with its captive parrot and future-summoning crystal compass, reveals a secret back room. It is here that she houses an orphaned New Orleans child, her great nephew Alphonse.[47] Frances, like Peters and every other significant character in this novel, is connected to the South by blood ties, as is her young charge. Her magic is her main device, and it brings people together in surprising ways. In one scene, for example, her magic connects her civically to the West End African Methodist Episcopal Church, where she is presumably a member. Readers are notified that "Madam Frances, spiritualistic soothsayer and marvelous mind-reader, had offered her services" to their fund-raising fair.[48] This is significant because even magic and mind reading can be molded into black ecclesiological incorporation.

Frances and Peters belong to a generation of blacks who have mostly died out. In fact, they prove to be the last black generation of this place—the holdouts—recorded here in the turn-of-the-century black novel. At the time Contending Forces was published, black residences of Beacon Hill were being quickly overwritten by new demands for community spaces, especially from a growing population of Jewish migrants from Poland and Russia in the last decade of the century. Smaller buildings on the North Slope (as opposed to the south side of Beacon Hill) were torn down rapidly, starting around 1899, to be replaced by larger, more uniform buildings. Contending Forces records this history. Writing at a time when she likely felt the black influence on the North Slope diminishing, Hopkins inscribed the area into her novel as a way to ensure black place history was not forgotten due to residential shifts.[49] The dwellings and offices of Peters and Frances compose the spaces of daily life in the same fashion that their lifelines shape the form of the story. They are figures who localize space by simply using it; their modes of performance are their ongoing labor. Notably, too, they are not summoned to Hopkins's debate forums or the staged national conventions at the middle of her novel because they enact citizenship on less codifiable registers. But their presences speak to a place specificity that at the same time is a gathering of migrational threads and spatial routes. And their constellated knowledges are valuable as the creative expression of black practice geographies.

Churches of Circuitry

Beyond the boardinghouse, which brings native and migrant popula-tions together, lies Hopkins's second, and probably most important, scale of connection. As Beacon Hill's narrow cobblestone streets reveal, the most significant throughlines for connectivity within black Boston are Afro-Protestant churches. The churches interlink the local commu-nity spatially and temporally; they concentrate site-based memories. More specifically, they connect black Boston's antebellum generation to Hopkins's own at the end of the century. In *Contending Forces* these local churches legitimate African Americans in both private and community pursuits in ways denied to them by the broader national culture. Bos-ton's black churches are scales of association. They integrate Beacon Hill into the lives of blacks living in the South End. They are also sites on the Underground Railroad, connecting blacks in the Northeast to those escaping slavery. One clear example of this latter connection is the net-work that is the church on X Street, the fictional corollary of what was Boston's Tremont Temple Baptist Church at Charles Street. In the novel, Hopkins uses the actual edifice of the church as a ground of projection for black Boston's franchise on a usable past—and a sustainable future.

Black churches are first cast as open systems. They are cultural and religious embroideries, embodying heterogeneity across time. The X Street church, she informs the reader, was physically founded on the structure of an old white church, the Third Baptist Church of Boston, later known as the Charles Street Baptist Church. In the mid-1830s the white church's segregationist tradition was challenged by local black and white abolitionists, most famously the white parishioner Timothy Gilbert, who was expelled after breaking rank with the pew assign-ments. The Tremont Temple Baptist Church came into being after black parishioners, required to sit in separate galleries, withdrew from the racist white Baptist congregation. With limited finances and no money for a new church building, the congregants initially relocated to an old theatre. But following black emancipation, their numbers grew rapidly, with many black recruits from the postwar South joining the church. The original white church with its depleted congregation became insolvent, and its building was put up for sale after the Civil War. Ultimately, the reconstituted black church community went on to purchase the building from the white proprietors in 1876, renaming it the Charles Street African Methodist Episcopal Church. Hopkins writes: "Thus the despised people, who were not allowed a seat outside of the galleries, now owned and occupied the scene of their former humiliation. It was a solemn and wonderful dispensation of Providence."[50] Tremont Temple is today considered to be the first integrated church in America.[51] Like the boarding-house, its success is in no small part due to the emancipation generation, whose settlement in Boston helped sustain the congregation. Such a structure as the Tremont Temple is a network for histories; it is a space of negotiated territory.

Hopkins also shapes into her story line two other churches in the West End, significant for their direct and organized work on behalf of black freedom. Again, these structures form a bridge between black Northern sympathies and blacks in the South. One church she discusses is today considered the oldest black church in the country: "On the J. Street side the old St. Paul's Baptist Church is situated. This historic old building was the first church the colored people owned in Massachusetts."[52] The church was built with black labor and black community money. Even the building's materials and workmanship attest to a community's collective willpower and hard work. As the novel claims: "Twenty years ago an old Negress—a centenarian—was living who had herself picked up bricks in the streets of Boston in the early morning, and carried them to the spot where the building was being erected. She did this because although too poor to give money toward furthering the enterprise, she felt that she must contribute in some way to the erection of this first colored house of worship in this part of the country."[53]

St. Paul's also proved to be an important site for defining intellectual resistance to slavery in antebellum national history. In this capacity, it became known as the Abolitionist Church: "St. Paul's Church became the sacred edifice where the desire for freedom was fostered in the heart of the Negro."[54] At St. Paul's, William Lloyd Garrison founded the offices of the New England Anti-Slavery Society in 1832, something which could not have been done without the organization of black churchgoers. Later the former indentured servant Maria W. Stewart would make history at the church as the first African American woman recorded as speaking before a mixed "promiscuous" audience of men and women on a political topic.[55] Frederick Douglass, Harriet Tubman, and Sojourner Truth—along with those whom Hopkins called "the white champions" of the antislavery cause, supporters like Charles Sumner and Wendell Phillips—

used the Meeting House to deliver speeches against antebellum chattel slavery. Transcribed, their rhetoric constitutes some of the most powerful vindications of human rights and social justice over politically unifying expediency in the nineteenth century. In 1898, just prior to the publication of *Contending Forces*, the church's congregation moved to lower Roxbury. Churches are mobile, but building sites are not. St. Paul's as an edifice remained on Beacon Hill, a testament to a history Hopkins wanted to record. It is best known today as the African Meeting House, and its current address is 8 Smith Street, on Beacon Hill.

Last, another church represents scales of affective belonging for those in transit, seeking a home. Metonymically, it reads as a place of patronage for wayfarers and those who go on journeys. On the North Slope "near the head of G. and P. Streets" was the sister church to the Abolitionist Church—the Twelfth Baptist Church, an offshoot of St. Paul's. Hopkins describes it as "world renowned under its beloved pastor and founder, Leonard Grimes."[56] This church was yet another geographical hallmark of the black South in the North. Grimes was a figure who bridged the divide between North and South. Like Martin Delany, he was born free in Virginia. In 1840 he was sentenced to hard labor at the Virginia Penitentiary for driving a slave woman, Patty, and her six children to freedom in Washington, D.C.[57] But after the internment, his labor for freedom was not done. Working his way North, he became pastor of the Boston church, where he continued to support the Underground Railroad. Grimes is famous for using his church office to aid escaped slaves, providing them with lodging and food, and helping ensure their travel to freedom. The church's activities became more prominent after the 1850 passage of the Fugitive Slave Law. Church collections and savings were used to finance slaves' passages to Canada or, when this could not be achieved, pay ransom.[58] The church was known among local blacks and beyond as the Fugitive Church, a sort of counterpart to the Abolitionist Church. Over a century later, after its congregation left Beacon Hill for lower Roxbury in 1958, it was home to the young Martin Luther King Jr., while a theology student at Boston University, and also to his future wife, Coretta Scott.

This historical walking tour of local churches, on the one hand, reads as a celebration of black Boston's history. It is an occasion for Hopkins to uncover the footprints of African American enterprise and attachments in Boston through its architectural traces. As Hazel Carby states in her classic *Reconstructing Womanhood*, Hopkins aimed to re-awaken the "political agitation and resistance of the early anti-slavery movement."[59] But in another sense, what the author develops is a type of counter-landscape, a story of place not quite coterminous with more widely disseminated, representative, late-century histories of Massachusetts. Hopkins does this by turning out a series of settings that celebrate Boston's revolutionary routes, but not those fortified in the struggle for national independence during the War for American Independence. Instead, she looks back to a more recent antebellum generation.[60] Steering her revision, she writes: "The history of Massachusetts is forever linked with that of the Anti-slavery Movement, and the Anti-slavery Movement is entwined about the familiar street-corners of the old West End."[61] This is the history she geographically reconstructs, and then connects to place indexes. So rather than indicating civic genealogies of Anglo-Massachusetts history making such as the Old State House, where citizens gathered in 1776 to hear the Declaration of Independence read from the balcony (scripted dissent as incorporation), or enlisting Paul Revere's modest downtown home (grassroots intervention) or Boston's most celebrated church—the Old North Church, used to signal the British march to Lexington—she locates a radical, revolutionary history in the early nineteenth-century geographical signages of black Boston.

Beyond connecting the lives of South End blacks to Beacon Hill, Hopkins builds a geographical history with staunch connectivity to her contemporary readership.[62] The churches serve as sustaining black cultural institutions. They were primary sites for enacting citizenship, exercised politically and economically. African Americans without formal incorporation in the United States—denied access to equal schools, employment, and, in the case of women (like their white counterparts), denied national enfranchisement through the ballot—were able to exercise civic identities through the offices of the church. The relatively horizontal leadership structures of the black Baptist and African Methodist Episcopal churches also promoted ready access to positions of leadership for lay persons. Cornel West has argued that "the primary political appeal of the Methodists and especially Baptists for blacks was their church polity and organizational form, free from hierarchical control, open and easy access to leadership roles, and relatively loose, uncomplicated requirements for church membership."[63] This is evidenced—or, at any rate, enacted—in *Contending Forces*. Although Du Bois is credited in most African American histories with having produced the earliest sociological study of the black church as an anthropological institution in *The Souls of Black Folk* (1903), three years earlier Hopkins inscribed it in a variety of forms into her fiction as the first social institution for African Americans in the United States.

Lastly, the West End churches function as cultural signposts for geographic flow, for what Hopkins depicted as a community in transition. This transition was reflected in black Boston's boardinghouses, migrant population, and intercity residential shifts. It thus becomes the challenge of the local community to make its buildings and shared spaces relevant for a twentieth-century future. As *Contending Forces* demonstrates, physical places index culture; they gather times. Accordingly, the churches prove most meaningful not as repositories of the glorious past, but as wellsprings for civic transformation. As a setting, the Tremont Temple on X Street, whose antebellum role Hopkins commemorated, is always under pressure to keep itself relevant to the lives of contemporary African Americans. Finances for maintaining this church in a central area of a populous metropolitan space were never extraneous to its pieced-together self-definition. Actually, this is presented as the ongoing work of Tremont's supporters: to constantly find ways to shape the space in relation to the needs of its people. In Hopkins's fiction, current events are shown to thrust the church into action in present time—a half-century after the formative beginning of the abolitionist movement.

Puritan Hagiographies and Politically Representative Models

At the midway point of *Contending Forces*, black churches, already presented as enfranchised organizational units, are transformed into key players in a counter-civic society. The transformation comes in the wake of a rash of unpunished Southern lynchings, loosely exonerated in newspaper dispatches as "the justice of the populace" or "salutary lessons for the Negro."[64] Such news electrifies black Boston into a politically charged arena. It galvanizes the congregants of the X Street Church into arranging a national emergency symposium of the American Colored League, a fictional organization based on T. Thomas Fortune's late nineteenth-century Afro-American League.[65] This special meeting inaugurates a second and very different staging of public sphere. It actually has little to do with people being drawn together as extensions of their capital- or labor-driven interests, for example, people gathering together became they live together for the purpose of work as they do in the Smith boardinghouse. This public sphere is expressly for the purpose of debate, and to this end, it nets widely across class and town lines throughout New England. In terms of illustrating a practice geography, an arena of presence-based interaction mediated by participant interests, a couple things take place in the outlines of this civic forum. First, Boston is made to stand for black New England, much like William Dean Howells in his "American Authorship" retrospective of 1871 claimed Boston did for literary New England. Indeed, for all the issues of representation and delegacy raised in the debate chapters, there is never any debate that this major forum will take place anywhere but Boston. Boston is the assumed nucleus.

Another point about the civic architecture of this particular deliberative public sphere is that it gains its magnitude as a civic geography through the same black ecclesiological structures that line Boston's streets. The church setting gives the debate forum its outward form and platform; and the forum, in turn, enlarges the functions of the church. So rather than incorporate religious sympathies and objectives into the aims of the nation-state, Hopkins politicizes the church. She turns it into a central setting for African American political organization. The process notably recalls what Sacvan Bercovitch identifies in *The Puritan Origins of the American Self* as the work of federal hagiography, the print-driven work of figuration. Such literary/print processes do the work of making, or "ensigning," individuals as not just figures of a community, but leaders by writ of textual placement. For Bercovitch this organizational "inversion" was exemplified in the work of Cotton Mather at the beginning of the eighteenth century.[66] In some thirteen chapters on governors, magistrates, and appointments in New England in volume 2 of *Magnalia Christi Americana* and "The Lives of Sixty Famous Divines, by whose ministry the Churches of New-England have been planted and continued," in volume 3, Mather laboriously built up the lives of Puritan founders.[67] Combined in print, they became what could be fittingly called a conglomerate, or a kind of emblematic backstory of America's heroic leadership. Church history, the record of synods, the bylaws of Harvard University, and the rolls of its graduating classes were thus materialized via print into a kind of mobile story of New World history. In a much livelier, and no less fictitious way, a parallel pattern of interaction is evoked by Hopkins.

Although obviously working through different conventions and through a later periodicity, Hopkins takes up a similar expanse of time as Mather (approximately half a century) and folds nation into a black Protestant, ecclesiological church structure. Describing the church on X Street's environment, she elaborates the ways it adapts the vestiges of nation. Its platform is "heavily draped in American flags, supplemented by wide bands of mourning. Pictures of the antislavery apostles peered out at the audience from the folds of the national colors. Speakers and representative citizens were seated upon the platform, and visiting delegates occupied seats in close proximity."[68] In *Contending Forces*, the legacy of abolitionist forerunners is mobilized as religious display, signifying yet again that in Hopkins's model of a counter-civil society, a division or disassociation between black intellectual and spiritual-religious lives is artificial. Instead, political and religious leaders alike are made corporate—made into a body that exceeds individuals' positionality—by what Hopkins shows to be their explicit record of commitments. It is a record reflected in her commentary on the walking tour, a record made by the ways congregants and pastors alike support policies applicable to their community, and by the stories that are handed down about bringing the disenfranchised into civic-support networks.

Church organization in Boston's black community thus provides a means for blacks to claim structural civic authority—as a premise for legal authority—over their own lives. This is an important point in the authors's construction of a Massachusetts-based participatory democracy for post-Reconstruction African Americans. Separation of church and state, made maxim in modern republicanism, is not then demarcated in the practice of religion.[69] Further, it is not demarcated in civic geographies, the claims to space and representation that Hopkins makes for black political action. For black Boston's political organizations, times of crisis are times of closing ranks. Nor is the church sharply separated from the functions of the state. In fact, it is attached to the workings (real and projected) of a black counter-state in a way that seemingly undermines any sharp separation between state and civil society. According to the feminist critique of Nancy Fraser, this kind of separation in modern societies would promote weak publics, anyway. In a weak public, deliberation basically amounts to opinion forming but not actual decision making. Writes Fraser, "Any conception of the public sphere that requires a sharp separation between civil society and the state will be unable to manage forms of self-management, interpublic coordination and political accountability that are essential to democratic society."[70]

Writing at the end of the nineteenth century, Hopkins, too, seems to have recognized that such divides for a people already outside the official discourse would be like debates in front of a locked door. They would just be more barriers to entry—deliberative closures—especially for a disenfranchised group seeking both representation and redress. Fraser's points about an alternate public sphere speak to the late-century situation in black Boston, where African Americans sought statist agency, among other reasons, in order to gain meaningful opportunities within the economy, and for protection of property. (This might be categorized by Fraser as a form of "redistribution.")[71] Evelyn Brooks Higginbotham's work makes a clear case that in an era (1880–1920) marked by the most intensive segregation in the Northeast, the black Baptist church was a deliberative space that both opposed and mediated the dominant white society:. She writes, "More effectively than any other institution the church stood between individual blacks, on the one hand, and the state with its racially alienating institutions, on the other."[72]

As Hopkins demonstrated, black churches were routes to public life for African Americans. The values attached to the Tremont Temple, St. Paul's African Meeting House, and Twelfth Baptist Church are forms of support extended specifically to those not protected by law. The national emergency meeting, called to order from within the church building, to a significant extent actually anticipates the civil rights movement of a half-century later. For one thing, the Afro-American League was best known as the precursor of the Niagara Movement and the National Association for the Advancement of Colored People (NAACP). In addition, the black church also proved to be a rallying point for the redress of basic African American rights. In the 1955 campaigns, Montgomery's Dexter Avenue Baptist Church (pastored by the twenty-six-year-old Martin Luther King Jr.) was at once the spiritual and political epicenter for the national call for change, just like the same Fugitive Church to which King belonged in Boston helped structure and support black abolitionism.

The X Street meeting yields insight into the black church apparatus, but it proves even further significant for the way it illustrates connection between the church as a structure, the church as a corpus, and the architectures of civic activism. Fiction was one way for Hopkins to make salient the various forms of convergence and to bring shape and location to ideas, with the aim of directing character and plot to some formative conclusion. Hopkins exercises these possibilities in Contending Forces. The Tremont meeting is a forum for one of the most compelling questions presented in the novel. It deals with the intersection of national life and regional, civic life. Hopkins asks: How can blacks in Boston best define their own culture? How do they add to a national culture?

Booker T. Washington, W. E. B. Du Bois, and
the Colored League: Politics of Place

Questions about local needs and civic consciousness are initially broached through recasting two very contrasting visions for post-Reconstruction free black communities. One such plan can be attributed to Booker T. Washington, Hopkins's colleague and archrival at the Colored American. The other, more subtly, reflects the contemporary thinking of W. E. B. Du Bois, a figure thinly veiled in Contending Forces as Will Smith, the son of the boardinghouse owner, Mrs. Smith. Referencing the thinking of both groups, Hopkins chooses the most viable script for Boston's local black community at the opening of the new century. It is a battle of rhetoric, and one figure is depicted as coming away with the clear advantage.

The Washington proxy is fitted to the plot in the figure of Dr. Arthur Lewis, the Boston-born founder of a large industrial education school in Louisiana and the man whom boardinghouse keeper Dora Smith eventually marries at the end of the novel (after rebuffing her local lawyer fiancé, John Langley). The marriage between Lewis and Smith is also a marriage of minds because unlike several other key women in the text, including Sappho Clark, Dora is content to reside outside the political public sphere. Eschewing women's involvement in politics, she maintains that economic development must precede the franchise, quoting the phrase "if you want honey, you must have money."[73] Her views are noteworthy because they are prerequisites for the kind of thinking fostered by the Lewis-Washington camp, which asked its constituents to reject politics—at least for the time being. The Washington figure, Arthur Lewis, who takes the stage before Will Smith, claims that "politics is the bane of the Negro's existence" and that it is "better and wiser to tend the weeds in the garden than to water the exotic in the window. We should strive to obtain the education of the industrial school, seeking there our level, content to abide there."[74] The speech, as Hopkins depicts it, is received with general disappointment.

Hopkins viewed Booker T. Washington as a purveyor of Northern white patronage for services that would not benefit the lives of blacks in Northern cities like Boston. Rather, she used both her fiction and biographical writings to argue that Washington's most productive work could be done in the new South, specifically in Alabama at Tuskegee. In her 1901 biographical sketch of Washington, she claimed "Dr. Washington and Tuskegee are one."[75] She even transmogrified the man into place: "Tuskegee is the soul of the man outlined in wood, in brick and stone, pulsating with the life of the human hive." In *Contending Forces* the Washington figure is depicted as somebody seeking representative status in New England, but stubbornly married to a specific geographical context and situation—the African school of Industrial and Agricultural Development—his "beloved industrial and agricultural school for blacks in the South."[76] His personhood and said-honorable goals are thus mislocated. They do not serve the complexity of such a place as black Boston—a city, she points out, he visits only annually with a "quartette of singers who were also members of the school" for the purpose of fundraising.[77]

In considering Washington's position as a race leader and his sphere of influence, Hopkins negotiated the different demands of distinct regions within the national landscape. She argued:

One man's meat is another man's poison. The colored people north of Mason and Dixon's lines [*sic*] are conspicuous of their advancement along all the lines which are distinctive features in the formation of the polished exterior of the good citizens of such a republic as ours. Among the best circles of this community are found the highest types of intellectual, moral, religious and social improvement. What becomes of such a class as this when hampered by rules and laws made to fit the needs of the Black Belt? Laws of life and living which cannot be forced, ought not to be forced, upon the large class of colored citizens whom embody within themselves the highest development of American citizenship.[78]

Contending Forces thus argues for a civic model of place as a multiplicity of interactions, a product of relations. The point that Hopkins's fiction and editorial work polarized was that places were affective. They had their own contexts, generated through physical encounters and layered interactions, and could not simply fit into some prefabricated social plan. To use geographer Doreen Massey's terminology, a place is specific and cannot simply contract into a pre-formed model, developed in some other space, and presumed to fit all.[79] Hopkins also harbored certain clear objections to Washington's patronage politics.[80] She pointed to the apologist tendencies engendered by the Washington agenda, including an abandoning of the pursuits of social equality and political representation in favor of economic development. In her February 1903 *Christian Recorder* political editorial, "The Latest Phases of the Race Problem in American," she blasted "the spirit of commercialism" of William McKinley's presidency as nullifying "political ethics" and fatally undermining black elective franchise, political rights, and black appointments to civil office, like postmasters and revenue collectors.[81] She considered Washington an advocate of conciliation programs for whites, and, at the same time, the benefactor of substantial contributions from white philanthropists. Because of his influence, he was able to exercise authority as a spokesman for the broader black community in areas like labor, philanthropy, education, and social affairs. Hopkins further suggested that support for the industrial school model had become a kind of outlet for a sublimated racism in Massachusetts: "Massachusetts is noted for being willing to see fair play: she hears the complaints of the Negro, and listens with attention to the accusations of the Southern whites, weighs the one against the other, and, naturally enough, the scales tip in favor of the white brother. From one class the Negro suffers in the state and is contemptuously flouted; from another he receives the hearty word of encouragement, backed by the all-powerful dollar which goes to feed such universities as Hampton, Tuskegee, and the like."[82]

On a personal level, Hopkins viewed Booker T. Washington less kindly than she did the fictional Arthur Lewis. It was Washington who eventually took ownership of Hopkins's prized *Colored American Magazine* in 1904 and moved the company from Boston to New York. He also changed the direction of the paper from a magazine about literature and race relations in the United States to a Washington party journal, running a series on the values of vocational education. Hanna Wallinger, Hopkins's biographer, writes that the changes engendered by Washington's buy-out of the fledgling *Colored American* promptly led to the destruction of the magazine. "While the emphasis of the magazine shifted from literature to current affairs, news of fraternal orders, education and business affairs, it lost a great part of its readership. Its circulation dropped considerably."[83] Magazine sales, which had averaged from 800 to 1,500 copies in Boston dropped to around 200 a month in New York. In a letter to William Trotter, Hopkins wrote: "One cannot help a feeling of honest indignation for a man who would be a party to defraud a helpless race of an organ of free speech."[84]

By contrast, Massachusetts's own Du Bois (represented by native son, the South End's Will Smith) gains leverage in the deliberative public sphere with a more realistic plan for black northern free communities. Will's appeal clearly sinks home: "When he had finished there was not a dry eye in that vast audience."[85] Will, like Du Bois, calls for higher education opportunities for blacks and for greater representation in politics. Indeed, Will identifies the same pernicious effects of Washington's policies on turn-of-the-century African Americans that Du Bois himself cited in "Of Mr. Booker T. Washington and Others." "Mr. Washington distinctly asks that black people give up, at least for the present, three things," Du Bois wrote. "First, political power, Second, insistence on civil rights, Third, higher education of Negro youth,—and concentrate all their energies on industrial education, the accumulation of wealth, and the conciliation of the South."[86] The fictional Will Smith cites nearly the identical results of this policy as Du Bois listed in his own 1903 essay: black disenfranchisement; legalized segregation, resulting in vast civil inequalities for African Americans; and the removal of aid from institutions of higher learning for blacks. To lose, or simply give up on, civic affiliation is to let go of the most meaningful spaces of life practice. Unsheltered by white privilege, blacks cannot afford to do this. Hopkins's rechanneling of the Du Boisian position is ultimately attractive in the cityscape of *Contending Forces* because it mobilizes the local bourgeois black experience toward viable action and, at the same time, is not limned by the exigencies of the local. Put another way, Will Smith represents the possibility of meeting local needs, and the possibility for venturing beyond scales of familiarity.

Yet while Hopkins's attentiveness to the broader ramifications of local political developments gives insights into the views of a forum, there is a certain incongruence within her presentation of region. There is something rather facile about casting external localities as seedbeds of modern political corruption and target sites for exploitative race-based economics from the position of being heirs to a "remarkable history" of New England activism, a position she goes to lengths to establish. It is perhaps even more presumptuous to suggest that the choicest setting for seeking a resolution and redress of such intricate injustices that had taken root in her depiction of a general "South" will be Boston.

For her careful attention to Boston's multitiered sociological structures, there is no attempt to define any real complexity or plurality within the South. Rather, as black Boston's needs and points of leverage are accorded increasing specificity throughout the novel, her depiction of a wide South appears persistently monological. This may be attributable to several factors, including the fact that Hopkins never traveled outside the Northeast. Unlike Reconstruction authors such as Ida Wells or Frances Harper, Hopkins had no firsthand experience of life in any of the former slave states. She could not color in any of these spaces with the same degree of realism and detail that she could apply to Boston.

However, to Hopkins's credit, she devoted much of *Contending Forces* to detailing the embeddedness of the South in the Northeast landscape, from churches built by black migrants to Boston's public spaces and residences. Moreover, in light of her choice of Boston as a sort of federated black bourgeois resolution center, we should not overlook the fact that the position of blacks in Boston would be difficult to cast as somehow privileged. African Americans had to take initiative and organize wherever they could. This is actually Hopkins's point in the Colored League section. Local action had its shortcomings, but it was preferable to indecisive festering. Writing in an era marked by obviously embattled race relations in the country and the consolidation of Jim Crow practices, Hopkins sought to learn from the failures of Reconstruction as she created a local model for social commitment and democratic reorganization.

In addition, Hopkins did not fail to overlook some of the limitations most prevalent in versions of local thinking. Her greatest criticism of the "merely local" was directed toward Boston's black politicians, whose undertakings (and, for Hopkins, whose characters) embodied the smallness and lack of extension most infecting regional initiative. As she depicted it, it was in the interest of Boston's politicians to maintain quietude among local blacks and to sustain the status quo in employment.

This, of course, disadvantaged African Americans tremendously. But black politicians were susceptible to the same exclusivity. One character, the local black politician John Langley, is shown to concede when it most matters, succumbing to the partisanship and self-promotion involved in elite leadership. He agrees to defuse demand for redress in the lynching furor in exchange for the receipt of district emergency money and a bid for the city solicitor position.[87] In Hopkins's speech at the William Lloyd Garrison centennial, five years after the publication of *Contending Forces*, she excoriated the ways political alliances could be purchased in Boston, "when the price of manhood is a good dinner, a fine position, a smile of approval and a pat on the back from the man of influence, of a fat endowment."[88]

Women's Civic Society/Women's Space

Finally, the divide between economic rights and the political disenfranchisement that Hopkins highlighted in the debate at the Colored League is played out nowhere more explicitly than in the person of Sappho Clark, living within community bounds at No. 500 D Street. Her case is constructed by Hopkins to vindicate the need for black political enfranchisement as more primary and necessary than what the Washington proxy calls "the humanizing influence of the dollar, judiciously expended."[89] Her story also makes immediate the stakes of the debate: that strategies for better governance in the South are not external concerns at all but exist in reciprocal relation to the identities of New England blacks. Sappho's startling story—told by Luke Sawyer, a stately, Louisiana-born Colored League member, reflects all this. First, readers learn that Sappho's real name is Mabelle Beaubean. She was kidnapped by her white uncle and imprisoned in a Louisiana brothel. After three weeks of searching, her father, "a colored planter," found her in a house of ill repute in New Orleans. He confronts his white half-brother with his crime. But the half-brother equates his actions only with money and offers to pay $1,000 for his "damage." Appalled at this offer, Beaubean's father threatens the half-brother with such locution as this: "I leave you to carry my case into the federal courts and appeal for justice."[90] The starchy language though cues two important legal points, central to Hopkins's stance on black citizenship: First, capital alone will not produce equal treatment, since not everything can be reduced to money; in such exigencies as the Beaubeans', capital does very little. And second, an appeal to federal justice is a breach of community understanding. It is a violation of what Hopkins casts as a white, Louisiana civic code. As a result, a mob sets the home on fire, kills the family, and Mabelle alone flees the scene, reaching the Sisters of the Holy Family Catholic convent in New Orleans. There she gives birth to a child. Though presumed dead by the friends of the Beaubeans, her secret history follows her to Boston, where her young son resides with the local black fortune-teller, Madam Frances, actually a distant black aunt. Though the threadlines of this drama are certainly diffusive, the author's placement of Sappho's exposition within the debate chapters makes the political message quite explicit: The pursuit of money without representation is suicidal. It offers no protection from mob violence. In fact, black economic gains actually inspire violence.

In the Mabelle Beaubean story, the Colored League finds kindling for their calls to action: "Under such conditions as I have described, contentment, amity—call it by what name you will—is impossible; justice alone remains to us."[91] Yet in their midst, the actual character, who has found a second life in Boston as the pseudonymous Sappho Clark, escapes their attention. For dramatic effect she even faints in the Tremont Temple auditorium and is ushered out. But most of the rapt, "grief-convulsed" audience fail to recognize her, and certainly fail to connect her to the delegate's story. Ultimately, the male-dominated discourse of the Colored League does not provide the reconstituted Sappho with any real agency or promote the kind of healing she needs, healing that will be crucial to her survival as well as the future of her secret child, Alphonse.

Theirs is the space of representative public identities, where before even speaking Luke Sawyer affirms his credentials as a member of the Williamstown, Massachusetts, branch of the league: "he handed his papers to the chairman."[92] But what Sappho seeks is a space of reinvention where presence can, in effect, be embodied. As Seyla Benhabib has memorably argued, "all struggles against oppression in the modern world begin by redefining what had previously been considered private, nonpublic, and nonpolitical issues as matters of public concern, as issues of justice, as sites of power that need discursive legitimation."[93] Sappho's experiences in Boston are targeted to disrupt the incorporeal surface of civic organization. Only through a reclamation of her body can she disrupt the shell of an imposed and irrelevant civics. The novel suggests then that women must seek ownership of their stories, their claims to history, to reach a more meaningful expanse of legitimation. For black women, this is not some facile or normative project. It takes the support of other women.

What *Contending Forces* also makes vivid is that for their meetings and representative assemblies, both sides of the Washington and Du Bois debate failed to account for the potential of local women as embodied, race constituents. And to a greater degree, they failed to take women seriously as race leaders in social and economic matters. In terms of bourgeois black leadership, Hopkins uses Sappho to point up short-comings, not only in Arthur Lewis's industrial education plan, but also in Will Smith's Du Boisian position. Though Smith carries the day at the Colored League, Hopkins differed markedly with Du Bois on the concept of the elite talented tenth. Du Bois wrote at the beginning of "The Talented Tenth" that "the Negro Race, like all races, is going to be saved by its exceptional men. . . . The talented tenth rises and pulls all that are worth saving up to their vantage ground."[94] This was clearly different from Hopkins's vision of black advancement, which she would go on to present as a Boston case study in the work of women's organiza-tions. She did not enlist Du Bois's maxim of "reaching back to uplift our less fortunate brethren" as a model for working in a local community. Perhaps Hopkins found such thinking too condescending. It was also overtly black male-centered and tended to marginalize women's involve-ment in the political sphere. Instead, what *Contending Forces* suggests at the end is that the foundation for a black participatory democracy could be developed through a more extensive modeling of publics, a vision influenced particularly by women's civic geographies.

Although Hopkins largely supported Du Bois, he did not adequately account for the work of women in the project of defining community direction and models of exchange. Du Bois repeatedly failed to credit women in both his social activism and his writing—women like Anna Julia Cooper, whose direct quotes he credited to himself in *Darkwater: Voices from within the Veil*, his essay collection about his personal history of activism on race, class, and economic issues in contemporary America.[95] He also made no mention of women like Ida B. Wells, whose work he drew on extensively to build his own antilynching campaign. In an 1898 essay Hopkins likely knew well, "The Study of the Negro Problems," he wrote that "these problems that we are . . . facing . . . will survive to curse the nation unless we grapple with them manfully and intelligently."[96] In her *Colored American Magazine* series, "Famous Women of the Negro Race," she identified a late-century attitude of black men toward women's involvement in politics: "We know that it is not 'popular' for a woman to speak or write in plain terms against political brutalities, that a woman should confine her efforts to woman's work in the home and church."[97] Nonetheless, she advised contemporary black women to think beyond these prescriptions: "The colored woman must have an intimate knowledge of every question that agitates the councils of the world; she must understand the solution of problems that involve the alteration of the boundaries of countries, and which make and unmake governments."[98]

It is fitting, then, that the final model of public sphere to emerge in *Contending Forces* is a women's public sphere. The novel casts a woman as the most active and powerful race leader in Boston. Her name is Mrs. Willis, and she is described as "the brilliant widow of a bright Negro politician," and the force behind his success.[99] In Hopkins's women's-era circle, Willis would have been a fictional proxy for Josephine St. Pierre Ruffin, a prominent Boston-based community worker and reformer, who devoted her work to reforming Jim Crow and advancing the case for women's suffrage.[100] And whereas Ruffin's New Era Club meetings were held at the Meeting House on 103 Charles Street (a home today preserved at that address), Hopkins moved them into the parlor of Mrs. Smith's boardinghouse. The boardinghouse, in fact, comes full circle. In her first novelistic appearance, Willis is seen managing the crowded parlor at the boardinghouse, where she has convened a fund-raising committee for the Tremont Temple annual church fair: "In her hands committees were as wax."[101] In business matters she is shrewd and uncompromising.[102]

Willis's modeling of a political space for women, in combination with the organizational presence of the African American women's club, lends notable contrast to the ways local identities and needs are constructed at the Colored League. Both organizations are inclusive to the extent they draw in members from all economic classes of society. However, what most delineates the women's club is that it provides a space where women are encouraged to assess their own subjectivity, their gendered identities within local life. And "local" goes some distance here.

It means a projectable range of human extension. It also means an angle on embodied attachments. It is a generative frame for people to talk about the ways they are received by the world.

Feminist scholars beginning with Adrienne Rich have used the term "politics of location" to describe not so much a place as a form of embodiment, an articulation of identity, and conditions for achieving critical agency as standpoints or locations. More recently, Aimee Carrillo Rowe has argued that "the sites of our belonging constitute how we see the world, what we value, who we are (becoming). The meaning of self is never individual, but a shifting set of relations that we move in and out of, often without reflection."[103] Rowe's points speak to the relational nature of self and the ways sites, or points of location, are composed of personal relations. And as Hopkins's portrayal of women's space shows, even the imagined and depersonalized public self is encompassed by geography. Indeed, in their larger project of reclaiming the local as a space of complexity and interconnectedness (as opposed to mere settledness), feminist geographers have insisted on the value of particularized and situated approaches to space, over macrodescriptions and geographical conventions of spatial fixity and invariable process. Geographers such as Gillian Rose and Susan Bordo have argued for a greater recognition of the inherently contradictory and fractious experiences that constitute place, as well as the contingency of various totalizing claims that give way to ideas of a standard forms in geography.[104]

What is particularly interesting about Contending Forces is that Hopkins presents debate forums and public sphere organization as the contingent activity of black everyday life. Everyday life is what constitutes the practice geographies of the novel—not some specific kind of offsetting into deliberative chambers. As Michael Warner has shown, "the ability to abstract oneself in public discussion has always been an unequally available resource. . . . The bourgeois public sphere has been structured from the outset by a logic of abstraction that provides a privilege for unmarked identities: the male, the white, the middle class, the normal."[105] Like the ecclesiological structures Hopkins builds into Contending Forces, what matters is the work of connectivity. And whatever geographies most flexibly compile this connectivity are the most likely to expand the cultural store of meaningful life movements.

As such, women's clubs are structured in the novel as engagement-based deliberative spheres. Participants consider "the events of interest to the Negro race which had transpired during the week throughout the country. These facts had previously been tabulated upon a blackboard which was placed upon an easel, and occupied a conspicuous position in the room. Each one was supposed to contribute anything of interest that she had read or heard in that time for the benefit of all."[106] Such representations of a blended rhetorical and ideographic kind of literacy, of course, speak to the collective nature of late-century literacy practices.[107] Beginning in the middle of the nineteenth century, women's clubs grew in popularity throughout the United States as a way for women to educate themselves, particularly in an era when women's opportunities in higher education remained generally limited.[108] The clubs were often structured around curriculums which emphasized the study of subjects like history or literature. In addition, they were important forums where women could deliver speeches and essays on social issues. Most women's clubs also shared a strong emphasis on voluntary community service, combining a desire for self-improvement with civic improvement.

But most centrally, it is through such literacies of location, through deliberating history and current political developments that Hopkins envisioned the workings of a counter-civic society. It could not be something based on self-abstraction, what Michael Warner terms the "principle of negativity" within notions of the bourgeois public sphere. Rather, it had to be built out of human connections. And it took form through interactions attached to use values, housing, education, and access to public utilities.[109] Indeed, the women's club meeting in Contending Forces is a site where raced, gendered, and classed women can assemble to interrogate the ways race has been constructed in their own local experiences. The women find a politics of location against prescriptions of self-abstraction. It is these rematerialized identities that they bring to their occupations and their church assemblies. Their major achievement is rebuilding conventions of community identity.

Hopkins depicts the Boston women as rejecting the most common axioms for the mixed-race female body as sites embodying white terror over interracialism and policed sanctimoniousness about racial purity. But even more pressing to the club women is the need to reject the rhetoric of local black leaders that exalts the pure Negro above the mulatto. One character in Contending Forces—Anna Stevens, "a school teacher of a very studious temperament"—recalls a noonday lecture at Tremont Temple in which the speaker suddenly cried: "Lo, the poor mulatto! Despised by the blacks of his own race, scorned by the whites! Let him go and hang himself!"[110] To this Mrs. Willis responds: "I would not worry about the fate of the mulatto, for the fate of the mulatto will be the fate of the entire race." Instead, the women approach race mixture as a local issue—not as something made in a Southern "back there," on the former plantation lands of the Americas, or something linked expressly to the violation of virtue. This recontextualization effectively becomes a dual space of agency, provided by the plotlines of the sentimental novel and the fictional discourse transcribed from the New Era women's club, through which Hopkins countered the trope of the tragic mulatta. The tragic mulatta of Contending Forces, Mabelle Beaubean, would have remained tragic and dead (and somehow holy in that enterprise) in the telling of the Colored League. Yet she is granted a counter-life in the Northeast in the larger story of Sappho Clark, a woman who takes a second life in the contacts and discourse of other women, who must find meaningful work and build a career, and who decides on her own to become involved in South End life. Contending Forces suggests that reading the mulatta figure as somehow in collusion with static racist ideologies fails to account for African Americans' own outflankings from Jim Crow, and also for the complex dynamics of contemporary place values (genius loci). Far from such interpretive traditions, Hopkins tried to reclaim the persona of the tragic mulatta and deploy her in modern, urban life. In this capacity, Sappho Clark challenges the kinds of national contradictions embodied by postbellum federal policy, as well as any forms of racial absolutism reflected within an African American literary tradition.[111]

Sappho's story is the final thematic puzzle piece in a novel built around the cataloguing of place and landmarks of black Boston life. She is an embodiment of the South in the North, bearing traces in her person of a secret history. She also brings with her a background of lynching, rape, and racial terror as a legacy of slavery that could not be erased through migration. Instead, these features of life are embedded in the landscape of modern cities. Throughout the novel, Hopkins aligns Sappho with the very nodes of black life in Boston. She has come as a boarder, without known roots, and she becomes involved in everything from church life, sewing circles, the women's club, and charity within the scape of the city. Her story provides a climactic case for revising the "distance decay" model associated with geographical care. She quite literally brings home the need for a relational understanding of region and local space, as well as the issues black Boston had to account for in the project Hopkins posed to it: a project of advancement along all lines steered by community direction. In the same way Sappho's tragedy points up the weaknesses in Washington's plan (particularly giving view to Hopkins's point: that enfranchisement was more urgent than industrial and economic gains), Sappho is also an example of the failure of a Du Boisian vision of black progress, which did not account for women's organization and enfranchisement as central to "uplift." She is a woman who finds herself through other women. Mobility saves Sappho in a way that African Americans since the eighteenth century have long understood. Sappho's own mobility is a structure of survival. Through relocation she locates grounds for reinvention. Place can provide a space of legitimacy to project a new self and change old orders.

Contending Forces proposes a corrective model of local life, one of dialogue and representative action. It is a model that refuses to depict regional identities through a topos of stasis or removal. Rather, local space interpolates other scales like gender-based organization, Jim Crow migrations, or the movement of capital and information. Contending Forces points out the need for a model of local thinking whereby wider social responsibility is not eroded by distance. This is a significant feature of the sort of civics Hopkins tries to depict, one in which progress is defined on a local register, as a measure of black citizens' participation in city life. Yet at the same time, it is a model built on cross-community exchanges. It is through such exchanges that black public life gets made and can proliferate multiple scales of action.

CHAPTER 5

CREOLE HETEROGLOSSIA

Counter-Regionalism and the New Orleans

Short Fiction of Alice Dunbar-Nelson

Regions are best viewed as initial contexts for themes that generate variable geographies, rather than as fixed geographies marked by pre-given themes. These themes are equally "real," equally coherent, but are results of our interests and not their causes.—ARJUN APPADURAI, "Grassroots Globalization and the Research Imagination"

American literary regionalism perhaps seems an unlikely starting place for examining the sorts of cosmopolitan discourses that have come to be associated with a postnational aesthetic. Unlike the modern landscapes of globalization—spatially indeterminate, but tracked with economic networks—the notion of region in the United States is mostly aligned with different paradigms. In contemporary thinking about region in both cultural studies and geography alike, it retains a kind of dormancy, a sense of spatial decidedness and finiteness.[1] In contrast to the wider, politically charged spaces of nation or the depersonalized global spheres of late capital, region holds a place in the popular imagination as something connected to the land and its folk. It is not a matter of size, at least not in the United States. Region can be large. It can be sprawling tracts of topography. Or it can be more intimate and internecine. But it implies two mutually reinforcing characteristics: a sectioning of the national via some form of tradition or local belonging and a spatiality that is stitched together, at least loosely, by a sense of shared values.

From within nineteenth-century U.S. popular literary culture, the movement historically most responsible for characterizing the postbellum American vernacular tradition as a repository of social nostalgia in an otherwise rapidly transforming national scene was widely known as regionalism or local color. Regionalism flourished as the dominant genre in U.S. print production shortly after the Civil War until the first decade of the twentieth century. It was a mobile, magazine form, targeting a middle-class, urban readership in Eastern seaboard publishing cities like New York and Boston. It also proved itself a powerful postbellum cultural force with a capacity to generate a fairly durable vision of what constituted American local life. Regionalist literature depicted region as something both spatially and temporally set apart from the more urbanized, mainstream social pressures of a fast, young nation. As critics such as Amy Kaplan and Richard Brodhead have observed, regionalism reaffirmed the possibility of a purer, more sustaining national landscape in an era otherwise marked by the rapid growth of mass-circular advertising, transportation technology, immigration, and urban population swells. Jennifer Greeson draws attention to the ways regionalism proliferated exceptionalist narratives of postbellum cultural history: "The denomination 'local color' itself indicates—as clearly as the name 'Civil War'—that this most popular form of postbellum writing explores a geopolitical specificity purely of the intra- or subnational variety."[2] Indeed, regionalism authenticated the existence of a national diversity from within.

Regionalism's diversity, on one level, appeared to be mostly organic insofar as it predated postbellum federal centralization. Importantly, it also predated the contemporary tides of mass immigration from Southern and Eastern Europe, Asia, and Russia. It was instead the sort of pre-existing diversity that could be found in the quaint-seeming and less-populated locales of the rural South, the far Northeast, and the sparsely populated Midwest. The people whom regionalist authors portrayed were coastal Maine villagers, Tennessee mountain folk, and pioneering prairie farmstead communities. On the whole, they were cast as emblems of a preindustrial Americana, and their languages were the dialects that circulated in postbellum America's quiet spaces. Region in turn-of-the century American literature thus came to stand for something not so much out of time as in its own time, a carved-out chronology that was largely self-contained. Regionalist writing, Richard Brodhead has suggested, took the form of a "cultural elegy" for a past that was quickly being supplanted by modern movements.[3]

Consequently, region in United States print culture *does* tend to be associated with precoded and nested modes of living. In various intermedial discourses, region is essentialized as both particular and bounded. It is commonly regarded as a kind of stage on which outside decisions can unfold, sometimes inciting resistance and sometimes little other than compliance. Regional representation constitutes an aesthetic retreat from the more rapidly developing global infrastructures that lend design to contemporary life. On some levels, at least, this appears as an outgrowth from a long elegiac tradition.

But in the interest of loosening region from an aestheticization attached to temporal stasis or social insularity, the literature of the first generation of postbellum African American fiction writers presents a compelling case. Within popular Southern regionalism, blacks entered into story lines as both situated and underdeveloped, especially in relation to the sorts of dynamic circulations and distributions of a rapidly evolving postbellum magazine culture.[4] They were siloed into spaces of an earlier epoch, usually the postplantation. Such spaces were, in turn, removed from any viable, progressive economics by overwhelming federal force during both the Civil War and its aftermath: early Reconstruction. In print production, this kind of spatial districting presented readers with a kind of time-fold for placing national blacks. What freed blacks from place also contained them in time. That is, African American figuration in popular print relied on black dialect and performances that were the product of living in a redolent, offset space. Black location stood in for a kind of passive placement. It was like the enveloping of time into place.

Yet the vogue of regional writing provided a point of access for African American authors to enter into the mass-periodical market with some measure of freedom in reshaping a history of exclusions. For authors like Charles Chesnutt, Paul Laurence Dunbar, and Alice Moore Dunbar-Nelson, region was a platform for deliberating national structures and recasting American social history for a people largely kept outside the official discourse. As their writings revealed, African American authors knew about social stratification, thinned opportunities, and color lines as much as practically anyone—and, consequently, region's value in their literature was less connected to its nostalgic containment of older orders. Rather, African American regionalists negotiated a literary tradition's expectations of an authentic black culture of the interior with the versions of place experience they encountered. Racial violence and social segregation were pivotal to black experience; they were subject forming.[5] And so in terraining the black subject via region, African American regionalist authors challenged core presumptions about the genre. They complicated region's spatialities and its vaunted quaintness. They also revealed interconnections between shifting national orders and the voices that circulated in local culture.

Nineteenth-century African American literature thus presents an occasion to consider region as an intensity of place affect. It was a site for embodiment and the scope of embodied practice. Region in African American writing actually takes on a double meaning. It is a frame for what can be known physically and sensibly through a subject's extension into a place. But it is also a space of discursive (inter)play. Region was a more elemental unit of place than nation insofar as it was revealed through forms that circulated beneath nation. But nor did it simply derive from a national form (a space in front of place) or a national rhetoric. Rather, as black novelists demonstrated, it might function as a repository of subnational resistance or, as Dunbar-Nelson's writing shows, a conduit of hemispheric culture. It might validate forms of identity and representation that were not formed in tandem with national hegemonies. Indeed, regional landscapes, not surprisingly, produced a range of tensions that were frequently not contained within region. And, as a brief overview of Chesnutt's and Dunbar's writing illustrates, such tensions contributed to very different types of literature.

Region as Repository/Place Dialectics

Chesnutt's most definitively regionalist fiction (published collectively in 1899 as *The Conjure Woman and Other Tales* under the prestigious Boston imprint Houghton Mifflin) drew out themes from black folklife to point up the complexities of place knowledge, its local routings and humors. Chesnutt blended African American folk modes of magic and superstition known variously as conjure, hoodoo, and sometimes goopher (as in his popular 1887 *Atlantic Monthly* story, "The Goophered Grapevine") with black oral traditions. Linguistically, through the cadences of story-telling and the dialect forms of plantation speech, Chesnutt inscribed a discourse that confounded white-dominant modes of reunification. For instance, *The Conjure Woman* brings together the frame narration of a northern carpetbagger, John, newly arrived at the scene of a ruined post-bellum plantation, and the tales of a master storyteller, a former plantation slave named Uncle Julius. Both figures hold contesting claims to ownership of the former plantation and vineyard surrounding it. What Chesnutt's interconnecting stories make apparent is that region was a key site in a wider contest for economic incorporation and entrepreneurial, landscape development in the postwar South. Julius and John symbolize two distinct forms of contending discourses. Julius represents the regionalist tradition, with a history rooted in the land and plantation genealogies of the South. His stories are his currency. They portray the endured experiences of local blacks, among these the women conjurers on the plot's outskirts, whose experiences he appropriates and turns into narrative material.[6] John holds legal ownership to the property, but has no history to link him to his new plantation home. He represents the national eye, the cultural tourist newly arrived in the Reconstruction South. As Chesnutt shows, the textualities of region exceed what the national eye apprehends.

The Ohio-born son of two former slaves, Dunbar also brought the vernacular speech of former slaves and the setting of the Southern plantations to his own writing. Even though Dunbar was prolific as an author of regional short fiction, publishing such collections as *The Uncalled* (1898), *Folks from Dixie* (also 1898), *The Strength of Gideon and Other Stories* (1900), and *The Fanatics* (1901), he is best remembered for his regionally influenced poetry, published between 1893 and 1905 in some eleven volumes.[7] Despite his considerable contributions to regionalist prose, one possible reason his short fiction has remained relatively unpopular (or even simply unknown) to modern readers is that it does not on the whole appear to differ markedly from what at the end of the century was considered one of the most prominent developments within regionalism: the plantation school of writing. Authors like Thomas Nelson Page popularized the plantation school tradition early on, with stories like "Marse Chan," featuring a stable of noble slave owners and happy Virginia slaves, a captioning of regional writing extended (and also complicated) in the local color stories of writer Joel Chandler Harris, author of the well-known Brer Rabbit tales, and in the plantation dialect poetry of Mississippian Irwin Russell. Similar themes appear in Dunbar's short fiction and plantation school regionalism. Among these were plantation contentment, pastimes enjoyed by slaves, and the loyalty of African Americans to their former enslavers.

But what is interesting about Dunbar is that region's resurgence in his very last work, the novel *The Sport of the Gods* (1902), forces the upheaval and hollowing out of what he initially appears to prescribe as plantation virtues. The novel reveals that when the form supporting these values has caved, so, too, does their currency. It also shows that adherence to postplantation modes (loyalty to former masters, contentment in white apportionments, and hard agricultural work as character building) only extends the psychological barriers to success for African Americans seeking to experience broader life. *The Sport of the Gods* is Dunbar's most pessimistic work, but it is also his most dynamic one. Its narrative about a plantation family forced to relocate to New York City accommodates the textual levels of disjunction between plantation life and the scales of production and consumption in the modern Northern city. And to a significant degree, this text anticipated the literature of the Harlem Renaissance, which years later came to assess the impact of the Great Migration on African American spiritual and social life in classic novels like Jean Toomer's *Cane* (1923) and Nella Larsen's *Quicksand* (1928). Like Chesnutt, Dunbar refused to treat region as a self-contained cultural unit. Rather, it was a place of contestation for national meaning; region was often (unwillingly) forced to negotiate its modalities and memories with other competing versions of life in an unsettled national culture that Dunbar shows is full of façades.

Yet neither of these authors particularize region's transnational signages or its tapestries of life beyond the national frame quite to the extent of Alice Moore Dunbar-Nelson. In the following pages I focus on the regional Creole literature of Dunbar-Nelson from the two collections of fiction she published in her lifetime: *Violets and Other Tales* (1895) and *The Goodness of St. Rocque* (1899). Born in New Orleans of mixed African American, Native American, and European American ancestry, Dunbar-Nelson wrote about the peoples and geography of the post-Reconstruction South. But—unlike black regionalists such as Charles Chesnutt and Paul Dunbar, to whom she was married from 1898 to 1902—she did not draw upon the rural South's plantation idiom, something linked to stasis and slave-based epistemologies. Instead, her writing is an occasion for examining the ways region functioned as a sort of open cell, a cultural landscape shot through with links to external histories.

As an author of regional fiction, Dunbar-Nelson is notable for the different textual ways she opened the scope and boundaries of regional writing to upend the notion of national unity. First, her representative landscapes read against suppositions about a backward-angled, static South, devitalized as a scene of modern action in a post-Reconstruction nation. Second, in her writing region signifies away from its more seemingly immobile features, its architecture, monuments, and fixed structures that would most give it solidity or distinctiveness. Rather, she was attracted to what contemporary cultural geographers refer to as the "process geographies" of the local, or deliberations about the ways places get produced rather than the outcomes of the production.[8] Put another way, process geographies are about the relations that come together to make place. They are about how practices produce *epistemes*. Process geographies consider place in relation to movement, to something geographers Mike Crang and Nigel Thrift call "*space as process* and in process."[9] Process geography offers a way to interpret region not as something fixed according to set traits of habitat, but rather as something dialectical that is always caught up in states of becoming. It is a way to think of region in terms more frequently accorded to sites of globalization—its connectedness to more mobile scales like immigration and the mobilization of capital, as well as information and idea exchanges.

In Dunbar-Nelson's Creole fiction, places are identified by their connections to conflicts and to the forms of organization that yield motion like trade and migration. In the stories I examine here, local scales mediate wider, transnational movements. This process ranges from the late nineteenth-century fruit trade with Central America—which, in turn, polarized African American and Irish labor within the New Orleans shipping industry—to the codification of Southern Louisiana Vodou practices in Creole culture.[10] Moreover, what sustains the cultural replication of folklife in Dunbar-Nelson's writing was actually something not typically associated with the category of regionalism at all. Instead, inherent in her depiction of region is what can perhaps best be identified as a core permeability. In a sense that mirrors region's own fluidity, her writing opens constructs like ethnicity and race to demonstrate their diffuseness and constructedness.

Local Interfaces: Life on the Docks

In the short story "Mr. Baptiste" from *The Goodness of St. Rocque*, her second and more complex collection of short fiction, Dunbar-Nelson transposes themes of local scale and personal diminutiveness against the larger scales of racialized conflict and industrialization. The story at its center is about the everyday life of a very small and old Creole man who occupies the hidden spaces of the city. He is a man of no apparent race or affiliation, but is instead described as "Latinised," "French," and "brown." He is ethnically indeterminate and socially amorphous, a figure who moves along surfaces, never appearing to disrupt convention and flow. He holds no singular profession but rather maintains a livelihood by doing odd jobs and errands. On his daily rounds, he "slips in through back doors," where he makes his visits and takes his meals.[11] He keeps to himself and commands no particular attention, nor does he generate any particular conflicts.

Yet Mr. Baptiste also exemplifies the different economic and social scales that coalesce within the space of region. His quiet livelihood among the city side streets, the author reveals, is made possible only by certain external contingencies. Each day Baptiste is known to frequent the local steamship levee, where the Morgan Line ships dock. These ships carry out the state's extensive international fruit trade from Central America. Moreover, Baptiste feeds himself daily by picking up baskets of imperfect fruit left behind on the docks, fruit that cannot be sold at market. And so it is that Mr. Baptiste, the most quaint and small of local Creole figures, has staked out a living vitally dependent on larger transnational trade circuits.

Baptiste has a second purpose in the story. He complicates the concept of ethnicity by demonstrating the ways such forms of identification are inherently variable and involved in more immediate and presence-based modes of self-fashioning. When the longshoremen and stevedores of the cotton ships go on strike, no merchandise can be unloaded, and the fruit Baptiste relies on is left to rot in the ships, neglected. It is at this juncture that the tenuousness of Baptiste's position between the cells of the conflict, so to speak, is polarized. What follows in Dunbar-Nelson's narrative is significant because it sets into motion a major race riot in New Orleans.[12] Assembled for their strike, the group of Irish workers is appalled to hear the steady sound of boats unloading from within the hold. They rush to the scene at the wharf in search of the scabs. "Scabs! Finnegan had said; and the word was passed along."[13] Prepared for battle, what the Irish strikers encounter makes a spectacle of the already-existing labor divisions between them and the newly hired men. On the ship's deck they witness a group of powerful black stevedores, "muscles standing out like cables through their blue cotton shirts, and sweat rolling from glossy black skins." The battle lines are instantly drawn in the imprint of color divisions demarcating the conflict. The Irish strikers throw a giant paving stone that destroys the cotton-compressing machine aboard the ship. The black workers, who own the ruined machines (and not, Dunbar-Nelson points out, the shipowners), in turn throw brickbats, iron, and wood at the Irish mob.

Race and ethnicity, the narrative demonstrates, are exploited by management to divide the workers and maintain control. Race thus functions as a sort of boundary or membrane that compartmentalizes the allocation of labor within local place. Yet Dunbar-Nelson is clear that race, in itself, does not initiate the conflict. It is a labor conflict with race as a signifier. To highlight the extra-regional element of the fight, the narrator steps far back from the riots. They become popular knowledge: "You remember, of course, how long the strike lasted, and how many battles were fought and lives lost before the final adjustment of affairs."[14] In terms of the story, the rioters on both sides of the divide constitute the dominant social narrative. It is the counter-story of Baptiste, however, which occupies the author's interest, and the capillary microsystem of Creole mercantilism: the "fishmen and vegetable marchands" lining the docks whose livelihoods and businesses are damaged by the riots.

In the same sense that Baptiste's reliance on cooperation between international trade and organized labor renders him vulnerable, so too does his position between the set racial boundaries of the conflict. The "Latinised," brown-skinned Baptiste ultimately falls between the lines of racial signification in the story. His ad hoc support of the black workers (who will presumably break the strike and bring forth the fruit) positions him symbolically against whiteness. Spotted by the Irish mob "weakly cheering the Negroes on," his Creole intermediacy is rendered black. "Cheering the niggers are you?," the Irish challenge him.[15] No more is he a *gens de coleur libres* (a free person of color), with a local privilege expressed as a kind of access. Instead, he is reborn as a contestant in the kinds of labor wars described by W. E. B. Du Bois as having "real underlying industrial causes obscured by political excuses and race hatred."[16] In Dunbar-Nelson's telling, this dynamic converges on Baptiste's very person. A striker named McMahon throws a brickbat deliberately in the direction of the bread stall where he takes refuge, and he crumples to the ground, killed instantly: "Fishmen and vegetable marchands gathered around him in a quick, sympathetic mass. The individual, the concrete bit of helpless humanity, had more interest for them than the vast, vague fighting mob beyond."[17] Ultimately Dunbar-Nelson memorializes Baptiste as the first and forgotten casualty of the riots, his fate determined by the interlocking spheres of conflict that plunge the scene into violent relief: "It was a fearsome war, and many forgot afterwards whose was the first life lost in the struggle,—poor little Mr. Baptiste's."[18]

Beyond its attention to heterogeneity and racial flux, "Mr. Baptiste" is a signal text insofar as it presents a kind of structural isomorphism between regionalism as a literary mode and the kinds of social forces at work in the industrial Jim Crow South, forces that could certainly undermine the coherence of any said-regional landscape. The story presents two arenas of conflict among the New Orleans working class, one based on the scales of imperial pan-Americanism—but recognized through industrial labor, and the other built up on old race binaries that in a port city at the mouth of international exchange were already shot through with disorder. The clash between these scales results in a key moment of "antiproduction," which reveals the ways in which the practical dynamics of local circulation are already established on distance.[19] Place coheres in the story only as a target of movement. And on another level, the story demonstrates the ways region itself is involved in producing hemispheric space. Region participates in international trade and relies on wider commercial networks to construct its own communities and local relations. Moreover, it models a circum-Atlantic frame that looks much less like flows and much more like turbulence; contestation defines place, and material gains are always somehow reducible to victors' spoils.

Further, in a climate where U.S. naval technology and African American ground troops (believed by the War Department to be more immunologically suited for tropical warfare) produced a decisive U.S. victory in the Spanish-American War of 1898, the fiction volatilizes the achievement that is pan-American commerce. It attaches the visual image of rotting fruit to the virile display of black masculinity. And synchronically, it makes ripeness the threat. Ripeness is black readiness. But readiness for what? The taut, laboring bodies aboard the ship, desperate for paying work, occupy the visual foreground of a city once governed and administered from Havana, Cuba. But they are certainly no more in possession of the terms of commercial port geographies than they were prior to African American victories at Santiago de Cuba. In fact, the black stevedore battalion, depicted in the story as vibrant and dimensional, pulsates very differently in its organized labor than the black Cuban troops commemorated in Dunbar's "The Conquerors: The Black Troops in Cuba" (1898). Dunbar's blacks are shown as "Grim with the dust of the battle, / and gray, / From the fight." Dunbar-Nelson's battalion is neither grim nor gray. The opposite, actually.

Yet what overlays black vitalism is the freight of empire. The riots that spill out from the ship and onto the docklands are, in effect, nodes of commercial instability, which powerfully bear on the geography of the local. As geographer Susan Roberts notes, "ports are the hinges or valves articulating the national economy with the global economy."[20] In the New Orleans port, the sun-spoiling fruit represents more than the asymmetries of surplus, which in the popular imagination of 1898 likely brought to mind new, ambiguous archipelagoes of U.S. power in Puerto Rico, the Philippines, or a newly known Spanish Guam. The cargo brings the labor of distanced groups together via the transport of commodities.

As Dunbar-Nelson tells it, it is also significant that the business of international shipping and the docklands of global capital had, in fact, largely served Baptiste and the Creole dock vendors until the time of the riots. The damages incurred by Creole merchants are connected to their absorption of international commercial culture, something that compromises their local autonomy and proves massive enough to erase the individual (represented as nonmechanized, heterogeneous Creoles like Baptiste). It is also significant that region is not passive in this process. Local life actually works as a sort of interface for a transnational framework. It is only as stable as what is under its surface.

Creole Tales and Vodou Vendors

Specifically regional customs in Dunbar-Nelson's New Orleans short fiction rarely prove to be purely local practices. Instead, they reference foreign origins. In two stories from the The Goodness of St. Rocque collection, "The Praline Women" and "Tony's Wife," the author depicts the southern Louisiana practice of lagniappe. Lagniappe is when a shop-keeper gives a small bonus with a purchase to promote patronage and good feeling. The practice, as well as the word's etymology, are reflective of a range of cultures. The term is thought to derive from the Spanish word for la ñapa (a tip or bonus) and the Quechua New World Spanish yapa (to give more or to increase). In the New Orleans Creole dialect, lagniappe takes on an Italian spelling, fitting with the city's large Sicilian population of shopkeepers from the 1840s onward.

Other local practices in New Orleans life reflect extra-national in-fluences, syncretized within domestic culture as quasi-religious ritu-als. In "Cupid and the Phonograph," a short story from a manuscript volume titled Stories of Women and Men (written between 1900 and 1910), Dunbar-Nelson detailed the custom of washing the front steps yellow to promote luck in the home and ward off evil: "Now your self-respecting Frenchtown housekeeper must needs wash her steps precisely at twelve on Fridays with the mysterious yellow wash which brings good luck the following week."[21] The eponymously titled story The Goodness of St. Rocque describes the one-story frame house of a clairvoyant known as "the Wiz-ened One," as marked by the same process. Upon approach, the story's protagonist Manuela notes, "the one little step was scrupulously yellow-washed, which denoted the occupants were cleanly as well as religious."[22]

The step-yellowing practice is significant for the ways it represents an inversion of private and public space. As public sphere theorists like Bruce Robbins have pointed out, the private as a type of symbol has tra-ditionally been associated with scenes of domesticity, the household, the familial, and female.[23] Luce Irigaray has also referred to what she calls the enveloping, secret, and opaque portrayal of women's creative space, qualities that make such places appear as "non-real" in politicized civil society.[24] Both Robbins and Irigaray identify constructions of women's space as something that signifies inward, and somehow back into itself. It is privatized and personal. It grows inward. In Dunbar-Nelson's de-piction of this practice, however, the domestic step-yellowing tradition represents something very different. Far from typifying a landlocked and self-reflexive feminine interiority, the ritual is an aestheticization of cultures that exceed the privatized home space and the regional environs of New Orleans altogether.

The yellow wash to promote luck was part of a spiritual practice that was brought to New Orleans from the former French colony of Saint-

Domingue (present-day Haiti) by West African slaves. It colored space, interiorizing it as blessed in the fused spirit of African animistic beliefs and planters' Catholic rituals, which came to be known, somewhat notoriously, as Vodou. During the Haitian Revolution (1792–1810), which overthrew slavery and established Haiti as a free black republic, some 10,000 refugees flocked to Louisiana, including planters, slaves, and *gens de couleur libres*. Most settled in the French-speaking Roman Catholic city of New Orleans.

New Orleans society was a fertile ground for the transformation of Vodou practices. For one thing, it was predominantly Catholic. Catholicism, as scholars of Haitian religion have pointed out, long served as a functional framework for the codification of Vodou religious practice. That is, at least a portion of the family of Vodou saints, known as Iwa, could be associated with Catholic patron saints.[25] For instance, Erzulie, the earth mother Iwa, was a corollary of the Virgin Mary, mother of Jesus; Dumballah, the snake Iwa, was Saint Patrick, and so forth.[26] In "The Goodness of Saint Rocque," Dunbar-Nelson shows the ways Vodun-inflected customs like the yellow wash interlinked themselves with Catholic practices in New Orleans Creole culture. Such scenes play out in "The Goodness of St. Rocque." Describing the front room of "The Mistress of Cards," she writes: "It was a small somber room within, with a bare yellow-washed floor and ragged curtains at the little window. In a corner was a diminutive alter [sic] draped with threadbare lace. The red glow of the taper lighted a cheap print of St. Joseph and a brazen crucifix."[27] New Orleans Vodou practices demand an association of symbol, spirit, and place. They are performances, legible to the initiated, but also signaling expectations of an encounter that is mystical. It cannot be encapsulated and cannot ever be only local since it is shaped by fluvial, trans-Atlantic currents, beyond the immediately contained.

Creole practices, Dunbar-Nelson's fiction suggests, connote the constructedness of local identities from the outside—as does the Creole lexicon. "The Praline Women," told in first-person by the title character, extends this point. It is written in Creole dialect, a French-Anglo language fusion. The story itself is a window into the daily life of Tante Marie, a street vendor who sits "by the side of the Archbishop's quaint little chapel on Royal Street," calling out to the passing crowds to buy her pralines: "Pralines, pralines. Ah, ma'amzelle, you buy? S'il vous plaît, ma'amzelle, ces pralines, dey be fine, ver' fresh."[28]

Yet Tante Marie does something further. She narrates life on the street; she is conversant with it. She is a mediating figure between local movement on Royal Street and Dunbar-Nelson's readership. In her running monologue, she identifies boundaries within regional community life and tries to bring to her table an "étrangér," a person she claims does not look like a local but rather the "Yankee-looking peo'p," "dat come down 'fo' de war." She also gives information about the daily comings and goings of a fellow merchant, an "Indian Squaw," whom she calls out to by the name of "Tonita." She goes on to spot a "lazy I'ishman" and tells a story about an Irishman asking her why she spoke the way she did. In turn she asks him why he speaks the way he does. The point is that she reports and reveals region and, in doing so, makes a stage for encounters between various nationalities and ethnic affiliations.

The themes of social mixture and social accretion reappear again and again in much of regionalist fiction. In fact, it becomes increasingly evident to readers of Dunbar-Nelson that the cultural uniqueness she tries to identify in the spaces of New Orleans is not about extracting a purer, undiluted Creole culture. Creole identity is rather the product of social overlap and in many cases, ethnic ambiguity. Despite efforts from Creole figures like Grandpère Colomés in the story "La Juanita" to keep his family line "proudly aloof from 'does Americain' from time immemorial," Dunbar-Nelson demonstrates how such ventures are nearly always fraught.[29] His granddaughter Juanita chooses Captain Mercer Grangeman for a beau, a young man the family disparages as "this Mercer, this pale-eyed youth." However, after proving his bravery on Lake Pontchartrain in a tropical Gulf storm, he receives honorary identity in Mandeville, a Louisiana stronghold of nineteenth-century Creole culture. Grandpère Colomés concludes, "Some time does American can mos' be lak one Frenchman."[30]

Ambiguous Race and Carnival Space

Most contemporary writing on creolization as acculturative process takes its start from the point that Creole identity is inherently dependent on ethnic mixture. Certainly contemporary cultural creolization theory shares metaphorical, if not contextual, affinity with black Atlantic scholarship. Both emphasize the forms of identity that converge through contacts across oceans. Both use the Atlantic as a frame to counter nation-state orientation and the artificially separated histories of Europe, Africa, North America, and the Caribbean.[31] The best-known literature about creolization and postcolonial textuality has been articulated by West Indian scholars such as Edouard Glissant and Kamau Brathwaite, whose writings both celebrate the liberating potential of Creole identity and the possibilities for chemistries of cross-cultural exchange. For Glissant, Creole identity is less about historical conditions than relational processes—what he identifies as a poetics of relation shaped through correspondences and embedded memories. Brathwaite also proposes a model of creolization that is about process and emergence, and also corporealization, "blood flow." He writes that a definition of creolization "can only derive from a proliferation of images: a multiplication of complex probes: a co-operative effort from us all." Nonetheless, this research represents a relatively new approach to the subject of Creole identity, and one quite at odds with the models that generally adhered in the early part of the century. West Indian scholarship on creolism, in Sidney Mintz's view, started so late specifically because this region "was considered theoretically unfruitful . . . its peoples supposedly lacked culture or were culturally bastardized."[32]

For Dunbar-Nelson, writing at the turn of the century about New Orleans life, the sense of polarity and dividedness that marked Creole identity was far more culturally prominent than the "relationality" and productive overlapping articulated by Glissant. In her two published short story collections, *Violets and Other Tales* and *The Goodness of St. Rocque*, she identified a history of the modern Creole that, despite claims of a long and well-established past, only came into its modern applicability after the Louisiana Purchase in 1803. Louisiana Creole identity prior to 1803 generally meant native born or locally produced. Yet it took on a charged political meaning after accession. Families with ancestral histories and property in New Orleans were among the most aggressive in asserting Creole identity as the basis for land rights against Anglo-Americans and European immigrants, especially from Ireland, Sicily, and Germany, who came to the city in large numbers after accession.[33]

It was perhaps the very mutability and mixture of Creole identity that in the nineteenth century generated the sorts of specificity and guardedness attached to its definition. Although the Creole is associated with a range of Francophile affiliations, the term was also asserted in Dunbar-Nelson's time to distinguish Louisiana natives from immigrants from

France who made their homes in the New World city, as well as Cajuns of Canadian backgrounds who settled west of New Orleans. These same Creoles, according to Joseph Tregle Jr., also sought to exclude "foreign French," who had arrived en masse in New Orleans after the revolution in St. Domingue.[34] In her essay "People of Color in Louisiana," Dunbar-Nelson herself explained Creole identity as something at once elusive and deliberately assigned with race as a principal signifier: "The native white Louisianaian [sic] will tell that a Creole is a white man, those ancestors contain some French or Spanish blood in their veins. . . . The Caucasian will shudder with horror at the idea of including a person of color in the definition, and the person of color will retort with his definition that a Creole is a native of Louisiana, in whose blood runs mixed strains of everything un-American, with the African strain slightly apparent. The true Creole is like the famous gumbo of the state, a little bit of everything, making a whole, delightfully flavored, quite distinctive, and wholly unique."[35]

New Orleans historian Virginia Domínguez offers a similar assessment of a stark racial divide: "Two types of Louisianians consequently identify themselves today as Creole. One is socially and legally white; the other, socially and legally colored. The white side by definition cannot accept the existence of colored Creoles; the colored side, by definition, cannot accept the white conception of Creole."[36]

This known social divide was a cogent factor in shaping the kind of regionalism Dunbar-Nelson wrote. More than anything, her regionalist writing gave expression to the uncertainty endemic to Creole identity as a site between different versions of racial and ethnic legitimation. In fact, Dunbar-Nelson's most definitively Creole characters defy attempts to be ethnically or racially fixed within the parameters of her fiction. For instance, in the story "Little Miss Sophie," from The Goodness of St. Rocque collection, the title character rides the Claiborne line streetcar through New Orleans with heavy burdens of sewing work. Although Miss Sophie is never identified by race, the reader is told she lives in the Third District, signifying her general poverty. She speaks both English and French and pays regular homage to the Virgin Mary; she is thus presumably a Catholic Creole. One day on the streetcar she overhears gossip about herself and her former lover, Louis Neale, now recently married and unable to collect his inheritance: "It seems that Neale had some little Creole love-affair some years ago and gave this ring to his dusky-eyed fiancée."[37] In the story "Sister Josepha," the protagonist is a woman named Camille, an orphan who has come of age in a New Orleans convent: "She grew up with the rest of the waifs; scraps of French and American civilization thrown together to develop a seemingly inconsistent miniature world."[38] Camille is described as "a glorious tropical beauty" who, stifled by boredom, works daily, filling lamps with her "small brown hands."[39]

To use a theme from Jean Fagan Yellin, Dunbar-Nelson's racially ambiguous characters perform significant cultural work. They are not cast as a way to avoid questions about race or deny black positivity. By writing about racially ambiguous characters, Dunbar-Nelson actually forced other scales of identification to the front of the fiction, something later writers like Toni Morrison would deploy in the only short story she ever published, "Recitatif." In "Recitatif," Morrison constantly subverts attempts to fix racial meaning on the identities of her two central characters by highlighting other features of economic-social identification over race, but, more importantly, the ambiguities of personal history and primary familial affiliation in relation to life choice. Dunbar-Nelson's choice of characters produces a similar effect. Race is something embedded into narratives of place. It is relational and conditioned by subjective experiences and expressions. With respect to her decision to encode and scramble the racial attributes of Creole identity, Kristina Brooks has suggested, "just as countless Creoles of color successfully passed for white in New Orleans at the turn of the century, several of Dunbar-Nelson's Creole characters are able to pass in their encounters with nonlocal readers. Choosing not to attribute a fixed racial identity to these characters, Dunbar-Nelson defines the Creole as uniquely and distinctly indefinable."[40]

The Goodness of St. Rocque on the whole eschews many determining codes of a deeply racialized Southern identity. These were codes that separated blacks and whites in regional as well as national spaces and, at the same time, codes that adhered in complex and questioning forms in the contemporary color-line regional fiction of authors such as Chesnutt, as well as later authors like William Faulkner and Flannery O'Connor. Like these writers, she expanded the space of the local through scenes of conflict. Yet her New Orleans stories suggest that inherent in spaces of cultural permeability and social confusion is a special freedom, a freedom similar to that articulated by modern critics like Werner Sollors. In

Beyond Ethnicity, Sollors argues that the concept of ethnicity in the United States functions as a sort of discourse that marks boundaries between registers of voluntary and inherited forms of identification. Modern American ethnic individuals, Sollors offers, can exercise the freedom to choose which inherited conventions of an identity are advantageous and which ones are dispensable. This connects to Dunbar-Nelson's aestheticization of the Creole. The Creole exceeds the backstory of Anglo-attribution by exercising a freedom of affiliation.

As Dunbar-Nelson depicts in her fiction, this affiliative freedom comes out during carnival time in New Orleans. In "A Carnival Jangle," she describes the February Tuesday of New Orleans Carnival, when youths in disguises overwhelm the city streets from Washington Square and Royal Street to Elysian Fields Avenue: "The streets swarm with humanity,—humanity in all shapes, manners, forms, laughing, pushing, jostling, crowding, a mass of men and women and children, as varied and assorted in their several individual peculiarities as ever a crowd that gathered in one locality since the days of Babel."[41]

It feels almost impossible to invoke the idea of carnival in literature without referencing the writing of Mikhail Bakhtin. It was Bakhtin who made carnival a lexical coalescence of times and modes. In his reading of François Rabelais, he found in the ritual spectacles of the Renaissance carnival an inversion of everyday life prohibitions and the "temporary suspension of all hierarchic distinctions and barriers among men." Bakhtin was interested in the ways the carnival experience represented a mode of resistance to social caste and order: "People who in life are separated by impenetrable hierarchical barriers enter into free and familiar contact on the carnival square."[42] For Dunbar-Nelson, actually writing before Bakhtin, carnival time represented the possibilities for radical transformation within the framework of regional (as opposed to Renaissance) custom. She writes: "There is fantasy and fancy and grotesqueness run wild in the costuming and behavior of the maskers."[43]

New Orleans's carnival was a demonstration of place in its transformative and transgressive potential. The focus was not preservation nor past memorialization, qualities traditionally associated with regionalist display. Rather, it was the capacity of region to reorganize itself, to open closed cells of convention, to debunk central authority and invert social barriers. This subversive potential of region was immensely attractive to

Dunbar-Nelson. It was an opportunity to invite new elements into the social topographies of local life. Like creolization, region was about its potential for reinterpretation. It was also a gesture toward new exchanges that flexed the boundaries of embodied forms—be they race or gender. For example, in "A Carnival Jangle," a young "demoiselle" identified as Flo joins the frenzy of the crowd, taking the form of a slender male troubadour. It is a guise brought together by region, by a walk-through into "one of the lowest-ceiled, dingiest and most ancient-looking" of the "old-world" disguise shops buried along Toulouse and St. Peter Streets.[44] The result of such transformation is "a dream of color and melody and fantasy gone wild in an effervescent bubble of beauty that shifts and changes and passes kaleidoscope-like before the bewildered eye."

Yet violence is never far removed from such scenes of overlap and social inversion. While the clash of carnival cultures can be productive, enriching and transforming the space of the local with pageantry and form, it also proves to be deadly. In the frenzy of bodies, Flo is mistaken for a rival male and stabbed between the shoulder blades. As the stories "Mr. Baptiste" and "A Carnival Jangle" demonstrate, violence almost always signals the fissure. It gestures the ripped surface when social membranes are radically crossed. Social membranes buffer internal orders. They are the containers, the preservers of law, tradition, and local myths. To operate within the membrane provides a form of social protection, oftentimes a cover of convention or a generic route for the kinds of side street anonymity exercised by figures like Baptiste. But region, like other fabricated forms, is polysemic, assimilable to outside forces and to internal reversals, to various oscillations and forms of crossing. Such movement is not without consequences for preconfigured orders. When social membranes are disrupted, the whole cell contorts. The result, the writing suggests, is a landscape of bounded chaos, modeled disorder, and desire.

Dunbar-Nelson's writing reveals her fascination with the ways New Orleans regional life did not let itself be refereed by the ideas of order belonging to what she called the "quieter democratic institution of our republic."[45] She describes Exchange Alley, a New Orleans pedestrian thoroughfare she called an "alley of Latinism," in her early short story from *Violets*, "Anarchy Alley": "There the great American institution, the wondrous monarch whom the country supports—the tramp—basks in superior comfort and contented, unmolested indolence. Idleness and labor, poverty and opulence, the honest, law-abiding workman, and the reckless, restless anarchist, jostle side by side, and brush each other's elbows in terms of equality as they do nowhere else."[46] What this representation illustrates is the affective intensity of a counter-regionalism, or a region as a context of connectivity. It is an idea of region as a migratory system, maybe best defined as an expressive space between binaries or standbys of meaning. The stories suggest that these very spaces of internationalism as difference, existing within regional life, are grounds for resisting narratives of nationalist conscription. Spaces like Exchange Alley exceed the ordered space of the national "republic," represented by "the grim solemnity of the main entrance of the Hotel Royal on St. Louis Street, ending with a sudden return to aristocracy, this stamping ground for anarchy."[47] In the same way local customs, from shopkeepers' *lagniappe* to washing the steps yellow at noontime, reflect the embeddedness of transnational practice in regional space, regional culture inhabits the borders of the national as a kind of heteroglossia. It does not so much subvert the national by diminishing its authority, but rather it exceeds the national; it pushes beyond the boundaries and narratives of any official historical culture.

Hence Dunbar-Nelson's New Orleans fiction can be read as a case for challenging certain long-held suppositions about regionalism's treatment of modern immigrant experience and narratives of postbellum national reunification. Contemporary critics have reacted mostly against the supposition that regional literatures constituted any real protest toward nationalist consolidation of local life and postwar forms of centralized federal control. Rather, they have argued after Richard Brodhead and Amy Kaplan that, to the contrary, regionialist literature was largely complicit with enshrining nationalist narratives.[48] Kaplan writes that regionalism's insertion as a staple form of popular print culture in the North led to a form of Northern solidification, "as an imagined community by consuming images of rural 'others' as both a nostalgic point of origin and measure of cosmopolitan development."[49] Regionalism, Brodhead suggested, accommodated the reading practices of the genteel, elite reader for whom "the immigrant became a phobic embodiment of all imagined threats to elite superiority, from cultural mongrelization and racial dilution to political anarchism and class war."[50] Both arguments point to regionalism's participation in a nationalist ideology of consensus. The consensus of the tourist, the modern outsider, finally obviates conflicts of representation within a national landscape. Indeed, the tourist's relationship to place is temporary, discontinuous from other experiences of daily life because it is not functionally obligated for living. The tourist wants to experience the strangeness of a place, its circuitry and voices—not for requisite work, but for a kind of aesthetic pleasure. The tourist is attracted to a culture for its measure of difference from a culture already lived and known.

For these reasons, the notion of a counter-regionalism is further useful because it complicates facile binarisms between the immigrant and native, as well as the local and global. As Dunbar-Nelson's writing demonstrates, nineteenth-century regional discourse is not simply spectrum discourse along an ethos of ancestral or redolent region. It is not about a thickness of temporal sedimentation, modes of characterization frequently associated with the genre. Far from these flattening modes of representation, her fiction offers an opportunity for considering the ways regional expression brings together different traces in the space of the local, schemes of international commerce and immigration, as well as street vending and streetcar circuitry. As Edward Casey has commented, "a place is more an *event* than a thing . . . places not only are, they *happen*."[51] Such points finally bear on an idea that black nineteenth-century writing makes stark. Locality is a contest. It is not, to use David Harvey's phrasing, a "passive outcom[e] of social processes."[52] It is something particular, made particular through its mixtures of time and embodiment: perception makes it. Place, as Casey fittingly puts it, is "an ingredient" in perception.[53]

By exploring region's sites of dissimilitude, its nonprocessability into some narrative of national development, authors such as Dunbar-Nelson could highlight an embattled sense of place's processes. To a greater degree than other period regionalists her work anticipated recent scholarship on creolization. Within region, she identified themes of transnational custom borrowing, carnival pageantry, cultural syncretism, and overlaps in speech patterns and dialects. These qualities of region were not presented to the reader as souvenirs of a place, expropriated for popular consumption; rather, they are shown as dialectical processes of a place in perpetual reinvention and movement. Dunbar-Nelson's writing finally suggests that the historical continuity of New Orleans life was sustained by its participation in wider circuits of transnational exchange.

··

POST SCALE

Place as Emergence

Place is emergent. It trespasses fixity. And its flows exceed the lines of any nested narratives of scale (from local to regional and national to transnational). In closing with this claim, I have in mind the work of recent humanist geographers who arrive at an outright rejection of traditional notions of geographical scale. Scale is itself a highly flexible term. But what seems outmoded from the start, at least for new directions in literary studies, is thinking about scale in its long-standing geographical sense—as something like sequences of vertical differentiation. For example, urban theorist Neil Brenner describes geographic scale as "territorial units stretching from the global, the supranational, and the national downwards to the regional, the metropolitan, the urban, the local, and the body."[1] In such a schema, the rigging of social space is most clearly inferred by size and, importantly, sums of power. Local decisions are effectively enveloped into wider economies of power. And power as a kind of agglomerative effect concentrates itself furthest away from the embodied self, from the individual on the street. Power is corporatized. I could also draw attention to a fitting visual analogue for scalar descent, something Andrew Herod and Melissa Wright have called the Russian doll model of scale.[2] Such a model conceptualizes place as a kind of nested leveling. But it also presents a closure of lower levels by higher ones; lower levels can be accessed only as parcels of the higher. As geographer Richie Howitt has argued, scale as a nested hierarchy "assumes or implies that the sum of all the small-scale parts produces the largest scale total."[3] Experience shows us differently, though.

One could go on. But rather than joining debates on how scales function, or trying to infuse them with horizontality, I have found in my own time that such unit-driven, leveling models of how space works ultimately do little to capture the complexities of place as it is inscribed in literature. I think it is a component of cultural-geographical apparatus that literary studies might do well to reject, particularly since literary cartographies multiply narratives about place relationships and character extension. Literature brings to the exploration of place nonquantifiable things like people's aspirations and memories. In a way, this recalls what Walter Benjamin took to be so compelling about the writings of Marcel Proust. He argued that Proust's "true interest is in the passage of time in its most real—that is space-bound—form."[4] Proust was important to Benjamin because he enlarged his study of the aesthetics of urban narrativity. In Proust, he encountered inventories of geographic sensation. Proust displayed the ways places accumulated traces of the past and continued to bear these out. Cities, written and rewritten, were filled with specters of memory, and literature as a medium could make more connectivity; it could saturate place with flows. As the readings here show, African American literature did something similar. It volatilized the presumably quiet spaces of the agrarian South and the nineteenth-century nonsites of human transit, nonspaces that were not acknowledged in the public record, except in profit ledgers. Literature could be, among other things, a kind of venue for tracing the texture of places as residual stories. It made plots from the kinds of hopes that were embodied in a place and histories of the losses. More broadly, what literature brought to geography were the poetics of recognition and revisitation.

In respect to further thinking past the architectures of bounded scale, another point is worth considering: African American textualities that are most deeply about place rarely convey it in the third-person omniscient, what social scientists call a "perspectivalism," or a kind of God's eye view from above and outside of experience. In the case of traditional scale, the organization almost always tallies up to some ultimate assumption. The ultimate assumption, if that is what to call it, is usually the global. And so, the implicit hierarchy is that everything radiates from the molt of the global. Now, industrial organization has relied on such models, and so have various foundationalist-driven systems. But black narratives in the nineteenth century (and in the twenty-first century, for that matter) mostly do not. Instead, the literature explored in these pages conveys spatialities as the courses of experience. Black literature accretes sites and symbols, and it is almost always involved in redistricting different hierarchies in environment. The final chapter on creolized region, which brings this book to a close, showcases the blending of different networks that comprise space in any interactive experience of it. Alice Dunbar-Nelson's creole stories illustrate the ways region layers different components of the hemispheric, the national, and the urban, and makes them relational tracings for the writer.

I mention Dunbar-Nelson, but in a way all the chapters in this book reach the same position: what matters most is connectivity. And they take the view that place is both material and discursive. Place is foremost a physical reality. It holds a great many events together. In fact, it yields the very terms by which we understand such flexible and broad life themes as movement, boundaries, and territory—all issues certainly pushed to a crisis in the black nineteenth century. The avatars of the early black novel very clearly understood the North American landscape to be something marked precipitously by dividing lines that were at once material, spiritual, and symbolic. Antebellum blacks, in particular, knew what it was like to be landlocked in a place with no clear paths leading out, subject to the impositions of the slaveholder's legal system and racist political economy. They knew what it was to be marked as other and physically conspicuous as an "American Negro," frequently subject to attack or, more patronizingly, punishment. They lived in the physical unyieldingness of place. The boundaries and barricades they encountered were not features of a landscape that could easily be abstracted away or attributed to mere orientation. But such obstacles also constitute a discursive terrain in black literature. It is a terrain that is rife with multiple counter-sites and creative spaces of dissension. Indeed, the stories and counter-maps examined in Black Atlas are less representative of some wider canon than they are performative: they redesignate the circulations of place—flows like migrations and capital—that were parceled into narratives of containment in dominant discourses. African American literature, I have argued, modalizes a real variety of spatial arrangements because the writing itself calls into quick relief much of what is presumed tacit in our thinking about geography and structures of belonging.

For instance, Gaston Bachelard in *Poetics of Space* has argued that the very layouts of the homes we inhabit, our earliest homes, teach us how to imagine being in the world. He writes: "In short, the house we were born in has engraved within us the hierarchy of various functions of inhabiting. We are the diagram of the functions of inhabiting that particular house, and all the other houses are but variations on a fundamental theme."[5] Bachelard's meditations revolve around soma's transport through structures of habitation. He also imagines the home as contouring our imaginations of intimacy and immensity. But for many, the whole house model can make for a fairly depressing determinism. Contemporary Chicana writers like Sandra Cisneros have, of course, recognized that such "communal knowledge" of bourgeois architectures did not match her experiences, and that "the metaphor of the *house* was totally wrong."[6] This would have been much more the case for the author of *The Bondswoman's Narrative*, Hannah Crafts, or for Harriet Wilson, author of *Our Nig*—or for nearly any of the U.S. fugitive slaves whose autobiographical records teach us much of what we know about black geographies of the interior.

Nineteenth-century African American autobiography and fiction recorded these experiences of confinement and systems of enclosure, often as epistemological conditions of the black literary voice ever reaching print in the first place. One recalls the nine feet long, seven feet wide, and three feet high center of *Incidents in the Life of a Slave Girl*: This was the Edenton, North Carolina, attic crawlspace where the fugitive Harriet Jacobs hid herself from other household occupants for seven years, venturing out only in the dark. Novelists like the nineteenth-century intellectual Martin Delany minutely imagined the airless holds of Baltimore clipper ships that became Atlantic slavers, describing in the novel *Blake* the "half suffocated beings closely packed in narrow stalls,"[7] and William Wells Brown drew his readers' attention to the bolted slave pens in major port cities of the U.S. South and District of Columbia.[8] The dimensions of the crate—two feet wide and eight inches deep—that Virginia slave Henry "Box" Brown had himself nailed into before being shipped to freedom in Philadelphia constitute a sort of subframe for his well-known, midcentury fugitive narrative. All told, much of what geography represented were the terms of black entrenchment.

Further, while place was marked by coded restrictions and claustrophobic corridors, the recorded passages of time for antebellum blacks were also tied to a sense of impassiveness, a heavy history of constraints. The search for a collective history as a wellspring for present action, a backstory of prediasporic freedom or the quested peoplehood that so preoccupied Martin Delany and propelled him through various aborted studies of Egyptology and claims of royal lineage in various African countries, did not yield any ready results in the space of the antebellum United States. There was no English-language almanac or recorded history to predate national black bondage. Africans came first to the Virginia Colony in 1619 without listed surnames, some tenuously termed indentured servants, and many living out their time in the New World as perennial slaves. By the founding of the American Republic in 1776, the slave population in the colonies was nearly 500,000.[9] Not until 1777 did the first of the thirteen colonies (Vermont) abolish slavery and enfranchise all adult males. The stories of nineteenth-century life with the radically shifting map of U.S. land possessions and the explosion of domestic slavery in a young nation are, of course, the material of a vast archive of slave narratives, fiction, and letters that *Black Atlas* draws on. But as is commonly known, by the time of the Civil War, the number of slaves in the United States had already grown to four million, and slaves comprised nearly 13 percent of the entire population of the country. Many lifetimes had passed in the struggle for defining the terms of national geography. And it was far from over. Reviewing the history of black experience in the United States from slavery through Emancipation and Reconstruction, W. E. B. Du Bois wrote in *The Souls of Black Folk* that "the vistas disclosed as yet no goal, no resting-place."[10]

At the same time, the authors I have discussed in this book did not limit themselves to thinking about geography in the given terms of dominant U.S. mappings. Nor did they adhere to standard geographic forms that gave coherence to the shapes of an emergent republic, itself radically undermined anyway during the black rise of the novel by its own midcentury federalist policies, internal cessions, and territorial acquisitions from independent Indian Nations and Mexico—as well as old imperial contenders, France and Spain. Whatever it meant as an idea, republic was radically in flux as a space. In fact, as racialized outsiders from white advantage, African Americans shared many reasons for seeking meaning beyond the enclosures of domestic race culture. The complexity of their diasporic counter-mappings, their routes around the iconic map of "one nation, indivisible," exceeds anything that can be summoned into one book or volume.

To be sure, then, Black Atlas is not positioned as some exhaustive study of the black territorial imaginary of empire—even though I take empire to be geographically ubiquitous: It rewires relations of hemisphere, between national mainland and island "interests," and relations of locality alike. Certainly, much of the literature, poetry, and critiques by twentieth-century postcolonial writers, especially after Frantz Fanon's Les Damnés de la Terre (The Wretched of the Earth; 1961), delineates the pervasiveness of empire through the conjunctions between land and language and word to world. Yet what we find is that the black novel genre did arise in relation to questions of geography, and that African American literature was an aestheticization of crucial concerns about black placement and placelessness in respect to material issues of territory. Therefore, I would be amiss if I did not close by emphasizing the valence of nation in these nineteenth-century texts. Nearly all of the African American literary texts examined in this book critiqued dominant notions of nationhood by pulling at a seam of national meaning. And even when their purviews appeared most diasporic in scope or most local in context, the authors all attended closely to the ways nation was written onto geography. Their writings show us how nation's preconditions and rhetorics influenced black planes of projection. They thought about national space very seriously.

I should also be clear that nineteenth-century African Americans—among them such pan-Africanist intellectuals as Alexander Crummell, Henry Highland Garnet, and Edward Wilmot Blyden—did not approach nation as a site of particularism or narrow fixity, as it is frequently accorded in more contemporary black diasporan treatments, especially after Paul Gilroy's panoramic The Black Atlantic. The Black Atlantic is probably the most field-defining work to merge black diasporan spatialities with literary studies in the past two decades. It presents the Atlantic as a frame to counter nation-state orientation and the artificially separated histories of Europe, Africa, North America, and the Caribbean. It also usefully extends Stuart Hall's argument that colonialism rewrites nation-centered grand narratives.[11] But Gilroy's important framework has also enabled some broad-brushed usages that constrict more particularized histories—against which loosely transnational identifications are made into sites of emergence. At the outset, Gilroy reminds readers that "the lure of ethnic particularism and nationalism has provided an ever present danger."[12] He later identifies such particularisms as "petty issues like language, religion, skin color, and to a lesser extent gender above and beyond which new alliances for black survival must be forged."[13]

In considering future directions for the study of geographical aesthetics and African American cultural history, I am led to ask: Are these issues really petty? Are they petty in the lived experience of any individual? The centrality of these themes to black ontology and representation (dating at least as far back as the earliest African American spiritual autobiographies published in the 1760s and continuing into the present twenty-first century) indicates, if anything, a greater need to reimagine and rearticulate the functions of language, gender, and religion, and the sites they arrange—instead of categorizing them as banal or less than valid modes for organizing experience.[14] In this vein, Sandra Gunning has pointed out that the "most recent privileging of disaspora identification almost to the point of romanticizing the revolutionary and subversive power of this identification threatens to elide the very real impact of color, status, region, and gendered experience as sites of intra-racial difference within the context of black diaspora."[15] Further, the desire to abandon the category of nation as a framework for black subjectivity tends toward the presupposition of a national wholism— albeit an admittedly fraught cohesion—or a *volkisch* normativity that needs to be broached from the outside for the extraction of wider cosmopolitan citizenship. But, as Saskia Sassen reminds us, "national space was never unitary or fully integrated to begin with, despite its institutional construction as such."[16] Official histories might enlist some original, organic form as a kind of underlay for the temporal crescendos of national history. (Any variant of national syndicalism briskly comes to mind.) But materially and affectively, national spatialities are polyphonous constructions. They do more than embed different histories; they proliferate them. Nation is thickly attached to the ways most people come to understand place and their various handles on coexistence. For this reason, it is geographically important.

Lastly, for authors such as William Wells Brown, Martin Delany, Frederick Douglass, Pauline Hopkins, Alice Dunbar-Nelson, and Charles Chesnutt, place stories were currencies. They were networks of meaning and exchange. In fact, as I have tried to show, place as contestation is not reducible to discursively arcing over nation with transnationalism or getting beneath it by appositionally identifying the structures through which people on the inside are made "other" or "outsider." Rather, it includes the potential for new mappings, where variegated stories grow and where, sometimes, more inclusive understandings can emerge. For these reasons, across the different readings I have tried to keep in the foreground an understanding perhaps most capaciously developed in the work of feminist geographers and their discussions of body space. It has to do with their insistence on the body as an arena of contestation and the ways the body is mediated by rhetoric. Nancy Duncan and Gillian Rose, in particular, have cautioned against what they take to be the common geographical tendency of "grounding spatial metaphors" as the real, as solid, concrete patterning.[17] Conversely, the nonreal is fluid, interiorized, indeterminate, feminine, and flux. It is all that surfeit that does not marshal into the bedrock of solidity. Such points are highly relevant in literary approaches to geography because they signal how questions of embodiment are at the center of spatial experience and that embodiment is freighted by geographical terminology and the weight of dominant usages. As I have tried to show through different textualities, places can be composed, and their codings can be taken apart. The terms of their makings can be reassigned. This is what deterritorializing literature does: It reconfigures the spatial codings of representations.

It makes sense, then, to end with the claim that places not only host conflicts but are themselves a product of conflict. Places thus stand in for what is at stake in how to negotiate a world and how to negotiate sharing a world. None of this changes the fact that geographies are highly topical things, with specific dates that matter. But maybe more interestingly, they are also something topological.[18] They bend and flex with movement. For nineteenth-century blacks this idea of place as flow, place as connectivity was, at best, a source of hope. It was in place that individuals were situated, embodied, gendered, and made subject or object. The possibility for new modes of representation might also be formed within the organization of space.

NOTES

....

Introduction. On Meaningful Worlds

1. Among this first generation of black novels are Frank J. Webb's *The Garies and Their Friends* (1857), Harriet Wilson's *Our Nig* (1859), and Martin Delany's *Blake* (1859–62).

2. Michel Foucault, *The Archaeology of Knowledge and the Discourse on Language*, 152.

3. The term "invention" is influenced by the rhetorical analysis of Kendall Phillips, "Spaces of Invention," 329.

4. Thadious Davis, *Southscapes*, 14.

5. Michel de Certeau, *The Practice of Everyday Life*, 115.

6. It seems fitting that the English word "space" derives from the Latin words *spatium*, meaning an interval or an expanse of time, and *ex-spatiari*, similar to wander or digress. Both roots connote a sense of directionless motion, a decentering effect. See the gloss on *ex-spatiari* in F. Ryland, *Johnson's Life of Milton*, 146. Also see "expiate" in T. R. Hoad, *The Concise Oxford Dictionary of English Etymology*. A similar etymology for "space" can be found in Mervyn Sprung, *Explorations in Life Sense*, 19.

7. Yi-Fu Tuan, *Space and Place*, 3–6.

8. Paul Dourish, "Re-Space-ing Place." See also Steve Harrison and Deborah Tatar, "Places," 99. Dourish's work, in particular, signals a movement in the field of informatics that advocates for a more phenomenological, place-forward approach to space, a kind of placial primacy.

9. Martin Heidegger, *Being and Time*, 102–4.

10. Anthony Giddens writes: "Place is best conceptualized by the idea of locale, which refers to the physical settings of social activity as situated geographically.... The advent of modernity increasingly tears space away from place by fostering relationships between absent 'others,' locationally distant from any given situation of face to face interaction" (*The Consequences of Modernity*, 18).

11. Tuan, *Space and Place*, 4.

12. Erica Carter, James Donald, Judith Squires, *Space and Place: Theories of Identity and Location*, xii.

13. This point is influenced by geographer Doreen Massey, who argues against core suppositions (by Henri Bergson and Ernesto Laclau, specifically) that space is something equivalent to representation. To use a phrase from Massey, such a view produces "a picture of the essentially dislocated world as somehow coherent" (*For Space*, 25). Laclau writes, "any representation of a dislocation involves its spatialization. The way to overcome the temporal, traumatic and unrepresentable nature of dislocation is to construct it as a moment in permanent structural relation with other moments, in which case the pure temporality of the 'event' is eliminated" (*New Reflections of the Revolution of Our Time*, 72). Massey cites challenges to Laclau's characterization of the spatial vis-à-vis the temporal from Richard Rorty, Gilles Deleuze and Félix Guattari, and geographers Timothy Ingold and Nigel Thrift. She goes on to suggest that poststructuralist critiques of mimetic representation might be fruitful for the study of geography: "As the text has been destabilized in literary theory so space might be destabilized in geography (and indeed in wider social theory)" (*For Space*, 28–29).

14. Robert Carr, *Black Nationalism in the New World*; John Gruesser, *The Empire Abroad and the Empire at Home*; Kirsten Gruesz, *Ambassadors of Culture*; David Kazanjian, *The Colonizing Trick*; Caroline Levander and Robert Levine, *Hemispheric American Studies*; and Nwankwo.

15. Robert Levine, *Dislocating Race and Nation*; see especially "Prologue: Undoings" (1–15).

16. John Ernest in *Liberation Historiography* makes the point that there can be no one Afro-American literary tradition any more than there is an Anglo tradition. He further argues that after the Civil War, many black writers turned from more oppositional historiographic discourses to more institutional ones, seeking a legitimization for their scholarly histories of black abolitionism, sacral spaces, and church histories as contributions to a more expansive U.S. democracy (*Liberation Historiography*, 330–31). Chapter 4 in this book is influenced by these claims.

17. Michael Curry, "Discursive Displacement and Seminal Ambiguity of Space and Place," 503–4.

18. Martin Delany, *North Star*, 12 January 1849: 2.

19. Sutton Griggs, *Imperium in Imperio*, 201.

20. Martin Delany, *Blake*, 305.

21. John C. Calhoun, "The Clay Compromise Measures," 189.

22. Kazanjian, *The Colonizing Trick*, 28–29.

23. *Plessy v. Ferguson*, 163 U.S. 537, 539 (1896). An excellent resource on the Dred Scott case is Don E. Fehrenbacher, *The Dred Scott Case* (see especially 347).

24. Bruno Latour, *Reassembling the Social: An Introduction to Actor-Network-Theory*, 108, 173.

25. David Harvey, *Cosmopolitanism and the Geographies of Freedom*, 557.

26. J. B. Harley, "Maps, Knowledge, and Power," in D. Cosgrove and S. Daniels eds., *The Iconography of Landscape*, 300.

27. Massey, *For Space*, 68.

28. Massey, *For Space*, 7.

29. Susan Gillman, *Blood Talk*, 119.

30. Walter Mignolo, "Globalization, Civilization Processes, and the Relocation of Languages and Cultures," 35.

31. Walter Mignolo, *Local Histories/Global Designs*, iv.

32. My conception of dominant discourses is influenced by Stuart Hall's "Encoding/Decoding." See also Hall's "Notes on Deconstructing the 'Popular.'"

33. Mike Crang and Nigel Thrift, Introduction, 3.

34. Edward Soja, *Postmodern Geographies*, 14.

35. Subsequent editions include *Clotelle: A Tale of the Southern States* (1864) and *Clotelle, Or the Colored Heroine: A Tale of the Southern States* (1867).

36. Hsuan Hsu, *Geography and the Production of Space in Nineteenth-Century American Literature*, 19. Though arguing from the perspective of scalar geographies, Hsu adeptly describes literature's mediating, reshaping position in bridging scales of bodily experience and the wider exigencies of the political and economic. For the studies underpinning Hsu's frame, see John Berger, *The Look of Things*; Neil Smith, *Uneven Development*; David Harvey, *Justice, Nature and the Geography of Difference*.

37. Ian James, *The Fragmentary Demand*, 107.

38. Katherine McKittrick, *Demonic Grounds*, 143.

Chapter 1. National Geographic

1. J. Noel Heermance, *William Wells Brown and Clotelle*, 164–65. See also Vernon Loggins, *The Negro Author*.

2. Addison Gayle argued that Brown's novel failed its nineteenth-century black readership as well as the broader project of the African American literary canon because it kept intact the images and symbols of a bourgeois romanticism. According to Gayle, *Clotel* failed to articulate a black specificity and collapsed racial difference by turning blacks into "people," "human beings," and "Negroes": "At a crucial time for black people, when the novel should have been engaged in redefining definitions, in moving to rebut both Mrs. [Harriet Beecher] Stowe and her detractors [Brown] is found lacking" (*The Way of the New World*, 6). In direct response to Gayle's indictment, Ann duCille writes: "It was a strategy of the times, this attempt to argue for equality . . . by pointing out the mutability of race and the absurdity of white society's color codes through the trope of the mulatto, tragic and heroic" ("Where in the World Is William Wells Brown?," 454).

3. Blyden Jackson and Bernard Bell situate their work in a larger project of addressing cultural and historical patterns arising across periodized histories of multiple black texts. For instance, Bell concludes his consideration of Brown with the comment that "it remained for Webb, Wilson, Chesnutt, Johnson, and other novelists to develop more deeply and fully the tragic mulatto theme and

character that Brown romantically introduced in the Afro-American novel" (*The Afro-American Novel and Its Tradition*, 42). See also Blyden Jackson, *A History of Afro-American Literature*, vol. 1.

4. John Ernest, *Resistance and Reformation in Nineteenth-Century African-American Literature*, 20.

5. The Bedford Cultural editions of *Clotel* edited by Robert S. Levine (2000, 2011) and Greenspan's *William Wells Brown: A Reader* are indications of a methodological shift in Brown studies—in effect, restaking the layers of anecdote, textual appropriations, and invention that circulate through the fiction as the very grounds for historicizing Brown's literature.

6. What *Clotel* demonstrates is that the early black novel could be a form for sewing cultural findings into a national text, a practice that Levine refers to as Brown's "bricolage" and "literary pastiche" ("Cultural and Historical Background," 7) and Ann duCille calls the shaping of "an 'unreal estate,' . . . an ideologically charged space, created by drawing together the variety of discursive fields—including 'the real' and 'the romantic,' the simple and the sensational, the allegorical and historical" ("Where in the World Is William Wells Brown?," 18).

7. Quoted in Kenneth Prewitt, "A Nation Imagined, A Nation Measured," 148.

8. Quoted in Joseph Ellis, *American Sphinx*, 202; and Peter Onuf, *Jefferson's Empire*, 181.

9. William Wells Brown, *Three Years in Europe*, 246.

10. William Wells Brown, *Clotel*, 190.

11. William Wells Brown, *The Travels of William Wells Brown*, 216.

12. John Cox (*Traveling South*), Cheryl Fish and Farah Griffin (*A Stranger in the Village*), and Stephen Lucasi have all pointed out how narrowly the genre of black travel writing has been defined, especially when the Middle Passage and international slave trade majorly configured black new world experience. Lucasi notes: "Unlike the previous generation of slave narrators who foregrounded the international spaces traversed by slaves, the 19th-century narrators primarily depicted stasis rather than movement—the fixed space of the plantation rather than the mobile or dynamic space of the slave ship—as the locus of slavery's horrors" ("William Wells Brown's Narrative and Traveling Subjectivity," 525).

13. William Wells Brown, *Narrative of the Life and Escape*, 91.

14. Frederick Douglass, *My Bondage and My Freedom*, 1855, 373.

15. Edlie Wong's work poses broader questions about the ways freedom and mobility are interlinked in legal discourses, reconfiguring the legal implications of travel through slaveholders' attempts to bring propertied persons into said-free jurisdictions (see Wong, *Neither Fugitive nor Free*). For an overview of the distinctions between clandestine movement by fugitives and overt legal challenges to the slavery institution afforded by relocation, see Edlie Wong, "Introduction," 1, 18.

16. William Wells Brown, *The American Fugitive in Europe*, 60.

17. W. Brown, *The American Fugitive in Europe*, 60–61.

18. Brown's affiliation with William Lloyd Garrison began at least as early as 1844, when Brown delivered his first speech at the tenth anniversary meeting of the American Anti-Slavery Society, held in New York. The society sponsored Brown as an antislavery lecturing agent during the 1840s and 1850s. It was also responsible for publishing his 1842 *Narrative of William Wells Brown, A Fugitive Slave*, a particularly successful publication that underwent four American editions and then five British editions, all before 1850. Brown's connections to Garrison and Wendell Phillips, in particular, were instrumental in shaping his skepticism toward the entire political apparatus of the United States, including its electoral process, and in fortifying his belief in the value of individual experiences to effect a moral revolution in the consciousness of his readers.

19. Mark Simpson, *Trafficking Subjects*, viii.

20. William Wells Brown, "Don't Come to England," reprinted in the *Liberator*, July 25, 1851.

21. W. Brown, *The American Fugitive in Europe*, 39.

22. Equiano wrote of his North American encounter with a Virginia planter: "While I was in this plantation the gentleman, to whom I suppose the estate belonged, being unwell, I was one day sent for to his dwelling house to fan him; when I came into the room where he was I was very much affrighted at some things I saw, and the more so as I had seen a black woman slave as I came through the house, who was cooking the dinner, and the poor creature was cruelly loaded with various kinds of iron machines; she had one particularly on her head, which locked her mouth so fast that she could scarcely speak; and could not eat nor drink. I was much astonished and shocked at this contrivance, which I afterwards learned was called the iron muzzle" (*The Interesting Narrative of the Life of Olaudah Equiano*, 64–65).

23. Equiano, *The Interesting Narrative*, 213.

24. Edward Casey's point, that "a place is something for which we continually have to discover or invent new forms of understanding, new concepts in the literal sense of ways of 'grasping-together'" ("How to Get from Space to Place in a Fairly Short Stretch of Time," 26), seems an apt descriptor for Brown's place inscriptions, which combine the work of authorship and activism.

25. Frederick Douglass, "The Fugitive Slave Law," transcribed speech to the National Free Soil Convention at Pittsburgh, August 11, 1852. *Frederick Douglass' Paper*, August 11, 1852.

26. William Wells Brown, *Three Years in Europe*, 248.

27. W. Brown, *Three Years in Europe*, 247–48.

28. The Missouri Compromise was revoked by the Kansas-Nebraska Act, which passed U.S. Congress on May 30, 1854. The act called for popular sovereignty in legislating slavery's spread into new western territories. Specifically, popular sovereignty allowed people in the territories of Kansas and Nebraska to decide for themselves if they wanted to allow slavery. This effectively repealed the Missouri

Compromise of 1820 because the earlier agreement prohibited slavery north of latitude 36°30', except within the boundaries of Missouri, Brown's home state. In 1857 the Missouri Compromise was altogether thrown out in the Supreme Court's Dred Scott decision. The court declared that the 1820 Missouri Compromise was unconstitutional and that slavery was permitted in all of the country's territories.

29. Currer is Brown's fictional proxy for the historical Sally Hemings. See Annette Gordon-Reed, *Thomas Jefferson and Sally Hemings*.

30. It was, in fact, five years prior to *Clotel*'s publication that Brown first encountered an anonymous poem, "Jefferson's Daughter," reprinted in the May 1848 issue of William Lloyd Garrison's *Liberator* (the poem first appeared in July 1839 in *Tait's Edinburgh Magazine*). The poem lamented that a daughter of the late Thomas Jefferson had been sold at a New Orleans slave market for $1,000. It accused antebellum Americans of being "blasphemers of Liberty's name," honoring the memory of the Revolutionary War as the nation's heroic quest to overthrow British tyranny, yet practicing dehumanizing slavery at home. For his part, Brown would go on to republish "Jefferson's Daughter" as a rather scandalous centerpiece in a compilation of forty-eight antislavery songs, which he called *The Anti-Slavery Harp; A Collection of Songs for Anti-Slavery Meetings* (1848). Five years later in *Clotel*, Brown extended the conceit of the short poem. About one-third of the songs in Brown's collection were taken from antislavery newspapers. See William Farrison, *William Wells Brown*, 123–26.

31. This idea that revision is not merely temporal adapation, trending, or cultural reaction, but more like its own alternative orderings, reminds readers of the spatial negotiations at play in various invocations of a story's plot. Different settings mobilize different scopes of signification and different ranges of meaning. As a kind of longitudinal, surface reading of *Clotel*, *Miralda*, and *Clotelle* shows, Brown's revisioning highlights the diachronous relationship between place making and authorship. Anna Brickhouse's work provides an interesting critical angle on tracking print histories. She writes: "We tend to understand literary revisionism primarily as a temporal issue: as the instance of a prior text adapted imaginatively to the cultural or aesthetic circumstances of a later moment. But revisionism is the product of—and itself produces—spatial effects" ("Autobiografia de un esclavo, 'El negro mártir,' and the Revisionist Geographies of Abolitionism," in *American Cultural Geographies*, 211).

32. Brown reprinted the Benjamin Banneker and Thomas Jefferson letter exchange in *The Black Man, His Antecedents, His Genius, and His Achievements*.

33. Jefferson's first city-planning document was his bill for moving the capital from Williamsburg to Richmond. The plans included a Parthenon-styled Virginia Capital at the peak of Shockhoe Hill and, according to Frederick Nichols and Ralph Griswold, "contained precedent-shattering innovations reaching far beyond the traditional functions of a legislator or architect" (*Thomas Jefferson, Landscape Architect*, 12). These included provisions for planning squares, streets,

and public buildings, and "for the first time in America, separat[ing] the three branches of government in buildings on squares of their own" (Nichols and Griswold, 12–15). Jefferson's plans ultimately proved too grandiose to be implemented by the Virginia Assembly in his absence while in France in 1784, but the plan was finally adopted in Washington, D.C. See Fiske Kimball, "Thomas Jefferson and the First Monument of Classical Revival in America," 473–74.

34. Gearóid Ó Tuathail and John Agnew, "Geopolitics and Discourse," 190.

35. *Clotel* is frequently cited as the leading text for text what came to be known as the tragic mulatta trope: The beautiful, imperiled, and passably white heroine of Brown's tale, riven by a divided racial inheritance and inhabiting a space between black and white domesticities, is a stock figure in the genre. For reconfigurations of the tragic mulatta tradition, see Jean Fagan Yellin, *The Intricate Knot*. Also see Rafia Zafar, *We Wear the Mask*. More recently, Eve Allegra Raimon writes: "Contemporary criticism of the tragic mulatta tends to project backward a transhistorical and fixed sense of U.S. ideologies of racial difference. In fact, the tradition employing the mulatta character came into being at the very time enduring notions of race were crystallizing in the new republic" (Raimon, *The "Tragic Mulatta" Revisited*, 4).

36. Brown never concealed his admiration for midcentury sentimental women writers. He included the long poem, "The Leap from the Long Bridge" (1851), by Grace Greenwood (Sarah J. Clarke), in the scenes depicting Clotel's death, which he also reproduced in his novel. The poem later constituted the thematic backbone for Brown's drama, *The Escape; or, A Leap for Freedom?* (1858), which traded on the same theme of an escape from slavery and a final showdown between liberty and tyranny. Brown rhapsodized Harriet Beecher Stowe's *Uncle Tom's Cabin* floridly in an 1853 letter published in the *Liberator* as having "come down upon the dark abodes of slavery like a morning's sunlight, unfolding to view its enormities in a manner which has fastened all eyes upon the 'peculiar institution'" (June 3, 1853).

37. Harriet Jacobs, *Incidents in the Life of a Slave Girl*, 145.

38. Brown transcribed portions of Lydia Maria Child's "The Quadroons" into several chapters of his novel. Child's story was originally published in *The Liberty Bell* in 1842 and was later revised for *Fact and Fiction: A Collection of Stories* (1847).

39. Midori Takagi, "Rearing Wolves to Our Own Destruction."

40. W. Brown, *Clotel*, 100.

41. William Gleason, *Sites Unseen*, 3.

42. Charles Dickens, *American Notes*. See also Rodney Stenning Edgecombe, "Topographic Disaffection in Dickens's *American Notes* and *Martin Chuzzlewit*"; Kris Lackey, "Eighteenth-Century Aesthetic Theory and the Nineteenth-Century Traveler in Trans-Allegheny America."

43. For more on Tredegar Iron Works as a microcosm of the culture war between free labor and bond labor, see Charles Dew, *Ironmaker to the Confederacy*; and Gregg Kimball's more recent *American City, Southern Place*.

44. Michael Hardt and Antonio Negri, *Empire*, 122. The authors continue: "Slav-

ery, servitude and all the other guises of coercive organization—from coolieism in the Pacific and peonage in Latin America to apartheid in South Africa—are all essential elements internal to the process of capital development."

45. Seymour Drescher, *Capitalism and Antislavery*, v–vi.

46. Ann Laura Stoler, "Intimidations of Empire," 3.

47. Stoler, "Intimidations of Empire," 2.

48. Ann Laura Stoler, "Tense and Tender Ties." See also Ann Laura Stoler, *Carnal Knowledge and Imperial Power*.

49. Robert Reid-Pharr, *Conjugal Union*, 134–35. Both Nancy Armstrong (*Desire and Domestic Fiction*) and David Leverenz (*Manhood and the American Renaissance*) have described how the bourgeois domestic sphere is represented in antebellum fiction as a sort of unified public subject; it is a site for fashioning competing values, interests, and social positions that are consequently replayed and restaged politically.

50. Quoted in James Wilmer, *Lincoln's Generals*, 25–26.

51. Bruno Latour, *Reassembling the Social*, 120.

52. Brown, *Clotel*, 149.

53. Arjun Appadurai writes: "The large regions that dominate our current maps for area studies are not permanent geographical facts. They are problematic heuristic devices for the study of global geographic and cultural processes" ("Grassroots Globalization and the Research Imagination," 7–8).

54. Frederick Douglass, *Narrative of the Life of Frederick Douglass*, 37.

55. Christopher Waldrep, *Vicksburg's Long Shadow*, 2. Following his identification as a forger in 1859, Red Jack was tried, convicted, and sentenced to prison for twenty years in 1860. *Vicksburg Weekly Citizen*, October 31, 1859. Waldrep notes that until his capture, Red Jack "had sold so many phony passes for a dollar and a half each that slave owners noticed an uptick in the number of runaways" (*Vicksburg's Long Shadow*, 2).

56. Peter Hinks has compiled a list of letters and newspaper reports related to the circulation of Walker's pamphlet into port cities of the South. See David Walker, *David Walker's Appeal*, 90–106.

57. Brown was the first person to report the ingenious escape of the Crafts in a letter in 1849, which was printed in Garrison's *Liberator* in an article titled "Singular Escape" (January 12, 1849, 7). As Edward Farrison, Brown's biographer, points out, the story was in turn picked up by the *New York Herald* (January 17, 1849) and other newspapers from Pennsylvania to Massachusetts (*William Wells Brown*, 181). Admiring the ingenuity of the husband-and-wife team, Brown helped install the fugitive couple on the Massachusetts Anti-Slavery Society's lecture circuit through 1849, later arranging for them to join him on his antislavery tour in Europe, as he was writing *Clotel*. In 1860 William Craft published the story that Brown first made public: *Running a Thousand Miles for Freedom; or, The Escape of William and Ellen Craft from Slavery*.

58. Iuliu "Julius" Herscovici's self-published 613-page *The Jews of Vicksburg, Mississippi* (2007) provides an extensive treatment of nineteenth-century Jewish immigration to Mississippi from Europe and the early establishments of Jewish congregations in the city.

59. Christopher Morris, *Becoming Southern*, 249.

60. See Claudia Goldin, *Urban Slavery in the American South 1820–1860*; Richard Wade, *Slavery in the Cities*.

61. William Craft, *Running a Thousand Miles for Freedom*, 29.

62. W. Brown, *Clotel*, 169.

63. This near encounter is obviously inspired by the Crafts's own overnight stay in a Charleston hotel where Calhoun was reputed to have been staying at the same time (Craft, *Running a Thousand Miles to Freedom*, 51–52).

64. Increasingly, advocates of cosmopolitanism seek to distinguish their aims from those of universalism. Kwame Anthony Appiah aligns what he repeatedly identifies as a malign universalism with world-order fundamentalism and resistance to local allegiances. Cosmopolitanism, on the other hand, acknowledges translocal solidarities as well as the particularities of difference. See Appiah, *Cosmopolitanism*. In contrast, Seyla Benhabib argues that "the real challenge of cosmopolitanism . . . is the reconciliation of universalistic norms with democratic politics, in favor of an undifferentiated concept of the masses or of the multitude" ("Reclaiming Universalism," 6). For the most developed analysis of Brown and the limits of cosmopolitanism, see Martha Schoolman, "Violent Places."

65. Describing New Orleans, Brown wrote, "before the slaves were exhibited for sale, they were dressed and driven out into the yard. Some were set to dancing, some to jumping, some to singing, and some to playing cards. This was done to make them appear cheerful and happy." His own work was in the staging: "My business was to see that they were placed in those situations before the arrival of the purchasers, and I have often set them to dancing when their cheeks were wet with tears" (*Narrative*, 45–46). See also Walter Johnson, *Soul by Soul*, 1–3.

66. W. Brown, *Narrative of William W. Brown*, 61.

67. Brown described his work with Walker: "On our way down, and before we reached Rodney, the place where we made our first stop, I had to prepare the old slaves for market. I was ordered to have the old men's whiskers shaved off, and the gray hairs plucked out, where they were not too numerous, in which case he had a preparation of blacking to color it, and with a blacking-brush we would put it on" (*Narrative*, 43).

68. W. Brown, *Clotel*, 149.

69. Martin Delany, *Blake*, 11.

70. Joseph Holt Ingraham, a New England writer who visited the Forks of the Road slave market about 1834, wrote that slaves there "are not sold at auction, or all at once, but singly, or in parties, as purchasers may be inclined to buy." Quoted in Jim Barnett and Clark Burkett, "Forks in the Road." Likewise, classified

advertisements placed by Forks of the Road slave traders in Natchez newspapers simply announced the availability of slaves for purchase, indicating a casual, first-come-first-served approach to marketing slaves: "Lacking the competitive, public spectacle atmosphere of an auction, individual buyers and sellers were free to quietly strike a bargain" (Barnett and Burkett, "Forks in the Road").

71. Eric Gardner, *Unexpected Places*, 25; see especially "Black St. Louis in the 1840s and 1850s."

72. Kenneth Warren, "A Reply to My Critics," 403.

73. Elisha Valentine, "History of Elisha Valentine," 14–18.

74. David Johnson, "History of David Johnson and Wife, Fugitive Slaves from the State of—," 24–27.

75. Andrew Jackson, *Narrative and Writings of Andrew Jackson*, 17.

76. W. Brown, *Clotel*, 165.

77. W. Brown, *Clotel*, 165–66.

78. John Cox argues that freedom of mobility in the emergent states of America was aligned with "the right to travel among various states . . . one of the first individual freedoms establishe[d]" (*Traveling South*, 2). Cox points out that this was not a right extended to slaves, indentured servants, or fugitives. Rather, for mobile populations travel was "constitutive of American freedom and identity, serving as proof of their status (or lack thereof) as American citizens" (Cox, *Traveling South*, 18). This reading is based on Article 4 of the Articles of Confederation.

79. W. Brown, *Clotel*, 166.

80. W. Brown, *Clotel*, 215–16.

81. W. Brown, *Clotel*, 216. Although Brown does not make this point, the Quaker story could not have taken place during the time Brown was writing *Clotel*—at least not without serious legal repercussions for the Quaker farmer and his hired man.

82. Interestingly, Elizabeth Comstock told a very similar story. Comstock was an antislavery Quaker, born—like Brown—in 1815. She moved between Canada West, Michigan, and New York State. Her antislavery selections were edited and compiled by her sister, Caroline Hare, and published in 1895—some ten years after Brown's death. Comstock writes of a "beautiful octoroon," sold at auction to a "young profligate from the far south, who paid 1,800 dollars for her" (*Life and Letters of Elizabeth Comstock*, 67). Comstock accords agency to the young woman, who "manifested no repugnance, but appeared pleased," and she promptly makes her escape by night (*Life and Letters of Elizabeth Comstock*, 67). However, the focal figure in her account is the Ohio Quaker who leads the distressed refugee through a small back door of his barn to the Underground Railroad and then begins nailing several boards across the large barn doors. The story included details similar to the property dramas enacted in Brown's *Clotel*. The slaveholders are lectured by the Quaker: "Young man, thou art now in a free state; we have laws in Ohio, and it is a penitentiary offence to break open another man's premises. . . . Thou wilt have to bring a constable and a warrant." The slaveholders search for the person and

document "in a strange country where no one seemed disposed to aid them, or give them reliable information as to the way" (*Life and Letters of Elizabeth Comstock*, 68–69). In Comstock's telling, the Quaker also insists that they bring a carpenter, too, for "he would expect to recover damages if anything was injured" on his newly painted barn (*Life and Letters of Elizabeth Comstock*, 68–69). The sun sets on the enterprise and, as in *Clotel*, no slave is found when the barn doors are thrown open.

83. John Calhoun, "The Clay Compromise Measures," 189.

84. The conflict between labor, land, and capital, which Calhoun claimed would be resolved in a virtual plantation republic, prompted a great deal of U.S. literature. George Fitzhugh, a Virginia plantation owner, published influential sociological studies that reinforced the belief that Southern slaves fared considerably better than northern "wage slaves." Fitzhugh posited that economic values determined virtues, and hence that northern capitalism bred deficient temperament and was destructive to morality: "Temperance, frugality, thrift, attention to business, industry and skill in making bargains are virtues in high repute, because they enable us to supplant others and increase our own wealth." Fitzhugh, *Sociology for the South* reprinted in *Clotel* (W. Brown, *Clotel*, 398).

85. John Calhoun, *Speeches of John C. Calhoun*, 629–32.

86. W. Brown, *Clotel*, 186.

87. W. Brown, *Clotel*, 191. The economics of slavery was a prominent concern in nearly all antebellum African American fiction, and it was particularly apparent in the novels that treated black life in the antebellum Northeast, like Webb's *The Garies and Their Friends* and Wilson's *Our Nig*.

88. Farrison, *William Wells Brown*, 173.

89. William Wells Brown, *A Description of William Wells Brown's Original Panoramic Views*, iii. In *The Afro-American Novel and Its Tradition*, Bernard Bell more expansively examines Brown's uses of humor, satire, folklore, and code-switching narrative modes in *Clotel*.

90. Frederick Douglass, "What to the Slave Is the Fourth of July?," in the appendix of *My Bondage and My Freedom*. See also Frederick Douglass, "The Meaning of July Fourth for the Negro" (July 5, 1852), in Eric Foner, *The Life and Writings of Frederick Douglass*, 2:201; John Blassingame, *Douglass Papers*, 359–88.

91. John Stauffer, *The Works of James McCune Smith*, 147.

92. John Ernest, *Resistance and Reformation in Nineteenth-Century African-American Literature*, 21.

93. John Ernest, *Liberation Historiography*, 334.

94. W. Brown, *Clotel*, 110. For more on the generic conventions of frontier humor and its depiction of early U.S. landscapes, see James H. Justus, *Fetching the Old Southwest*; Andrew Silver, *Minstrelsy and Murder*; Gretchen Martin, "A Louisiana Swamp Doctor's Diagnosis"; Henry Clay Lewis, *Odd Leaves from the Life of a Louisiana Swamp Doctor* (especially the introduction by the editor, Edwin Arnold);

Hennig Cohen and William B. Dillingham, *Humor of the Old Southwest*. Contemporary writing on the frontier by the African American/Indian mountaineer and self-proclaimed Crow chief James P. Beckwourth also drew upon exaggeration, extreme environments, and trading-post wit, including stories of fights with wild beasts, Indian ruses, and mountaineer camp follies. Like Brown, Beckwourth came of age in Missouri, but he was never enslaved. See James Beckwourth, *The Life and Adventures of James P. Beckwourth as Told to Thomas D. Bonner.*

95. W. Brown, *Clotel*, 117.

96. Brown's rattlesnake inclusions appear to draw on the newspaper sketches of William C. Hall, who depicted life in the Yazoo Hills, near Satartia in Mississippi. Hall lived in that area for a time, until his hyperbolic writings of religious camp revivals and satirical portraits of identifiable locals, such as "How Sally Hooter Got Snake-Bit," purportedly forced him to flee for New Orleans. There he continued to publish his Yazoo-based stories for the widely circulated *True Delta* newspaper. A biographical sketch of the author appears in Franklin L. Riley, ed., *Publications of the Mississippi Historical Society*, Vol. X, 301–2. See also William Hall, "How Mike Hooter Came Very Near 'Wolloping' Arch Coony" in Lamar and Charlton, *Polly Peablossom's Wedding and Other Tales*, 146–53.

97. W. Brown, *Clotel*, 118.

98. An avid newspaper reader, Brown likely encountered the popular burlesque sermons of William Penn Brannan (1825–66), a Cincinnati newspaper writer and portrait painter who, like Brown, traveled down the Mississippi River to New Orleans. Brannan worked under various pseudonyms, including Vandyke Brown, and is best remembered for sermons such as "Where the Lion Roareth and the Wang-Doodle Mourneth," which revealed less about the Bible or scriptural understandings than the idiomatic characteristics and sayings of regional life.

99. W. Brown, *Clotel*, 117.

100. W. Brown, *Clotel*, 116.

101. W. Brown, *Clotel*, 119.

102. W. Brown, *Clotel*, 106.

103. William Wells Brown, *The Negro in the American Rebellion*, 143.

104. Martin Brückner and Hsuan Hsu, *American Literary Geographies*, 13.

105. W. Brown, *Clotel*, 46.

106. Abraham Lincoln, *Abraham Lincoln*, 1:426; 2:213.

107. In the first inaugural address, Lincoln said: "Again, if the United States be not a government proper, but an association of States in the nature of contract merely, can it, as a contract, be peaceably unmade, by less than all the parties who made it? One party to a contract may violate it—break it, so to speak; but does it not require all to lawfully rescind it? Descending from these general principles, we find the proposition that, in legal contemplation, the Union is perpetual, confirmed by the history of the Union itself. . . . It follows from these views that no State, upon its own mere motion, can lawfully get out of the Union,—that *resolves*

and *ordinances* to that effect are legally void, and that acts of violence, within any State or States, against the authority of the United States, are insurrectionary or revolutionary, according to circumstances"*(Abraham Lincoln,* 2:217–18).

108. Lincoln, *Abraham Lincoln,* 2:213. Ezra Greenspan observes: "Like most anti-slavery activists, in spring 1860 Brown had preferred Senator William Seward of New York to the little-known former representative from Illinois as the Republican Party's presidential nominee" (*William Wells Brown: A Reader,* 329).

109. In *Abraham Lincoln and the Second American Revolution,* James McPherson argues that Lincoln believed it would take the abolition of slavery and the restoration of the Union to fulfill the founders' aims—in effect, making valid the promise of the first American War for Independence.

110. Onuf, *Jefferson's Empire,* 181–82.

111. Martin Brückner, *The Geographic Revolution in Early America,* 134.

112. Charles Dew, *Apostles of Disunion;* Maury Klein, *Days of Defiance.*

113. Thomas Jefferson, *Notes on Virginia,* 162, 163.

114. Thomas Jefferson, *Notes on the State of Virginia,* query 19.

115. Leo Marx, *The Machine in the Garden,* 143.

116. Marx, *The Machine in the Garden,* 143–44.

117. Throughout the fiction, Clotel's ability to transgress the color line is never an automatic aegis of protection in the social economy of Brown's novel. In fact, several of Brown's leading African American characters, described in terms of their whiteness and general adherence when at all possible to bourgeois Victorian ideals of decorum and virtue, are extraordinarily ill suited to success. Like Clotel, they are mostly unable to survive the vicissitudes of a world that fails to operate according to the laws that govern their own high-mindedness.

118. Michel Foucault, *Power/Knowledge,* 149.

119. Jefferson closely oversaw Benjamin Henry Latrobe's execution of the plans for the Capitol. See Saul K. Padover, *Thomas Jefferson and the National Capital,* 232.

120. Edward Abdy, *Journal of a Residence and Tour in the United States.*

121. See Letter no. 22 in Brown, *Three Years in Europe,* 1852.

122. Though Brown's conception of national identity was not (anachronistically) modern, it was certainly contemporary. His treatment of nation was decidedly in keeping with the Romantic nationalist currents that dominated social thought in contemporary historiography. Brown was a voracious reader of European and U.S. history by, among others, the British writers Edward Gibbon, historian of the Enlightenment, and Thomas Babington Macaulay. Brown was also deeply interested in the work of the Victorian antislavery historian and biographer William Roscoe, whose *Life and Pontificate of Leo X* serves as the linchpin for Brown's uniting the two lost lovers—Clotel's daughter, Mary, and Horatio Green—in the final pages of *Clotel.* In addition, Brown was drawn to George Bancroft's monumental ten-volume *A History of the United States* (1834–74; revised into 6 vol. by the author in 1876 and 1883–85). Although admiring Bancroft as

the premier nineteenth-century United States historian and statesman, Brown was troubled by his failure to account for African American contributions to the United States. This omission would inspire Brown to write his own history: *The Negro in the American Rebellion*.

Chapter 2. Indigenes of Territory

1. Despite opposition to African American emigration from leading black intellectuals like Frederick Douglass and James McCune Smith, it would take the Civil War to slow the tide of interest. This was also testament to the wide-reaching hopes for national renewal and greater black equality that blacks attached to the Civil War. Finally, in the decade of the 1870s, after the federally authorized end of Reconstruction (with devastating consequences for southern blacks), emigration activity once again more publicly resumed. Liberian colonists like Edward Wilmot Blyden and Alexander Crummell petitioned African Americans to join them to build Liberia into a black beacon of light. In 1876 Delany formed the Liberian Exodus Joint Stock Steam Ship Company to bring blacks from South Carolina and Georgia to Africa. The expedition was bankrupted almost from the start.

2. Robert Sack writes: "Territoriality in humans is best understood as a spatial strategy to affect, influence, or control resources and people, by controlling area" (*Human Territoriality*, 1).

3. Henson observed: "I was not the only one who had escaped from the States, and had settled on the first spot in Canada which they had reached. Several hundreds of colored persons were in the neighborhood; and, in the first joy of their deliverance, were going on in a way which, I could see, led to little or no progress in improvement. They were content to have the proceeds of their labor at their own command, and had not the ambition for, or the perception of what was within their easy reach, if they did but know it" (*Truth Stranger than Fiction*, 138–39). His realization prompted a resolution to encourage the community to "invest our earnings in land, and undertake the task—which, though no light one certainly would yet soon reward us for our effort—of settling upon wild lands which we could call our own; and where every tree which we felled, and every bushel of corn we raised, would be for ourselves; in other words, where we could secure all the profits of our own labor" (*Truth Stranger than Fiction*, 139–40). Much of the narrative details these efforts to make a viable, economic, land-based community in Canada West.

4. Chapters 1–23 and 29–31 were originally published in the *Anglo-African Magazine* from January to July 1859. The remaining chapters of part 1 were first published when Delany reprinted *Blake* in the *Weekly Anglo-African* from November 1861 to May 1862. Only the first forty odd chapters of part 2 have been recovered. The novel was thought to be lost until Floyd J. Miller, then a doctoral student in history

at the University of Minnesota, uncovered the almost complete text of *Blake* (first chapters 24–28 and then chapters 32–74), resulting in the publication of the novel in book form.

5. Quoted in Frances Rollin, "Life and Public Service of Martin R. Delany," 80.

6. Gayatri Spivak, "Can the Subaltern Speak?"; Gilles Deleuze and Félix Guattari, *Anti-Oedipus*; *Kafka*; and *A Thousand Plateaus*.

7. Deleuze and Guattari, *Anti-Oedipus*, 145–53.

8. Robert Resch describes this fluidity in their territorial assemblages well: "Territorialization constitutes all social phenomena," he writes, "yet it lacks any unified or central locus, logic, or meaning. Difference, being ontologically prior and antithetical to society, resists the coding process, and therefore all forms of territorialization are inherently unstable and incomplete" (*Althusser and the Renewal of Marxist Social Theory*, 230).

9. Deleuze and Guattari, *Anti-Oedipus*, 257.

10. The *Anglo-African Magazine* also featured contributions by Frederick Douglass, Sarah Mapps Douglass, James McCune Smith, and Frances Ellen Watkins (later Harper), among others.

11. Hiram Chittenden, *The American Fur Trade of the Far West*, 2:689–90; Francis Parkman, *The Oregon Trail*, 124–25; Dale Morgan, *Jebediah Smith and the Opening of the West*, 156. Elinor Wilson details the means by which Beckwourth gained the appellation "gaudy liar" (*Jim Beckwourth*, 3–10).

12. Delmont Oswald, "Introduction," vii–xiii.

13. A black nationalist reading might take as its focus the essential qualities of Africanness, black autonomy, or African American exceptionalism found in Delany's work as hallmarks of an evolved cultural tradition. While scholarly attention has drifted from many of these essentialist issues, this earlier tradition of Delany scholarship still represented timely work in bringing out a black literary aesthetic (that was never singular to begin with) from under the mostly Anglo canon of American letters. Some of these attributes account for Delany's enlistment as a nineteenth-century forebear for academic black nationalism (Essien Udon, Sterling Stucky), where the casting lines of segregation and integration were leading issues.

14. This wealth of recent criticism attending to the complexity of Delany's intra-national fashioning has been important in the creation of a more expansive, nonessentialist black studies. See Andy Doolen, "Martin Delany"; Jeffory Clymer, "Martin Delany's *Blake* and the Transnational Politics of Property."

15. Delany's detailed attention to African American community-making strategies has been examined in newer, revisionist literary-historiographic perspectives. Important among these are the critical frames developed by John Ernest, Glenn Hendler, Stephanie LeMenager, Jordan Alexander Stein, and Katy Chiles.

16. Pheng Cheah in *Spectral Nationality* describes a postessentialist ideal of nation by reconstructing what he calls an ontology of "organismic vitalism" from

nineteenth-century Idealists (especially Kant, Fitche, and Hegel). Cheah rejects the irrationality attached to Romantic "organic" collectives—a term he applies to both societies and cultures—and posits the nation form as a kind of out working of a political ideal, as a rational vehicle for seeking freedom in form, and something that can be drawn upon by different indigenous collectives.) For the general arc of Cheah's argument, see especially *Spectral Nationality*, part 1: "Culture as Freedom: Territorializations and Deterriorializations." I am indebted to Jordan Alexander Stein's application of Cheah's work in his argument about abolitionist print histories. Stein opens with the controversial Liberian departure scene in *Uncle Tom's Cabin* to consider the ways such mid-nineteenth-century contemporaries as Sarah J. Hale and Martin Delany treated race and religion ("Christian teleology") as the grounds for national affiliation ("A Christian Nation Calls for Its Wandering Children," 849–73).

17. "A New Map," *North Star*, December 8, 1848. See also "Free Soil Map," *North Star*, March 9, 1849. Delany resigned as coeditor of the newspaper in June 1849 and returned to Pittsburgh in anticipation of pursuing his studies in medicine.

18. John Lewis, *Lewis' Free Soil, Slavery, and Territorial Map of the United States*. Lewis used war service statistics and a literacy table taken from the U.S. Census of 1840 to compare both the "comparatively feeble" efforts of Southern citizens in the War for Independence and the number of whites able to read and write in slave states, compared to free states, themes William Wells Brown put to use in *Clotel*.

19. John Lewis, *Lewis' Free Soil, Slavery, and Territorial Map of the United States*. The map depicted slavery's extension across physical space through statist territorial arrangements. Lewis asks: "Had Georgia a moral right, in ceding its Western Territory to the Union in 1798, to insist on closing it against the ordinance of 1787, and thus dooming it to the causes of slavery?" Or, the map reads, "had the Slave States, in 1804, a moral right to close Louisiana against this ordinance, thus dooming it to the same mischief? Or when Missouri was admitted, to inflict the same blight upon that State, and to extend it over all the territory, south of latitude 36°30'?"

20. Martin Delany, *Official Report of the Niger Valley Exploring Party*, 237–38.

21. Blake is not degraded through habits of mind or strategies of dependence instilled by knowing only slavery. As Jon-Christian Suggs has argued, the real difference for Delany between a slave and a free man "lay in the relation between authority to . . . action" (*Whispered Consolations*, 101–2).

22. Martin Delany, *The Condition*, 50.

23. Delany, *The Condition*, 207. Here Delany characterized the positions of natives of Ireland and Germany, "depressed and downcast" in their native soil but undergoing what he described as a "physiological" change, upon migration to the United States (*The Condition*, 207–8).

24. Martin Delany, "Political Destiny," 278. The next line in the Hamilton-Gordon speech ("The pickpocket who robs us is not to be let off just because he

offers to restore our purse") refers to Britain's insistence on carrying out a war with Russia, despite the initial provocation for war being reversed (quoted in "Political Destiny," 278).

25. Delany, The Condition, 278.

26. Martin Delany, "Political Aspect," 289–90.

27. Delany, Blake, 262.

28. Delany, Official Report, 345.

29. Quoted in Delany, "Political Destiny," 278.

30. Gilles Deleuze and Félix Guattari, "What Is a Minor Literature?"

31. Delany, Blake, 109.

32. Jake Mattox interprets Blake's speedy and unobstructed travels as proof of black success in site claiming, something Mattox flexibly calls "mobile occupation," or a means of affecting different forms of discursive and physical settlement ("The Mayor of San Juan del Norte?"). Such a reading is important because it underscores the connection between movement and territory, mapping and making. Drawing on the work of Glenn Hendler, Mattox suggestively treats Delany's use of mobility as a projection of emigration goals: "A literal and discursive mobile occupation could underwrite the nation's claim to spaces and routes that formed the networks of emerging empire even as, for Delany, such processes could be intended to resist precisely those hegemonic claims of the U. S. nation" ("The Mayor of San Juan del Norte?," 529).

33. Delany, Blake, 68.

34. Delany, Blake, 80.

35. Delany, Blake, 86.

36. Deleuze and Guattari, A Thousand Plateaus, 177–78.

37. Deleuze and Guattari, A Thousand Plateaus, 158–60.

38. Deleuze and Guattari, "What Is a Minor Literature?" 16.

39. Nigel Thrift, "Intensities of Feeling," 59.

40. Edward Soja, Postmodern Geographies, 151.

41. Martin Brückner enlists Thomas Jefferson's adaptation of the 1806 Lewis and Clark report, presenting the status of their Missouri expeditions to the American public for the first time as a means of gaining support. In doing so, Brückner argues, Jefferson represented travel with statist instrumentalism. Place knowledges represented by the maps were not neutral illustrations of space. Rather, "in quoting geographical coordinates, the cartographic grid, and the map, the American president took possession of the narratives not only as a state-funded project but also as the basis of political capital" (Brückner, The Geographic Revolution in Early America, 206). See also Myra Jehlen, "The Literature of Colonization," 1:156.

42. Robert Levine has noted that Blake's teachings in astrology imply his black Masonic character (Martin Delany and Frederick Douglass and the Politics of Representative Identity, 195, note 292). Levine connects this to Martin Bernal's point, that "nineteenth-century Africanists regularly argued that astronomy was invented

by Egyptians; astronomical and astrological figures were thus central to antebellum black Freemasonry" (*Black Athena: The Afroasiatic Roots of Classical Civilization*, 226).

43. Delany gave few details of his first voyage to Liberia in May 1859. But he did thank the officers of the *Mendi* for "facilitating my microscopic and other examinations and inquires, during the voyage" and commented on their facility in "collecting scientific information by astronomical, meteorological, and other observations" (*Official Report*, 253). In chapter 3 of *Official Report*, he envisioned meteorology as connected to exploration and observation.

44. Delany, *Blake*, 133.

45. In another table Delany compiled, intended to assert the numerical dominance of the populations of the black race in "the Western Continent," from the Caribbean to Central and South America, he wrote: "This is a fixed fact in the zodiac of the political heavens, that the blacks and colored people are the stars which must ever most conspicuously twinkle in the firmament of this division of the Western Hemisphere" ("Political Destiny," 258).

46. "Free Soil Map," *North Star*, March 9, 1849.

47. Delany, *Blake*, 133.

48. Delany, *Blake*, 133.

49. Striated space is authoritarian, canalized, hierarchical. It is a space of achievement, though not a space of becoming. See Deleuze and Guattari, *A Thousand Plateaus*, 486.

50. Emphasizing the sort of sublimated moral economy Delany wished to achieve through his characterization of a White Gap, John Ernest observes: "The transformation of commercial discourse into a vehicle for revolutionary moral reform is characteristic of Delany's strategies throughout *Blake* . . . the passage to the reinvention of power by way of the appropriation of moral discourse and authority" (*Resistance and Reformation in Nineteenth-Century African-American Literature*, 124). As Ernest's reading suggests, passage through the White Gap is passage through the white codes governing conduct and commerce. It requires an understanding of the sorts of relations and arrangements that preside in given places, arrangements that make up the social infrastructure of space.

51. Delany, *Blake*, 203.

52. Delany, *Blake*, 43.

53. Delany, *Blake*, 84.

54. More recently, *The Life and Adventures* has been discussed in the growing field of black frontier studies by Michael K. Anderson, Blake Almendinger, and Noreen Grover Lape, among others, for its constructions of masculinity, racial passing, and the gaps such passing produces between representation and experience.

55. Beckwourth, *The Life and Adventures*, 534.

56. Beckwourth, *The Life and Adventures*, 51.

57. Deleuze and Guattari, *Anti-Oedipus*, 372.

58. See Deleuze and Guattari, *Anti-Oedipus*, especially 372–82, beginning with the capitalist formation of sovereignty to a deterritorializing critique of capitalism's growth and operations. Deleuze and Guattari argue that localizing concerns to wages and improvements supports the capitalist machine, and that the profit ventures of capitalism "pass through the mesh of the axiomatic, underneath the recodings and the reterritorializations," expanding its aims biologically, symbolically, and beyond (*Anti-Oedipus*, 375).

59. Beckwourth, *Life and Adventures*, 121.

60. Thomas D. Bonner, "Preface," 3.

61. The most colorful analysis of Bonner's temperance efforts, illuminated by his corpus of published work, can be found in Elinor Wilson, *Jim Beckwourth*, 133–46.

62. William Andrews, *To Tell a Free Story*, 22.

63. Andrews, *To Tell a Free Story*, 23. "We had formed the opinion . . . that Captain Beckwourth was a rough, illiterate backwoodsman, but we were most agreeably surprised to find him a polished gentleman, possessing a fund of general information which few can boast" (quoted in *Rocky Mountain News*, 1 December 1859).

64. Bonner, "Preface," iv.

65. Noreen Grover Lape makes the point that the collaboration results in a hybrid Western form of frontier romance, composed of war and captivity narratives, with an emphasis of cultural crossings or "excursions between cultures" and the plight of civilization facing savagery (*West of the Border*, 23).

66. Blake Allmendinger, *Imagining the African American West*, 2.

67. Oswald, introduction, 601. See also Carl Wheat, *California in 1851*, 1:87–88, 88–93.

68. "Story of James P. Beckwourth," *Harper's New Monthly Magazine*, Vol. xiii (June to November), 1865, 455.

69. See T. D. Bonner, *The Temperance Harp*. Themes of temperance enter Beckwourth's text in chapter 31, which describes the devastating effects of whisky or firewater on the Cheyenne, who were actually supplied by the text's hero, Beckwourth himself.

70. Beckwourth, *The Life and Adventures*, 529.

71. Beckwourth, *The Life and Adventures*, 232–33.

72. Beckwourth, *The Life and Adventures*, 14.

73. Beckwourth, *The Life and Adventures*, 382.

74. My concept of absolutism in citizenship is influenced by James Clifford, *Routes*, 8–10.

75. Beckwourth, *The Life and Adventures*, 51–52.

76. E. Wilson, *Jim Beckwourth*, 38.

77. Beckwourth, *The Life and Adventures*, 534.

78. Beckwourth, *The Life and Adventures*, 233.

79. Beckwourth, *The Life and Adventures*, 347.

80. Beckwourth, *The Life and Adventures*, 347–48.

81. Beckwourth, *The Life and Adventures*, 348.

82. Beckwourth, *The Life and Adventures*, 347–48.

83. Beckwourth, *The Life and Adventures*, 214. Noreen Grover Lape further points out that the fur trade relied on no single currency and no fixed scale of value: "Beckwourth enabled these transactions by claiming dual racial identities and maintaining simultaneous national and tribal allegiances" (*West of the Border*, 5).

84. As I show in the following chapter, Delany believed that midcentury U.S. chattel slavery existed at the nexus of a hemispheric slave system.

85. Delany, *The Condition*, 12.

86. Paul Gilroy, "There Ain't No Black in the Union Jack," 158.

87. Delany, *The Condition*, 11.

88. R. Radhakrishnan argues that globalization actually does little to promote the functional dissolution of the nation-state as it has often been reputed to do, but rather is intrinsically tied to the work of nationalism insofar as it "takes the form of the dismantling of subaltern nationalisms by developed nationalisms" ("Globalization, Desire, and the Politics of Representation," 316).

89. Delany, *Blake*, 85.

90. Grant Foreman, *The Five Civilized Tribes*. See also Barbara Krauthamer, "In Their 'Native Country.'"

91. The Chickasaw campaigned for nearly two decades to separate themselves from the Choctaw and delimit their borders, and managed to do so by 1856, when they appointed their own governor and set up an electoral government.

92. Clara Kidwell, *Choctaws and Missionaries in Mississippi*.

93. Delany, *Blake*, 86.

94. "The African Diaspora in Indian Country," 10.

95. Delany, *Blake*, 287.

96. Delany, *Blake*, 87.

97. Indian Commissioner William Medill wrote in 1848: "The policy already begun and relied on to accomplish objects so momentous . . . is . . . to colonize our Indian tribe[s] beyond the reach, for some years, of our white population; confining each within a small district of country, so that as the game decreases and becomes scarce, the adults will gradually be compelled to resort to agriculture and other kinds of labor to obtain subsistence, in which aid may be afforded and facilities furnished them out of the means obtained by the sale of their former possessions." "Indian Commissioner Medill on Indian Colonies" from the Annual Report of the Commission of Indian Affairs, November 30, 1848. House Executive Document no. 1, 30th Congress, 2d, sess., serial 537: 385–89 in Francis Paul Prucha, *Documents of United States Indian Policy*, 77.

98. My description of border knowledges is influenced by feminist epistemologist Linda Martín Alcoff, who distinguishes between Walter Mignolo's border

thinking and theories of situated knowing such as those associated with Donna Haraway and Lorraine Code. The latter are attentive to both the development of knowledge for epistemological agents and the conditions of being knowers. But what Alcoff identifies in Mignolo's more normative epistemology is not a theory about the noninterchangeability of individually situated knowers, about showing knowledge as always locatable and partial. Rather, it is "a theory about epistemic resources that accompany a very specific site" ("Mignolo's Epistemology of Coloniality," 93). "Border knowledges," writes Alcoff, are "those that emerged from the encounter itself, not simply from a local context of any sort" ("Mignolo's Epistemology of Coloniality," 93). See also Walter Mignolo, "The Geopolitics of Knowledge and the Colonial Difference" and *Local Histories/Global Designs*.

99. Taiaiake Alfred, *Peace, Power, Righteousness*, 59.

100. Vine Deloria Jr., "Self-Determination and the Concept of Sovereignty," 122.

101. Beckwourth, *The Life and Adventures*, 324.

102. Beckwourth, *The Life and Adventures*, 324.

103. Though Beckwourth cites the War Department, Indian Affairs had by that time been turned over to the Department of the Interior, created in 1849. U.S. Statutes at Large, 9:395.

104. Quoted in "Indian Commisioner Medill on Indian Colonies" from the Annual Report of the Commission of Indian Affairs, November 30, 1848. House Executive Document no. 1, 30th Congress, 2d, sess., serial 537, 385–89, in Prucha, *Documents of United States Indian Policy*, 76.

105. Maureen Konkle, "Indigenous Ownership and the Emergence of U.S. Liberal Imperialism," 298.

106. Beckwourth, *The Life and Adventures*, 531.

107. Deleuze and Guattari, *A Thousand Plateaus*, 509.

108. Deleuze and Guattari, *A Thousand Plateaus*, 220.

109. William Andrews, "Annotated Bibliography of Afro-American Autobiography," in *To Tell a Free Story: The First Century of Afro-American Autobiography, 1760–1865*, 333–47; Beckwourth, *The Life and Adventures*, 33.

110. Beckwourth, *The Life and Adventures*, 444.

111. Henry Inman, *The Old Santa Fe Trail*, 437. Inman corroborates Beckwourth's accomplishments as a trader, stating, "His success as a trader among the various tribes of Indians has never been surpassed; for his close intimacy with them made him know what would best please their taste, and they bought of him when other traders stood idly at their stockades" (quoted in Oswald, editor's note in Beckwourth, *The Life and Adventures*, note 583).

112. Beckwourth, *The Life and Adventures*, 346–47.

113. See Wilson, "The Everglades," 86–87, 174–80; Oswald, editor's note in Beckwourth, *The Life and Adventures*, 617–18.

114. Beckwourth's testimony to the military commission investigating the mur-

der of peaceful Cheyennes on November 29, 1864 at Sand Creek is detailed in "The Sand Creek Massacre."

115. Beckwourth suggested that the most efficient means of killing Western Indians was by killing buffalo: "They can shoot them, poison them, dig pitt-falls for them, and resort to numberless other contrivances to efface the devoted animal" (*The Life and Adventures*, 533).

116. Beckwourth, *The Life and Adventures*, 533.

117. Beckwourth, *The Life and Adventures*, 233.

118. John Agnew, *Place and Politics*.

119. Beckwourth, *The Life and Adventures*, 348.

120. Beckwourth, *The Life and Adventures*, 530.

121. Beckwourth, *The Life and Adventures*, 530.

122. Beckwourth, *The Life and Adventures*, 530.

123. Beckwourth, *The Life and Adventures*, 158.

124. Beckwourth, *The Life and Adventures*, 530.

125. Beckwourth, *The Life and Adventures*, 197–98.

126. Matt Cohen, *The Networked Wilderness*, 7.

127. Deloria, "Self-Determination and the Concept of Sovereignty," 122.

128. Beckwourth, *The Life and Adventures*, 155.

129. Beckwourth, *The Life and Adventures*, 529.

130. Beckwourth, *The Life and Adventures*, 516.

131. Beckwourth, *The Life and Adventures*, 516.

132. Beckwourth, *The Life and Adventures*, 519.

133. Beckwourth, *The Life and Adventures*, 519.

134. Martin Brückner considers "geographical literacy," an aptitude for reading maps and cartographic processes, to be a "literary competence," along with the ways the learned subject engages in the "internalizing of geography as a kind of language" (*The Geographic Revolution in Early America*, 4). He thus argues for the map's centrality in American subject formation in the early republic, "within the intertwined technologies of land and print management" (*The Geographic Revolution in Early America*, 12).

135. Beckwourth, *The Life and Adventures*, 529.

136. Beckwourth, *The Life and Adventures*, 120.

137. See Anthony Giddens, *The Consequences of Modernity*, 63–65 on time-space distanciation as stretched relations between local and distant social forms.

138. Lawrence Buell considers how "the significance of environmentality is defined by the self-conscious sense of an inevitable but uncertain and shifting relation between being and physical contest," focusing on the concept of place as a way to draw out this relation (*The Future of Environmental Criticism*, 62).

Chapter 3. This House of Gathering

1. Carolyn Porter, "What We Know That We Don't Know," 521. Porter's call for a relational approach to American studies is cited in Robert Levine and Caroline Levander, "Introduction," and Emory Elliot, "Diversity in the United States and Abroad."

2. Gustavo Pérez Firmat, "Cheek to Cheek." See also Jane Desmond and Virginia Domínguez, "Resituating American Studies in a Critical Internationalism."

3. See José David Saldívar, "Nuestra América's Borders." For instance, Paul Gilles writes: "The hemispheric redescription of space also points, then, toward an equivalent remapping of time, a delineation of alternative genealogies for American literary history" ("Commentary," 652). Wai Chee Dimock further traces the evolution of hemispheric American studies and calls to "denaturalize" an already non-unified Americanness by both "mapping it against other coordinates" and "situating it within an alternate set of relations, linking it to a history older and broader than the territory and chronology of any single nation" ("Hemispheric Islam," 30).

4. Itala Vivan, "Geography, Literature, and the African Territory," 52.

5. Brückner argues "that in theory and practice the construction of the American subject was grounded in the textual experience of geography" (The Geographic Revolution in Early America, 6).

6. Brückner, The Geographic Revolution, 7.

7. See Kirsten Silva Gruesz, Ambassadors of Culture. For diachronic cartographies of New Orleans as a "pivot" to the wider Americas from the end of the nineteenth century to contemporary times, see Gruesz, "The Mercurial Space of 'Central' America." For European troping of American spaces from the perspective of Latin American cultural history, see Ileana Rodríguez, Transatlantic Topographies.

8. Denis Wood argues that maps are more than representational; they advance propositions (Rethinking the Power of Maps, especially chapter 2). For more on process geography, see especially Mike Crang and Nigel Thrift, Thinking Geographies; Doreen Massey, For Space. See also Edward Soja, Seeking Spatial Justice.

9. Polk appealed to Monroe's bold (at-the-time untenable without British naval support) proclamations from 1823, actually intended against Spain, to support U.S. military takeover of the Yucatán and annexation of Cuba some twenty years later (see Jay Cox, The Monroe Doctrine, especially chapter 3). For the relationship between the Monroe Doctrine and American literature, see Gretchen Murphy, Hemispheric Imaginings.

10. A powerful description of Delany's position in the early 1850s can be found in Robert Levine, Martin Delany, Frederick Douglass, and the Politics of Representative Identity, chap. 2, "A Nation within a Nation: Debating Uncle Tom's Cabin and Black Emigration."

11. See Bruce Harvey, American Geographics; also see Robert Carr, Black Nationalism in the New World.

12. My terminology here is influenced by Gilles Deleuze and Félix Guattari, *Anti-Oedipus*.

13. Timothy Oakes, "Place and the Paradox of Modernity," 510.

14. Bruno Latour, *Reassembling the Social*, 55.

15. Martin Delany, "Annexation of Cuba," *North Star*, April 27, 1849.

16. Q, "Cuba," *Liberator*, September 17, 1847.

17. Quoted in "The Scheme Unfolding the Future," *National Era*, August 12, 1847. The *American Literary Magazine* reported that "Cuba lies within very tempting distance of our own soil. It is only one hundred miles from the Florida coast and a poetical fancy might easily imagine that it had really been drifted away from our own continent and ought to be reclaimed as a waif of our own" ("Cuba," 109).

18. Martin Delany, *The Condition, Elevation, Emigration and Destiny of the Colored People of the United States*, 203.

19. Delany, *Blake*, 261.

20. Delany, *Blake*, 193.

21. Delany, *Blake*, 287.

22. Gearóid Ó Tuathail, *Critical Geopolitics*, 64.

23. Ó Tuathail, *Critical Geopolitics*, 59.

24. Ó Tuathail, *Critical Geopolitics*, 67.

25. Ó Tuathail, *Critical Geopolitics*, 68.

26. Eric Sundquist (*To Wake the Nations*) and Jean Yellin (*The Intricate Knot*) have argued that Delany began *Blake* in 1852 or 1853 as a revisionary counter-story to *Uncle Tom's Cabin*; the serial form of the novel suggests a second half written at a later date. Robert Levine demonstrates that the bulk of the text was produced between 1856 and 1859 (*Martin Delany*, 177). Patricia Okker contends that although the majority of the novel was completed prior to 1859, *Blake*'s two serializations in the inaugural issue of the *Anglo-African Magazine* in January 1859 and in the *Weekly Anglo-African* from November 1861 through May 1862 can convincingly be considered "separate texts" (*Social Stories*, 103). She argues that the presidency of Lincoln and the growing coverage of war dominated the later print runs and changed the context and representational claims surrounding the text.

27. "A New Map," *North Star*, December 8, 1848; "Free Soil Map," *North Star*, March 9, 1849.

28. G. W. Elliott, *Map of the United States, Showing by Colors the Area of Freedom and Slavery, and the Territories Whose Destiny Is Yet to be Decided, Exhibiting Also the Missouri Compromise Line, and the Routes of Colonel Fremont in His Famous Explorations*; William C. Reynolds, *Reynolds's Political Map of the United States*.

29. J. H. Colton was commissioned by the Bolivian government in the late 1850s to produce and deliver 2,500 large-format maps of the country. This is a saga in its own right, involving Bolivia's failure to pay, Colton's subsequent bankruptcy, and his eventual compensation, which restored his fortune. Colton's lawyer, Hinton

Rowan Helper, addresses Andean diplomacy and his client's claims in detailed length in "The Colton Claim against Bolivia."

30. See Borden Dent, *Cartography—Thematic Map Design*, especially chapter 13, on patterning visual planes in thematic mapping.

31. An excellent source on the emergence of modern mapping and printing technologies is Seymour Schwartz and Ralph Ehrenberg, *The Mapping of America*. For map technologies after the formative period of national cartography, see chapter 9, which discusses the rise of geological maps, California mining camp maps, and the technologies of image transfer.

32. Walter Ristow, *American Maps and Mapmakers*, 316.

33. John Short points out that maps were composite forms, building on sketches, notes, earlier maps, and available indigenous material (*Representing the Republic*, 34).

34. Delany, *The Condition*, 191.

35. Thayer and Colton maps were built from templates used and updated for about a decade. (For instance, the 1859 edition of Colton's two-sheet map of the United States was first issued in 1848.) Apart from the new boundaries added to the United States West and the addition of further travel routes, the map's composition and figural organization would look familiar to any viewer of his work throughout the earlier part of decade. Thus beyond its compound authorship and compounding of inscriptions/inscriptive devices, the map tells a story over time, much as a serial novel would do. But maps temporalize most directly through an angle on geography.

36. Names listed as signed on maps.

37. Jean Baudrillard, "Simulacra and Simulations," 151–62. Read according to Baudrillard's formulations, Californian gold deposits in the Atlantic might be representations of third-stage sign, a sign without a corresponding reality beneath, a "pacified . . . digest on the American way of life, panegyric to American values, idealized transposition of a contradictory reality" (154).

38. Borden Dent observes that the three elements of planar visual organization in thematic maps are balance or arrangement, focus of attention, and internal organization (*Cartography—Thematic Map Design*, chapter 13).

39. Carole Davies and Monica Jardine, "Imperial Geographies and Caribbean Nationalism."

40. See Antonio Benitez Rojo, *The Repeating Island*.

41. Walter Mignolo, *Local Histories/Global Designs*, ix.

42. Anthony Bogues, "Preface," v–vi. Bogues argues against a story of a leveling, homogenizing modernity "as a singular universal process that . . . drags both the colony and postcolony kicking and screaming into the present age and into a singular uniform process" (v).

43. Quoted in Michelle Stephens, "Black Transnationalism and the Politics of National Identity," 596.

44. Delany, *Blake*, 173.

45. Delany, *Blake*, 288.

46. Delany, *Blake*, 289.

47. Frederick Douglass, *Life and Times of Frederick Douglass*, 730. Douglass noted that "Haïti is no stranger to Americans or to American prejudice. Our white fellow-countrymen have taken little pains to conceal their sentiments. This objection to my color and this demand for a white man to succeed me spring from the very feeling which Haïti herself contradicts and detests."

48. Frederick Douglass, *Life and Times*, 731–32; see especially chapter 12. For a developed reading of Douglass that polarizes the dilemmas of recognition and affiliation in respect to Haiti, see Ifeoma Nwankwo, *Black Cosmopolitanism*, 140–43.

49. See Gordon S. Brown, *Toussaint's Clause*. See also Sibylle Fischer, *Modernity Disavowed*.

50. Michael Drexler, "Haiti, Modernity, and US Identities," 457–58. See also David Scott, *Conscripts of Modernity*.

51. Delany, *Blake*, 265.

52. Delany, *Blake*, 266.

53. Delany, *Blake*, 263.

54. Delany, *Blake*, 258.

55. Delany, *Blake*, 241.

56. Delany, *Blake*, 256.

57. Susan Gillman, "The Epistemology of Slave Conspiracy," 119.

58. Eric Sundquist, *To Wake the Nations*, 184–85.

59. Sundquist's concept of a mirror state is also suggestive of nineteenth-century African American literature's broader challenges to white periodicity (*To Wake the Nations*, 184–86).

60. Delany, *Blake*, 158.

61. Delany, *Blake*, 276.

62. Negro laws are discussed in chapter 74, late in the novel. Floyd Miller comments that Delany's "clearly didactic portrayal of Creoles subordinating their own biases for the greater good of black-led rebellion is at variance with the large numbers of Creoles who in actuality feared 'Africanization' (Introduction, xxiii).

63. The Ladder Conspiracy (*Conspiración de La Escalera*) is depicted in the novel as a cluster of events from the 1844 reactionary campaign of torture and execution of mostly blacks and mulattos. Events of 1844 further strained relations with Britain since the Spanish state alleged that British consul to Cuba, David Turnbull, had incited the rebellion (something reported in *Blake* as unlikely). The campaign was also responsible for the execution of Cuba's acclaimed poet Plácido (Gabriel de la Concepción Valdés), whom Delany casts as Blake's "yellow" cousin. See Delany, *Blake*, 193.

64. Delany, *Blake*, 310.

65. Aline Helg, "Race and Black Mobilization in Colonial and Early Independent Cuba," 54. See also George Andrews, *Afro-Latin America*.

66. For a thorough history of midcentury U.S. attempts to acquire Cuba, see Philip S. Foner, *A History of Cuba and Its Relations to the United States*.

67. Quoted in Charles Brown, *Agents of Manifest Destiny*, 109.

68. Wellington Williams, *The Traveler's and Tourist's Guide through the United States of America, Canada, Etc.*, iv.

69. See Wellington Williams, *A New Map of the United States*. This emphasis on popular destinations could account for the three insets in the map. The first appears directed to tourists; it is the Canada-U.S. junction at Niagara Falls. (The vastly popular Niagara Falls had just opened its first suspension bridge across the gorge in 1848.) The second inset was of the trans-Mississippi West, updated with boundaries drawn after the Compromise of 1850. It included California, Oregon, New Mexico, and Utah, important inclusions in a publication boasting that it featured three routes from New York to California. The third inset was slaveholding Cuba.

70. "The Ostend Report," 261–66. See also Sundquist's reading of the Ostend Report, *To Wake the Nations*, 183.

71. Matthew Guterl, "An American Mediterranean," 100.

72. Delany, *Blake*, 238.

73. Delany, *Blake*, 305.

74. Nwankwo, *Black Cosmopolitanism*, 77.

75. Delany, *Blake*, 305.

76. Delany, *Blake*, 282.

77. Cuba did not enter into Delany's political writing in any depth until a decade after the Ladder Conspiracy and Placido's execution. See "Political Destiny" (1854).

78. "Insurrection in Cuba," *North Star*, July 7, 1848.

79. William J. Watkins, "Cuba and the Administration," *Frederick Douglass' Paper*, May 26, 1854.

80. George Weston, "Will the South Dissolve the Union," *Anti-Slavery Bugle*, July 5.

81. See George Andrews, *Afro-Latin America*.

82. Delany, *Blake*, 294.

83. Delany's was not a transnationalism of cosmopolitan correspondence, linked to the circulation of journalism or the work of language and letters (translation) in bringing different diasporan groups and individuals into contact. Sandra Gunning makes the cogent point that nineteenth-century black cosmopolitanism cannot be read as a backstory for 1920s modernist, black cosmopolitanism (*Moving Home*).

84. Jean Cole observes: "In the course of the novel, Delany stresses the fact that the ability to move—through space, but also among different classes and races—is a fundamental aspect of freedom" ("Theresa and Blake," 165).

85. Delany, *Blake*, 62.

86. Delany was born to a free mother and a slave father who eventually purchased his freedom.

87. "Submarine Telegraph," *New Orleans Daily Creole*, December 24, 1856.

88. Delany, *Blake*, 295.

89. Martin Delany, "Annexation of Cuba," *North Star*, April 1849.

90. Delany, *Blake*, 305.

91. Delany, *Blake*, 305.

92. "Cuba," *American Literary Magazine*, 109.

93. Caroline Levander, "Confederate Cuba," 823.

94. Kirsten Gruesz points to the ways the Gulf of Mexico came to be defined in "The Gulf of Mexico System and the 'Latinness' of New Orleans."

95. Delany, "Political Destiny," 255–58.

96. Delany, *The Condition*, 169; *Official Report*, 263 and 346; *Blake*, 262.

97. Delany, *Official Report*, 288–89.

98. Delany, *The Condition*, 211.

99. Ronald Bogue, *Deleuze's Way*, 36.

100. Delany, *Blake*, 224.

101. Delany, *Blake*, 239.

102. Delany, *Blake*, 172.

103. Delany, *Blake*, 238–39.

104. See Delany, *Official Report*, 252–64. See also Martin R. Delany, "Niger Valley," *Chatham Tri-Weekly*, January 18, 1861.

105. While the eighteenth-century North Atlantic slave trade is frequently regarded as a kind of triangulation between Europe (particularly England and Spain), Africa, and the Americas, Delany's nineteenth-century depiction of illegal commercial activity notably occludes Europe. Only Britain is effectively brought into the fray. The British position in the Atlantic slave trade is double-edged: On the one hand, between 1651 and 1807, they were responsible for transporting an estimated 1,900,000 slaves to their Caribbean colonies. Yet Britain was the only nation Delany viewed as enforcing the ban on international slavery, stationing naval squadrons along coastal areas in both the Caribbean and along Western Africa, places like Gallinas, Sherbro, and Sierra Leone. Further, it is pursuit by a British ship that results in the greatest loss to black life depicted in this novel. Six hundred weakened slaves in the hold of the *Vulture* are thrown into the sea to avoid capture by lightening the ship's cargo load.

106. Delany, *Blake*, 238.

107. Delany, *Blake*, 238.

108. Andy Doolen argues that this transatlantic space emphasizes an economy of power that exceeds nation and "accumulates new territories" (*Fugitive Empire*, 165).

109. Transfer technologies were publicized in *Frederick Douglass' Paper*. In Febru-

ary 1854 it reported: "Eleven vessels are fitting out in different parts of Cuba for the coast of Africa to engage in the slave trade. It is stated that seven have sailed from Boston, Baltimore, and New York, within a few weeks, with the same intention." "Gleanings of News," *Frederick Douglass' Paper*, February 17, 1854.

110. See Jeffory Clymer, "Martin Delany's *Blake* and the Transnational Politics of Property." Clymer reads mercantilism and conflicts between competing imperial powers as central to debates over slave bodies and slave production.

111. Delany, *Blake*, 194.

112. The novel's presentation of ship masts on the open seas is a visualization for capital flows. Delany dramatizes how the *Vulture*, a refitted Baltimore clipper, flies the flags of various countries for protection against British West India cruisers (*Blake*, 203). The image of the mis-signifying phantom ship is also a metaphor for international commerce. The *Vulture* was a moving representation of the postnational politics of capital transportability.

113. In an interview with Tommie Shelby, Paul Gilroy makes the following point on "oceanic" framing: "In our idiom, most of the time, the connection between culture and land is so strong, and I think that attention to the fluidity of culture, to its liquid characteristics, this remains important, too." Tommie Shelby, "Cosmopolitanism, Blackness, and Utopias," 121.

Chapter 4. Civic Geographies and Intentional Communities

1. Hopkins moved to New York City for a short time in 1904 due to the demands of an employer.

2. For a discussion of the distinction between ethnic and moral communities, and a rethinking of core presuppositions of cosmopolitan citizenship, see Brook Thomas, "Civic Multiculturalism and the Myth of Liberal Consent."

3. It was from the press offices on West Canton Street in the South End that Hopkins built her career as one of the most important women in turn-of-the-century African American journalism. In the years leading up to 1900, she established herself as one of the most frequent contributors to Boston's *Colored American Magazine*, which today is recognized as the country's first literary magazine to be owned and operated by African Americans. She was a shareholder of the Colored Co-Operative Publishing Company, the magazine's parent firm, and also a member of its Board of Directors. She was editor of the magazine's Women's Department and, in 1901–3, its editor in chief. In addition to contributing field correspondence, editorials, and short stories to the magazine, Hopkins recognized the *Colored American*'s value as a forum for presenting her novels to the larger reading public.

4. Webb's *The Garies and Their Friends* (1857), Delany's *Blake* (1859–61), and Wilson's *Our Nig* (1859) could be listed here as major and representative earlier works.

5. Houston Baker Jr., *Workings of the Spirit*.

6. In moving from a consideration of Brown, Delany, and Beckwourth to the later writing of Hopkins, it is important to acknowledge overlapping and parallel black literary genealogies. Although the years between 1867 and James Howard's *Bond and Free* (1886) may not have given rise to the same volume of African American literary production as the decade leading up to the Civil War or the later print production from the 1890s and the rise of the new century, African American novels were still produced during this time. The work of Frances Smith Foster, who brought to contemporary readers the serial novels from the *Christian Recorder*; Hazel Carby; Henry Louis Gates Jr.; and, more recently, Melba Joyce Boyd, Dixon Bruce, and—from the perspective of relocation as recovery—Eric Gardner has been instrumental in expanding the textual bases for black literature.

7. For a developed discussion of the representation of sexual partnering and coupling conventions in African American literature as producing the discursive black bourgeois, see Ann DuCille, *The Coupling Convention*.

8. Pauline Hopkins, *Contending Forces*, 115.

9. Charles Chesnutt, *The House Behind the Cedars*, 60.

10. In novels of the first generation, place is often more reflexive. In a fashion nearly opposite to that of a character like Rena Walden, for instance, Delany's eponymous Blake flattens space discursively. He is not a nuanced device for invoking what might be described as situationist cartographies, which defamiliarize sweeps of coherence with a particularized angle. Instead, Blake is an arch overwriter. His aim is to deterritorialize white slaveholder spaces by tunneling beneath them and redirecting their codes of organization.

11. Hazel Carby makes an important point: Unlike *Contending Forces*, Hopkins's serial fiction is "situated within a white rather than a black social order" (introduction, xxxvii). This indicates that the template of concerns will be different, and that the questions about belonging (including questions of alliances or citizenship) will also be framed toward different attainments.

12. William Dean Howells, *Literary Friends and Acquaintances*, www.Gutenberg.com.

13. Howells, *Literary Friends and Acquaintances*.

14. Hopkins, *Contending Forces*, 82.

15. Urban historians cite Boston as undergoing a period of massive decentralization that began in 1880 and lasted throughout the twentieth century. During this time, surrounding suburban territories grew in population faster than that of the city, and the city's total area population declined in comparison. This residential shift can be observed in Hopkins's metropolitan Boston. Leo Schnore and Peter Knights attribute the expansion of the city's peripheries in the late nineteenth century to the "influence of the street railroad" ("Residence and Social Structure," 249). The streetcars preceded the popularization of automobile ownership, which has largely been credited with the explosion of the American suburb.

16. In *Boston Confronts Jim Crow*, Mark Schneider concludes that the city's postbellum migrants were mainly from the upper South and had bypassed closer coastal cities because of Boston's unique advantages, in particular educational opportunities available to them and their children.

17. Elizabeth Pleck, *Black Migration and Poverty*, 30–32.

18. Most Boston residents in the late nineteenth century were employed in industry, trade, or service occupations. Black men from Hopkins's South End worked as barbers, cooks, waiters, and clothes dealers. With the increasing growth of heavy steam engine industry in central Boston and along the harbor front, they also found employment as mechanics, construction workers, and railroad machinists. A limited few were lawyers, entrepreneurs, and business proprietors. Women from the South End were employed as teachers, tailors, dressmakers, and factory operatives. See Pleck, *Black Migration and Poverty*.

19. Hopkins, *Contending Forces*, 83.

20. A respected and reasonably well-remunerated position for single black women was in the field of stenography. Stenography as a trade gave African Americans a valued mobility; it could be practiced in various cities and was less contingent on the dictates and growth of any single employer. It was a trade practiced by Hopkins herself and Charles Chesnutt, her contemporary. In her biography of her father, Mary Chesnutt called stenography a sort of "magic carpet to take him to the North, to the land of opportunity, to life" (*Charles Waddell Chesnutt*, 26), and Hopkins worked as a stenographer at a Boston law firm and the Massachusetts Institute of Technology. It was a supplementary career that helped her support herself until the time of her death, at age seventy-one. The profession allowed blacks to cross between black and white societies without holding a service position.

21. Hopkins, *Contending Forces*, 83.

22. Hopkins, *Contending Forces*, 231.

23. W. E. B. Du Bois, "The Black North; A Social Study: Boston," *New York Times*, December 8, 1901.

24. Du Bois, *The American Negro*, 37.

25. Mark Peel writes: "By 1900 almost one quarter of the small-house owners and renters in the South End took in at least five paying tenants. Boston's most rapid lodging-house development thus occurred in neighborhoods that allowed easy access to jobs and urban services and that contained family homes free for conversion into tenant housing" ("On the Margins," 820).

26. Michel de Certeau, *The Practice of Everyday Life*, 117–18.

27. Jürgen Habermas, *The Structural Transformation of the Public Sphere*.

28. On a restructured, proletarian public sphere, see Oskar Negt and Alexander Kluge, *Public Sphere and Experience*. For inclusiveness and representative organizational claims for those excluded from worker-reform policies by their categorization as contingent or nonpolitical, see Saskia Sassen, *Territory, Authority, Rights*, 277–321.

29. In terms of building from black public sphere to transformative directions for black geography as spaces of lived negotiation and emergence, Thadious Davis's groundbreaking *Southscapes* warrants particular mention. Central to any consideration of black public sphere are Houston Baker Jr., "Critical Memory and the Black Public Sphere," *Critical Memory*; and the now-classic Evelyn Higginbotham, *Righteous Discontent*. For lucid evaluations of public sphere at the intersection of black literary and popular cultures, see Gillian Johns, "Jim Trueblood and His Critic-Readers"; Kevin Quashie, "The Trouble with Publicness."

30. Hopkins, *Contending Forces*, 86.

31. Hopkins, *Contending Forces*, 243.

32. Habermas, *The Structural Transformation of the Public Sphere*, 175–76.

33. Hopkins, *Contending Forces*, 104.

34. Hopkins, *Contending Forces*, 106.

35. Baker, *Workings of the Spirit*, 9.

36. Harper's serial novel *Minnie's Sacrifice* addresses similar issues related to what could be called a women's vertical community. Such communities do not presuppose a flat, horizontal structure where leadership is shared. They have their alpha figures and agenda steerers. See especially Colleen O'Brien, "'The White Women All Go for Sex'"; Jean Cole, "Information Wanted"; and Leslie Lewis, "Biracial Promise and the New South in *Minnie's Sacrifice*."

37. Hopkins, *Contending Forces*, 91.

38. Hopkins, *Contending Forces*, 102.

39. The Montfort clan is ruined by white proslavery vigilantes, who murder the family patriarch, rape his wife, and consign the children to slavery. One of these children manages to escape the South and reach federalist-era Boston. Hopkins wrote: "He stood beside the stone wall that enclosed the historic Boston Common, and as he watched the cows chewing their peaceful cuds and inhaled deep draughts of freedom's air, he vowed to die rather than return" (*Contending Forces*, 78). (Her description of Boston Common is historically accurate; grazing cows were banned by ordinance only in 1830.) The reader is told that Montfort settles for a time among the "colored people of the community" (Hopkins, *Contending Forces*).

40. Hopkins, *Contending Forces*, 84.

41. During the course of the novel, Smith is said to have earned a doctorate from Harvard University and completed his postdoctoral studies at Heidelberg. In this respect, he is patterned after Du Bois, who earned his doctorate from Harvard and continued his studies at the University of Berlin.

42. Hopkins, *Contending Forces*, 129.

43. A significant early site is the home of the antebellum community leaders and abolitionists Lewis and Harriet Hayden, a residence at 66 Phillips Street (then Southac Street). The Hayden house is a structure that symbolizes the convergences between North and South in antislavery activism. The Hayden family included Union soldiers and recruiters. Like the other structures Hopkins describes, the

house also symbolizes the local black community's resistance to slavery, in this case two decades before the outbreak of the Civil War, during the volatile abolition years. Here the family gave refuge to such well-known fugitives as William and Ellen Craft, who boarded with them in Boston in 1849 after their harrowing escape from Macon, Georgia. In 1853 Harriet Beecher Stowe visited the Hayden's home when she was researching "The Key to Uncle Tom's Cabin." Regarded as a friend, she experienced firsthand one of Massachusetts's foremost hubs on the Underground Railroad, and would go on to include Lewis Hayden's own narrative in the book's release the following year.

44. The area described was bounded by Pinckney, Cambridge, Joy, and Charles Streets.

45. Hopkins, *Contending Forces*, 13–14.

46. Hopkins, *Contending Forces*, 131.

47. Hopkins, *Contending Forces*, 201–2.

48. Hopkins, *Contending Forces*, 197.

49. In the period between 1890 and 1900, many of the residential buildings on the North Slope were demolished, to be replaced by structures more closely resembling the buildings on the south side of Beacon Hill. The newer buildings were squarer in shape, more uniform, and considerably larger; one might occupy the space of two to three of the older structures. As a result, the buildings on Beacon Hill in the early twentieth century became more homogeneous in appearance. See Lawrence Kennedy, *Planning the City upon a Hill*; Philip Bergen, *Old Boston in Early Photographs*.

50. Hopkins, *Contending Forces*, 130. The Charles Street African Methodist Episcopal Church remained at that location until 1939. It was the last black institution to leave Beacon Hill. Today it is located at Elm Hill Avenue and Warren Street, in Roxbury.

51. For more on Tremont's transformative structures, see Jeanne Kilde, *When Church Became Theatre*.

52. Hopkins, *Contending Forces*, 275.

53. Hopkins, *Contending Forces*, 276.

54. Hopkins, *Contending Forces*, 276.

55. See also Jean Yellin and John Van Horne, *The Abolitionist Sisterhood*; Carla Peterson, *Doers of the Word*.

56. Hopkins, *Contending Forces*, 277.

57. This parallelism could not have been lost on Delany, whose own mother, Patti Peace, arranged for a driver to carry her and her five young children into the free state of Pennsylvania from Charles Town, Virginia, some twenty years earlier, in 1822.

58. Grimes wrote the ransom check for $1,300 for Anthony Burns, a twenty-one-year-old fugitive slave who had escaped from Virginia. Burns was taken into custody in Boston at the injunction of his master, Charles F. Suttle, of Virginia. His arrest

created massive civil disruptions in Boston. The rioting that followed Burns's arrest sparked what historian Albert Von Frank called "a pocket revolution" (*The Trials of Anthony Burns*, 99), led by Leonard Grimes, Theodore Parker, and Thomas Wentworth Higginson, among others. During the failed attempt to free Burns, a sheriff's deputy was killed. As Burns was walked handcuffed through the streets of Boston, it took a heavy contingent of federal troops to escort him onto the ship returning him South. Some fifty thousand people lined the streets, shouting "Kidnapper," "Slave Catcher," "Shame! Shame!" (Von Frank, *The Trials of Anthony Burns*, 99).

59. Hazel Carby, *Reconstructing Womanhood*, 127–28.

60. To a notable extent, Boston's antislavery tradition in the antebellum era is celebrated in *Contending Forces* as a cooperative achievement of black and white leaders. Blacks lay claim to the abolitionist movement as a central component of their unique legacy in national events, but they also honor white fighters in the cause for emancipation. Hopkins writes: "There such men as Garrison and Phillips defied the vengeance of howling mobs that thirsted for the lives of the Negro champions" (*Contending Forces*, 276).

61. Hopkins, *Contending Forces*, 277–78.

62. See Carby, introduction, xxxv.

63. Cornel West, *Prophesy Deliverance!*, 36.

64. Hopkins, *Contending Forces*, 223–24. Like her contemporary Ida Wells, Hopkins argued that racial violence was tactical, political terror. It was an attempt by certain groups of individuals (including those in law enforcement, who were assigned to protect the populace) to regain regional control in a power vacuum, during an era marked by large-scale national displacement and reorganization. See Hopkins's transcriptions of a Congregational Club meeting at Tremont Temple in Boston on May 22, 1899, in Hanna Wallinger, *Pauline E. Hopkins*, 165.

65. T. Thomas Fortune founded the Afro-American League in 1890 as an equal rights organization. Like Hopkins, Fortune worked as a journalist, writing for the *Amsterdam News* and the *Norfolk Journal and Guide*. He was also an editor of Marcus Garvey's *Negro World*.

66. Sacvan Bercovitch, *The Puritan Origins of the American Self*.

67. *Magnalia Christi Americana: The Ecclesiastical History of New England from Its First Planting, In the Year 1620, Unto the Year of Our Lord 1698*, originally published in 1702, is Cotton Mather's seven-volume historical study of the Puritans in New England. A description of Mather's method and an overview of the project as a whole can be found in "An Attestation to this Church History of New-England" (13–17) and "The General Introduction" (26–38) in the first American edition.

68. Hopkins, *Contending Forces*, 243–44.

69. Based on an exchange of letters between President Thomas Jefferson and the Baptist Association of Danbury, Connecticut, in 1801.

70. Nancy Fraser, "Rethinking the Public Sphere," 92. See also Geoff Eley, "Nations, Publics, and Political Cultures."

71. Nancy Fraser, "Rethinking Recognition," 107–8.

72. Higginbotham, *Righteous Discontent*, 9.

73. Hopkins, *Contending Forces*, 126.

74. Hopkins, *Contending Forces*, 251.

75. Pauline Hopkins, "Booker T. Washington," 436.

76. Hopkins, *Contending Forces*, 288.

77. Hopkins, *Contending Forces*, 242.

78. Hopkins, *Contending Forces*, 289.

79. Doreen Massey, *For Space*, 11.

80. In a chapter called "Raising Money" in *Up From Slavery*, Washington concentrated on his fund-raising work in Boston. He wrote: "In the city of Boston I have rarely called upon an individual for funds that I have not been thanked for calling, usually before I could get an opportunity to thank the donor for the money. In that city the donors seem to feel, in a large degree, that an honour is being conferred upon them in their being permitted to give. Nowhere else have I met with, in so large a measure, this fine and Christlike spirit as in the city of Boston, although there are many notable instances of it outside that city. I repeat my belief that the world is growing in the direction of giving. I repeat that the main rule by which I have been guided in collecting money is to do my full duty in regard to giving people who have money an opportunity to help" (313).

81. Ira Dworkin, *Daughter of the Revolution*, 218.

82. Dworkin, *Daughter of the Revolution*, 224–5.

83. Wallinger, *Pauline E. Hopkins*, 92.

84. Quoted in Wallinger, *Pauline E. Hopkins*, 90.

85. Hopkins, *Contending Forces*, 272.

86. W. E. B. Du Bois, "Of Mr. Booker T. Washington and Others" in *The Souls of Black Folks*, 40–42.

87. Hopkins, *Contending Forces*, 237–38.

88. Pauline Hopkins, "Speech at the William Lloyd Garrison Centennial," 4.

89. Hopkins, *Contending Forces*, 251.

90. Hopkins, *Contending Forces*, 261.

91. Hopkins, *Contending Forces*, 262.

92. Hopkins, *Contending Forces*, 255.

93. Seyla Benhabib, "Models of Public Space," 100.

94. Du Bois, "The Talented Tenth" in Booker T. Washington, et al., *The Negro Problem*, 45.

95. Du Bois quoted Anna Julia Cooper's proclamation that "only the black woman can say 'when and where I enter, . . . then and there the whole Negro race enters with me'" but failed to credit Cooper as its source (*Darkwater*, 100–101).

96. W. E. B. Du Bois, "The Study of the Negro Problems," 6. Du Bois could account for the work of black women in many arenas, but not as intellectual and political leaders. Hazel Carby argues, Du Bois's rigidly gendered prescriptions

accounted for what she calls his "complete failure to imagine black women as intellectuals and race leaders" (*Race Men*, 10).

97. Pauline Hopkins, "Famous Women of the Negro Race," *Colored American Magazine* 4.4 (March 1902): 277–80, 277.

98. Hopkins, "Famous Women of the Negro Race," 277.

99. Hopkins, *Contending Forces*, 197.

100. Ruffin was known in her time as the wife of the first African American graduate of Harvard Law School and Boston's first black municipal judge, George Ruffin. She was also involved in recruiting black soldiers for the Union Army during the Civil War. After the death of her husband, she founded the *Woman's Era*, the country's first newspaper published by and for African American women. Hopkins knew Josephine Ruffin directly through the women's club circuit in Boston. Hopkins was listed as a club secretary for the New Era Club in Boston, founded by Ruffin in 1894. Hopkins also read portions of *Contending Forces* at a Japanese tea event she organized to promote her new novel to Boston clubwomen (Elizabeth McHenry, *Forgotten Readers*, 370n85). The *National Association Notes* of April 1900 reported: "An entertaining and interesting afternoon was spent at a Japanese Tea, given to Miss Pauline Hopkins, to aid her in the publication of her novel, *Contending Forces*, portions of which she read."

101. Hopkins, *Contending Forces*, 147.

102. Hopkins, *Contending Forces*, 144. Hopkins, "Club Life among Colored Women."

103. Amy Rowe, "Be Longing," 16.

104. In *Feminism and Geography*, Gillian Rose has identified what she calls a trend of "social-scientific masculinity" in geographic discourses that reject the local as nostalgic and residual. In *The Male Body*, Susan Bordo explores the issue of male objectification through popular visual culture and media. Both authors argue that gender is implicated in the construction of geography and that the organization of place (as in woman's place and the domestic sphere) is a formative element in the construction of gender.

105. Michael Warner, "The Mass Public and the Mass Subject," 251, 250.

106. Hopkins, *Contending Forces*, 143.

107. Elizabeth McHenry documents the collective literacy practices of mid-nineteenth-century African Americans as a means to "facilitate involvement in the public sphere" (*Forgotten Readers*, 182). Collective literacy, I argue, itself enacts public sphere.

108. The National Association of Colored Women was formed by a merger in 1896 of the National Federation of Afro-American Women and the National League of Colored Women. Both organizations were outgrowths of the women's club movement. The organization's two leading members were Josephine Ruffin and Mary Church Terrell. Together, they expanded the organization to a membership of some 300,000 women. They directed campaigns to address such issues as

women's suffrage, Jim Crow laws, media depictions of African Americans, and lynching crimes.

109. David Harvey writes: "All the commodities we buy in a capitalist society have a use value and exchange value . . . To the degree they are often at odds with each other they constitute a contradiction, which can, on occasion, give rise to a crisis. The use values are infinitely varied (even for the same item), while the exchange value (under normal conditions) is uniform and qualitatively identical" (*Seventeen Contradictions*, 15).

110. Hopkins, *Contending Forces*, 151.

111. For more on the ways scholars have reclaimed the trope of the tragic mulatta, see Jean Yellin, *The Intricate Knot*, and Rafia Zafar, *We Wear the Mask*. More recently, Eve Raimon has written: "Contemporary criticism of the 'tragic mulatta' tends to project backward a transhistorical and fixed sense of U.S. ideologies of racial difference. In fact, the tradition employing the mulatta character came into being at the very time enduring notions of race were crystallizing in the new republic" (*The "Tragic Mulatta" Revisited*, 4).

Chapter 5. Creole Heteroglossia

1. David Harvey suggests that an emphasis on localism in postmodern cultural reclamation efforts often results in insularity, political conservatism, and forms of cultural chauvinism (*The Condition of Postmodernity*, 3). Feminist geographers beginning with Doreen Massey have challenged such thinking as being premised on ideas that region represents historical fixity and immobility. Massey writes: "There is a specificity of place which derives from the fact that each place is the focus of a distinct *mixture* of wider and more local social relations" (*Space, Place, and Gender*, 156).

2. Jennifer Greeson, "Expropriating *The Great South*," 116.

3. Richard Brodhead, *Cultures of Letters*, 120.

4. For a particularly interesting approach to regionalism as a mobile network of commodity culture, and something explicitly not about region, see Brad Evans, "Howellsian Chic."

5. Gloria Hull, Dunbar-Nelson's biographer, writes that in response to her proposal to expand her short story "Stones of the Village" into a novel, Bliss Perry, editor of the *Atlantic Monthly*, "offered his opinion that at present the American public had a 'dislike' for treatment of 'the color line'" (*Works*, xxxvi).

6. For a nuanced view of Chesnutt's conjure women and the spatialization of spirit writing, see Houston Baker, "Workings of the Spirit."

7. Although much of Dunbar's poetry was written in standard English verse and reflected the influence of William Wordsworth and Robert Burns as well as the American poets James Whitcomb Riley and Henry Wadsworth Longfellow, his poetry that received the most critical attention was written to affect Southern

black dialect forms. (Dunbar was himself born in Ohio.) The poems invoked the landscape of the rural South and scenes of the plough and in the sun-scorched "medders." In "The Banjo Song" from his first collection, *Oak and Ivy* (1893) he tried to emulate the speech of a black plantation musician: "Den my fam'ly gadders roun' me,/In de fadin' o' de light,/Ez I strike de strings to try 'em/Ef dey all is tuned er-right" (*The Collected Poetry of Paul Laurence Dunbar*, 20).

8. The concept of process geography can be attributed in its earliest formulations to Doreen Massey, "Geography Matters" (1984), and to the later writings of John Agnew, "Representing Space" (1993); Michael Brown, "The Possibility of Local Autonomy" (1993); and Alain Lipietz, "The "Local and the Global" (1993).

9. Mike Crang and Nigel Thrift, *Thinking Geographies*, 3.

10. Hsuan Hsu's influential essay on Sarah Orne Jewett makes a similar argument: Region is produced by global scales of capital (Hsu, "Literature and Regional Production").

11. Alice Dunbar-Nelson, *Works*, 113.

12. Kristina Brooks has noted that Dunbar-Nelson's account of the strike in "Mr. Baptiste" is based on the New Orleans labor riots of 1892, which began when British shippers substituted black workers for white who packed cotton bales onto ships in port. Several men were killed, and there was heavy damage to property ("Alice Dunbar Nelson's Local Colors of Ethnicity, Class, and Place," 13).

13. Dunbar-Nelson, *Works*, 120.

14. Dunbar-Nelson, *Works*, 123–24.

15. Dunbar-Nelson, *Works*, 122.

16. W. E. B. Du Bois, *Black Reconstruction in America*, 688.

17. Dunbar-Nelson, *Works*, 123. The history of the Irish emerging as white in the nineteenth century as a case for pointing out the social constructedness of race has been well addressed in a range of literature. Both David Roediger and Noel Ignatiev have argued that for the Irish immigrants, whiteness worked as a color "wage" to elevate whites in the eyes of their employers and at the same time devalue African Americans as "others." Such observations follow the thinking of Du Bois, who identified the "public and psychological wage" that came from being a part of the dominant race. W. E. B. Du Bois, *Black Reconstruction in America*, 700.

18. Dunbar-Nelson, *Works*, 124. This presents different terms of conflict than might be distilled from a reading of George Washington Cable's popular 1870s-era Louisiana Creole stories in *Scribner's Monthly*. As Jennifer Greeson has observed, Cable's Creoles present a "characterological stasis" ("Expropriating *The Great South* and Exporting 'Local Color,'" 129). Left to their own degenerative cycles, they brew in their subtropical torpor. Outside action from a national outsider or the U.S. administration frequently mobilizes the plots, not Creole initiative.

19. Gilles Deleuze and Félix Guattari, *Anti-Oedipus*, 8. The authors' theory of flow is useful here because they refuse to separate textuality from exchanges of

violence and social struggles, which are overtly bodily as opposed to linguistically signifying. Instead, Deleuze and Guattari argue that all production stems substantively (not figuratively) from machinic processes, from flows of consumption and production. Only when these flows are disrupted by moments of "antiproduction" can an insistence on physicality, concrete context, or local demand be forced to the front of capitalist assemblage.

20. Susan Roberts, "Economic Landscapes," 336.

21. Alice Dunbar-Nelson, *Works*, 88.

22. Dunbar-Nelson, *Works*, 7.

23. See, for example, Bruce Robbins, *The Phantom Public Sphere*, xiii.

24. Luce Irigaray, *Elemental Passions*, 25.

25. In *Tell My Horse*, Zora Neale Hurston claims the opposite.

26. According to Leslie Desmangles, "this syncretistic nature of Voudou was disturbing to the church. Voudou assemblies were a cause for alarm among the colonists, for not only were they profane in their use of objects stolen from the church, but the planters feared that they would serve as catalysts for slave insurrections" (*The Faces of the Gods*, 27).

27. Dunbar-Nelson, *Works*, 7.

28. Dunbar-Nelson, *Works*, 175.

29. Dunbar-Nelson, *Works*, 203.

30. Dunbar-Nelson, *Works*, 208.

31. See Stuart Hall, "Subjects in History." The colonial framework idea also appears in an earlier text by Hall, "Cultural Identity and Diaspora."

32. Sidney Mintz, "Enduring Substances, Trying Theories," 303.

33. With their varied genealogies and contested international histories, Louisiana Creoles were a subject of considerable interest in late-century regional writing. The short fiction of authors like Dunbar-Nelson, Cable, Kate Chopin, and Grace Elizabeth King all looked to the geography of New Orleans and its environs to depict the comings and goings of specifically regional characters. What these authors share is that each constructed modern Creole identity in their fiction as something specific to the geographic and social locale of Louisiana.

34. Joseph Tregle, Jr., "Creoles and Americans," 171.

35. Alice Dunbar-Nelson, "People of Color in Louisiana," Part I, 8–9.

36. Virginia Domínguez, *White by Definition*, 149.

37. Dunbar-Nelson, *Works*, 147.

38. Dunbar-Nelson, *Works*, 157–58.

39. Dunbar-Nelson, *Works*, 158. Critics like Violet Harrington Bryan and Gloria Hull have suggested that the racial ambiguity in Dunbar-Nelson's fiction may have been a feature of her own ambivalence about race and perhaps a "feeling of shame about some circumstance(s) of her birth" (Hull, *Works*, xxix). Yet Dunbar-Nelson's involvement in African-American social activism and journalism largely refutes

such criticism of racial shame or ambivalence. In 1913 she worked for and helped edit the African Methodist Episcopal *Church Review*. She also edited and published collections of writing distinctly organized around the theme of race, like *Masterpieces of Negro Eloquence* (1914) and "People of Color in Louisiana," which was originally published in the *Journal of Negro History*. In 1922 Dunbar-Nelson headed the Anti-Lynching Crusaders in Delaware in support of the Dyer Anti-Lynching Bill and authored a two-part article on Delaware in "These 'Colored' United States," in the *Messenger*. She became increasingly involved with the black women's club movement, working both federally, under the umbrella organization called the National Federation of Colored Women's Clubs, and on a state level from a range of cities, including New York, Washington, D.C., Philadelphia, and Wilmington.

40. Brooks, "Alice Dunbar Nelson's Local Colors of Ethnicity, Class, and Place," 8.

41. Dunbar-Nelson, *Works*, 127.

42. Mikhail Bakhtin, *Rabelais and His World*, 123.

43. Dunbar-Nelson, *Works*, 131.

44. Dunbar-Nelson, *Works*, 128.

45. Dunbar-Nelson, *Works*, 62.

46. Dunbar-Nelson, *Works*, 56–57.

47. Dunbar-Nelson, *Works*, 62.

48. The work of Sandra Zagarell ("Troubling Regionalism"), Elizabeth Ammons (*Conflicting Stories*), and June Howard (*New Essays on The Country of the Pointed Firs*) extends in a number of ways the Brodhead and Kaplan "national agenda of reunion" thesis.

49. Amy Kaplan, "Nation, Region, and Empire," 251.

50. Brodhead, *Cultures of Letters*, 134.

51. Edward Casey, "How to Get from Space to Place in a Fairly Short Stretch of Time," 26, 27.

52. David Harvey, "The Sociological and Geographical Imaginations," 213.

53. Casey, "How to Get from Space to Place," 18.

Epilogue

1. Neil Brenner, *New State Spaces*, 9.

2. Andrew Herod and Melissa Wright, "Placing Scale."

3. Richie Howitt, "A World in a Grain of Sand," 36. See also Richie Howitt, "Scale and the Other."

4. Walter Benjamin, "The Image of Proust," 213.

5. Gaston Bachelard, *The Poetics of Space*, 15.

6. Jim Sagel, "Sandra Cisneros," 74–75. See also Sandra Cisneros, *The House on Mango Street*; Julián Olivares, "Sandra Cisneros' *The House on Mango Street*, and the Poetics of Space."

7. Martin Delany, *Blake*, 223.

8. William Wells Brown, *Clotel*, 226.

9. Ira Berlin, *Many Thousands Gone*.

10. W. E. B. Du Bois, *The Souls of Black Folk*, 14.

11. Stuart Hall, "Subjects in History." The colonial framework idea also appears in an earlier text by Hall, "Cultural Identity and Diaspora."

12. Paul Gilroy, *The Black Atlantic*, 4.

13. Gilroy, *The Black Atlantic*, 28.

14. I am referring to texts like Briton Hammon's *Narrative of the Uncommon Sufferings, and Surprising Deliverance of Briton Hammon, a Negro Man* (1760) and John Marrant's much-reproduced *A Journal of the Rev. John Marrant* (1790). These narratives are included in William Andrews, "Annotated Bibliography of Afro-American Autobiography."

15. Sandra Gunning, "Nancy Prince and the Politics of Mobility, Home and Diasporic (Mis)Identification," 33.

16. Saskia Sassen, "Spatialities and Temporalities of the Global," 219. Sassen cites Garret Mattingly's thinking on the doctrine of extraterritoriality as a way to accommodate the extension of state authority beyond the boundaries of national territory and to account for the "nonunitary condition of the national." See Garret Mattingly, *Renaissance Diplomacy*.

17. Nancy Duncan, "Introduction: (Re)placings," *BodySpace*, 3. See also Gillian Rose, who draws on the work of Judith Butler and Luce Irigaray to argue that "the distinction between the real and non-real is characterized as a performance of power, and . . . the distinction between real and non-real space is constructed in terms which are also gendered, and that this hierarchical engendering of spaces is naturalized by the claim that only one of those spaces is real." She further argues that "the distinction produces instabilities which undermine the distinction itself" ("Masculinist Theory and Feminist Masquerade" in *BodySpace*, 58).

18. In "Spatial Stories," Michel de Certeau describes the "space of operations" of the story as topological, "concerning the deformation of figures." This might be contrasted with something that is topical, which he summarizes as "defining places" (*The Practice of Everyday Life*, 129).

BIBLIOGRAPHY

Maps

Elliott, G. W. Map of the United States, Showing by Colors the Area of Freedom and Slavery, and the Territories Whose Destiny Is Yet to be Decided, Exhibiting Also the Missouri Compromise Line, and the Routes of Colonel Fremont in His Famous Explorations. New York: G. W. Elliott, 1856.

Johnson, Alvin J., and D. Griffing Johnson. A New Map of the Union, with the Adjacent Islands & Countries, from Authentic Sources. New York: D. Griffing and Alvin J. Johnson, 1857.

Johnson, D. Griffing. Johnson's New Illustrated & Embellished County Map of the Republics of North America with the Adjacent Islands & Countries, Compiled Drawn & Engraved from U. States Land & Coast Surveys, British Admiralty & Other Reliable Sources. Designed by Alvin J. Johnson and engraved by D. Griffing Johnson, J. H. Goldthwait, W. S. Barnard, Wm. Wright, G. Rae Smith, F. H. King, James Duthie, and J. L. White. New York: D. Griffing and Alvin J. Johnson, 1859.

Lewis, John C. Lewis' Free Soil, Slavery, and Territorial Map of the United States. New York: John Lewis, 1848.

Reynolds, William C. Reynolds's Political Map of the United States. New York: Wm. C. Reynolds and J. C. Jones, 1856.

Thayer, B. W., and Joseph H. Colton. Colton's Map of the United States of America, the British Provinces, Mexico, the West Indies and Central America. New York: Thayer and Colton, 1859.

Williams, Wellington. A New Map of the United States upon which Are Delineated the Vast Works of International Communication, Routes across the Continent, &c. showing Canada and the Island of Cuba. Philadelphia: Lippincott and Grambo, 1851.

Williams, Wellington. The Traveler's and Tourist's Guide through the United States of America, Canada, Etc. Containing the Routes of Travel by Steamboat, Stage and Canal; Together with Descriptions of, and Routes to, the Principal Places of Fashionable and Healthful Resort; with Other Valuable Information. Accompanied by an Entirely New and Authentic Map of the United States, Including California, Oregon, Etc., and a Map of the Island of Cuba. Philadelphia: Lippincott and Grambo, 1851.

Primary and Secondary Sources

Abdy, Edward Strutt. *Journal of a Residence and Tour in the United States, from April, 1833 to October, 1834.* Vol. 2. London: John Murray, 1835.

Agnew, John. "Representing Space: Space, Scale and Culture in Social Science." In *Place/Culture/Representation,* edited by James Duncan and David Ley, 251–71. New York: Routledge, 1993.

Agnew, John. *Place and Politics: The Geographical Mediation of State and Society.* London: Allen and Unwin, 1987.

Alcoff, Linda Martín. "Mignolo's Epistemology of Coloniality." *CR: The New Centennial Review* 7, no. 3 (2007): 79–101.

Alfred, Taiaiake. *Peace, Power, Righteousness: An Indigenous Manifesto.* Don Mills, Ontario, CN: Oxford University Press, 1999.

Allmendinger, Blake. *Imagining the African American West.* Lincoln: University of Nebraska Press, 2005.

Ammons, Elizabeth. *Conflicting Stories: American Women Writers at the Turn into the Twentieth Century.* New York: Oxford University Press, 1991.

Anderson, Benedict. *Imagined Communities: Reflections on the Origin and Spread of Nationalism.* Rev. ed. New York: Verso, 1991.

Anderson, Victor. *Beyond Ontological Blackness: An Essay on African American Religious and Cultural Criticism.* New York: Continuum, 1995.

Andrew, William L. "Annotated Bibliography of Afro-American Autobiography." In *To Tell a Free Story: The First Century of Afro-American Autobiography, 1760–1865,* 333–47. Urbana: University of Illinois Press, 1986.

Andrews, George Reid. *Afro-Latin America, 1800–2000.* New York: Oxford University Press, 2004.

Anzaldúa, Gloria. *Borderlands/La Frontera: The New Mestiza.* San Francisco: Spinsters, 1987.

Appadurai, Arjun. "Disjuncture and Difference in the Global Cultural Economy." In *Colonial Discourse and Post-Colonial Theory,* edited by Patrick Williams and Laura Chrisman, 324–39. New York: Columbia University Press, 1994.

Appadurai, Arjun. "Grassroots Globalization and the Research Imagination." *Public Culture* 12, no. 1 (2000): 1–19.

Appiah, Kwame Anthony. *Cosmopolitanism: Ethics in a World of Strangers.* New York: W. W. Norton, 2006.

Armstrong, Nancy. *Desire and Domestic Fiction: A Political History of the Novel.* New York: Oxford University Press, 1987.

Augé, Marc. *Non-Places: Introduction to an Anthropology of Supermodernity.* Translated by John Howe. London: Verso, 1995.

Bachelard, Gaston. *The Poetics of Space.* Translated by Maria Jolas. Boston: Beacon, 1994.

Baker, Houston A., Jr. "Critical Memory and the Black Public Sphere." In *The Black*

Public Sphere: A Public Culture Book, edited by the Black Public Sphere Collective, 7–37. Chicago: University of Chicago Press, 1995.

Baker, Houston A., Jr. "Workings of the Spirit: Conjure in the Space of Black Women's Creativity." In Workings of the Spirit: Conjure and the Space of Black Women's Creativity. Phototext by Elizabeth Alexander and Patricia Redmond. Chicago: University of Chicago Press, 1991.

Bakhtin, Mikhail. Rabelais and His World. Translated by Hélène Iswolsky. Bloomington: Indiana University Press, 1984.

Balibar, Etienne, and Immanuel Wallerstein. Race, Nation, Class: Ambiguous Identities. Translated by Chris Turner. London: Verso, 1991.

Ball, Charles. Slavery in the United States: A Narrative of the Life and Adventures of Charles Ball, a Black Man, Who Lived Forty Years in Maryland, South Carolina and Georgia, as a Slave under Various Masters, and Was One Year in the Navy with Commodore Barney, during the Late War. New York: John S. Taylor, 1837.

Barnett, Jim, and Clark Burkett. "Forks in the Road." Journal of Mississippi History. Vol. 63, no. 3 (2001).

Baudrillard, Jean. "Simulacra and Simulations." In Modernism/Postmodernism, edited by Peter Brooker, 151–62. London: Longman, 1992.

Beckwourth, James P. The Life and Adventures of James P. Beckwourth as Told to Thomas D. Bonner. 1854. Lincoln: University of Nebraska Press, 1981.

Bell, Bernard W. The Afro-American Novel and Its Tradition. Amherst: University of Massachusetts Press, 1987.

Benhabib, Seyla. "Reclaiming Universalism: Negotiating Republican Self-Determination and Cosmopolitan Norms." Tanner Lecture Series on Human Values, the University of California, Berkeley. March 15–19, 2004.

Benhabib, Seyla. "Models of Public Space: Hannah Arendt, the Liberal Tradition, and Jürgen Habermas." In Habermas and the Public Sphere, edited by Craig Calhoun, 73–98. Cambridge, MA: MIT Press, 1992.

Benjamin, Walter. "The Image of Proust." In Illuminations. Translated by Harry Zohn. New York: Schocken, 1968.

Bennett, Jane. Vibrant Matter: A Political Ecology of Things. Durham, NC: Duke University Press, 2010.

Bercovitch, Sacvan. The American Jeremiad. Madison: University of Wisconsin Press, 1978.

Bergen, Philip, comp. Old Boston in Early Photographs, 1850–1918: 174 Prints from the Collection of the Bostonian Society. New York: Dover, 1990.

Berlin, Ira. Many Thousands Gone: The First Two Centuries of Slavery in North America. Cambridge, MA: Belknap Press of Harvard University Press, 1998.

Bibb, Henry. Narrative of the Life and Adventures of Henry Bibb, an American Slave, Written by Himself. New York: the author, 1849.

Bleiker, Roland. Popular Dissent, Human Agency, and Global Politics. Cambridge: Cambridge University Press, 2000.

Bogue, Ronald. *Deleuze's Way: Essays in Transverse Ethics and Aesthetics*. Burlington, VT: Ashgate, 2007.

Bogues, Anthony. "Preface: The Frame of the Nation." *Small Axe* 6, no. 1 (2002): v–vii.

Bolster, W. Jeffrey. *Black Jacks: African American Seamen in the Age of Sail*. Cambridge, MA: Harvard University Press, 1997.

Bongie, Chris. *Islands and Exiles: The Creole Identities of Post/Colonial Literature*. Stanford, CA: Stanford University Press, 1998.

Bonner, T. D. *The Temperance Harp: A Collection of Songs*. Northampton, MA: Printed for the Proprietor, 1842.

Bordo, Susan. *The Male Body: A Look at Men in Public and in Private*. New York: Farrar, Straus and Giroux, 1999.

Brenner, Neil. *New State Spaces: Urban Governance and the Rescaling of Statehood*. New York: Oxford University Press, 2005.

Brodhead, Richard H. *Cultures of Letters: Scenes of Reading and Writing in Nineteenth-Century America*. Chicago: University of Chicago Press, 1993.

Brooks, Kristina. "Alice Dunbar Nelson's Local Colors of Ethnicity, Class, and Place." *MELUS* 23, no. 2 (1998): 3–26.

Brown, Charles H. *Agents of Manifest Destiny: The Life and Times of Filibusters*. Chapel Hill: University of North Carolina Press, 1980.

Brown, Gordon S. *Toussaint's Clause: The Founding Fathers and the Haitian Revolution*. Jackson: University Press of Mississippi, 2005.

Brown, Josephine. *Biography of an American, by His Daughter*. Boston: R. F. Wallcut, 1856.

Brown, Henry "Box." *Narrative of the Life of Henry Box Brown, Written by Himself*. Manchester, UK: Lee and Glynn, 1851.

Brown, Michael P. "The Possibility of Local Autonomy." *Urban Geography* 13 (1993): 257–79.

Brown, William Wells. *The American Fugitive in Europe: Sketches of Places and People Abroad*. Boston: John P. Jewett, 1855.

Brown, William Wells. *The Black Man, His Antecedents, His Genius, and His Achievements*. New York: Thomas Hamilton, 1863.

Brown, William Wells. *Clotel; or, The President's Daughter* (1853). Edited by Robert S. Levine. Boston: Bedford, 2000.

Brown, William Wells. *Clotelle; or, The Colored Heroine: A Tale of the Southern States*. Burke, VA: Mnemosyne, 1998.

Brown, William Wells. *A Description of William Wells Brown's Original Panoramic Views of Scenes in the Life of an American Slave, from His Birth in Slavery to His Death or His Escape to His First Home of Freedom on British Soil*. London: Charles Gilpin, n.d.

Brown, William Wells. *The Escape; or, A Leap for Freedom: A Drama in Five Acts*. 1858. Edited by John Ernest. Knoxville: University of Tennessee, 2001.

Brown, William Wells. *My Southern Home; or, The South and Its People*. 1880. New York: Negro Universities Press, 1969.

Brown, William Wells. *Narrative of William W. Brown, A Fugitive Slave: Written by Himself* (1847). Mineola, NY: Dover, 2003.

Brown, William Wells. *The Negro in the American Rebellion: His Heroism and His Fidelity*. Miami, FL: Mnemosyne, 1969.

Brown, William Wells. *Three Years in Europe; or, Places I Have Seen and People I Have Met*. London: Charles Gilpin, 1852.

Brown, William Wells. *The Travels of William Wells Brown* (1855). Edited by Paul Jefferson. New York: Markus Wiener, 1991.

Brückner, Martin. *The Geographic Revolution in Early America: Maps, Literacy, and National Identity*. Chapel Hill: University of North Carolina Press for the Omohundro Institute of Early American History and Culture, 2006.

Brückner, Martin, and Hsuan L. Hsu, eds. *American Literary Geographies: Spatial Practice and Cultural Production 1500–1900*. Newark: University of Delaware Press, 2007.

Bryan, Violet Harrington. "Race and Gender in the Early Works of Alice Dunbar-Nelson." In *Louisiana Women Writers*, edited by Dorothy H. Brown and Barbara C. Ewell, 120–38. Baton Rouge: Louisiana State University Press, 1992.

Buell, Lawrence. *The Future of Environmental Criticism: Environmental Crisis and the Literary Imagination*. Malden, MA: Blackwell, 2005.

Calhoun, John C. "The Clay Compromise Measures." In *The Papers of John C. Calhoun*, edited by Robert L. Meriweather et al. Columbia: University of South Carolina Press, 1959.

Calhoun, John C. *Speeches of John C. Calhoun, Delivered in the House of Representatives, and in the Senate of the United States*. Edited by Richard K. Cralle. New York: D. Appleton, 1864.

Carby, Hazel V. *Race Men: The W. E. B. Du Bois Lectures*. Cambridge, MA: Harvard University Press, 1998.

Carby, Hazel V. Introduction to Pauline Hopkins. In *The Magazine Novels of Pauline Hopkins*, xxxv–xxxvii. New York: Oxford University Press, 1988.

Carby, Hazel V. *Reconstructing Womanhood: The Emergence of the Afro-American Woman Novelist*. New York: Oxford University Press, 1987.

Carr, Robert. *Black Nationalism in the New World: Reading the African American and West Indian Experience*. Durham, NC: Duke University Press, 2002.

Carretta, Vincent, and Philip Gould, eds. *Genius in Bondage: Literature of the Early Black Atlantic*. Lexington: University Press of Kentucky, 2001.

Carretta, Vincent, ed. *Unchained Voices: An Anthology of Black Authors in the English-Speaking World of the 18th Century*. Lexington: University Press of Kentucky, 1996.

Carter, Erica, James Donald, and Judith Squires, eds. *Space and Place: Theories of Identity and Location*. London: Lawrence and Wishart, 1993.

Casey, Edward S. "How to Get from Space to Place in a Fairly Short Stretch of Time: Phenomenological Prolegomena." In *Senses of Place*. Santa Fe, NM: School of American Research Press, 1997.

Castells, Manuel. *The City and the Grassroots: A Cross-Cultural Theory of Urban Social Movements*. Berkeley: University of California Press, 1983.

Chaterjee, Partha. *The Nation and Its Fragments: Colonial and Post-Colonial Histories*. Princeton, NJ: Princeton University Press, 1993.

Chesnutt, Charles Waddell. *"To Be an Author": Letters of Charles W. Chesnutt, 1889–1905*. Edited by Joseph R. McElrath Jr. and Robert C. Leitz. Princeton, NJ: Princeton University Press, 1997.

Chesnutt, Charles Waddell. *The House Behind the Cedars*. Athens, GA: University of Georgia Press, 1988.

Chesnutt, Charles Waddell. *The Conjure Woman, and Other Conjure Tales*. Edited by Richard H. Brodhead. Durham, NC: Duke University Press, 1993.

Chesnutt, Helen Mary. *Charles Waddell Chesnutt: Pioneer of the Color Line*. Chapel Hill: University of North Carolina Press, 1952.

Chittenden, Hiram. *The American Fur Trade of the Far West*. 2 vols. Stanford, CA: Academic Reprints, 1954.

Cisneros, Sandra. *The House on Mango Street*. New York: Vintage, 1991.

Clifford, James. *Routes: Travel and Translation in the Late Twentieth Century*. Cambridge, MA: Harvard University Press, 1997.

Clymer, Jeffory. "Martin Delany's *Blake* and the Transnational Politics of Property." *American Literary History* 15, no. 4 (Winter 2003): 709–31.

Cohen, Hennig, and William B. Dillingham, eds. *Humor of the Old Southwest*. 3rd ed. Athens: University of Georgia Press, 1994.

Cohen, Matt. *The Networked Wilderness: Communicating in Early New England*. Minneapolis: University of Minnesota Press, 2009.

Cole, Jean Lee. "Information Wanted: *The Curse of Caste, Minnie's Sacrifice*, and *The Christian Recorder*." *African American Review* 40, no. 4 (2006): 731–42.

Cole, Jean Lee. "Theresa and Blake: Mobility and Resistance in Antebellum African American Serialized Fiction." *Callaloo* 34, no. 1 (2011): 158–75.

Comstock, Elizabeth. *Life and Letters of Elizabeth Comstock*. Edited and compiled by Caroline Hare. London: Headley Brothers, 1895.

Cosgrove, Dennis, and Peter Jackson. "New Directions in Cultural Geography." *Area* 19 (1987): 95–101.

Cox, Jay. *The Monroe Doctrine: Empire and Nation in Nineteenth-Century America*. New York: Hill and Wang, 2011.

Cox, John D. *Traveling South: Travel Narratives and the Construction of American Identity*. Athens: University of Georgia Press, 2005.

Craft, William. *Running a Thousand Miles for Freedom; or, The Escape of William and Ellen Craft from Slavery*. London: William Twedie, 1860.

Crane, Gregg D. *Race, Citizenship, and Law in American Literature*. New York: Cambridge University Press, 2002.

Crang, Mike, and Nigel Thrift. Introduction to *Thinking Space*, edited by Mike Crang and Nigel Thrift, 1–30. London: Routledge, 2003.

Crang, Mike, and Nigel Thrift. *Thinking Geographies*. London: Routledge, 2000.

"Cuba." *American Literary Magazine* 5, no. 2 (1849): 109.

Cuffee, Paul. *Narrative of the Life and Adventures of Paul Cuffe, Pequot Indian: During Thirty Years Spent at Sea, and in Traveling to Foreign Lands*. Vernon, NY: Horace N. Bill, 1839.

Curry, Michael R. "Discursive Displacement and Seminal Ambiguity of Space and Place." In *Handbook of New Media*, edited by Leah Lievrouw and Sonia Livingstone, 502–17. Los Angeles: Sage, 2002.

Dainotto, Roberto Maria. *Place in Literature: Regions, Cultures, Communities*. Ithaca, NY: Cornell University Press, 2000.

Davies, Carole Boyce, and Monica Jardine. "Imperial Geographies and Caribbean Nationalism: At the Border between 'a Dying Colonialism' and U.S. Hegemony." *CR: The New Centennial Review* 3, no. 3 (2003): 152–54.

Davis, Arthur. Introduction to William Wells Brown, *Clotel; or the President's Daughter: A Narrative of Slave Life in the United States*, vii–xvi. New York: Collier, 1970.

Davis, Thadious. *Southscapes: Geographies of Race, Region, and Literature*. Chapel Hill: University of North Carolina Press, 2011.

De Certeau, Michel. *The Practice of Everyday Life*. Translated by Steven Rendall. Berkeley: University of California Press, 1984.

Delany, Martin R. *Blake; or, the Huts of America: A Tale of the Mississippi Valley, the Southern United States, and Cuba*. 1859–62. Reprinted as *Blake; or, the Huts of America*, edited by Floyd J. Miller. Boston: Beacon, 1970.

Delany, Martin R. *The Condition, Elevation, Emigration and Destiny of the Colored People of the United States*. 1852. New York: Arno, 1968.

Delany, Martin R. *Official Report of the Niger Valley Exploring Party*. 1861. In *Martin R. Delany: A Documentary Reader*, edited by Robert S. Levine. Chapel Hill: University of North Carolina Press, 2003.

Delany, Martin R. "Political Aspect of the Colored People of the United States." 1855. In *Martin R. Delany: A Documentary Reader*, edited by Robert S. Levine. Chapel Hill: University of North Carolina Press, 2003.

Delany, Martin R. "Political Destiny of the Colored Race on the American Continent." 1854. In *Martin R. Delany: A Documentary Reader*, edited by Robert S. Levine. Chapel Hill: University of North Carolina Press, 2003.

Deleuze, Gilles, and Félix Guattari. *Anti-Oedipus: Capitalism and Schizophrenia*. Translated by Robert Hurley, Mark Seem, and Helen Lane. London: Penguin, 2009.

Deleuze, Gilles, and Félix Guattari. *Kafka: Toward a Minor Literature*. Translated by Dana Polan. Minneapolis: University of Minnesota Press, 1986.

Deleuze, Gilles, and Félix Guattari. *A Thousand Plateaus*. Translated by Brian Massumi. Minneapolis: University of Minnesota Press, 1987.

Deleuze, Gilles, and Félix Guattari. *What Is Philosophy?* Translated by Hugh Tomlinson and Graham Burchell. New York: Columbia University Press, 1990.

Deloria, Vine, Jr. "Self-Determination and the Concept of Sovereignty." In *Native*

American Sovereignty, edited by John R. Wunder, 118–24. New York: Garland, 1996.

Dent, Borden D. Cartography-Thematic Map Design. 5th ed. Boston: McGraw-Hill, 1999.

Desmangles, Leslie G. The Faces of the Gods: Vodou and Roman Catholicism in Haiti. Chapel Hill: University of North Carolina Press, 1992.

Desmond, Jane C., and Virginia R. Domínguez. "Resituating American Studies in a Critical Internationalism." American Quarterly 48, no. 3 (1996): 475–90.

Dew, Charles B. Apostles of Disunion: Southern Secession Commissioners and the Causes of the Civil War. Charlottesville: University Press of Virginia, 2001.

Dew, Charles B. Ironmaker to the Confederacy: Joseph R. Anderson and the Tredegar Iron Works. New Haven, CT: Yale University Press, 1966.

Dickens, Charles. American Notes. 1874. Edited by John Lance Griffith. Charlottesville: Electronic Text Center, University of Virginia Library, 1996.

Dimock, Wai Chee. "Hemispheric Islam: Continents and Centuries for American Literature." American Literary History 21, no. 1 (2009): 28–52.

Domínguez, Virginia. White by Definition: Social Classification in Creole Louisiana. New Brunswick, NJ: Rutgers University Press, 1986.

Doolen, Andy. Fugitive Empire: Locating Early American Imperialism. Minneapolis: University of Minnesota Press, 2005.

Doolen, Andy. "Martin Delany, 'Be Cautious of the Word Rebel': Race, Transnationalism, and the Struggle for History in Martin Delany's Blake; Or, the Huts of America." American Literature 81 (March 2009): 153–79.

Douglass, Frederick. Life and Times of Frederick Douglass, Written by Himself. Introduction by George L. Ruffin. New rev. ed. Boston: D. E. Wolfe and Fiske, 1892.

Douglass, Frederick. My Bondage and My Freedom. 1855. Edited by William L. Andrews. Urbana: University of Illinois Press, 1987.

Douglass, Frederick. Narrative of the Life of Frederick Douglass, an American Slave, Written by Himself. Boston: Anti-Slavery Office, 1845.

Dourish, Paul. "Re-Space-ing Place: 'Place' and 'Space' Ten Years On." In CSCW'06: Proceedings of the 2006 20th Anniversary Conference on Computer Supported Cooperative Work. November 4–8, 2006. Banff, Alberta, Canada.

Drescher, Seymour. Capitalism and Antislavery. New York: Oxford University Press, 1987.

Drexler, Michael J. "Haiti, Modernity, and US Identities." Early American Literature 43, no. 2 (2008): 453–65.

Du Bois, W. E. B. The American Negro: His History and Literature. New York: Arno, 1969.

Du Bois, W. E. B. Black Reconstruction in America. Introduction by David Levering Lewis. New York: Touchstone, 1995.

Du Bois, W. E. B. Darkwater: Voices from within the Veil. Mineola, NY: Dover, 1999.

Du Bois, W. E. B. The Souls of Black Folk (1903). Edited by Henry Louis Gates Jr. and Terri Hume Oliver. New York: W. W. Norton, 1999.

Du Bois, W. E. B. "The Study of the Negro Problems." *Annals of the American Academy of Political and Social Science* (1898).

Du Bois, W. E. B. "The Talented Tenth. In *The Negro Problem: A Series of Articles by Representative American Negroes of Today*, edited by Booker T. Washington et al., 31–76. New York: James Pott, 1903.

DuCille, Ann. *The Coupling Convention: Sex, Text, and Tradition in Black Women's Fiction.* New York: Oxford University Press, 1993.

DuCille, Ann. "Where in the World Is William Wells Brown? Thomas Jefferson, Sally Hemings, and the DNA of African-American Literary History." *American Literary History* 12, no. 3 (2000): 443–62.

Dunbar, Paul Laurence. *The Collected Poetry of Paul Laurence Dunbar.* Edited by Joanne M. Braxton. Charlottesville: University Press of Virginia, 1993.

Dunbar, Paul Laurence. *In His Own Voice: The Dramatic and Other Uncollected Works of Paul Laurence Dunbar.* Edited by Herbert W. Martin. Athens: Ohio University Press, 2002.

Dunbar-Nelson, Alice. "People of Color in Louisiana." In *Creole: The History and Legacy*, edited by Sybil Kein, 3–41. Baton Rouge: Louisiana State University Press, 2000.

Dunbar-Nelson, Alice. *The Works of Alice Dunbar-Nelson.* Edited by Gloria T. Hull. 3 vols. New York: Oxford University Press, 1988.

Duncan, Nancy, ed. *Body Space: Destabilizing Geographies of Gender and Sexuality.* New York: Routledge, 1996.

Dworkin, Ira. *Daughter of the Revolution: The Major Nonfiction Works of Pauline E. Hopkins.* New Brunswick, NJ: Rutgers University Press, 2007.

Edgecombe, Rodney Stenning. "Topographic Disaffection in Dickens's *American Notes* and *Martin Chuzzlewit*." *Journal of English and Germanic Philology* 93, no. 1 (1994): 35–54.

Eley, Geoff. "Nations, Publics, and Political Cultures: Placing Habermas in the Nineteenth Century." In *Habermas and the Public Sphere*, edited by Craig Calhoun, 289–339. Cambridge, MA: MIT Press, 1992.

Elliot, Emory. "Diversity in the United States and Abroad: What Does It Mean When American Studies Is Transnational?" *American Quarterly* 59, no. 1 (2007): 1–22.

Ellis, Joseph. *American Sphinx: The Character of Thomas Jefferson.* New York: Alfred A. Knopf, 1997.

Equiano, Olaudah. *The Interesting Narrative of the Life of Olaudah Equiano, or Gustavus Vassa, the African. Written by Himself.* Vol. 1. New York: W. Durell, 1791.

Ernest, John. *Liberation Historiography: African American Writers and the Challenge of History, 1794–1861.* Chapel Hill: University of North Carolina Press, 2004.

Ernest, John. *Resistance and Reformation in Nineteenth-Century African-American Literature.* Jackson: University of Mississippi Press, 1995.

Evans, Brad. "Howellsian Chic: The Local Color of Cosmopolitanism." *English Literary History* 71, no. 3 (2004): 778–812.

Faragher, John Mack. "The Frontier Trail: Rethinking Turner and Reimagining the American West."*American Historical Review* 98, no. 1 (1993): 106–17.

Farrison, William Edward. *William Wells Brown: Author and Reformer.* Chicago: University of Chicago Press, 1969.

Fehrenbacher, Don E. *The Dred Scott Case: Its Significance in American Law and Politics.* New York: Oxford University Press, 1978.

Fetterley, Judith, and Marjorie Pryse. *Writing out of Place: Regionalism, Women, and American Literary Culture.* Urbana: University of Illinois Press, 2003.

Finseth, Ian. "Geographic Consciousness in the American Slave Narrative." In *American Literary Geographies: Spatial Practice and Cultural Production 1500–1900,* edited by Martin Brückner and Hsuan Hsu. Newark: University of Delaware Press, 2007.

Fischer, Sibylle. *Modernity Disavowed: Haiti and the Cultures of Slavery in the Age of Revolution.* Durham, NC: Duke University Press, 2004.

Fish, Cheryl J., and Farah J. Griffin, eds. *A Stranger in the Village: Two Centuries of African-American Travel Writing.* Boston: Beacon, 1998.

Fitzhugh, George. *Sociology for the South, or the Failure of Free Society.* Richmond, VA: A. Morris, 1854.

Foner, Philip S. *A History of Cuba and Its Relations to the United States.* New York: International Publishers, 1963.

Foner, Philip S. *The Life and Writings of Frederick Douglass.* 5 vols. New York: International Publishers, 1950–75.

Foreman, Grant. *The Five Civilized Tribes: Cherokee, Chickasaw, Choctaw, Creek, Seminole.* Norman: University of Oklahoma Press, 1934.

Foucault, Michel. *The Archaeology of Knowledge and the Discourse on Language.* Translated by A. M. Sheridan Smith. New York: Pantheon, 1972.

Foucault, Michel. *Language, Counter-Memory, Practice.* Edited by D. F. Bouchard. Ithaca, NY: Cornell University Press, 1977.

Foucault, Michel. *Power/Knowledge: Selected Interviews and Other Writings, 1972–1977.* Edited and translated by Colin Gordon. New York: Pantheon, 1980.

Fraser, Nancy. *Justice Interruptus: Critical Reflections on the "Postsocialist" Condition.* New York: Routledge, 1997.

Fraser, Nancy. "Rethinking Recognition." *New Left Review* 3 (May–June 2000): 107–20.

Fraser, Nancy. "Rethinking the Public Sphere: A Contribution to the Critique of Actual Democracy." In *Habermas and the Public Sphere,* edited by Craig Calhoun, 10–137. Cambridge, MA: MIT Press, 1992.

Friedman, Susan Stanford. *Mappings: Feminism and the Cultural Geographies of Encounter.* Princeton, NJ: Princeton University Press, 1998.

Gardner, Eric. *Unexpected Places: Relocating Nineteenth-Century African American Literature.* Jackson: University Press of Mississippi, 2009.

Gayle, Addison. *The Way of the New World: The Black Novel in America.* Garden City, NY: Anchor, 1975.

Geertz, Clifford. "Common Sense as a Cultural System." In *Local Knowledge: Further Essays in Interpretive Anthropology*, 73–93. New York: Basic, 1983.

Geertz, Clifford. "'From the Native's Point of View': On the Nature of Anthropological Understanding." In *Local Knowledge: Further Essays in Interpretive Anthropology*, 55–72. New York: Basic, 1983.

Giddens, Anthony. *The Consequences of Modernity*. Oxford: Polity, 1990.

Gilles, Paul. "Commentary: Hemispheric Partiality." *American Literary History* 18, no. 3 (2006): 648–55.

Gillman, Susan. *Blood Talk: American Race Melodrama and the Culture of the Occult*. Chicago: University of Chicago Press, 2003.

Gillman, Susan. "The Epistemology of Slave Conspiracy." *Modern Fiction Studies* 49, no. 1 (2003): 101–23.

Gilroy, Paul. *The Black Atlantic: Modernity and Double Consciousness*. Cambridge, MA: Harvard University Press, 2000.

Gilroy, Paul. *"There Ain't No Black in the Union Jack": The Cultural Politics of Race and Nation*. Chicago: University of Chicago Press, 1991.

Gleason, William A. *Sites Unseen: Architecture, Race, and American Literature*. New York: New York University Press, 2011.

Glissant, Edouard. *Caribbean Discourse: Selected Essays*. Translated by J. Michael Dash. Charlottesville: University Press of Virginia, 1989.

Goldin, Claudia Dale. *Urban Slavery in the American South 1820–1860: A Quantitative History*. Chicago: University of Chicago Press, 1976.

Gordon-Reed, Annette. *Thomas Jefferson and Sally Hemings: An American Controversy*. Charlottesville: University Press of Virginia, 1997.

Greenspan, Ezra. *Poetics of Relation*. Translated by Betsy Wing. Ann Arbor: University of Michigan Press, 1997.

Greenspan, Ezra. *William Wells Brown: A Reader*. Athens: University of Georgia Press, 2008.

Greeson, Jennifer. "Expropriating The Great South and Exporting 'Local Color': Global and Hemispheric Imaginaries of the First Reconstruction." In *Hemispheric American Studies*, edited by. Caroline F. Levander and Robert S. Levine, 116–139. New Brunswick, NJ: Rutgers University Press, 2008.

Gruenewald, David. "Foundations of Place: A Multidisciplinary Framework for Place-Conscious Education." *American Educational Research Journal* 40, no. 4 (2003): 619–54.

Gruesser, John Cullen. *The Empire Abroad and the Empire at Home: African American Literature and the Era of Overseas Expansion*. Athens: University of Georgia Press, 2012.

Gruesz, Kirsten Silva. *Ambassadors of Culture: The Transamerican Origins of Latino Writing*. Princeton, NJ: Princeton University Press, 2002.

Gruesz, Kirsten Silva. "The Gulf of Mexico System and the 'Latinness' of New Orleans." *American Literary History* 18, no. 3 (2006): 468–95.

Gunning, Sandra. *Moving Home: Gender, Travel and Writing in the Early African Diaspora*. Durham, NC: Duke University Press, forthcoming.

Gunning, Sandra. "Nancy Prince and the Politics of Mobility, Home and Diasporic (Mis)Identification." *American Quarterly* 53, no. 1 (2001) 32–69.

Guterl, Matthew Pratt. "An American Mediterranean: Haiti, Cuba, and the American South." In *Hemispheric American Studies*, edited by Caroline Levander and Robert S. Levine, 96–115. New Brunswick, NJ: Rutgers University Press, 2007.

Gutiérrez, David G. "Significant to Whom? Mexican Americans and the History of the American West." *Western Historical Quarterly* 24, no. 4 (1993) 519–39.

Habermas, Jürgen. *The Postnational Constellation: Political Essays*, edited and translated by Max Pensky. Cambridge, MA: MIT Press, 2001.

Habermas, Jürgen. *The Structural Transformation of the Public Sphere: An Inquiry into a Category of Bourgeois Society*, translated by Thomas Burger and Frederick Lawrence. Cambridge, MA: MIT Press, 1989.

Hall, Stuart. "Cultural Identity and Diaspora." In *Identity, Community, Culture, Difference*, edited by Jonathon Rutherford, 222–37. London: Lawrence and Wishart, 1990.

Hall, Stuart. "Encoding/Decoding." In *Culture, Media, Language*, edited by Stuart Hall, Dorothy Hobson, Andrew Lowe, and Paul Willis, 128–38. London: Hutchinson, 1980.

Hall, Stuart. "The Local and the Global: Globalization and Ethnicity." In *Dangerous Liaisons: Gender, Nation, and Postcolonial Perspectives*, edited by Anne McClintock, Aamir Mufti, and Ella Shohat, 173–87. Minneapolis: University of Minnesota Press, 1997.

Hall, Stuart. "Subjects in History: Making Diasporic Identities." In *The House That Race Built*, edited by Wahneema Lubiano, 289–99. New York: Pantheon, 1997.

Hall, William C. "How Mike Hooter Came Very Near 'Wolloping' Arch Coony." In *Polly Peablossom's Wedding and Other Tales*, edited by J. B. Lamar and R. M. Charlton, 146–53. Philadelphia: Getz and Buck, 1854.

Hardt, Michael, and Antonio Negri. *Empire*. Cambridge, MA: Harvard University Press, 2000.

Harlan, Louis R., ed. *The Booker T. Washington Papers*. Vol. 1: *The Autobiographical Writings*. Urbana: University of Illinois Press, 1972.

Harley, J. B. "Maps, Knowledge, and Power." In *The Iconography of Landscape: Essays on the Symbolic Representation, Design and Use of Past Environments*, edited by Denis Cosgrove and Stephen Daniels, 277–312. Cambridge: Cambridge University Press, 1988.

Harrison, Steve R., and Deborah G. Tatar. "Places: People, Events, Loci—the Relation of Semantic Frames in the Construction of Place." *Computer Supported Cooperative Work* 17, nos. 2–3 (2008): 97–133.

Harvey, Bruce. *American Geographics: U.S. National Narratives and the Representation of the Non-European World, 1830–1865*. Stanford, CA: Stanford University Press, 2001.

Harvey, David. *The Condition of Postmodernity. An Enquiry into the Origins of Cultural Change*. Oxford: Wiley Blackwell, 1991.

Harvey, David. "Cosmopolitanism and the Banality of Geographical Evils." *Public Culture* 12, no. 2 (2000): 529–64.

Harvey, David. *Justice, Nature and the Geography of Difference.* Oxford: Blackwell, 1996.

Harvey, David. *Seventeen Contradictions and the End of Capitalism.* New York: Oxford University Press, 2014.

Harvey, David. "The Sociological and Geographical Imaginations." *International Journal of Politics, Culture, and Society* 18, nos. 3–4 (2005): 211–55.

Hayden, William. *Narrative of William Hayden, Containing a Faithful Account of His Travels for a Number of Years, Whilst a Slave, in the South: Written by Himself.* Cincinnati, Ohio: the author, 1846.

Heermance, J. Noel. *William Wells Brown and Clotelle: A Portrait of the Artist in the First Negro Novel.* Hamden, CT: Archon, 1969.

Heidegger, Martin. *Being and Time.* Translated by Joan Stambaugh and revised by Dennis J. Schmidt. Albany: State University of New York Press, 2010.

Held, David. *Cosmopolitanism: A Defense.* Cambridge: Polity, 2003.

Held, David. *Democracy and the Global Order: From the Modern State to Cosmopolitan Governance.* Stanford, CA: Stanford University Press, 1995.

Helg, Aline. "Race and Black Mobilization in Colonial and Early Independent Cuba: A Comparative Perspective." *Ethnohistory* 44, no. 1 (1997): 53–74.

Helper, Hinton Rowan. "The Colton Claim against Bolivia." In *Oddments of Andean Diplomacy and Other Oddments*, 23–271. St. Louis, MO: W. S. Bryan, 1879.

Hendler, Glenn, *Public Sentiments: Structures of Feeling in Nineteenth-Century American Literature.* Chapel Hill: University of North Carolina Press, 2001.

Henson, Josiah. *Truth Stranger than Fiction: Father Henson's Story of His Own Life.* Boston: John P. Jewett, 1858.

Herder, J. G. *Outlines of a Philosophy of the History of Man.* Translated by T. Churchill. New York: Bergman Publishers, 1800.

Herder, J. G. "Essay on the Origin of Language." In *On the Origin of Language*, translated by John Moran and Alexander Gode, 87–166. Chicago: University of Chicago Press, 1966.

Herod, Andrew, and Melissa W. Wright. "Placing Scale: An Introduction." In *Geographies of Power: Placing Scale*, edited by Andrew Herod and Melissa W. Wright, 1–14. Malden, MA: Blackwell, 2002.

Higginbotham, Evelyn Brooks. *Righteous Discontent: The Women's Movement in the Black Baptist Church, 1880–1920.* Cambridge, MA: Harvard University Press, 1993.

Hoad, T. F., ed. *The Concise Oxford Dictionary of English Etymology.* Oxford: Oxford University Press, 1993.

Hobsbawm, Eric J. *Nations and Nationalism since 1780.* Cambridge: Cambridge University Press, 1990.

Hopkins, Pauline. "Booker T. Washington." *Colored American Magazine* (1901): 436–41.

Hopkins, Pauline. "Club Life among Colored Women." *Colored American Magazine* (August 1902): 273–77.

Hopkins, Pauline. *Contending Forces: A Romance Illustrative of Negro Life North and South.* 1900. Introduction by Richard Yarborough. Reprint. New York: Oxford University Press, 1988.

Hopkins, Pauline. "Famous Women of the Negro Race." *Colored American Magazine* 4.4 (March 1902): 277–80.

Hopkins, Pauline. *The Magazine Novels of Pauline Hopkins.* Introduction by Hazel V. Carby. New York: Oxford University Press, 1988.

Hopkins, Pauline. "Speech at the William Lloyd Garrison Centennial." *Guardian*, 16 (December 1905): 1, 4.

Horsman, Reginald. *Race and Manifest Destiny: The Origins of American Racial Anglo-Saxonism.* Cambridge, MA: Harvard University Press, 1981.

Howard, June, ed. *New Essays on The Country of the Pointed Firs.* New York: Cambridge University Press, 1994.

Howells, William Dean. *Literary Friends and Acquaintances: A Personal Retrospect of American Authorship.* 1900. Edited by David Widger. Reprint. Project Gutenberg, 2004.

Howitt, Richie. "Scale and the Other: Levinas and Geography." *Geoforum* 33 (2002): 299–313.

Howitt, Richie. "A World in a Grain of Sand: Towards a Reconceptualization of Geographical Scale." *Australian Geographer*, 24 (1993): 33–44.

Hsu, Hsuan L. *Geography and the Production of Space in Nineteenth-Century American Literature.* New York: Cambridge University Press, 2010.

Hsu, Hsuan L. "Literature and Regional Production." *American Literary History* 17, no. 1 (2005): 36–69.

Hurston, Zora Neale. *Tell My Horse: Voodoo and Life in Haiti and Jamaica.* New York: Harper Perennial Modern Classics, 2008.

Inman, Henry. *The Old Santa Fe Trail: The Story of a Great Highway.* New York: Macmillan, 1897.

Irigaray, Luce. *Speculum of the Other Woman.* Translated by G. C. Gill. Ithaca, NY: Cornell University Press, 1985.

Jackson, Andrew. *Narrative and Writings of Andrew Jackson, of Kentucky; Containing an Account of His Birth, and Twenty-Six Years of His Life while a Slave; His Escape; Five Years of Freedom, Together with Anecdotes Relating to Slavery; Journal of One Year's Travels; Sketches, etc. Narrated by Himself; Written by a Friend.* Syracuse, NY: Daily and Weekly Star Office, 1847.

Jackson, Blyden. *A History of Afro-American Literature.* Vol. 1: *The Long Beginning, 1746–1895.* Baton Rouge: Louisiana State University Press, 1989.

Jacobs, Harriet. *Incidents in the Life of a Slave Girl: Written by Herself*, edited by L. Maria Child. Boston: the author, 1861.

James, Ian. *The Fragmentary Demand: An Introduction to the Philosophy of Jean-Luc Nancy.* Stanford, CA: Stanford University Press, 2006.

Jefferson, Thomas. *Notes on the State of Virginia.* Vol. 2 of *From The Writings of Thomas*

Jefferson. Charlottesville: Electronic Text Center, University of Virginia Library, 2000.

Johns, Gillian. "Jim Trueblood and His Critic-Readers: Ralph Ellison's Rhetoric of Dramatic Irony and Tall Humor in the Mid-Century American Literary Public Sphere." *Texas Studies in Literature and Language* 49, no. 3 (2007): 230–64.

Johnson, David. "History of David Johnson and Wife, Fugitive Slaves from the State of—." In *Hair-Breadth Escapes from Slavery to Freedom*, edited by William Troy. Manchester, NH: W. Bremner, 1861.

Johnson, Michael K. *Black Masculinity and the Frontier Myth in American Literature*. Norman: University of Oklahoma Press, 2002.

Johnson, Walter. *Soul by Soul: Life inside the Antebellum Slave Market*. Cambridge, MA: Harvard University Press, 1999.

Justus, James H. *Fetching the Old Southwest: Humorous Writing from Longstreet to Twain*. Columbia: University of Missouri Press, 2004.

Kaplan, Amy. "Nation, Region, and Empire." In *The Columbia History of the American Novel*, edited by Emory Elliott, 240–66. New York: Columbia University Press, 1991.

Kaplan, Amy. *The Social Construction of American Realism*. Chicago: University of Chicago, 1988.

Kaplan, Amy, and Donald Pease. *Cultures of United States Imperialism*. Durham, NC: Duke University Press, 1993.

Kazanjian, David. *The Colonizing Trick: National Culture and Imperial Citizenship in Early America*. Minneapolis: University of Minnesota Press, 2003.

Kennedy, Lawrence W. *Planning the City upon a Hill*. Amherst: University of Massachusetts Press, 1992.

Kidwell, Clara Sue. *Choctaws and Missionaries in Mississippi, 1818–1918*. Norman: University of Oklahoma Press, 1997.

Kilde, Jeanne Halgren. *When Church Became Theatre: The Transformation of Evangelical Architecture and Worship in Nineteenth-Century America*. New York: Oxford University Press, 2005.

Kimball, Fiske. "Thomas Jefferson and the First Monument of Classical Revival in America." *Journal of the American Institute of Architects* 3 (November 1915): 473–74.

Kimball, Gregg D. *American City, Southern Place: A Cultural History of Antebellum Richmond*. Athens: University of Georgia Press, 2000.

Klein, Maury. *Days of Defiance: Sumter, Secession, and the Coming of the Civil War*. New York: Alfred A. Knopf, 1997.

Knadler, Stephen P. *Remapping Citizenship and the Nation in African-American Literature*. New York: Routledge, 2010.

Koldony, Annette. *The Land before Her: Fantasy and Experience of the American Frontiers, 1630–1860*. Chapel Hill: University of North Carolina Press, 1984.

Koldony, Annette. *The Lay of the Land: Metaphor as Experience and History in American Life and Letters*. Chapel Hill: University of North Carolina Press, 1975.

Koldony, Annette. "Letting Go of Our Grand Obsessions: Notes toward a New Literary History of the American Frontiers." *American Literature* 64, no. 1 (1992): 1–18.

Konkle, Maureen. "Indigenous Ownership and the Emergence of U.S. Liberal Imperialism." *American Indian Quarterly* 32, no. 3 (2008): 297–323.

Krauthamer, Barbara. "In Their 'Native Country': Freedpeople's Understandings of Culture and Citizenship in the Choctaw and Chickasaw Nations." In *Crossing Waters, Crossing Worlds: The African Diaspora in Indian Country*, edited by Tiya A. Miles and Sharon P. Holland, 100–120. Durham, NC: Duke University Press, 2006.

Lackey, Kris. "Eighteenth-Century Aesthetic Theory and the Nineteenth-Century Traveler in Trans-Allegheny America: F. Trollope, Dickens, Irving, and Parkman." *American Studies* 32, no. 1 (1991): 22–48.

Laclau, Ernesto. *New Reflections of the Revolution of Our Time*. London: Verso, 1990.

Lane, Lunsford. *The Narrative of Lunsford Lane, Formerly of Raleigh, N.C. Embracing an Account of His Early Life, the Redemption by Purchase of Himself and Family from Slavery, and His Banishment from the Place of His Birth for the Crime of Wearing a Colored Skin*. Boston: the author, 1842.

Lape, Noreen Grover. *West of the Border: The Multicultural Literature of the Western American Frontiers*. Athens: Ohio University Press, 2000.

Latour, Bruno. *Reassembling the Social: An Introduction to Actor Network Theory*. New York: Oxford University Press, 2005.

Latour, Bruno. *We Have Never Been Modern*. Translated by C. Porter. London: Harvester Wheatsheaf, 1993.

Lee, Debbie. *Slavery and the Romantic Imagination*. Philadelphia: University of Pennsylvania Press, 2002.

Levander, Caroline. "Confederate Cuba." *American Literature* 78, no. 4 (2006): 821–45.

Levander, Caroline, and Robert S. Levine, eds. *Hemispheric American Studies*. New Brunswick, NJ: Rutgers University Press, 2007.

Leverenz, David. *Manhood and the American Renaissance*. Ithaca, NY: Cornell University Press, 1989.

Levine, Robert S. *Dislocating Race and Nation: Episodes in Nineteenth-Century American Literary Nationalism*. Chapel Hill: University of North Carolina Press, 2008.

Levine, Robert S. *Martin Delany, Frederick Douglass, and the Politics of Representative Identity*. Chapel Hill: University of North Carolina Press, 1997.

Levine, Robert S., and Caroline Levander. "Introduction: Hemispheric American Literary History." *American Literary History* 18, no. 3 (2006): 397–405.

Lewis, Henry Clay. *Odd Leaves from the Life of a Louisiana Swamp Doctor*. Edited by Edwin T. Arnold. Baton Rouge: Louisiana University Press, 1997.

Lewis, Leslie. "Biracial Promise and the New South in *Minnie's Sacrifice*: A Protocol for Reading Julia Collins's *Curse of Caste*." *African American Review* 40, no. 4 (2006): 755–68.

Limerick, Patricia Nelson. *The Legacy of Conquest: The Unbroken Past of the American West*. New York: Norton, 1987.

Limerick, Patricia Nelson. *Something in the Soil: Legacies and Reckonings in the New West*. New York: Norton, 2001.

Lincoln, Abraham. *Abraham Lincoln: Speeches and Writings*. Edited by Don E. Fehrenbacher. 2 vols. New York: Library of America, 1989.

Linebaugh, Peter, and Marcus Rediker. *The Many-Headed Hydra*. Boston: Beacon, 2000.

Lipietz, Alain. "The Local and the Global: Regional Individuality or Interregionalism?" *Transactions of the Institute of British Geographers* 18 (1993): 8–18.

Loggins, Vernon. *The Negro Author: His Development in America*. New York: Columbia University Press, 1931.

Lucasi, Stephen. "William Wells Brown's Narrative and Traveling Subjectivity." *African American Review* 41, no. 3 (2007) 521–39.

Martin, Gretchen. "A Louisiana Swamp Doctor's Diagnosis: Romantic Fatality and the Frontier Roots of Realism." *Southern Literary Journal* 37, no. 2 (2005): 17–39.

Marx, Leo. *The Machine in the Garden: Technology and the Pastoral Ideal in America*. 1964. New York: Oxford University Press, 2000.

Massey, Doreen. *For Space*. London: Sage, 2006.

Massey, Doreen. "Geography Matters." In *Geography Matters: A Reader*, edited by Doreen Massey and John Allen, 1–11. New York: Cambridge University Press, 1984.

Massey, Doreen. *Space, Place and Gender*. Minneapolis: University of Minnesota Press, 1994.

Mather, Cotton. *Magnalia Christi Americana: The Ecclesiastical History of New England from Its First Planting, In the Year 1620, Unto the Year of Our Lord 1698*. 1702. Introduction by Thomas Robins, translation of Hebrew, Greek, and Latin by Lucius Robinson. 7 vols. Hartford, CT: Silas and Andrus and Son, 1853.

Mattingly, Garret. *Renaissance Diplomacy*. New York: Dover, 1988.

Mattox, Jake. "The Mayor of San Juan del Norte? Nicaragua, Martin Delany, and the 'Cotton' Americans." *American Literature* 81, no. (2009): 527–54.

McHenry, Elizabeth. *Forgotten Readers: Recovering the Lost History of African American Literary Societies*. Durham, NC: Duke University Press, 2002.

McPherson, James. *Abraham Lincoln and the Second American Revolution*. New York: Oxford University Press, 1991.

Merleau-Ponty, Maurice. *Signs*. Translated with an Introduction by Richard C. McCleary. Evanston, IL: Northwestern University Press, 1964.

Mignolo, Walter D. "The Geopolitics of Knowledge and the Colonial Difference." *South Atlantic Quarterly* 101, no. 1 (winter 2002): 57–97.

Mignolo, Walter D. "Globalization, Civilization Processes, and the Relocation of Languages and Cultures." In *The Cultures of Globalization*, edited by. Fredric Jameson and Masao Myoshi, 32–53. Durham, NC: Duke University Press, 1998.

Mignolo, Walter D. *Local Histories/Global Designs: Coloniality, Subaltern Knowledges, and Border Thinking*. Princeton, NJ: Princeton University Press, 2000.

Miller, Floyd J. Introduction to Martin Delany, *Blake; or, the Huts of America*, edited by Floyd J. Miller. xi-xxix. Boston: Beacon, 1970.

Mintz, Sidney. "Enduring Substances, Trying Theories: The Caribbean Region as Oikoumene." *RAI* 2 (1996): 289–311.

Moretti, Franco. *Atlas of the European Novel 1800–1900*. New York: Verso, 1999.

Morgan, Dale L. *Jebediah Smith and the Opening of the West*. Lincoln: University of Nebraska Press.

Morris, Christopher. *Becoming Southern: The Evolution of a Way of Life, Warren County and Vicksburg, Mississippi, 1770–1860*. New York: Oxford University Press, 1995.

Morrison, Toni. "Recitatif." In *Confirmation: An Anthology of African American Women*, edited by Amiri Baraka and Amina Baraka, 243–61. New York: Morrow, 1983.

Morton, Timothy. *Realist Magic: Objects, Ontology, Causality*. Ann Arbor, MI: Open Humanities Press, 2013.

Moses, Wilson J. *The Wings of Ethiopia: Studies in African-American Life and Letters*. Ames: Iowa State University Press, 1990.

Mulvey, Christopher. "The Fugitive Self and the New World of the North: William Wells Brown's Discovery of America." In *The Black Columbiad: Defining Moments in African American Literature and Culture*, edited by Werner Sollors and Maria Diedrich, 99–111. Cambridge, MA: Harvard University Press, 1994.

Mulvey, Christopher, ed. *Clotel by William Wells Brown: An Electronic Scholarly Edition*. Charlottesville: University of Georgia Press, 2006.

Murphy, Gretchen. *Hemispheric Imaginings: The Monroe Doctrine and Narratives of U.S. Empire*. Durham, NC: Duke University Press, 2005.

Nancy, Jean-Luc. *The Inoperative Community*. Minneapolis: University of Minnesota Press, 1991.

Negt, Oskar, and Alexander Kluge. *Public Sphere and Experience: Toward an Analysis of the Bourgeois and Proletarian Public Sphere*. Translated by Peter Labanyi, Jamie Owen Daniel, and Assenka Oksiloff. Minneapolis: University of Minnesota Press, 1993.

Nwankwo, Ifeoma. *Black Cosmopolitanism: Racial Consciousness and Transnational Identity in the Nineteenth-Century Americas*. Philadelphia: University of Pennsylvania Press, 2005.

Oakes, Timothy. "Place and the Paradox of Modernity." *Annals of the Association of American Geographers* 87, no. 3 (1997): 509–31.

O'Brien, Colleen C. "'The White Women All Go for Sex': Frances Harper on Suffrage, Citizenship, and the Reconstruction South." *African American Review* 43, no. 4 (2009): 605–20.

Okker, Patricia. *Social Stories: The Magazine Novel in Nineteenth-Century America*. Charlottesville: University of Virginia Press, 2003.

Olivares, Julián. "Sandra Cisneros' *The House on Mango Street*, and the Poetics of

Space." In *Chicana Creativity and Criticism: New Frontiers in American Literature*, edited by María Herrera-Sobek and Helena María Viramontes, 233–44. Albuquerque: University of New Mexico Press, 1996.

Onuf, Peter S. *Jefferson's Empire: The Language of American Nationhood*. Charlottesville: University of Virginia Press, 2000.

"The Ostend Report." 1854. In *The Works of James Buchanan Comprising His Speeches, State Papers, and Private Correspondences*, edited by John Bassett Moore, 261–66. New York: Antiquarian, 1960.

Oswald, Delmont R. Introduction to James P. Beckwourth, *The Life and Adventures of James P. Beckwourth as Told to Thomas D. Bonner*, vii–xiii. Lincoln: University of Nebraska Press, 1972.

Ó Tuathail, Gearóid, and John Agnew. "Geopolitics and Discourse: Practical Geopolitical Reasoning in American Foreign Policy." *Political Geography* 2 (1992): 190–204.

Padover, Saul K. *Thomas Jefferson and the National Capital Containing Notes and Correspondence Exchanged between Jefferson, Washington, L'Enfant, Ellicott, Hallett, Thornton, Latrobe, the Commissioners, and Others, Relating to the Founding, Surveying, Planning, Designing, Constructing, and Administering of the City of Washington, 1783–1818.* Washington, DC: Government Printing Office, 1946.

Parkman, Francis. *The Oregon Trail*. 6th ed., rev. Boston: Little, Brown, 1877.

Peel, Mark. "On the Margins: Lodgers and Borders in Boston, 1860–1900." *Journal of American History* 72, no. 4 (1986): 813–34.

Pérez Firmat, Gustavo, ed. *Do the Americas Have a Common Literature?* Durham, NC: Duke University Press 1990.

Peterson, Carla L. *Doers of the Word: African-American Women Speakers and Writers in the World (1830–1880)*. New Brunswick, NJ: Rutgers University Press, 2008.

Phillips, Kendall R. "Spaces of Invention: Dissension, Freedom, and Thought in Foucault." *Philosophy and Rhetoric* 35, no. 4 (2002): 328–44.

Pleck, Elizabeth Hafkin. *Black Migration and Poverty: Boston 1865–1900*. New York: Academic, 1979.

Porter, Carolyn. "What We Know That We Don't Know: Remapping American Literary Studies." *American Literary History* 6, no. 3 (1994): 467–526.

Prewitt, Kenneth. "A Nation Imagined, A Nation Measured." In *Across the Continent: Jefferson, Lewis and Clark, and the Making of America*, edited by Douglas Seefeldt, Jeffrey L. Hantman, and Peter S. Onuf, 132–68. Charlottesville: University of Virginia Press, 2005.

Prucha, Francis Paul. *Documents of United States Indian Policy*. 3rd ed. Omaha: University of Nebraska Press, 2000.

Quashie, Kevin Everod. "The Trouble with Publicness: Toward a Theory of Black Quiet." *African American Review* 43, nos. 2–3 (2009): 329–43.

Radhakrishnan, R. "Adjudicating Hybridity, Co-ordinating Betweenness," *Jouvert* 5, no. 1 (2000): n.p.

Radhakrishnan, R. "Globalization, Desire, and the Politics of Representation." *Comparative Literature* 53, no. 4 (2001): 315–32.

Rael, Patrick. "Black Theodicy: African Americans and Nationalism in the Antebellum North." *North Star* 3, no. 2 (2000).

Raimon, Eve Allegra. *The "Tragic Mulatta" Revisited: Race and Nationalism in Nineteenth-Century Antislavery Fiction.* New Brunswick, NJ: Rutgers University Press, 2004.

Reid-Pharr, Robert F. *Conjugal Union: The Body, The House, and the Black American.* New York: Oxford University Press, 1999.

Resch, Robert Paul. *Althusser and the Renewal of Marxist Social Theory.* Berkeley: University of California Press, 1992.

Reynolds, David S. *Beneath the American Renaissance: The Subversive Imagination in the Age of Emerson and Melville.* Cambridge, MA: Harvard University Press, 1989.

Rifkin, Mark. *Manifesting America: The Imperial Construction of U.S. National Space.* New York: Oxford University Press, 2009.

Riley, Franklin L., ed. *Publications of the Mississippi Historical Society.* Vol. X. Oxford, MS: Printed for the Society, 1909.

Ristow, Walter. *American Maps and Mapmakers: Commercial Cartography in the Nineteenth Century.* Detroit, MI: Wayne State University Press, 1985.

Roberts, Susan. "Economic Landscapes." In *A Companion to Cultural Geography,* edited by James Duncan, Nuala Johnson, and Richard Schein, 331–36. Malden, MA: Blackwell, 2004.

Robbins, Bruce, ed. *The Phantom Public Sphere.* Minneapolis: University of Minnesota Press, 1993.

Rodríguez, Ileana. *Transatlantic Topographies: Islands, Highlands, Jungles.* Minneapolis: University of Minnesota Press, 2004.

Roediger, David R. *The Wages of Whiteness: Race and the Making of the American Working Class.* New York: Verso, 1991.

Rojo, Antonio Benitez. *The Repeating Island: The Caribbean and Postmodern Performance.* Translated by James E. Maraniss. Durham, NC: Duke University Press, 1992.

Rollin, Frances A. "Life and Public Service of Martin R. Delany" (1868). In *Two Biographies by African American Women,* edited by William L. Andrews. New York: Oxford University Press, 1991.

Rose, Gillian. *Feminism and Geography: The Limits of Geographical Knowledge.* Minneapolis: University of Minnesota Press, 1993.

Rowe, Aimee Carrillo. "Be Longing: Toward a Feminist Politics of Relation." *National Women's Studies Association Journal* 17, no. 2 (2005): 15–46.

Ryland, F. *Johnson's Life of Milton with Introduction and Notes.* London: George Bell and Sons, 1894.

Sack, Robert David. *Human Territoriality: Its Theory and History.* Cambridge: Cambridge University Press, 1986.

Sagel, Jim. "Sandra Cisneros." *Publishers Weekly,* March 29, 1991, 74–75.

Said, Edward. *Culture and Interpretation*. New York: Alfred A. Knopf, 1993.

Sassen, Saskia. "Spatialities and Temporalities of the Global: Elements for a Theorization." *Public Culture* 12, no. 1 (2000): 215–32.

Sassen, Saskia. *Territory, Authority, Rights: From Medieval to Global Assemblages*. Princeton, NJ: Princeton University Press, 2006.

Schein, Richard H. "The Place of Landscape: A Conceptual Framework for Interpreting an American Scene." *Annals of the Association of American Geographers* 87, no. 4 (1997): 660–80.

Schneider, Mark R. *Boston Confronts Jim Crow, 1890–1920*. Boston: Northeastern University Press, 1997.

Schnore, Leo F., and Peter R. Knights. "Residence and Social Structure: Boston in the Antebellum Period." In *Nineteenth-Century Cities: Essays in the New Urban History*, edited by Stephan Thernstrom and Richard Sennett. New Haven, CT: Yale University Press, 1969.

Schoolman, Martha. "Violent Places: Three Years in Europe and the Question of William Wells Brown's Cosmopolitanism." *ESQ* 58, no. 1 (2012).

Schwartz, Seymour, and Ralph Ehrenberg. *The Mapping of America*. New York: Harry N. Abrams, 1980.

Scott, David. *Conscripts of Modernity: The Tragedy of Colonial Enlightenment*. Durham, NC: Duke University Press, 2004.

Shelby, Tommie. "Cosmopolitanism, Blackness, and Utopias: A Conversation with Paul Gilroy. *Transition* 98 (2008): 116–35.

Short, John R. *Representing the Republic: Mapping the United States, 1600–1900*. London: Reaktion, 2001.

Silver, Andrew. *Minstrelsy and Murder: The Crisis of Southern Humor, 1835–1925*. Baton Rouge: Louisiana State University Press, 2006.

Simpson, Mark. *Trafficking Subjects: The Politics of Mobility in Nineteenth-Century America*. Minneapolis: University of Minnesota Press, 2005.

Slotkin, Richard. *The Fatal Environment: The Myth of the Frontier in the Age of Industrialization, 1800–1890*. New York: Atheneum, 1985.

Slotkin, Richard. *Gunfighter Nation: The Myth of the Frontier in Twentieth Century America*. New York: Atheneum, 1992.

Slotkin, Richard. *Regeneration through Violence: The Mythology of the American Frontier, 1600–1860*. Middletown, CT: Wesleyan University Press, 1973.

Smith, Neil. *Uneven Development: Nature, Capital, and the Production of Space*. 2nd ed. Oxford: Blackwell, 1990.

Soja, Edward W. *Postmodern Geographies: The Reassertion of Space in Critical Social Theory*. New York: Verso, 1989.

Soja, Edward W. *Seeking Spatial Justice*. Minneapolis: University of Minnesota Press, 2010.

Soja, Edward W., and Barbara Hooper. "The Spaces That Difference Makes: Some

Notes on the Geographical Margins of the New Cultural Politics." In *Place and Politics of Identity*, edited by Michael Keith and Steve Pile, 180–202. London: Routledge, 1993.

Sollors, Werner. *Beyond Ethnicity: Consent and Descent in American Culture*. New York: Oxford University Press, 1986.

Spivak, Gayatri Chakravorty. *Critique of Post-Colonial Reason: Toward a History of the Vanishing Present*. Cambridge, MA: Harvard University Press, 1999.

Sprung, Mervyn. *Explorations in Life Sense*. Albany: State University of New York Press, 1994.

Stauffer, John, ed. *The Works of James McCune Smith: Black Intellectual and Abolitionist*. New York: Oxford University Press, 2006.

Stein, Jordan. "A Christian Nation Calls for Its Wandering Children: Life, Liberty, Liberia." In *American Literary History*, 849–73. New York: Oxford University Press, 2007.

Stephens, Michelle. "Black Transnationalism and the Politics of National Identity: West Indian Intellectuals in Harlem in the Age of War and Revolution." *American Quarterly* 50, no. 3 (1998): 592–608.

Stephens, Michelle. "Re-Imagining the Shape and Borders of Black Political Space." *Radical History Review* 87 (2003): 169–82.

Stepto, Robert B. *From Behind the Veil: A Study of Afro-American Narrative*. Urbana: University of Illinois Press, 1979.

Stewart, Charles. "Syncretism and Its Synonyms: Reflections on Cultural Mixture." *Diacritics* 29, no. 3 (1999): 40–62.

Stoler, Ann Laura. *Carnal Knowledge and Imperial Power: Race and the Intimate in Colonial Rule*. Berkeley: University of California Press, 2002.

Stoler, Ann Laura. "Intimidations of Empire: Predicaments of the Tactile and Unseen." In *Haunted by Empire: Geographies of Intimacy in North American History*, edited by Ann Laura Stoler, 1–22. Durham, NC: Duke University Press, 2006.

Stoler, Ann Laura. "Tense and Tender Ties: The Politics of Comparison in North American History and (Post) Colonial Studies." *Journal of American History* 88, no. 3 (2001): 829–65.

Stuckey, Sterling. *Slave Culture: Nationalist Theory and the Foundations of Black America*. New York: Oxford University Press, 1988.

Suggs, Jon-Christian. *Whispered Consolations: Law and Narrative in African American Life*. Ann Arbor: University of Michigan Press, 2000.

Sundquist, Eric. *To Wake the Nations: Race in the Making of American Literature*. Cambridge, MA: Harvard University Press, 1993.

Takagi, Midori. "*Rearing Wolves to Our Own Destruction": Slavery in Richmond, Virginia, 1782–1865*. Charlottesville: University Press of Virginia, 1999.

Thiong'o, Ngugi wa. "Enactments of Power: The Politics of Performance Space." *TDR* 41, no. 3 (1997): 11–30.

Thomas, Brook. "Civic Multiculturalism and the Myth of Liberal Consent: A Comparative Analysis." *CR: The New Centennial Review* 1, no. 3 (2001): 1–35.

Thrift, Nigel. "Intensities of Feeling: Towards a Spatial Politics of Affect." *Geografiska Annaler, Series B, Human Geography* 86, no. 1 (2004): 57–78.

Thrift, Nigel. *Non-Representational Theory: Space, Politics, Affect.* London: Routledge, 2007.

Tregle, Joseph G., Jr. "Creoles and Americans." In *Creole New Orleans: Race and Americanization*, edited by Arnold Hirsch and Joseph Logsdon, 131–85. Baton Rouge: Louisiana State University Press, 1992.

Tuan, Yi-Fu. *Humanist Geography: An Individual's Search for Meaning.* Staunton, VA: George F. Thompson Publishing Company, 2012.

Tuan, Yi-Fu. *Space and Place: The Perspective of Experience.* Minneapolis: University of Minnesota Press, 1977.

United States Army Courts of Inquiry. "The Sand Creek Massacre." In *Report of the Secretary of War*, 68–74. S. Exec. Doc. No. 26, 39th Cong., 2nd Sess. (1864).

Valentine, Elisha. "History of Elisha Valentine, a Fugitive Slave from the State of North Carolina." In *Hair-Breadth Escapes from Slavery to Freedom*, edited by William Troy. Manchester, Ontario, CN: W. Bremner, 1861.

Vivan, Itala. "Geography, Literature, and the African Territory: Some Observations on the Western Map and the Representation of Territory in the South African Literary Imagination." *Research in African Literatures* 31, no. 2 (2000): 49–70.

Von Frank, Albert. *The Trials of Anthony Burns: Freedom and Slavery in Emerson's Boston.* Cambridge, MA: Harvard University Press, 1998.

Wade, Richard. *Slavery in the Cities: The South 1820–1860.* New York: Oxford University Press, 1967.

Waldrep, Christopher. *Vicksburg's Long Shadow: The Civil War Legacy of Race and Remembrance.* Lanham, MD: Rowman and Littlefield, 2005.

Walker, David. *David Walker's Appeal.* 1829. Edited by Peter Hinks. University Park: Penn State Press, 2002.

Wallinger, Hanna. *Pauline E. Hopkins: A Literary Biography.* Athens: University of Georgia Press, 2005.

Ward, Samuel Ringgold. *Autobiography of a Fugitive Negro: His Anti-Slavery Labours in the United States, Canada, and England.* London: John Snow, 1855.

Warner, Michael. "The Mass Public and the Mass Subject." In *American Literary Studies: A Methodological Reader*, edited by Michael A. Elliot and Claudia Stokes, 245–63. New York: New York University Press, 2003.

Warren, Kenneth W. "A Reply to My Critics." *PMLA* 128, no. 2 (2013): 403–8.

Warren, Kenneth W. *What Was African American Literature?* Cambridge, MA: Harvard University Press, 2011.

Washington, Booker T. "Industrial Education: Will It Solve the Negro Problem?" *Colored American Magazine* 7, no. 2 (February 1904): 87–95.

Washington, Booker T, et. al. *The Negro Problem: A Series of Articles by Representative American Negroes of Today*. New York: James Pott, 1903.

Washington, Booker T. *Up from Slavery*. 1901. New York: Airmont, 1967.

Webb, Frank. *The Garies and Their Friends*. Baltimore: Johns Hopkins University Press, 1997.

Weber, Max. *From Max Weber: Essays in Sociology*. Edited and translated by H. H. Gerth and C. Wright Mills. New York: Oxford University Press, 1958.

Wells, Ida B. *Crusade for Justice: The Autobiography of Ida B. Wells*. Edited by Alfreda M. Duster. Chicago: University of Chicago Press, 1970.

Wells, Ida B. "Lynching and the Excuse for It." 1901. In *Rape: An Exchange of Views*, edited by Bettina Aptheker, 29. New York: American Institute for Marxist Studies, 1977.

West, Cornel. *Prophesy Deliverance! An African American Revolutionary Christianity*. 1982. Louisville, KY: Westminster Press, 2002.

Whatmore, Sarah. *Hybrid Geographies: Natures Cultures Spaces*. London: Sage, 2002.

Wheat, Carl I., ed. *California in 1851: The Letters of Dame Shirley*. 2 vols. San Francisco: Grabhorn, 1933.

Wilmer, James L. *Lincoln's General*. Vol. 1 of *Generals in Blue and Gray*. Westport, CT: Greenwood, 2004.

Wilson, Elinor. *Jim Beckwourth: Black Mountain Man and War Chief of the Crows*. Norman: University of Oklahoma Press, 1984.

Wilson, Harriet. *Our Nig: or, Sketches from the Life of a Free Black*, edited by Henry Louis Gates, Jr. and Richard J. Ellis. New York: Vintage, 2011.

Wilson, Ivy. *Specters of Democracy: Blackness and the Aesthetics of Politics in the Antebellum U.S.* New York: Oxford University Press, 2011.

Wong, Edlie L. *Neither Fugitive nor Free: Atlantic Slavery, Freedom Suits, and the Legal Culture of Travel*. New York: New York University Press, 2009.

Wood, Denis. *Rethinking the Power of Maps*. New York: Guilford, 2010.

Wrobel, David M. "Beyond the Frontier-Region Dichotomy." *Pacific Historical Review* 65, no. 3 (1996): 401–30.

Yellin, Jean Fagan. *The Intricate Knot: Black Figures in American Literature, 1776–1863*. New York: New York University Press, 1972.

Yellin, Jean Fagan, and John C. Van Horne, eds. *The Abolitionist Sisterhood: Women's Political Culture in Antebellum America*. Ithaca, NY: Cornell University Press, 2004.

Zafar, Rafia. *We Wear the Mask: African Americans Write American Literature, 1760–1870*. New York: Columbia University Press, 1997.

Zagarell, Sandra A. "Troubling Regionalism: Rural Life and the Cosmopolitan Eye in Jewett's 'Deephaven.'" *American Literary History* 10, no. 4 (1998): 639–63.

INDEX

Abdy, Edward Strutt, 67

Abraham Lincoln and the Second American Revolution (McPherson), 231n109

Adams, John, 129

"Address in Independence Hall in Philadelphia, Pennsylvania" (Lincoln), 62–63

African American literature: Atlantic travels in, 27–30, 54–55, 146; color line in, 154; place in, 1–3, 8–10, 25–26, 35, 213–18; rise of the black novel and, 1–2, 154–56; second wave of, 154–55; territory and deterritorialization in, 3–4, 69–71; travel in, 55

"The African Diaspora in Indian Country" (Miles and Holland), 98

African Meeting House (St. Paul's Baptist Church) (Boston), 170–71, 176

Afro-American League, 173, 176

Afro-American Novel and Its Tradition, The (Bell), 229n89

Agnew, John, 36

agrarianism, 17, 26, 59–60, 64–65, 178

Albert, James (Ukasaw Gronniosaw), 30–31

Alcoff, Linda Martín, 238–39n98

Alfred, Taiaiake, 100

Allmendinger, Blake, 91

A.M.E. Church Review, The (magazine), 258n39

America and Other Poems (Whitfield), 70

"American Authorship" (Howells), 174

American Fugitive in Europe, The (Brown), 28, 30

American Literary Geographies (Brückner and Hsu), 61–62

American Literary Magazine (journal), 144, 242n7

American Negro, The (Du Bois), 160–61

American Notes (Dickens), 38

Ammons, Elizabeth, 258n48

Amsterdam News (newspaper), 252n65

"Anarchy Alley" (Dunbar-Nelson), 208–9

Anderson, Michael K., 236n54

Andrews, William, 90, 102

Anglo-African Magazine (black journal): *Blake* and, 34, 71, 75, 85, 232n4, 242n26; *Miralda* and, 34

"Annexation of Cuba" (Delany), 114, 143

Anti-Lynching Crusaders, 258n39

Anti-Oedipus (Deleuze and Guattari), 89

Anti-Slavery Bugle (newspaper), 141

Anti-Slavery Harp, The (Brown), 224n30

Appadurai, Arjun, 226n53

"An Appeal to the People of Great Britain and the World" (Brown), 27

Appiah, Kwame Anthony, 227n64

Aristotle, 54

Armstrong, Nancy, 226n49
Ashley, William H., 93
Atlantic Monthly (magazine), 158,
   193–94, 255n5

Bachelard, Gaston, 214
Baker, Houston A., Jr., 155, 162, 164
Bakhtin, Mikhail, 207
Bancroft, George, 231–32n122
"The Banjo Song" (Dunbar), 256n7
Banneker, Benjamin, 36
Barbé-Marbois, François, Marquis de,
   35
Baudrillard, Jean, 124–25
Beckwourth, James P.: frontier humor
   and, 230n94; nation and, 71, 75–76,
   108; Native Americans and, 74, 76,
   94–95, 95, 100–107; photograph of,
   97; territory and, 13, 71–74, 75–76,
   85, 88–95, 100–109. See also *The Life
   and Adventures of James P. Beckwourth*
   (Beckwourth)
Beckwourth Pass, 71, 107
Bell, Bernard W., 24, 229n89
Benhabib, Seyla, 183, 227n64
Benjamin, Walter, 212
Benton, Thomas, 140–41
Bercovitch, Sacvan, 153, 174
Bergson, Henri, 220n13
Bernal, Martin, 235–36n42
Beyond Ethnicity (Sollors), 206–7
Bibb, Henry, 46, 70
Black Atlantic, The (Gilroy), 216–17
black church, 153, 169–77
black geography, 2, 5, 12–13, 20, 22–23,
   49–50, 55, 58–59, 70–79, 108–9,
   112–16, 157, 213–16
Black Migration and Poverty (Pleck), 160
"The Black North in 1901: A Social
   Study" (Du Bois), 160–61
Black Power, 24
black public sphere: in *Contending*

Forces, 13, 154, 161–66, 173–77; in *Iola
   Leroy*, 162–63
Black Public Sphere Collective, 162
black women's club movement:
   Dunbar-Nelson and, 258n39; Hopkins and, 153, 185–88
Blake (Delany): audience of, 9; confinement in, 214; Cuba in, 114–15,
   130–35, 139–41; Haiti in, 127–28,
   129–30; instructional counter-atlas
   in, 5 73, 83–88; mapping in, 77–78,
   112–14, 126–27; Native Americans
   in, 98–99; publication of, 71, 75;
   "pure black" in, 92; slavery in,
   80–84; territory and deterritorialization in, 71–74, 75, 76–77, 79–87,
   97–100, 108–9; transit in, 142–44,
   146–50
Blake Almendinger, 236n54
Blyden, Edward Wilmot, 216, 232n1
Bogue, Ronald, 145–46
Bolivia, 242–43n29
Bond and Free (Howard), 155
Bondswoman's Narrative, The (Crafts),
   214
Bonner, Thomas D., 71, 75–76, 90–91,
   102
Bordo, Susan, 186, 254n104
Boston: black churches in, 169–73;
   black population of, 153, 160–61;
   in *Contending Forces*, 152–53, 156–61,
   166–69, 180–82; literary situation
   of, 158–59
Boston Confronts Jim Crow (Schneider),
   249n16
Boyd, Melba Joyce, 248n6
Brannan, William Penn, 230n98
Brathwaite, Kamau, 204
Brenner, Neil, 211
Brickhouse, Anna, 224n31
Brodhead, Richard, 191, 192, 209
Brooks, Kristina, 206, 256n12

Brown, Henry "Box," 214

Brown, William Wells: as antislavery lecturer in Britain and France, 12, 27–33; as city slave, 43, 46; Crafts and, 44; Fugitive Slave Act and, 27, 32–33; on Haitian emigration, 70; nation and, 25–27; rise of the black novel and, 1–2, 24–25, 34–35, 154; on slave pens, 47, 66–68, 214

Brown, William Wells, writings: *The American Fugitive in Europe*, 28, 30; *The Anti-Slavery Harp*, 224n30; "An Appeal to the People of Great Britain and the World," 27; *A Description of William Wells Brown's Original Panoramic Views*, 57–58, 60; *The Escape*, 225n36; *Miralda, or the Beautiful Quadroon*, 34; *My Southern Home*, 29, 48, 53; *Three Years in Europe*, 28, 32, 67. See also *Clotel* (Brown)

Bruce, Dixon, 248n6

Brückner, Martin: on geographical literacy, 240n134; on Jefferson, 64, 235n41; on maps, 111; on place studies through literature, 61–62

Bryan, Violet Harrington, 257n39

Buell, Lawrence, 240n138

Burns, Anthony, 251–52n58

Burns, Robert, 255–56n7

Butler, Judith, 259n17

Cable, George Washington, 256n18, 257n33

Calhoun, John C., 11, 45, 53–54

Canada West, 70, 92, 133, 141, 152, 228n82

Cane (Toomer), 195

capital: Beckwourth and, 94; in *Blake*, 81, 86–89, 135, 139, 144, 147–49; Calhoun on, 229n84; in *Clotel*, 37–41; in *Contending Forces*, 182–83; deterritorialization and, 4; in Dunbar-Nelson's

regionalist fiction, 200; mapping and, 125; Native Americans and, 99–100; power and, 43; process geography and, 14; slavery and, 10–11

Carby, Hazel, 171–72, 248n6, 248n11, 253–54n96

carnival, 207–8

"A Carnival Jangle" (Dunbar-Nelson), 207–8

Carr, Robert, 112–13

Carter, Erica, 7

cartography. See maps and mapping

Casey, Edward S., 32, 210, 223n24

Cataract (weekly paper), 90

Catholicism, 202

Certeau, Michel de, 6, 161, 259n18

Cheah, Pheng, 233–34n16

Chesnutt, Charles Waddell: Reconstruction and, 12; regionalism and, 192–94, 206; stenography and, 249n20; tragic race heroes by, 157

Chesnutt, Charles Waddell, writings: *The Conjure Woman and Other Tales*, 167, 193–94; *House Behind the Cedars*, 157; *The Marrow of Tradition*, 157

Chesnutt, Mary, 249n20

Child, Lydia Maria, 37, 41

Chiles, Katy, 233n15

Chittenden, Hiram, 76

Chivington, John, 103

Chopin, Kate, 257n33

chorography, 10

Christian Recorder (magazine), 179, 248n6

Cisneros, Sandra, 214

Civil War: causes of, 68; in *Clotel*, 34–35; Delany and, 77; maps and, 117–18; Reconstruction and, 12; regionalism and, 191–92; Richmond and, 38–39; slave traffic and, 47; slavery and, 215

Clotel (Brown): audience of, 9; black mobility and counter-transit in, 48–54; discourses on national geography in, 25–27, 30, 32–34; editions of, 25, 34–35; as first novel by an African American author, 2; frontier humor in, 59–61; literacy in, 234n17; Natchez in, 47; Ohio River sketches in, 50–54; panoramic dissimilitude in, 58–59; reception of, 24–25; Richmond in, 36, 37–38, 39–41, 42; rise of the black novel and, 154–55; Rodney in, 46–47; "Sketch of the Author's Life" in, 28; on slavery, 27; St. Louis in, 47–48; Vicksburg in, 41–46; Washington, DC, in, 62, 66–68; Wheeling in, 55–57

Clotelle: A Tale of the Southern States (1864) (Brown), 34

Clotelle, Or the Colored Heroine: A Tale of the Southern States (1867) (Brown), 34–35

Clymer, Jeffory, 76, 247n110

Code, Lorraine, 238–39n98

Cohen, Matt, 106

Cole, Jean Lee, 245n84

Colored American Magazine (magazine): Hopkins and, 156, 177, 185, 247n3; Washington and, 179–80

Colored Co-Operative Publishing Company, 247n3

Colton, Joseph Hutchins: *Colton's Map* and, 121–22, 122–23, 125, 132–33; as copyright consolidator, 120; map of Bolivia and, 242–43n29

Colton's Map of the United States of America, the British Provinces, Mexico, the West Indies and Central America (Colton and Thayer), 121–22, 122–23, 125, 132–33

Compromise of 1850. *See* Fugitive Slave Act (1850)

Comstock, Elizabeth, 228–29n82

Condition, Elevation, Emigration and Des- *tiny of the Colored People of the United States, The* (Delany): on Cuba, 116, 141; on diaspora, 97; on freemen, 80; mapping and, 145; mobility in, 142; on Native Americans, 96–97, 99; reception of, 74–75

"Confederate Cuba" (Levander), 144

Conflicting Stories (Ammons), 258n48

Conjure Woman and Other Tales, The (Chesnutt), 167, 193–94

"The Conquerors: The Black Troops in Cuba" (Dunbar), 200

Conscripts of Modernity (Drexler), 129

Contending Forces (Hopkins): black church in, 153, 169–77; black public sphere in, 13, 154, 161–66, 173–77; Boston in, 152–53, 156–61, 166–69, 180–82; Du Bois proxy in, 177, 180, 184; rise of the black novel and, 154–56; Washington proxy in, 177–80; women's civic society in, 153, 182–88

Cooper, Anna Julia, 184

Cooper, James Fenimore, 89

counter-transit, 49–54, 146

Cox, John D., 222n12, 228n78

Craft, Ellen, 44, 251n43

Craft, William, 44, 45, 251n43

Crafts, Hannah, 214

Crang, Mike, 16, 196

creolization and Creole identity, 22, 203–7

Critical Geopolitics (Ó Tuathail), 116

Crow Indians, 76, 94–95, 95, 100–107, 104

Cruikshank, George, 57

Crummell, Alexander, 129, 216, 232n1

Cuba: in African American literature, 112; in *Blake*, 114–15, 130–35, 139–41; in "The Conquerors: The Black Troops in Cuba," 200; mapping of, 125–26, 136–39; in "Mr. Baptiste," 200; United States and, 135–39

"Cuba" (Liberator article), 114–15
Cugoano, Quobna Ottobah, 30–31
Cultures of United States Imperialism
(Kaplan and Pease), 110
Cumberland Road, 55
"Cupid and the Phonograph" (Dunbar-Nelson), 201
Curry, Michael R., 9–10

Damnés de la Terre, Les (*The Wretched of the Earth*) (Fanon), 216
Darkwater (Du Bois), 184
David Walker's Appeal (Walker), 36
Davies, Carole Boyce, 125–26
Davis, Jefferson, 41
Davis, Thadious, 5–6, 162, 250n29
Declaration of Independence, 35, 62–63, 172
Deerslayer, The (Cooper), 89
Delany, Martin R.: on black dispora, 12–13; on Canadian land procurement, 70; on Cuba, 114–16, 130–35, 139–41; as journalist, 141; life and accomplishments of, 74–75, 151–52; mapping and, 48–49, 112–16, 120–21, 126–27, 145–50; on Natchez, 47; nation and, 26, 71, 76–87, 93, 96–97, 98, 108; Native Americans and, 95–100; Niger Valley Exploring Party and, 70, 75; *North Star* and, 11, 75, 114, 135, 143; reception of, 76–77; rise of the black novel and, 1; search for a collective history by, 215; on slavery, 10–11, 148–49; territory and, 71–74, 75, 76–77, 79–87, 97–100, 108–9; Theban Society and, 83
Delany, Martin R., writings: "Annexation of Cuba," 114, 143; *Official Report of the Niger Valley Exploring Party*, 142, 145; "Political Aspect of the Colored People of the United States," 80–81; "Political Destiny

of the Colored Race on the American Continent," 75, 80, 135, 142, 245n77; "Redemption of Cuba," 143. *See also Blake* (Delany)
Deleuze, Gilles: on deterritorialization, 72–74, 89, 101; on flow, 256–57n19; on Kafka, 81; on lines of flight, 84–85; Massey on, 220n13
Deloria, Vine, Jr., 100, 106
Dent, Borden, 243n38
Derrida, Jacques, 116
Description of William Wells Brown's Original Panoramic Views, A (Brown), 57–58, 60
Desire and Domestic Fiction (Armstrong), 226n49
Desmangles, Leslie, 257n26
Dessalines, Jean-Jacques, 141
deterritorialization. *See* territory and deterritorialization
Dexter Avenue Baptist Church (Montgomery), 176
Diario, El (morning journal), 141
Dickens, Charles, 28, 38
Dimock, Wai Chee, 241n3
Dislocating Race and Nation (Levine), 8
Dixon, Melvin, 2
Do the Americas Have a Common Literature? (Pérez Firmat), 110
Dobie, J. Frank, 76
domestic sites and households, 36–37, 40–41, 214
Domínguez, Virginia, 205
Donald, James, 7
Doolen, Andy, 76, 246n108
Douglass, Frederick: *Anglo-African Magazine* and, 233n10; on city slaves, 42, 43; on Fugitive Slave Act, 32; on Haiti, 128–29; *North Star* and, 11, 78, 117; St. Paul's Baptist Church and, 170–71; travels to England and Northern Ireland, 28, 29

Douglass, Frederick, writings: *The Life and Times of Frederick Douglass*, 128; "What to the Slave Is the Fourth of July?" (Douglass), 58–59

Douglass, Sarah Mapps, 233n10

Dourish, Paul, 6, 219n8

Dred Scott v. Sandford (1857), 69–70, 132, 224n28

Drescher, Seymour, 40

Drexler, Michael J., 129

Du Bois, W. E. B.: on city blacks, 160–61; Hopkins and, 153, 177, 180, 184–85; on labor wars, 198–99, 256n17; women and, 184–85

Du Bois, W. E. B., writings: *The American Negro*, 160–61; "The Black North in 1901: A Social Study," 160; *Darkwater*, 184; "Of Mr. Booker T. Washington and Others," 180; *The Souls of Black Folk*, 173, 215; "The Study of the Negro Problems," 184–85; "The Talented Tenth," 184

duCille, Ann, 222n6

Dumballah, 202

Dunbar, Paul Laurence: Dunbar-Nelson and, 195; regionalism and, 192–93, 194–95

Dunbar, Paul Laurence, writings: "The Banjo Song," 256n7; "The Conquerors: The Black Troops in Cuba," 200; *The Fanatics*, 194; *Folks from Dixie*, 194; *Oak and Ivy*, 256n7; *The Sport of the Gods*, 157, 160, 195; *The Strength of Gideon and Other Stories*, 194; *The Uncalled*, 194

Dunbar-Nelson, Alice Moore: on Creole identity, 205; Dunbar and, 195; geographical scale and, 213; Reconstruction and, 12; regionalism and, 13, 167, 192–93, 195–210

Dunbar-Nelson, Alice Moore, writings: "Anarchy Alley," 208–9; "A Carnival Jangle," 207–8; "Cupid and the Phonograph," 201; "The Goodness of Saint Rocque," 201, 202; *The Goodness of St. Rocque*, 195–96, 197–201, 202–3, 204–8; "La Juanita," 203; "Little Miss Sophie," 205–6; *Masterpieces of Negro Eloquence*, 258n39; "Mr. Baptiste," 197–200, 208; "People of Color in Louisiana," 205, 258n39; "The Praline Women," 200–201, 202–3; "Sister Josepha," 206; "Stones of the Village," 255n5; *Stories of Women and Men*, 201; "Tony's Wife," 200–201; *Violets and Other Tales*, 195–96, 204–5, 208–9

Duncan, Nancy, 218

Dyer Anti-Lynching Bill, 258n39

Elaw, Zilpha, 54–55

Elliott, G. W., 117

empire: Brown and, 61; in *Clotel*, 40; Cuba and, 115, 130, 200; Delany on, 80–81; as geographically ubiquitous, 216; mapping and, 125; territory and, 72–73, 108–9, 111–13

environment, 6, 109, 213

"The Epistemology of Slave Conspiracy" (Gillman), 132

Equiano, Olaudah, 30–31

Ernest, John, 25, 59, 220n16, 233n15, 236n50

Erzulie, 202

Escape, The (Brown), 225n36

ethnicity: Creole identity and, 203–7; in Dunbar-Nelson's regionalist fiction, 196, 198–99

Fact and Fiction (Child), 225n38

"Famous Women of the Negro Race" (Hopkins), 156, 185

Fanatics, The (Dunbar), 194

Fanon, Frantz, 216

Farrison, William Edward, 57, 226n57

Faulkner, William, 206

Feminism and Geography (Rose), 254n104

feminist geography, 21, 40–41, 175–76, 183–89, 218, 238n98, 255n1, 259n17

Fish, Cheryl, 222n12

Fitzhugh, George, 229n84

flow: African American literature and, 4–5, 29, 48, 54–55; in Blake, 83, 86–88, 127–28, 133; in Chesnutt's fiction, 133; in Clotel, 53; in Contending Forces, 173; in Dunbar-Nelson's regionalist fiction, 197, 199; non-representational geographies and, 13; place and, 22, 211–13; politics of location and, 43–44; process geography and, 14–16

Folks from Dixie (Dunbar), 194

Foote, Julia, 54–55

Foreman, Grant, 97–98

Fort Towson, Arkansas, 97–98

Fortune, T. Thomas, 173

Foster, Frances Smith, 248n6

Foucault, Michel, 4, 43, 66, 72

Fraser, Nancy, 175–76

Frederick Douglass' Paper (newspaper), 30, 140–41, 246–47n109

Freedmen's Bureau (South Carolina), 72, 77

Frémont, John Charles, 93

From Behind the Veil (Stepto), 155

frontier: Beckwourth and, 13, 88–89, 92, 101; Bonner and, 91; Fort Towson and, 97–98

frontier humor, 59–61

A Frontier Lady (Royce), 89

Fugitive Slave Act (1850), 27, 32–33, 69, 171

Gadsden Purchase (1853), 10

Gardner, Eric, 8, 48, 248n6

Garies and Their Friends, The (Webb), 37, 70–71, 156

Garnet, Henry Highland, 216

Garrison, William Lloyd, 28, 170. See also The Liberator (anti-slavery newspaper)

Garvey, Marcus, 252n65

Gasché, Rodolphe, 116

Gates, Henry Louis, Jr., 91, 248n6

Gayle, Addison, 221n2

genres: black rise of the novel and, 1–2, 9–10, 25–26, 31–32, 35, 59–60; geography and, 20–21, 215–16; regionalism and, 21–22, 190–92, 210–11

Geographic Revolution in Early America (Brückner), 111

geographical scale: African American literature and, 3, 8–9; black church and, 169–71; in Clotel, 34–35, 40, 66–67; in Contending Forces, 189; Cuba and, 114; definitions of, 211–13; in Dunbar-Nelson's regionalist fiction, 196–97, 199, 206; mapping and, 126; Thrift on, 85

geography, 3, 6–7, 9–10. See also maps and mapping; place; space; territory and deterritorialization

Geography and the Production of Space in Nineteenth-Century American Literature (Hsu), 23

geopolitics, 32–33, 67, 116–17

Gibbon, Edward, 231n122

Giddens, Anthony, 6, 109, 219n10

Gilbert, Timothy, 169

Gilles, Paul, 241n3

Gillman, Susan, 14, 132

Gilroy, Paul, 76, 97, 216–17, 247n113

Gleason, William A., 38

Glissant, Edouard, 204

Goldin, Claudia Dale, 45

"The Goodness of Saint Rocque" (Dunbar-Nelson), 201, 202

Goodness of St. Rocque, The (Dunbar-Nelson), 195–96, 197–201, 202–3, 204–8
"The Goophered Grapevine" (Chesnutt), 193–94
Gramsci, Antonio, 43
Great Migration, 195
Greenspan, Ezra, 25, 222n5, 231n108
Greenwood, Grace, (Sarah J. Clarke), 225n36
Greeson, Jennifer, 191, 256n18
Griffin, Farah, 222n12
Griggs, Sutton, 11
Grimes, Leonard, 171, 252n58
Griswold, Ralph, 224–25n33
Gruesz, Kirsten Silva, 111
Guattari, Félix: on deterritorialization, 72–74, 89, 101; on flow, 256–57n19; on Kafka, 81; on lines of flight, 84–85; Massey on, 220n13
Gunning, Sandra, 217

Habermas, Jürgen, 161–62, 163
Hagar's Daughter (Hopkins), 152
Haiti: in *Blake*, 127–28, 129–30; W.W. Brown on, 62, 70; Douglass and, 128–29; United States and, 129
Haitian Revolution (1792–1810), 202
Hale, Edward Everett, 158
Hale, Sarah J., 234n16
Hall, William C., 230n96
Hamilton, Alexander, 129
Hamilton-Gordon, George, 80
Hammon, Briton, 54, 259n14
Haraway, Donna, 238–39n98
Hardt, Michael, 39
Hare, Caroline, 228n82
Harlan, John Marshall, 12
Harlem Renaissance, 195
Harley, J. B., 14
Harper, Frances: *Anglo-African Magazine* and, 233n10; experience of life in former slave states of, 181; rise of the black novel and, 155
Harper, Frances, writings: *Iola Leroy*, 35, 155, 156, 162–63; *Minnie's Sacrifice*, 154–55, 156, 250n36; *Shadows Uplifted*, 155; *Sowing and Reaping*, 155; *Trial and Triumph*, 155
Harper's New Monthly Magazine (magazine), 91
Harris, Joel Chandler, 194–95
Harvey, Bruce, 112–13
Harvey, David, 14, 43, 255n1, 255n109
Hawthorne, Nathaniel, 158
Hayden, Lewis and Harriet, 166, 250–51n43
Hayes, Rutherford, 77
Heermance, J. Noel, 24
Heidegger, Martin, 6
Helg, Aline, 135
Helper, Hinton Rowan, 242–43n29
Hemings, Sally, 224n29
Hendler, Glenn, 233n15
Henson, Josiah, 70
Herod, Andrew, 211
Herscovici, Iuliu "Julius," 227n58
Higginbotham, Evelyn Brooks, 176
Higginson, Thomas Wentworth, 252n58
Hinks, Peter, 226n56
History of the United States, A (Bancroft), 231–32n122
Holland, Sharon, 98
Holly, James, 70
Holmes, Oliver Wendell, 158
Hopkins, Pauline: black women's club movement and, 153, 185–88; *Colored American Magazine* and, 156, 177, 185; Du Bois and, 153, 177, 180, 184–85; life of, 151–52; Native Americans and, 99–100; Washington and, 153, 155–56, 177–80
Hopkins, Pauline, writings: "Famous

Women of the Negro Race," 156, 185; *Hagar's Daughter*, 152; "The Latest Phases of the Race Problem in American," 179; *Of One Blood*, 152, 157; *Winona*, 99–100, 152, 157. See also *Contending Forces* (Hopkins)

House Behind the Cedars (Chesnutt), 157

"House Divided" (Lincoln), 62

Howard, James, 155

Howard, June, 258n48

Howe, Julia Ward, 158

Howells, William Dean, 158, 174

Howitt, Richie, 211–12

Hsu, Hsuan L., 23, 61–62, 221n36, 256n10

Hugo, Victor, 28

Hull, Gloria, 255n5, 257n39

Hurston, Zora Neale, 257n25

Ignatiev, Noel, 256n17

Imperium in Imperio (Griggs), 11

Incidents in the Life of a Slave Girl (Jacobs), 37, 41, 214

Ingold, Timothy, 220n13

Ingraham, Joseph Holt, 227n70

Inman, Henry, 239n111

Interesting Narrative, The (Equiano), 31

Intricate Knot, The (Yellin), 242n26

Iola Leroy (Harper), 35, 155, 156, 162–63

Irigaray, Luce, 201, 259n17

Irish immigrants, 44, 159

Italian immigrants, 44

Iwa, 202

Jackson, Andrew, 50

Jackson, Blyden, 24

Jacobs, Harriet, 37, 41, 214

James, Ian, 23

Jameson, Fredric, 6

Jardine, Monica, 125–26

Jefferson, Thomas: agrarianism and, 26; Brown and, 63–66; Haiti and, 129; Lewis and Clark report and, 235n41; as portrayed in *Clotel*, 33–34, 35–36, 37

"Jefferson's Daughter" (anonymous poem), 224n30

Jewett, Sarah Orne, 256n10

Jewish immigrants, 44, 168, 227n58

Jews of Vicksburg, Mississippi, The (Herscovici), 227n58

Johnson, Alvin Jewett, 120. *See also A New Map of the Union* (A.J. Johnson and D.G. Johnson)

Johnson, D. Griffing: Colton and, 120; life and accomplishments of, 118–19; *A New Map of the Union* and, 122, 123–25, 123–24, 142; *Republics of North America* and, 122–23, 125, 134, 142

Johnson, David, 50

Journal of Negro History (journal), 258n39

Journal of the Rev. John Marrant, A (Marrant), 259n14

"La Juanita" (Dunbar-Nelson), 203

Kafka, Franz, 81

Kansas-Nebraska Act (1854), 69, 223–24n28

Kaplan, Amy, 110, 191, 209

Kazanjian, David, 11

King, Grace Elizabeth, 257n33

King, Martin Luther, Jr., 171, 176

Knadler, Stephen P., 7

Knights, Peter, 248n15

Konkle, Maureen, 101

Laclau, Ernesto, 220n13

Ladder Conspiracy (Conspiración de La Escalera), 135, 140

lagniappe, 200–201

Lape, Noreen Grover, 236n54, 237n65, 238n83

Larsen, Nella, 195

"The Latest Phases of the Race Problem in American" (Hopkins), 179

Latour, Bruno, 13, 42, 113

"The Leap from the Long Bridge" (Greenwood), 225n36

Lee, Jarena, 54–55

Lefebvre, Henri, 6, 43

LeMenager, Stephanie, 233n15

Levander, Caroline, 7, 144

Leverenz, David, 226n49

Levine, Robert S.: on Blake, 235–36n42; on Clotel, 25, 222n5, 222n6; on Delany, 76; on qualities of a national culture, 8

Lewis, John C. See Lewis' Free Soil, Slavery, and Territorial Map of the United States (Lewis)

Lewis' Free Soil, Slavery, and Territorial Map of the United States (Lewis), 78–79, 78, 117, 139

Liberation Historiography (Ernest), 59, 220n16

Liberator, The (anti-slavery newspaper): Brown and, 28, 225n36, 226n57; on Crafts, 226n57; on Cuba, 114–15; "Jefferson's Daughter" in, 224n30

Liberty Bell, The (annual gift book), 225n38

Life and Adventures of James P. Beckwourth, The (Beckwourth), 71–74, 75–76, 85, 88–95, 100–109

Life and Pontificate of Leo X (Roscoe), 231n122

Life and Times of Frederick Douglass, The (Douglass), 128

Lincoln, Abraham, 62–63

"Literary Boston as I Knew It" (Howells), 158

"Little Miss Sophie" (Dunbar-Nelson), 205–6

local color. See regionalism

Longfellow, Henry Wadsworth, 158, 255–56n7

Lopez, Narcíso, 136, 138–39, 147

Louisiana Purchase (1803), 129, 204

Lowell, James Russell, 158

Lucasi, Stephen, 222n12

Macaulay, Thomas Babington, 231n122

Magnalia Christi Americana (Mather), 174–75

Male Body, The (Bordo), 254n104

Manhood and the American Renaissance (Leverenz), 226n49

Map of the United States (Elliott), 117

Map of the Upper Great Plains and Rocky Mountains Region (de Smet), 104

maps and mapping: in Blake, 77–78, 112–14, 126–27; Colton's Map of the United States of America, the British Provinces, Mexico, the West Indies and Central America (Colton and Thayer), 121–22, 122–23, 125, 132–33; Delany and, 48–49, 112–16; imperialist claims and, 111–12, 116–21, 136–39; Lewis' Free Soil, Slavery, and Territorial Map of the United States, 78–79, 78, 117, 139; Map of the United States (Elliott), 117; Map of the Upper Great Plains and Rocky Mountains Region (de Smet), 104; A New Map of the United States (Williams), 136–37, 137–38; Political Map of the United States (Reynolds), 117, 118; postnational American literary studies and, 110–11; territorialization and deterritorialization in, 111–13, 145–46; titling and vignettes in, 122–25

Marrant, John, 259n14

Marrow of Tradition, The (Chesnutt), 157

"Marse Chan" (Page), 194–95

Marx, Leo, 65–66

Massey, Doreen: on place, 14, 179; on power as territorialized, 43; on region, 255n1; on space, 220n13

Masterpieces of Negro Eloquence (Dunbar-Nelson), 258n39

Mather, Cotton, 174–75

Mattingly, Garret, 259n16

Mattox, Jake, 76, 235n32

McHenry, Elizabeth, 254n107

McKinley, William, 179

McKittrick, Katherine, 23

McPherson, James, 231n109

Medill, William, 100, 238n97

Messenger, The (magazine), 258n39

Mexican Cession (1848), 10

Middle Passage, 30–31, 146–48

Mignolo, Walter D., 14–15, 126, 238–39n98

Miles, Tiya, 98

Miller, Floyd J., 232–33n4, 244n62

Minnie's Sacrifice (Harper), 154–55, 156, 250n36

Miralda, or the Beautiful Quadroon (Brown), 34

Missouri Compromise (1820), 32–33, 69

Monroe, James, 26

Monroe Doctrine, 112

Morris, Christopher, 45

Morrison, Toni, 206

mountaineers, 91–94

"Mr. Baptiste" (Dunbar-Nelson), 197–200, 208

Mulvey, Christopher, 25

My Southern Home (Brown), 29, 48, 53

Mystery, The (newspaper), 141

Nancy, Jean-Luc, 23

Narrative of the Life of Frederick Douglass (Douglass), 42

Narrative of the Uncommon Sufferings, and Surprising Deliverance of Briton Ham- mon, a Negro Man (Hammon), 259n14

Narrative of William W. Brown, A Fugitive Slave (Brown): publication and editions of, 223n18; reception of, 33; slavery as plave performance in, 28–29; St. Louis in, 48, 58

Natchez, Mississippi, 42, 47

nation and national spaces: in African American literature, 216–17; Beckwourth and, 71, 75–76, 108; in Chesnutt's fiction, 194; in *Clotel*, 25–28, 30, 32–34, 60–61, 67–68; in *Contending Forces*, 165, 169, 174–75, 177–78; creolization and, 203–4; Delany and, 26, 71, 76–87, 93, 96–97, 98, 108; in Dunbar-Nelson's regionalist fiction, 195–96, 205–6, 209–10; geographical scale and, 3; in *Iola Leroy*, 162–63; Lewis Map and, 79; Native Americans and, 74, 96, 97–98; periodicity and, 7–8; process geography and, 14–16; regionalism and, 190–93; slavery and, 10–12; spaces of dissension and, 17. See also empire; geographical scale; maps and mapping; territory and deterritorialization

National Association for the Advancement of Colored People (NAACP), 176

National Emigration Convention of Colored Men (Cleveland, 1854), 79, 145

National Era (newspaper), 141

National Federation of Afro-American Women, 254n108

National Federation of Colored Women's Clubs, 258n39

National Free Soil Convention (Pittsburgh), 32

National League of Colored Women, 254n108

Native Americans: Beckwourth and, 74, 76, 94–95, 95, 100–107; conceptions of space by, 74; Delany and, 95–100; Hopkins and, 99–100; slavery and, 98–99

Nebraska Territory, 10, 69, 223n28

Negri, Antonio, 39

Negro World (newspaper), 252n65

New England Anti-Slavery Society, 170

New Essays on The Country of the Pointed Firs (Howard), 258n48

New Map of the Union, A (A.J. Johnson and D.G. Johnson), 122, 123–25, 123–24, 142

New Map of the United States, A (Williams), 136–37, 137–38

New Mexico, 10

New Orleans, Louisiana: creolization and Creole identity in, 203–7; in Dunbar-Nelson's regionalist fiction, 197–210; Vodou in, 201–3

New Orleans Daily Creole (newspaper), 143

New York Evangelist (newspaper), 140

New York Herald (newspaper), 226n57

New York Sun (newspaper), 115

New York Times (newspaper), 160

Niagara Movement, 176

Nichols, Frederick, 224–25n33

Nicomachean Ethics (Aristotle), 54

Niger Valley Exploring Party, 70, 75

nonrepresentational geographies, 13, 16, 49

Norcom, James, 37

Norfolk Journal and Guide (newspaper), 252n65

North Star (newspaper): on Cuba, 140; Delany and, 11, 75, 114, 135, 143; Douglass and, 11, 78, 117; Lewis Map in, 78, 79, 117, 139

Notes on Canada West (Shadd), 70

Notes on the State of Virginia (Jefferson), 35–36, 63–66

Nwankwo, Ifeoma, 76, 139

Oak and Ivy (Dunbar), 256n7

Oakes, Timothy, 113

O'Connor, Flannery, 206

"Of Mr. Booker T. Washington and Others" (Du Bois), 180

Of One Blood (Hopkins), 152, 157

Official Report of the Niger Valley Exploring Party (Delany), 142, 145

Ohio River, 50–54

Okker, Patricia, 242n26

Old North Church (Boston), 172

Onuf, Peter S., 63–64

Order of the Lone Star, 136

Ostend Report (1854), 138

Ó Tuathail, Gearóid, 36, 116

Our Nig (Wilson), 37, 70–71, 214

Page, Thomas Nelson, 194–95

panic cartographies, 15, 26, 53, 59–60

panoramic dissimilitude, 54–59

Parker, Theodore, 252n58

Parkman, Francis, 76

Pathfinder, The (Cooper), 89

Peace, Patti, 251n57

Pease, Donald, 110

Peel, Mark, 249n25

Pennington, James W. C., 54–55

"People of Color in Louisiana" (Dunbar-Nelson), 205, 258n39

Pérez Firmat, Gustavo, 110

periodicity, 1, 7–8, 48–49, 130, 154–56, 244n59

Perry, Bliss, 255n5

perspectivalism, 212–13

Phillips, Wendell, 170–71, 223n18

Pierce, Franklin, 10, 136

place: as actor, 16; in African American literature, 1–3, 8–10, 25–26, 35, 49, 192–93, 213–18; in *Clotel*, 26–27, 29–32, 36, 39–40, 42, 46–54, 62, 68; feminist scholarship on, 186; Hopkins and, 152–53, 155–62, 166–67, 172–73, 178–79, 188–89; Massey on, 14, 179; process geography and, 14–16; slavery and, 28–29; space and, 6–7. *See also* maps and mapping; regionalism; territory and deterritorialization

Plácido (Gabriel de la Concepción Valdés), 244n63, 245n77

plantation school tradition, 194–95

Pleck, Elizabeth Hafkin, 160

Plessy v. Ferguson (1896), 12

Poetics of Space (Bachelard), 214

"Political Aspect of the Colored People of the United States" (Delany), 80–81

"Political Destiny of the Colored Race on the American Continent" (Delany), 75, 80, 135, 142, 245n77

Political Map of the United States (Reynolds), 117, 118

politics of location, 43, 186–87

Polk, James, 112, 135–36

Porter, Carolyn, 110

Postmodern Geographies (Soja), 16

postnational American literary studies, 88, 110–11

power, 4–6, 12, 43–44; balance of, 54–55; cartographic, 14–15; circulatory, 52, 62, 83–85; geography and 43, 61, 211–12; imperial, 73–4, 125–29, 200; slaveholder 33–34, 67, 78–81; statist, 40, 100, 101, 120–21

power geometries, 18, 61, 66

Power/Knowledge (Foucault), 66, 109, 114, 121

practice-based geographies, 152, 174, 186–87

"The Praline Women" (Dunbar-Nelson), 200–201, 202–3

process geography, 1–5, 7, 13–16, 19, 74, 87, 119, 145–46, 196, 203–4, 210, 241n8

Proust, Marcel, 212

Provincial Freeman (newspaper), 70, 141

Ptolemy, 10

public sphere, 161–62, 163. *See also* black public sphere

Pueblo, Colorado, 71

Puritan Origins of the American Self, The (Bercovitch), 174

"The Quadroons" (Child), 37, 41

Quakers (Society of Friends), 52–53, 228n81, 228n82

Quicksand (Larsen), 195

Rabelais, François, 207

race: Creole identity and, 203–7; in Dunbar-Nelson's regionalist fiction, 196, 198–99

Radhakrishnan, R., 97, 238n88

Raimon, Eve Allegra, 225n35, 255n111

"Recitatif" (Morrison), 206

Reconstructing Womanhood (Carby), 171–72

"Redemption of Cuba" (Delany), 143

Redpath, James, 34

regionalism: African American writers and, 21–22; Brown and, 25–26, 59–62; Chesnutt and, 192–94, 206; Dunbar and, 192–93, 194–95; Dunbar-Nelson and, 13, 167, 190–96, 195–210; Hopkins and, 153–54, 158, 166–67, 181–82, 189; nationalist narratives in, 209–10; notion of region and national diversity in, 190–92

Reid-Pharr, Robert F., 41

Remapping Citizenship and Nation in African American Literature (Knadler), 7

Republican (newspaper), 79

Republics of North America (D.G. Johnson), 122–23, 125, 134, 142
Resch, Robert, 233n8
Revere, Paul, 172
Reynolds, William C., 117, 118
Rich, Adrienne, 186
Richmond, Virginia: in *Clotel*, 36, 37–38, 39–41, 42; slavery in, 38–39
Ride out the Wilderness (Dixon), 2
Riley, James Whitcomb, 255–56n7
Robbins, Bruce, 201
Robbins, Hollis, 25
Roberts, Susan, 200
Rodney, Mississippi, 46–47
Rodríguez, Ileana, 111
Roediger, David R., 256n17
Rorty, Richard, 220n13
Roscoe, William, 231n122
Rose, Gillian, 186, 218, 254n104, 259n17
Rowe, Aimee Carrillo, 186
Royce, Sarah, 89
Ruffin, George, 254n100
Ruffin, Josephine St. Pierre, 185, 254–55n108
Running a Thousand Miles for Freedom (W. Craft), 44, 226n57
Russell, Irwin, 194–95

Sack, Robert David, 232n2
Said, Edward, 43
Schneider, Mark R., 249n16
Schnore, Leo, 248n15
Scott, Coretta, 171
Scott, David, 129
Scribner's Monthly (magazine), 256n18
Seminole Wars, 103
Shadd, Mary Ann, 70
Shadows Uplifted (Harper), 155
Signifying Monkey, The (Gates), 91
Simpson, Louis, 126
Simpson, Mark, 29

"Sister Josepha" (Dunbar-Nelson), 206
slave narratives, 70, 155; and Ohio River stories, 48–54
slavery: Beckwourth and, 76; in *Blake*, 80–84; Brown as antislavery lecturer and, 27–33; Calhoun on, 53–54; city slaves and, 42–45, 46; *Dred Scott* decision and, 67–70, 132, 224n28; fugitive narratives and, 50; Jefferson and, 65; land and, 10–12; in Lewis Map, 79; mapping and, 112–16; Middle Passage and, 30–31, 146; Native Americans and, 98–99; number of slaves in the United States, 215; as place performance, 28–29; in Richmond, 38–39; slave markets and, 46–48
Smet, Pierre-Jean de, 104
Smith, James McCune, 59, 233n10
Smith, Venture, 30–31, 54
Society of Friends (Quakers), 52–53, 228n81, 228n82
Soja, Edward W., 16
Sollors, Werner, 206–7
Souls of Black Folk, The (Du Bois), 173, 215
Southscapes (Davis), 5–6, 250n29
Sowing and Reaping (Harper), 155
space: in African American literature, 2–4, 22–23; Brown and, 47–59, 60–61, 67–68; dissension and, 4–10, 17; Foucault on, 66; Native Americans and, 74; panic cartographies and, 26; place and, 6–7; process geography and, 14–16; slavery and, 12–13. *See also* black public sphere; domestic sites and households; nation; territory and deterritorialization
spaces of dissension, 4–10, 17
Spanish-American War (1898), 199–200

Specters of Democracy (Wilson), 7–8
Spectral Nationality (Cheah), 233–34n16
Spivak, Gayatri Chakravorty, 72
Sport of the Gods, The (Dunbar), 157, 160, 195
Squires, Judith, 7
St. Louis, Missouri: in Clotel, 47–48; in The Life and Adventures of James P. Beckwourth, 92–93; in Narrative of William W. Brown, A Fugitive Slave, 58
St. Paul's Baptist Church (Boston), 170–71, 176
Stein, Jordan Alexander, 233n15, 234n16
stenography, 249n20
Stephens, Michelle, 126
Stepto, Robert B., 155
Stewart, Maria W., 170
Stoler, Ann Laura, 40
"Stones of the Village" (Dunbar-Nelson), 255n5
Stories of Women and Men (Dunbar-Nelson), 201
Stowe, Harriet Beecher, 57, 158, 225n36, 234n16, 242n26
Strength of Gideon and Other Stories, The (Dunbar), 194
Structural Transformation of the Public Sphere, The (Habermas), 161–62
"The Study of the Negro Problems" (Du Bois), 184–85
Suggs, Jon-Christian, 234n21
Sumner, Charles, 170–71
Sundquist, Eric, 76, 132, 242n26
Sutter's Sawmill, 124
Suttle, Charles F., 251–52n58

Tait's Edinburgh Magazine (British magazine), 224n30
Takagi, Midori, 38
"The Talented Tenth" (Du Bois), 184
Tell My Horse (Hurston), 257n25
temperance, 90, 91, 102

Temperance Harp, The (Bonner), 90
Tennyson, Alfred, 28
Terrell, Mary Church, 254–55n108
territory and deterritorialization: in African American literature, 3–4, 69–71; in Blake, 71–74, 75, 76–77, 79–87, 97–100, 108–9; Deleuze and Guattari on, 72–74, 89; in The Life and Adventures of James P. Beckwourth, 71–74, 75–76, 85, 88–95, 100–109; maps and, 111–13, 145–46
Thayer, B. W. See Colton's Map of the United States of America, the British Provinces, Mexico, the West Indies and Central America (Colton and Thayer)
Theban Society, 83
Third Baptist Church (later Charles Street Baptist Church) (Boston), 169–70
Thousand Plateaus, A (Deleuze and Guattari), 84–85
Three Years in Europe (Brown), 28, 32, 67
Thrift, Nigel, 16, 85, 196, 220n13
To Wake the Nations (Sundquist), 242n26
Tocqueville, Alexis de, 28
"Tony's Wife" (Dunbar-Nelson), 200–201
Toomer, Jean, 195
topography, 9–10, 39, 43, 93–94, 135, 190
Toussaint Clause (1799), 129
Toussaint l'Ouverture, François-Dominique, 141
tragic mulatta trope: in Clotel, 24, 225n35; in Contending Forces, 188
Traveler's and Tourist's Guide through the United States of America (Williams), 136–37
Tredegar Iron Works, 38–39
Tregle, Joseph G., Jr., 205
Tremont Temple Baptist Church (Boston), 169, 173, 176

Trial and Triumph (Harper), 155
Trotter, William, 180
"Troubling Regionalism" (Zagarell), 258n48
Truth, Sojourner, 54–55, 170–71
Truth Stranger than Fiction (Henson), 70
Tuan, Yi-Fu, 6
Tubman, Harriet, 170–71
Turnbull, David, 244n63
Tuskegee Normal and Industrial Institute, 178
Twelfth Baptist Church (Boston), 171, 176

Uncalled, The (Dunbar), 194
Uncle Tom's Cabin (Stowe), 57, 225n36, 234n16, 242n26
Underground Railroad, 29, 171
Unexpected Places (Gardner), 8
Up From Slavery (Washington), 253n80
Utah, 10

Valentine, Elisha, 50
Vermont, 215
Vicksburg, Virginia, 41–46
Violets and Other Tales (Dunbar-Nelson), 195–96, 204–5, 208–9
Virginia Colony, 215
Vivan, Itala, 111
Vodou, 201–3
Voice of the Fugitive (newspaper), 70
Von Frank, Albert, 252n58

Wade, Richard, 45
Waldrep, Christopher, 42, 226n55
Walker, David, 36, 43
Walker, James, 46
Wallinger, Hanna, 179–80
Ward, Samuel Ringgold, 70
Warner, Michael, 186, 187

Warren, Kenneth W., 49
Washington, Booker T.: *Colored American Magazine* and, 179–80; Hopkins and, 153, 155–56, 177–80
Washington, D.C., 62, 66–68
Watkins, William, 140–41
weak publics, 175–76
Webb, Frank J., 1, 37, 70–71, 156
Weekly Anglo-African (magazine), 117, 232n4, 242n26
Wells, Ida B., 184, 252n64
West, Cornel, 172
Weston, George, 141
"What is a Minor Literature?" (Deleuze and Guattari), 85
"What to the Slave Is the Fourth of July?" (Douglass), 58–59
"What We Know That We Don't Know" (Porter), 110
Wheeling, Virginia, 55–57
Whitfield, James Monroe, 70
Whittier, John Greenleaf, 158
William Wells Brown (Greenspan), 222n5
Williams, Roger, 106
Williams, Wellington, 136–37, 137–38
Wilson, Elinor, 93, 233n11
Wilson, Harriet, 1, 37, 70–71, 214
Wilson, Ivy, 7–8
Winona (Hopkins), 99–100, 152, 157
Wong, Edlie L., 222n15
Wood, Denis, 241n8
Wordsworth, William, 255–56n7
World Peace Conference (Paris, 1849), 28–29
Wright, Melissa, 211

Yellin, Jean Fagan, 206, 242n26

Zagarell, Sandra A., 258n48